DATE DUE

DEMCO 38-296

A NEW CRITICAL HISTORY OF
OLD ENGLISH LITERATURE

Front Panel of the Franks Casket. Courtesy of the British Museum.
(see discussion of *Deor*, chapter 12)

The left section depicts a scene from Germanic story: Weland the Smith after he has killed King Niðhad's sons and made cups of their skulls (one torso lies behind his feet). He seems to be holding one cup with tongs and proffering the other to Beaduhild, the King's daughter, who is accompanied by an attendant. Weland's brother Egill (?) is catching birds with which to make wings for their escape. The right section represents the Christian subjects of the Adoration of the Magi, runes for *Magi* appearing in the top center of the section.

A runic inscription in alliterative verse runs around the panel. It bears no relation to either Christian or Germanic subject in the compartments, but says in effect: "The ocean cast up the fish on the cliff-bank; the whale became sad [or, the ocean became turbid] where he swam aground on the shingle. Whale's bone."

A NEW CRITICAL HISTORY OF OLD ENGLISH LITERATURE

Stanley B. Greenfield and
Daniel G. Calder

*With a survey of the Anglo-Latin background by
Michael Lapidge*

NEW YORK UNIVERSITY PRESS
NEW YORK AND LONDON

Library of Congress Cataloging-in-Publication Data

Greenfield, Stanley B., 1922–
   A new critical history of old English literature.

   Bibliography: p.
   Includes index.
   1. Anglo-Saxon literature—History and criticism.
I. Calder, Daniel Gillmore.   II. Title.
PR173.G73   1986   829'.09   85-25941
ISBN 0-8147-3002-7 (alk. paper)

Clothbound editions of New York University Press
books are Smyth-sewn and printed on permanent
and durable acid-free paper.

c 10 9 8 7 6 5 4 3 2

Book design by K. Venezio

To Thelma Greenfield
and Margaret and Gillmore Calder

Contents

Preface to
the New Edition

We gratefully acknowledge the assistance given us in preparing this new, greatly revised version of Greenfield's *A Critical History of Old English Literature*. But first we should outline the areas of our separate tasks: Calder is responsible for the sections on Anglo-Saxon prose, Greenfield for the chapters on Anglo-Saxon poetry. As we note on the title page, Lapidge has contributed a survey of the Anglo-Latin background. Greenfield and Calder have read each other's work again and again, and each has made significant contributions to the other's part. Henry A. Kelly read the chapters on prose and made valuable suggestions. Jeannette Gilkison typed most of the book and offered us cheerful service, as she has often done. Matthew Miller and John Bernhardt put in long hours checking the many quotations and references, and to them we also extend our appreciation. The staffs of the University of Oregon Library and the University Research Library at UCLA have also been unfailingly helpful. We would especially like to thank Colin Jones of the New York University Press, who has given us considerable freedom to revise and expand the first edition as we saw best.

All translations in this book are our own, except that those of the Latin sources and analogues of the poetry are taken from

Calder/Allen 1976. For a few translations of Latin background material we have used (and cited) other works. Part of this project was underwritten by research grants from the Academic Senate of UCLA. For all errors of fact and blunders of style that remain, we take full responsibility.

Eugene, Oregon   Stanley B. Greenfield
Los Angeles, California   Daniel G. Calder

Acknowledgments

The maps of England in the tenth century and of the early kingdoms of the southern English are reproduced by permission of Cambridge University Press from P. H. Blair's *An Introduction to Anglo-Saxon England*. The *Beowulf* facsimile is reproduced by permission of The Early English Text Society and the Trustees of the British Library. The photograph of the Franks Casket (frontispiece) is reproduced by permission of the Trustees of the British Museum from a photograph in David M. Wilson, *Anglo-Saxon Art* (Thames and Hudson, 1984), illustration 37.

Acknowledgments are gratefully made to Southern Illinois University Press, for permission to reprint translations from Stanley B. Greenfield, *A Readable Beowulf* © 1982; and to D. S. Brewer Ltd., for permission to reprint translations from Michael J. B. Allen and Daniel G. Calder, *Sources and Analogues of Old English Poetry: The Major Latin Texts in Translation* © 1976.

Preface to
the Original Edition

It is a great pleasure to acknowledge the aid and comfort afforded me by various people in the course of writing this *Critical History*. First, to Kemp Malone and Charles Dunn, for recommending me for the volume to the General Editor, Oscar Cargill, and to Mr. Cargill for his encouragement at various stages of the enterprise. Then, to James E. Cross and Dorothy Bethurum, who carefully read the Introduction and the chapters on the prose, making suggestions both as to fact and style that have proved invaluable. To the staff of the University of Oregon Library for their cooperation, and to Mrs. Roxanne Erb and Sue Hamilton for their kindness and diligence in typing the manuscript. I am indebted most of all to Arthur G. Brodeur, Thelma C. Greenfield, and Jess B. Bessinger, Jr., who painstakingly read the entire manuscript; their tactful suggestions have spared my readers many an unconscious ambiguity of meaning and many a graceless phrasing, as well as spared me many a later blush at factual oversights. Such errors of fact and difficulties of style as remain I must acknowledge as my own.

Eugene, Oregon   Stanley B. Greenfield

A NEW CRITICAL HISTORY OF
OLD ENGLISH LITERATURE

Introduction

Anglo-Saxon prose and poetry are the major literary achievement of the early Middle Ages. In no other medieval vernacular language does such a hoard of verbal treasures exist for such an extended period (c. 700–1100). While some of the Germanic and Celtic nations produced works of high art, they cannot match the encyclopedic breadth of the Anglo-Saxons, who triumphed in almost every genre. They inherited a rich oral tradition from their Germanic ancestors; they absorbed the theological doctrine and rhetoric of their Christian Roman teachers. Yet they experimented and created new forms, while remaining true to this dual heritage. The result is a corpus of astonishing variety. We are fortunate to possess as many examples from these centuries as we do; if we had more of what must have been an even greater original creation, our wonder would grow in proportion.[1]

The singularity of their accomplishment is not only to be measured against that of neighboring or related peoples; it is also noteworthy within the history of English literature. Old English prose and poetry furnish a sense of depth and continuity in English thought, since the basic Christian tradition underlies most writing from the seventh to the nineteenth centuries. Microcosm and macrocosm, *ubi sunt*, consolation, Trinitarianism—these are some ideas and motifs that Old English texts share with the works of writers like Donne, Milton, Arnold, and Tennyson. But despite this community of thematic interest, Old English literature, for the most part, stands alone. While subsequent English prose may show some development out of its Anglo-Saxon origins, Old English poetry presents stylistically a unique body of material in which oral poetic techniques fuse with literary or rhetorical methods. Later poets, such as Hopkins and Pound, may have imitated a few of what they perceived as the striking qualities of Old English verse, yet this form of flattery still leaves the ancient patterns intact and unaffected. In truth, there is not a great deal of continuity from the Anglo-Saxon to what we have come to know as the "English literary tradition." What does exist is often artificial and contrived, and fails to evoke the spirit of the originals. When we review what the Anglo-Saxons did create within a span of four centuries, we must concentrate on it more or less by itself.

Some of the problems facing the historian of this literature are self-evident: the necessity of filling in historical background; of determining how much culture is "literary," or important for literary understanding; of assessing the relevance of Latin writings composed by Anglo-Saxons; of explaining certain linguistic features; and of establishing a proper sequence for the presentation of the works.[2] More properly the domain of the literary historian is commentary on poetic and prose styles, on genres and traditions, on metrics and prosody, as well as assessment of individual works and authors. Complicating the task are chronological problems with most of the poetry (the major surviving manuscripts all date from c. 1000) and a good deal of the prose, the anonymity of the authors, and the great amount of borrowing from tradition and from one or two named writers.

Since this book is a drastic revision of an earlier work, it will be useful to detail the major alterations which we have introduced. First, we have eliminated the initial chapter on Anglo-Latin prose, replacing it with Michael Lapidge's general survey of Anglo-Latin literature, written specifically for this revision with an eye toward providing a background for Old English literature.[3] Second, we have tripled the amount of space devoted to Anglo-Saxon prose. This reflects the growing scholarship on prose texts, and the sense that they are important in their own right, as well as providing a broad cultural backdrop for the study of Old English poetry. Prose

has for too long been the step-child of Old English literary studies. Third, it has been our intention to encompass the whole of
Anglo-Saxon literature; many prose and poetic texts are included
which did not make an appearance in the first edition: *The Grave,
The Rime of King William,* the penitentials, and various religious
tracts, to name a few.

Our intention has also been to incorporate as much as possible
of the scholarship and criticism that has blossomed in the past
twenty years. Thus the book is three things—a synopsis, a critical
reading of texts, and a history of the criticism. All of this has had
to be accomplished in a severely compressed fashion, but on occasion—the readings of Caedmon's *Hymn,* Ælfric's homily "On the
Lord's Prayer," or some of the "Elegies," for example—we have
permitted ourselves more scope for treating textual and interpretive problems. In addition, we have tried to account for some of
the renewed interest in the history of the discipline, seen as a history of tastes, styles, and attitudes;[4] the quickening of interest in
the study of Anglo-Saxon literature in relation to other arts and
sciences;[5] the reassignment of authorship for more than one prose
text; and the explosion of Christian-allegorical and oral-formulaic
studies. To assist readers in this endeavor, we have added a lengthy
bibliography, so that they might know what, in our opinion, to
read first, before turning to the definitive Greenfield/Robinson
compilation.[6] Our bibliography is arranged alphabetically by au-
thors/editors and keyed to abbreviated footnote references.

Perhaps the study of Old English literature still finds that its
primary question is the same one Alcuin asked nearly twelve
hundred years ago: *Quid Hinieldus cum Christo?* "What has Ingeld
to do with Christ?" This famous remonstrance, made in a letter
written in 797 to Hygebald, bishop of Lindisfarne, concerning the
monks' fondness for listening to heroic song in the refectory rather
than to spiritual wisdom, still forces us to consider how we should
understand and describe that extraordinary corpus which emerged
from the encounter between an unlettered Germanic tribal aesthetic and the remnants of the classical tradition, itself transformed by the Christian religion. Old English literature is a pal-
impsest, and few periods in the history of English literature offer
the literary historian a greater challenge—to comprehend and ap-

preciate the layers as they accumulated over many centuries, understanding its historical context and yet using modern critical techniques.

NOTES

1. On the losses in the medieval period, see Wilson 1952. On extant materials, see Ker 1957. On continuity, or the lack thereof, see Chambers 1932; Wrenn 1958; Wilson 1959.

2. For the history and culture of the OE period, see Stenton 1971; Hunter Blair 1956; Whitelock 1979; Campbell, Jas. 1982. All have excellent bibliographies, and Whitelock 1979 not only has a general introduction but comments on different sections and on specific works translated therein. For further historical and cultural bibliography, see Bonser 1957. Of the many grammars and introductory texts, we recommend Quirk/Wrenn 1958; Cassidy/Ringler 1971; Mitchell/Robinson 1982. The definitive study of OE syntax is Mitchell 1985. The standard dictionary is Bosworth/Toller 1882; Clark Hall/Meritt 1960 provides a concise dictionary. A concordance to all OE prose and poetry is Healey/Venezky 1980. Of previous histories of OE literature we may cite Malone 1967; Anderson, G. 1966 (with some reservations); Wrenn 1967. Calder 1982 reviews nearly all the surveys and histories of OE literature.

3. It is, to date, the only complete history of Anglo-Latin literature, even though condensed. Since some of the Anglo-Latin material impinges on OE prose and some of the poetry, there is inevitable overlap between chapter 1 and those following.

4. On the history of the discipline, see Adams, E. 1917; Stanley 1975; Calder 1979b; Berkhout/Gatch 1982.

5. On the interrelationships of art and literature, see Leyerle 1967; Schroeder 1974.

6. See Greenfield/Robinson 1980.

The Anglo-Latin Background

Most surviving Old English literature was composed and transmitted by Christian churchmen. This statement probably holds true
even of apparently secular literature, but it is unquestionably true
of the obviously ecclesiastical literature: homilies, saints' lives,
translations of Christian-Latin texts, ecclesiastical legislation,
prayers. Any literate person in the Anglo-Saxon period would have
been trained by the Church, either in a monastery, cathedral, lesser
canonry, or small minster. If we are properly to understand Old
English literature, we must know something of the circumstances
and context in which it was composed; in short, we must study
the Anglo-Saxon church.[1]

In Anglo-Saxon times, the language of Christianity was Latin.
The word of God *per se* was transmitted in a Latin Bible. The sac-
raments of baptism, marriage, and burial were conducted in Latin,
as were the Mass and other church ceremonies, such as the consecration of a king. In monasteries, all parts of the Divine Office
(that is, the daily cycle of prayers and hymns) were in Latin;
moreover, monks were obliged to speak the language among
themselves. Learning to read and write necessarily implied the
study of Latin, and a critical examination of Old English literature
should best begin with some reflections on the workings of the

Anglo-Saxon school. Since most of our rather sparse evidence pertains to monastic schools, we may consider a typical monastic education.

The young oblate or novice was received into the monastery at approximately the age of seven. From the outset he was expected to participate in the Divine Office, even though he would not at first have been able to understand a word. Since the Office consists almost entirely of psalmody and hymnody, the beginner would first have committed the Latin psalter to memory. His teacher would have aided memorization by means of literal explanations: hence, presumably, the complete Old English interlinear glosses of Latin texts in many Anglo-Saxon psalters. So too with the hymns. Because they were mostly composed in late antiquity and presented greater syntactical difficulties than the psalms, they were often recast in simple Latin prose and then provided with word-for-word interlinear glosses.[2]

By the time he had committed to memory long tracts from the Latin psalter and hymnal, the young student was ready for the rules of Latin grammar. In the early Anglo-Saxon period the teacher would have relied principally on the *Ars Minor* of Donatus, a fourth-century Latin grammarian, together with various Late Latin commentaries on Donatus. However, since these works were meant for Latin-speaking audiences and did not meet the needs of English-speaking students, a number of Anglo-Saxon scholars compiled Latin grammars of their own: Boniface and Tatwine in the early period, Alcuin and Ælfric in the later.[3] At this stage the student would also have received some elementary instruction in Latin metrics; here again, since the metrical treatises handed down from late antiquity hardly sufficed for speakers of a Germanic tongue, Aldhelm, Bede, and Boniface set about composing elementary metrical treatises for their Anglo-Saxon students. The novice was expected to speak as well as read Latin, and apparently learned to do so from Latin "colloquies," that is, model dialogues between master and students concerning business of the day, intended to impart the vocabulary necessary to discuss daily affairs; in the later period Ælfric and his student, Ælfric Bata, composed such pedagogical exercises (see chapter 3).

After the novice had learned the rudiments of Latin grammar

and meter, he proceeded to those Latin texts which constituted the medieval curriculum, a course lasting some ten years. The novices read the texts with minute attention: word for word, line for line. Probably the master dictated a passage and the students transcribed it onto wax tablets; by class on the following day they had to learn the text thoroughly. They then erased the passage and replaced it with the next. The curriculum-texts came in order of difficulty. Of course, those studied would have varied from place to place and from time to time;[4] and our information for Anglo-Saxon England is incomplete.

Nevertheless, we may deduce from surviving booklists[5] and manuscripts[6] that the Anglo-Saxon curriculum included study of the following texts—listed in order of difficulty: the *Disticha Catonis*, a collection of two-line moral maxims by an unknown Late Latin poet; the *Epigrammata* of Prosper of Aquitaine (died c. 455), a collection of some 106 epigrams, each of which is a metrical version of a moral maxim by St. Augustine; the *Evangelia*, a hexametrical version of the gospel narrative of Christ's life by the early fourth-century Spanish priest Juvencus; the *Carmen Paschale* of the fifth-century poet Caelius Sedulius, whose poem is, like Juvencus', an account of Christ's life, but with extensive allegorical and typological amplification; the *Psychomachia*, by the fourth-century Spanish poet Prudentius, an allegorical account of the struggle between the Virtues and the Vices; the early sixth-century Roman poet Arator's *De Actibus Apostolorum*, a hexametrical account in two books of the lives of SS. Peter and Paul as told in the biblical Acts of the Apostles; and the *Poema de Mosaicae Historiae Gestis* by Alcimus Avitus of Vienne (fl. 500), a hexametrical version of Genesis, as far as the Crossing of the Red Sea.[7]

The curriculum may have included other texts as well. In particular, Vergil's *Aeneid* and Lucan's *Pharsalia* seem to have been known throughout the Anglo-Saxon period, and in the later part, the *Satires* of Persius and the *De Consolatio Philosophiae* of Boethius come to the fore. But the staple of the curriculum remained the Christian-Latin poems. Study of these poems would have determined the tastes of the literate Anglo-Saxon and affected the form of Old English literature. Specific examples of such influence are the translation of the *Disticha Catonis* into Old English (see chapter 3); the collections of maxims in verse *(Maxims I* and *II* and *Pre-cepts);* the number of surviving Christian allegories *(The Seafarer, The Phoenix,* and *Physiologus);* and the large proportion of Old English biblical verse-narrative, including all the poems of the Junius manuscript *(Genesis B* is very largely based on Alcimus Avitus) and *Judith.*

When the student had completed his secondary education in curriculum texts, he pursued either the study of the scientific quadrivium (geometry, arithmetic, astronomy, and harmony), or, if he became a monk, spent the remainder of his life reading Scripture and the patristic authorities. There is little evidence that the quadrivium was widely studied in Anglo-Saxon England, but meditation on the writings of Ambrose, Augustine, Jerome, and Gregory would have been the lifelong occupation of a monk.

The large body of surviving Anglo-Latin compositions proves that schools flourished in Anglo-Saxon England. The English were among the earliest non-Latin-speaking peoples in Europe who had to master Latin after their conversion to Christianity, a task which they undertook with great zeal. As a result, many Anglo-Latin writings spread throughout Europe during the early Middle Ages. Proud of their achievement, the Anglo-Saxons often composed a Latin which is characterized by a lavish display of vocabulary designed to impress by the arcane nature of its learning; it abounds in obscure, learned-sounding words, such as archaisms, grecisms, and neologisms. Because this vocabulary often derived from certain Greek-Latin glossaries known as *Hermeneumata,* the style is usually referred to as "hermeneutic."[8] This recherché style commended much Anglo-Latin literature to medieval audiences, but also makes it seem alien to modern literary taste. Nevertheless, we must remember that the literate Anglo-Saxon expressed himself in both Old English and Latin; if we are to understand properly the context of Old English literature, we must have some notion of the range and nature of Anglo-Latin literature.[9]

We shall begin this survey of Anglo-Latin writings with early Southumbria (Mercia, Wessex, and Kent), before moving on to consider Northumbria. We may assume that Latin schools were first established in England with the arrival in 597 of Augustine and the Roman monks dispatched by Pope Gregory the Great. The first task of these monks would have been the training of a native English clergy capable of reading the Latin Bible and performing the Latin liturgy. They obviously enjoyed some success, for a generation later, in the 630s, a bishop of East Anglia, assisted by masters and teachers from Kent, established a new school based on this Kentish model.[10] And by 644, Ithamar, bishop of Rochester, was consecrated as the first native bishop, followed soon by the first native archbishop, Deusdedit (655–64). Unfortunately, Augustine and his companions appear to have left no Latin writings, although a gospel-book they brought to England may still survive, and some of the earliest Anglo-Saxon charters may show the influence of chancery documents they first introduced into England (see chapter 4).[11]

The arrival of Theodore of Tarsus in 669 and of his colleague, the African Hadrian, shortly after put Latin learning in England on a more secure basis. Theodore became archbishop of Canterbury (669–90) and Hadrian abbot of the monastery of SS. Peter and Paul (later St. Augustine's) nearby. They established a school in Canterbury to which students from all over England flocked. Bede describes it in glowing terms:

> And because both of them were extremely learned in sacred and secular literature, they attracted a crowd of students into whose minds they daily poured the streams of wholesome learning. They gave their hearers instruction not only in the books of the holy Scripture but also in the art of meter, astronomy, and ecclesiastical computation. As evidence of this, some of their students still survive who know Latin and Greek just as well as their native tongue. Never had there been such happy times since the English first came to Britain. . . .[12]

Very few writings of Theodore (and none of Hadrian) survive, but later glossaries reveal the impact and range of his teaching. These preserve his explanations of various biblical passages and other texts, and display an amazing knowledge of earlier authorities, including many Greek patristic authors otherwise unknown in the Latin West.[13]

Among those who studied with Theodore and Hadrian was Aldhelm (died 709), who may justly be called the first English man of letters; indeed, it is doubtful whether the Anglo-Saxons ever produced a man of greater learning or literary enterprise. Aldhelm was born in Wessex, possibly around 640, of a noble family with royal connections. He studied at Canterbury in the early 670s, before becoming abbot of Malmesbury in 673 or 674 and eventually bishop of Sherborne in 706. The range of Aldhelm's Latin writings is impressive.[14] His prose writings include a collection of ten letters addressed to various persons on a variety of subjects: the question of Easter reckoning (in a letter to Geraint, king of Dumnonia), the difficulties of metrical and computistical studies (in a letter to the bishop of Wessex), and the advantages of English over Irish education (in letters to his students Heahfrith and Wihtfrith). He also addressed a massive epistle, the so-called *Epistola ad Acircium*, to King Aldfrith of Northumbria (685–705), with whom he evidently enjoyed a close relationship. The preface to this treatise contains a long discussion of the allegorical significance of the number 7; but two distinct yet complementary treatises on Latin metrics, the *De Metris* and *De Pedum Regulis*, make up its main part. Aldhelm was perhaps the earliest Anglo-Saxon to attempt to explain the difficulties of metrical composition for his students. The *Epistola ad Acircium* also includes a collection of 100 metrical *Enigmata* (see below), which illustrate the properties of the hexameter.

Aldhelm's longest and most influential work was a treatise on virginity *(De Virginitate)*, addressed to Abbess Hildelith and a sorority of nuns at Barking Abbey, near London. In its opening chapters Aldhelm follows several patristic authorities in recognizing three grades of virginity, though he departs from them in emphasizing the state of *castitas*. In his description, this state pertains to those who have formerly been married, but who have rejected their spouses in favor of the celibate life—the situation of some of the nuns at Barking. Following this lengthy theoretical discussion, Aldhelm gives brief accounts of exemplary male virgins, in rough chronological order: Old Testament virgins such as Elijah; New Testament ones such as John the Baptist; Christian martyrs and confessors of the early centuries. A similar list of female virgins follows this catalogue. Aldhelm ends by warning the nuns against the dangers of ostentatious dress.

Apart from the number of sources which Aldhelm drew upon,

this treatise's most striking feature is the prose style: long, almost Joycean, sentences studded with obscure vocabulary, interlaced word order, biblical similes, and alliteration. Aldhelm was apparently writing in a tradition of Late Latin continental prose; he was not following Irish models.[15] But whatever the source of inspiration his style had an immediate impact on English readers, and for the next four centuries many Anglo-Latin authors, notably Boniface and Byrhtferth (see below), modeled their prose on his.

As a Latin poet Aldhelm was also an influential innovator.[16] He appears, for example, to have pioneered a sort of Latin rhythmical verse called continuous octosyllables. He has left one lengthy poem in this verse form; it describes the cataclysmic effects of a mighty storm on a small church somewhere in southwest England. In addition, he was the first medieval Latin poet who was not a native speaker of Latin to be faced with the difficult task of composing extensive quantitative verse. Latin quantitative verse combines long and short syllables in a manner utterly distinct from Old English verse, which consists of stress-patterns and alliteration. An early medieval poet who did not speak Latin would have had to learn the quantity of Latin syllables painstakingly, and the process of combining them (not to mention the infinite complexities of hiatus, elision, and the rest) would have presented formidable problems. It is a mark of Aldhelm's achievement that he was able to master so foreign a medium.[17]

Aldhelm's surviving corpus of quantitative Latin verse consists of several works. First, there is a collection of *tituli*, which were intended for the dedication of various churches and altars. These *tituli* (or *Carmina Ecclesiastica*) throw considerable light on the form and structure of early Anglo-Saxon churches. One of them (no. V), ostensibly commemorating a series of altars dedicated to the twelve apostles, in fact gives brief accounts of how and where each apostle met his end. The poem is an interesting forerunner of the Old English *Fates of the Apostles* (see chapter 7). Aldhelm's longest poem, the *Carmen de Virginitate*, is a metrical counterpart to his earlier prose version. In composing such a verse counterpart, Aldhelm created an *opus geminatum* or "twin work," thus continuing an ancient tradition.[18] In particular he here imitated the Late Latin poet Caelius Sedulius, who composed a prose treatise to accompany his earlier *Carmen Paschale*. Aldhelm's *Carmen de Virginitate* is not, however, a slavish versification of the earlier prose work. He condensed drastically the theoretical discussion of virginity, made a number of additions and deletions to the catalogues of exemplary virgins, and added a final section describing an allegorical battle between the Vices and Virtues, which seems to be indebted to Prudentius' *Psychomachia*.

Perhaps Aldhelm's most influential poetic work was the collection of *Enigmata* inserted in the *Epistola ad Acircium*. Like the Late Latin poet Symphosius, Aldhelm wrote 100 *enigmata*. In view of the seriousness of Aldhelm's theme, the term should probably be rendered "Mysteries" rather than "Riddles," for Aldhelm set out to reveal the hidden links between all creation—animate and inanimate—and by means of an intricate web of interlocking themes and metaphors to lead the reader to contemplate God's Creation afresh. Drawing his subjects mainly from Pliny, Isidore, and his own observation of nature, Aldhelm wove them together in the final *enigma*, which is "Creation" itself.

These *Enigmata* were widely read in early medieval Europe, inspiring many imitators. Tatwine, a Mercian scholar who subsequently became archbishop of Canterbury (731–4), composed forty such *enigmata*.[19] They reflect the high seriousness of Aldhelm's collection and contain subtle ruminations on God and on man's means of comprehending His creation—the whole united by a vast acrostic which embraces all forty items. Another Anglo-Latin poet (very probably a Southumbrian as well), named Eusebius, completed Tatwine's collection by adding a further sixty *enigmata*.[20] But these lack the intellectual subtlety of Aldhelm's and Tatwine's, and many are simply uninspired versifications of subjects from the Latin *Physiologus* (Bestiary). Aldhelm's *Enigmata* also influenced Old English poets: several of them were translated into Anglo-Saxon. The *Lorica* (no. XXXIII)—Breastplate—was early translated into the Northumbrian dialect and survives as the so-called *Leiden Riddle*. A verse translation of the final *enigma*, "Creation" (no. C), is found among the Old English riddles in the Exeter Book, a collection of some 90 riddles which may have been assembled on the model of Aldhelm's group of 100 (see chapter 11).

Aldhelm was the most important and influential Southumbrian

author of the early period, but he was not an isolated figure. One of his students, the poet Æthilwald, composed four poems using continuous octosyllables in imitation of his teacher's *Carmen Rhythmicum*.[21] Another scholar, who was apparently Aldhelm's colleague or student, composed the fascinating *Liber Monstrorum*, a prose work consisting of three books, on monsters, beasts, and serpents respectively.[22] Whereas Aldhelm's *Enigmata* treat of the natural world in its normal manifestations, the *Liber Monstrorum* concerns itself with unnatural monstrosities—giants, Harpies, and Minotaurs, among others. The *Liber Monstrorum* includes a chapter on an extraordinarily tall man (hence a monster) called Hygelac (I.2); this is probably the earliest reference in an English source to Hygelac, the Geatish king and Beowulf's uncle.

Returning to the Mercian scholar Tatwine, we note that he also compiled an elementary *Ars Grammatica*,[23] one further reflection of the early Anglo-Saxon concern with pedagogy and the problems of teaching Latin grammar as a foreign language. From Mercia too came the Felix (otherwise unknown) who composed the *Vita S. Guthlaci* (c. 740), a verbose and occasionally difficult account of the Mercian nobleman Guthlac, who abandoned the world and became, on the model of St. Antony in Egypt, a lonely anchorite in the fens near present-day Crowland. There he waged a lifelong struggle against devilish apparitions.[24] Felix's work was one of the earliest Southumbrian saints' lives.[25] The elaborate Latin prose resembles Aldhelm's, and the work influenced Old English literature: it was translated into vernacular prose, served as the certain source of one poem in the Exeter Book *(Guthlac B)*, and may have inspired another *(Guthlac A)*.

As Latin culture became firmly established in Southumbrian monasteries during the late seventh century, some zealous English Christians began to turn their attention to the still pagan inhabitants of Germany; and from this time onwards there was increasing intercourse between Southumbria and the peoples of Germany and Friesland.[26] The greatest of these Southumbrian missionaries was Boniface, whose activities in Hesse and Thuringia earned him the title "Apostle of Germany."[27] Born near Exeter (c. 675) with the English name Wynfrith, he spent his adolescence studying Latin under one Wynberht at the monastery of

Nursling (Hants.). To these early years, presumably, belongs the composition of his elementary *Ars Grammatica*.[28] Boniface's *Ars* is distinguished by being the first Latin grammar to include full conjugations of all classes of Latin verbs—such useful information had been taken for granted by the Late Latin grammarians. He also wrote a collection of twenty metrical *enigmata*, each in the form of an acrostic, treating the Vices and Virtues.[29] Although he could have had a distinguished career as a grammarian and scholar, Boniface chose to pursue missionary work overseas; he left England forever in 719. While attempting to extend the influence of the church in Friesland, he was martyred, at Dokkum, in 754.

A large body of correspondence chronicles Boniface's continental career in detail. Assembled after his death by a close follower who remains anonymous, this collection includes letters by Boniface himself, as well as by a circle of correspondents in England, and by the various popes with whom Boniface had dealings.[30] These letters throw much light on the nature of the intellectual contacts between Boniface and his English well-wishers, in particular on the passage of books between English houses and Boniface in Germany. They reveal clearly the surprisingly high standard of literacy among otherwise unknown clergy of the time. Many of Boniface's letters implore support for his mission—through prayers, books, or helpers; and many helpers from Southumbria did travel to Germany to assist him. They have left traces in the record of Anglo-Latin literature. A number of letters by Lul, Boniface's successor as archbishop of Mainz and a former student at Malmesbury, are preserved in the corpus of Bonifatian correspondence.

Another English follower, one Willibald, composed a lengthy life of the saint (the *Vita S. Bonifatii*), probably at Mainz between 754 and 768. Another saint's life from the orbit of the Bonifatian mission is the eccentric *Vita SS. Willibaldi et Wynnebaldi*, written by an English nun of Heidenheim named Hygeburg. Willibald and Wynnebald were brothers from Wessex; Willibald (not to be confused with Boniface's hagiographer) became bishop of Eichstätt, and Wynnebald, abbot of Heidenheim. Hygeburg's *vita*, composed in a highly elaborate and unusual prose, provides a fascinating account of a journey made by Willibald to the Holy Land

and the eastern Mediterranean in the years 723–9. This work may fairly be described as the earliest travel-book from an English pen.[31] Through the agency of the Bonifatian mission, then, many Anglo-Latin works—notably the writings of Aldhelm and glossaries such as that known as the "Leiden Glossary"—were transmitted to the Continent. The "Leiden Glossary" is of particular importance, because its Latin-Old English lists preserve some of the earliest surviving Old English vocabulary; it was copied at St. Gallen c. 800.

In Northumbria somewhat different circumstances obtained. Paulinus' early mission met with initial success in the conversion of King Edwin (627); but this was short-lived, and by the mid-seventh century the only active center of learning in the north was Whitby, under the direction of the energetic Abbess Hild.[32] As at Canterbury before the advent of Theodore and Hadrian, help had to be sought from outside England; but whereas the Southumbrians turned to Rome, the Northumbrians turned to Ireland and Iona. The story of Aidan and his Irish monks at Lindisfarne is well known. Through them, Irish learning was brought to England. Late seventh-century manuscripts from Northumbria show its impress in both script and decoration, and Anglo-Latin literature from Northumbria also bears the stamp of Irish influence.

A number of late seventh- or early eighth-century Latin saints' lives survive to indicate that Northumbria enjoyed a high standard of Latin training. The anonymous *Vita S. Gregorii*, a life of Pope Gregory the Great, was produced at Whitby (680–704). This is one of the most idiosyncratic and engaging of all the Anglo-Latin *vitae*, and contains a version of the famous story of Gregory and the English slave boys, as well as numerous (and spurious) miracles involving the great pope. At Lindisfarne, between 699 and 705, an anonymous monk produced the *Vita S. Cuthberti*, a detailed and loving account of the holy life and miracles of St. Cuthbert (died 687), who, although an Englishman, lived his austerely religious life after the manner of an Irish hermit. A monk of Ripon, customarily referred to as "Eddius" Stephanus, composed (710–20?) the *Vita S. Wilfridi*, a life of the indefatigable Bishop Wilfrid (died 709). The work is in effect an *apologia* for Wilfrid, who, during the course of a stormy career, was expelled many times from various Northumbrian sees by several kings and ecclesiastical councils, and who invariably sought papal endorsement for his position. The *Vita S. Wilfridi* presents a vivid but partisan account of these struggles. Soon after the death of Abbot Ceolfrith (716), an anonymous monk at Wearmouth-Jarrow wrote the *Vita S. Ceolfridi;* this brief work gives a valuable glimpse of the origin and spiritual life of the monastery Ceolfrith helped to found.[33]

For more than a century Wearmouth-Jarrow outshone all other Northumbrian monasteries as a result of the learning and fame of its most celebrated monk, the Venerable Bede (672/3–735).[34] We know little of Bede's life beside what he himself tells us in an autobiographical chapter at the end of his *Historia Ecclesiastica* (V.24): that he was delivered as an oblate to Wearmouth-Jarrow aged seven, that he studied under Benedict Biscop and Ceolfrith and was successively ordained deacon and priest, and that otherwise he spent his entire life in that monastery studying the Scriptures, teaching, and writing. The range of Bede's learning was immense, as was the extent of his writing;[35] he embraced grammar, hagiography, natural science, computus (see below), history, biblical exegesis, and poetry as his intellectual province. But all his diverse works are marked by one characteristic—clarity of exposition. Bede was a teacher *par excellence,* and he devoted his greatest energy to the instruction of his monastic pupils. One of the most moving texts to have come down to us from the Latin Middle Ages is the account of Bede's last days by his student Cuthbert, the *Epistola Cuthberti de Obitu Bedae.*[36] Here we see Bede, bedridden and terminally ill, expounding to his circle of disciples the Gospel of St. John and explaining the deficiencies of Isidore's *De Natura Rerum* on the pretext that "I cannot have my children learning what is not true, and losing their labor on this when I am gone."[37] This sentiment animates nearly all of Bede's writing.

Three didactic works set off Bede's concern with pedagogy to advantage: a treatise on correct Latin spelling *(De Orthographia),* one on metrics *(De Arte Metrica)* and one on elementary cosmology *(De Natura Rerum).*[38] Bede drew the first from a wide range of grammatical authorities, but organized it in alphabetical order for ease of consultation. So too the *De Arte Metrica:* here Bede consulted many Late Latin grammarians, but took care to substitute examples from Christian Latin poets (especially those discussed above as "curriculum authors") where the earlier grammarians had cited classical Latin authors. In this way Bede made his work more appropriate for Christian teaching and more accessible to the students who were reading their way through the medieval curriculum. He also added an appendix *(De Schematibus et Tropis)* in which he described the numerous rhetorical figures and illustrated them with biblical examples. Because of its clarity and utility, Bede's *De Arte Metrica* became the principal textbook on Latin metrics in the early Middle Ages. Equally popular was the brief *De Natura Rerum*. In this work, probably one of his earliest, Bede assembled passages—mostly from Isidore and Pliny—on such subjects as the elements, the firmament, the motion of the planets, and eclipses. A notable feature of the *De Natura*, as it is preserved in some manuscripts, is a series of source-marks by which Bede scrupulously identified his sources.

Another aspect of Bede's pedagogy was his concern with computus, or what we might call ecclesiastical arithmetic. A subject of almost intolerable complexity, it consists of mathematical rules and procedures for calculating the dates of the movable feasts of the Christian year. The date of Easter was the most important of these, not only because of its central place in Christian history, but also because other dates depended upon it. By Bede's time, various procedures were in circulation, and in his view, many of them were dangerously wrong. He set out to demolish the erroneous ones and to expound the principles upon which to base correct ones. He wrote two treatises: a short, early work, *De Temporibus* (703), and the more expansive *De Temporum Ratione* (725);[39] apparently his students found the early work too condensed. Medieval computists all over Europe read *De Temporum Ratione,* and it survives in hundreds of manuscripts. In many ways it is still the most helpful exposition of this difficult subject.

Biblical exegesis, however, made up the bulk of Bede's literary output. He compiled commentaries on the following books of the Old Testament: Genesis, part of Exodus (chapters XXIV–XXX = *De Tabernaculo)*, parts of Samuel and Kings, parts of Chronicles (= *De Templo Salomonis)*, Ezra and Nehemiah, Tobit, Proverbs, Song of Songs and the minor prophet Habakkuk; of the New Testament he wrote commentaries on the gospels of Mark and Luke, two treatises on the Acts of the Apostles, a collection of patristic opinions on the Pauline Epistles, and commentaries on the seven Catholic Epistles and on Revelation.[40]

In these commentaries Bede was mostly concerned to assemble and sift the opinions of earlier Church Fathers rather than to venture his own; some of his exegetical works—for example, *In Genesim* and the *Collectaneum* on the Pauline Epistles—are little more than centos of quotations from patristic sources. By nature Bede favors philological and historical exposition and avoids the wilder excesses of allegorical interpretation. He prefers to interpret a biblical text literally, and will only attempt to extract an allegorical interpretation when he feels justified in so doing by recourse to other biblical texts. A typical instance occurs near the beginning of Book I of *In Ezram et Nehemiam;* Bede says he did not arrive at the mystical interpretation of King Cyrus as the Savior "by his own interpretation *(ex nostra coniectura)* but through the clear statements of the prophet Isaiah."[41] Normally Bede concentrates on explaining the meaning of Hebrew and Greek terms (basing himself on Jerome's treatises on Hebrew names), identifying biblical persons and places, and explaining historical references and allusions. One of Bede's mature works, the *Retractatio* or "Revision" of his earlier *Expositio* on the Acts of the Apostles (c. 709), best exemplifies these characteristics. In the later work Bede clarified numerous points of ambiguity which had earlier eluded him, by recourse to a Greek text of the Acts (the actual manuscript used by Bede survives in Oxford, Bodleian Library, Laud Grec. 35), and hence he was in a position to compare Jerome's Vulgate translation with the Greek original. In short, Bede's biblical commentaries provided what might be called philological and historical commentary; he wished to clarify the meaning of the Bible for his students. But this desire gave his commentaries wider appeal and some survive in hundreds of copies.

Bede's small corpus of Latin poetry also deserves mention.[42] Among his works he listed a book of epigrams and a book of hymns. These have not been preserved entire, but remnants of each exist, enough to indicate that Bede, like Aldhelm, composed *tituli* for the dedication of churches. He also composed, as a supplement to the Old Hymnal, a series of hymns for different liturgical feasts in the iambic dimeter of Ambrosian hymns. In the *Historia Ecclesiastica* he included two of his poems, one on St. Æthelthryth, the other an epitaph for Bishop Wilfrid. These, together with his metrical *Vita S. Cuthberti*, show him to have been thoroughly steeped in Vergil and the Christian-Latin poets, and to have been a more competent Latin versifier than Aldhelm. Perhaps he also composed the long moralizing poem on the Day of Judgment *(De Die Iudicii)*, which was widely read during the Middle Ages and was translated into Old English *(Judgment Day II—* see chapter 10) at a time near the millenium when men were thinking hard of the Judgment to come.

Bede was also active as a hagiographer.[43] His interest in this most widely practised of all early medieval literary genres manifests itself in the extensive reading program which lay behind his revision of the Hieronymian *Martyrology*. Unhappily, Bede's own *Martyrology* does not survive in complete and unadulterated form. In the metrical *Vita S. Cuthberti*, his earliest essay in hagiography, Bede provided a hexametrical version of the anonymous Lindisfarne *Vita S. Cuthberti*. Bede knew the tradition of prose and verse paraphrase, and in his poetic version of Cuthbert's life, he seems to have modelled himself on Arator's verse rendering of the Acts of the Apostles. Like Arator, Bede gives a prose summary of each event in Cuthbert's life, and then, in the accompanying verse, expands on its theological and moral significance. His verse *vita*, therefore, is not a close or literal rendition of the anonymous *vita*. Bede showed himself interested in the relationship between verse and prose on other occasions. He produced a prose version of the life of St. Felix, the patron saint of Nola, which had earlier been treated in verse by the Late Latin poet Paulinus of Nola. Another work of hagiography which Bede lists, but which has hitherto been presumed lost, is the *Passio S. Anastasii*, an account of a seventh-century Persian martyr. Bede thought that it had been badly translated from the Greek and he attempted to correct it. The recent discovery of Bede's corrected version should throw new light on his knowledge of Greek and his hagiographical methods.

Bede's prose *Vita S. Cuthberti* (c. 721) remains his best-known essay in hagiography. Here Bede shows that he understood well the aims of the hagiographer. His principal source, the anonymous Lindisfarne *Vita S. Cuthberti* once again, was written by a member of the community in which Cuthbert had lived, and it is full of personal reminiscences and incidental details. Such matters may be of great interest to modern historians, but Bede saw that they were inappropriate in a saint's *vita*. The hagiographer must demonstrate that the saint in question was a vessel of God's grace, residing only temporarily in a human frame, but eternally a member of the community of God's saints, who may intercede on behalf of those who pray to him. Thus it matters little whether the saint's human form was tall or short, hairy or smooth, or whether he was born at Lichfield or Lastingham; what does matter is his efficacy as a vessel of divine *virtus* and his ability to demonstrate this power through *virtutes* or miracles. Bede systematically set out to recast the earlier anonymous *vita* of Cuthbert, eliminating all its local detail and drawing attention, in many homiletic additions, to the saint's eternal virtues. Shorn of local detail, Bede's prose *Vita S. Cuthberti* appealed to an international medieval audience.

While Bede's pedagogical, exegetical, and hagiographical writings were extensive, it is as a historian that he is best known today.[44] Indeed, without Bede's historical works, our knowledge of early Anglo-Saxon England would be minimal. Bede's scholarly interest in computus led naturally to an interest in chronology and in the ages of the world. He wrote a brief letter to one Plegwine on the Six Ages of the World, and appended to his *De Temporum Ratione* a broader treatment of the same subject. This appendix is a chronicle in its own right, referred to as the *Chronica Maiora*,[45] since in his treatment of the sixth or present age Bede brought his account from the first year of Christ's life up to the death of Ceolfrith (716), abbot of Wearmouth-Jarrow. In compiling these *Chronica Maiora*, Bede drew on a variety of historical sources, notably the chronicles of Jerome, with continuations, and Rufinus' Latin translation of the Greek historian Eusebius' *Ecclesiastical History*. Bede's work on these *Chronica Maiora* was preparatory to his ultimate historical enterprise. Also preparatory was the brief *Historia Abbatum* (725–30),[46] an account of the foundation of Bede's own monastery at Wearmouth-Jarrow, and of its two principal abbots, Benedict Biscop and Ceolfrith.

But it is Bede's *Ecclesiastical History* (*Historia Ecclesiastica Gentis*

Anglorum)[47] which has secured his reputation for twelve centuries. This work, written at the end of his scholarly career, is universally regarded as a masterpiece of historical composition. Bede's immediate model appears to have been the *Ecclesiastical History* of Eusebius, although he also knew other Late Latin historical writings, such as Orosius (see chapter 3). However, rather than attempt a universal history like theirs, Bede decided to limit his scope to the English people, following the example of the *Historia Francorum* by Gregory of Tours. Bede's *Historia Ecclesiastica* is divided into five roughly equal books, and extends from Julius Caesar's attempted invasion of Britain in 60 B.C. to A.D. 731, the year in which Bede finished his work. Each of the books has an individual focus: the background to the Augustinian mission (I), Gregory the Great and the Augustinian mission, as far as Paulinus' return from Northumbria (II), the subsequent growth of the Northumbrian Church under Irish influence (III), Archbishop Theodore and Cuthbert (IV), and the present state of the Church in England (V). But into this broad historical framework Bede inserted an impressive variety of papal and episcopal correspondence, *acta* of church councils, anecdotes, metrical epitaphs, and many poetic quotations. He recounts at length the visions of holy men—Fursa and Dryhthelm, for example—and frequently departs from his narrative to record miracles. The whole work is unified mainly by its general concern with the growth of the Church in England. Yet in spite of its seeming lack of coherent organization, it makes compelling reading.[48] Bede has told many of the stories so well that they have become a permanent part of our literary heritage. Who has never heard the tale of Pope Gregory and the English slaveboys (II.1)? Or the comparison of man's life to the passage of a sparrow in and out of a hall on a wintry night (II.13)? Or the story of the illiterate peasant Caedmon and his miraculous gift of poetry (IV.24[22])? Like several of Bede's works, the *Historia Ecclesiastica* survives in hundreds of manuscripts, and was one of the Latin texts translated into Old English at the time of King Alfred's revival of learning in the late ninth century (see chapter 2).

In what may have been his last work, the *Epistola ad Ecgberhtum*, Bede wrote to Ecgberht, archbishop of York (732–66) and one of his former students, instructing him on a bishop's duties and on the need to study Latin. Ecgberht apparently took this advice to heart, for he penned a brief *Dialogus Ecclesiastice Institutionis*, a series of questions and answers on the relationship of secular to ecclesiastical law in matters such as the giving of oaths and the commission of capital crimes. A penitential has also been transmitted under Ecgberht's name and it may be an authentic work. These two items[49] reveal that Ecgberht was concerned with ecclesiastical discipline in his archdiocese; but we also know that he was a conscientious teacher.

His successor, Ælberht (767–78), continued his task of building up York as a center of learning. On several occasions he made trips abroad in search of books and amassed one of the finest libraries in Europe. No writings of Ælberht survive, but we know about his teaching and library from a lengthy poem by his most illustrious student, Alcuin. In his *Versus de Patribus, Regibus et Sanctis Euboricensis Ecclesiae* (On the Bishops, Kings and Saints of York),[50] Alcuin described the progress of the Christian Church in Northumbria, with particular attention to Deira and the see of York, from its beginnings up to Ælberht's death, two years after his retirement, in 780. For the earlier period Alcuin depended mainly on Bede's *History* and metrical *Vita S. Cuthberti;* for the latter part, especially the accounts of Ecgberht and Ælberht, Alcuin relied on his personal experience. The later sections thus contain a glowing description of Ælberht's teaching, and of the library he assembled (which was subsequently bequeathed to Alcuin), and an impassioned lament on his death.

Alcuin (died 804) was born near York and received his schooling there;[51] he would have been over forty at the time of Ælberht's death. For Eanbald, his colleague and Ælberht's episcopal successor, he travelled to Rome to fetch the *pallium*. On his return in 781 he met the emperor Charlemagne at Parma. This encounter proved of immense consequence for Carolingian learning: Charlemagne invited Alcuin to take charge of his palace school. Alcuin accepted the invitation, with the result that he left England in 782 and, except for a visit in 786 and a stay of three years (790–3), spent the remainder of his life on the Continent. He served as master of Charlemagne's palace school and toward the end of his life (796–804) as abbot of the wealthy monastery at Tours.

During the years of his continental sojourn Alcuin produced a vast corpus of Latin writings:[52] poems, letters, school texts, biblical exegeses, theological treatises, and hagiography. With few exceptions, possibly including the poem on York, none of his works was produced in England; they therefore throw only indirect light on Latin learning in eighth-century Northumbria. Of particular interest to students of Old English literature are some of Alcuin's Latin poems[53] and his treatise *De Virtutibus et Vitiis*. Alcuin's poems encompass a large array of subjects. Many of them are merely functional, such as epitaphs and inscriptions, but in some there is an intense, personal tone of reflection on the joys and beauty— but also the inevitable transience—of this earthly life (e.g., nos. IX, XI, XXIII, and LV–LVI). These poems are reminiscent of the Old English elegies, especially *The Wanderer* and *The Seafarer* (see chapter 12). The treatise *De Virtutibus et Vitiis*, a layman's handbook compiled from numerous sources, including Isidore and some pseudo-Augustinian homilies, was used by Ælfric in his *Catholic Homilies* and translated into Old English in the tenth century (see chapter 3).

The remainder of Alcuin's writings have perhaps less direct relevance to later Old English literature, but their importance for Carolingian learning is inestimable. As Charlemagne's principal advisor on matters ecclesiastical, liturgical, and educational, Alcuin was the architect of the "Carolingian Renaissance." We can easily trace Alcuin's involvement in Carolingian learning through the large collection of his letters: 230 survive from the time he spent on the Continent, about 200 of which date from the period of his abbacy.[54] Alcuin probably also drafted the circular letters issued by Charlemagne which set out the emperor's program for educational renewal and standardization. In addition, Alcuin wrote treatises on grammar (*Ars Grammatica*), rhetoric (*De Rhetorica*), and orthography (*De Orthographia*). He may even have been responsible for establishing the standard orthography and pronunciation of medieval Latin which obtained throughout the Middle Ages.[55] His brief treatise on dialectic (*De Dialectica*) has been seen as the earliest medieval attempt to assimilate the principles of Aristotelian logic.[56]

Alcuin's theological writings include the *De Virtutibus et Vitiis*, as well as a treatise *De Animae Ratione* (also used by Ælfric), and a longer work on Trinitarian theology, *De Trinitate*. As Charlemagne's spokesman on matters ecclesiastical, Alcuin was responsible for a number of dogmatic treatises against the heresy of Adoptianism (which held that Christ was not the true but only the adoptive son of God), a subject of intense debate in the late eighth century. He wrote an account of a relative, the Anglo-Saxon missionary to Friesland, Willibrord *(Vita S. Willibrordi)*; this he cast in both prose and verse after the models of Aldhelm and Bede. To Alcuin also belong the *vitae* of St. Martin, the patron saint of Tours, St. Vedastus, patron saint of Saint-Vaast, and St. Richarius of Saint-Riquier.[57] His exegetical commentaries cover Genesis, the Song of Songs, Ecclesiastes, the Gospel of John, and Revelation (unfinished). Alcuin had a great reputation for biblical scholarship among his contemporaries, and he was accordingly asked to produce a revised version of Jerome's Vulgate, since many errors had crept into the text as a result of scribal lapses and the vagaries of manuscript transmission. His revision involved elimination of errors in punctuation, grammar, and orthography, and his "corrected" text henceforth became standard.[58] In this undertaking, as in all his endeavors, Alcuin's main concern was with correctness, consistency, and order.

The impact of Alcuin's skill as teacher and scholar is reflected in the writings of his pupils, among them some of the most influential and learned men of the next generation, men such as Hrabanus Maurus, abbot of Fulda, and Hildebold, archbishop of Cologne. Two of Alcuin's English students who had followed the master to the Continent have left writings of their own: Hwita, better known as Candidus, and Frithugils.[59] Alcuin also remained in contact with his former pupils at York, some of whom sent him (for correction?) a lengthy poem on the life and miracles of St. Nynia, an early missionary of Whithorn (the *Miracula S. Nyniae*).[60] Little more than a pastiche of quotations from the curriculum poets, this exercise may have been written at York in the late eighth century. Another Northumbrian Latin poem composed at roughly this time was the so-called *De Abbatibus* by one Æthilwulf.[61] This poem details the foundation and abbots of an unidentified monastic cell of Lindisfarne. Like Alcuin's poem on the saints of York, it treats events in chronological order, and closes with an intimate vision of the cell's brethren, past and present, all reunited in heaven. From a reference to a bishop of Lindisfarne, the poem may be dated to 803–21.

Lindisfarne was sacked by the Vikings in 793: this disaster—lamented by Alcuin in a long, elegiac poem (no. II)—was the harbinger of a century of Viking activity. As a result of their attacks, the fortunes of the English church in the ninth century were at a low ebb. The Vikings are unlikely to have been the sole cause of the decline, but to judge from surviving specimens, it appears that very few manuscripts were copied during that century. Further, no Latin literature was written between Æthilwulf's poem and the revival of learning initiated by King Alfred. In a famous passage from the Preface to his English translation of Gregory's *Regula Pastoralis* 'The Pastoral Care,' Alfred noted that on his accession in 871 there was not a single man south of the Humber who could understand divine services in Latin, or translate from Latin into English. Alfred's statement receives striking confirmation from a series of original charters issued at Canterbury in the 860s, which reveal that the principal scribe there was an old man nearly blind, who could scarcely see to correct the appalling grammatical errors he committed.[62] Alfred took decisive measures to correct this situation (see chapter 2). Additionally, many books were brought to England from the Continent at this time, and thus began the gradual restocking of Anglo-Saxon libraries that had been depleted during the ninth century.

The educational revival begun by Alfred continued under his successors, his son Edward the Elder (899–924) and his grandson Æthelstan (924–39). They too were concerned with obtaining a literate clergy and with providing endowments of monasteries to make such literacy possible; they also maintained the flow of books and scholars into England from the Continent. As evidence of this revival, we find during Æthelstan's reign a number of Latin poems from various centers, some of them apparently composed by foreign clerics.[63] One such continental scholar may have been Frithegod, who composed his *Breviloquium Vitae Wilfredi* at Canterbury during the decade 948–58;[64] by any reckoning this is one of the most difficult medieval Latin poems. Archbishop Oda of Canterbury (died 958) had acquired St. Wilfrid's relics from Ripon during an expedition to the north in 948; to celebrate his acquisition he commissioned Frithegod to make a hexametrical version of the *Vita S. Wilfridi* by "Eddius" Stephanus (see above). Oda himself provided a prose preface in appropriately difficult Latin prose. Frithegod's poem is a masterpiece of the "hermeneutic" style, bristling with archaisms, grecisms, and neologisms in such profusion that many lines cannot be understood even with the guidance of the prose *vita*.

In a similar vein, but later in the century, the layman Æthelweard produced his *Chronicon* (978–88), a Latin prose translation of a (lost) version of the Anglo-Saxon Chronicles. Like Frithegod's, the Latin of Æthelweard is almost impenetrable, clotted with glossary words of all sorts and couched in incoherent Latin syntax. If we believe the preface that the work is by a layman, then it is a most astonishing production.[65] These two works set the standard for Latin style in verse and prose for the late Anglo-Saxon period. They attest clearly to the revival of learning in the tenth century, but illustrate that, in its extreme form, learning could become pretentious and arcane.

The Benedictine reform movement provided the impetus for the great burgeoning of English learning and literature—in both Latin and the vernacular—during the second half of the tenth century (see also chapter 3). In certain respects the English movement reenacted the Carolingian reform of ecclesiastical discipline initiated by Louis the Pious (died 840) and his ecclesiastical advisor, Benedict of Aniane. The *capitula* of an episcopal synod held by Louis and Benedict at Aachen in 817, together with such related documents as the *Memoriale qualiter* (a detailed exposition of a monk's daily duties), laid down the guidelines for the English reform; they were frequently copied in tenth-century England.

But the English movement was also inspired by more recent contact with the Continent. The three chief proponents of the English movement—Dunstan, Æthelwold and Oswald—each had close links with the Continent, Dunstan having spent time at St. Peter's in Ghent and Oswald having had a period of study at Fleury. Æthelwold, too, had wished to study at Fleury, but had been prevented by royal intervention.[66] Monks from Ghent and

Fleury supervised the compilation of the *Regularis Concordia;* this document, the monastic customary [collection of laws] designed to regulate Benedictine life in England, was issued after an ecclesiastical synod convened by King Edgar, perhaps in 973. If Æthelwold drafted the text, as seems likely, it was Dunstan, the archbishop of Canterbury, who inspired it.[67]

The beginning of the monastic movement in England is conventionally dated to 940, the year in which Dunstan assumed the abbacy of Glastonbury. An anonymous Anglo-Saxon monk .B. wrote his biography, the *Vita S. Dunstani,* between 995 and 1005; from it we learn that Dunstan was a scholar of outstanding ability.[68] He composed a number of Latin poems, and his handwriting may possibly be seen in several surviving manuscripts. But Dunstan was primarily effective as an administrator, and his long tenure of the archbishopric of Canterbury (960–88) saw the implementation of many of the ideas cherished by the English reformers.

Æthelwold's achievements surpassed those of Dunstan. He had studied briefly with Dunstan at Glastonbury and subsequently had restored the ruined monastery of Abingdon; in 963 he was appointed bishop of Winchester, and he ruled that see with indefatigable energy until his death in 984. Æthelwold's greatest efforts were put to increasing the prestige and revenues of the Old Minster (the cathedral church) at Winchester. He had been tutor to King Edgar, and through this personal connection obtained endowments for Winchester and for other monasteries as far afield as the fenland, such as Thorney and Peterborough. He undertook to rebuild the cathedral at Winchester on a scale then unsurpassed by any other church in Europe,[69] and arranged for the translation, in 971, of St. Swithun's relics to a lavish shrine in the Old Minster itself. St. Swithun had been an obscure ninth-century bishop of Winchester. In order to record this translation and the miracles which followed it, a Frankish monk at Winchester named Lantfred wrote—probably at Æthelwold's instigation—a lengthy prose account entitled the *Translatio et Miracula S. Swithuni.*[70]

In addition to these activities, Æthelwold was also a scholar and teacher of note.[71] He has left few Latin writings, but issued a painstakingly accurate English translation of the Benedictine *Rule.*

His concern with accuracy and consistency in translation was an important factor in the establishment of what has been called Standard Old English. His pedagogical excellence is also reflected in the students he trained. Godeman, for example, who subsequently became abbot of Thorney, composed a poem in Æthelwold's praise which serves as a preface to the famous "Benedictional of St. Æthelwold," the most lavishly illuminated extant manuscript from the late Anglo-Saxon period.[72] Another student of Æthelwold was Wulfstan the Cantor (not to be confused with Wulfstan the homilist). A number of his Latin writings have come down to us, including a prose *Vita S. Æthelwoldi*, composed shortly after the translation of Æthelwold's remains in 996, and a lengthy hexametrical version, the *Narratio Metrica de S. Swithuno*, of Lantfred's prose account of St. Swithun's miracles, probably finished in the same year.[73] This poem reveals Wulfstan as perhaps the most accomplished Latin metricist which Anglo-Saxon England produced. As precentor at Winchester, Wulfstan may also have composed various tropes for feasts celebrated there, and he may have been partly responsible for one of the famous "Winchester Tropers"—two lavish manuscripts containing tropes, that is, musical embellishments to the chants of the Mass.

Ælfric, too, was one of Æthelwold's students at Winchester, and we may suspect that Ælfric learned much of his concern for accuracy and clear exposition from his more flamboyant teacher. Best known for his Old English writings (see chapter 3), Ælfric was also a distinguished Latin scholar.[74] In his concern for clarity he repudiated the fashionable "hermeneutic" style affected by Lantfred and Wulfstan—and presumably by Æthelwold. Thus he produced simple prose abbreviations of both Lantfred's *Translatio et Miracula S. Swithuni* and Wulfstan's *Vita S. Æthelwoldi*. His pedagogical concerns led him to compile a Latin grammar, the first such work in a European vernacular. The large number of manuscripts which preserve it attest to its utility. Another teaching book is his brief *Colloquium*, or manual of Latin conversation. Brilliantly cast in the form of a series of dialogues between various artisans and the teacher, these dialogues enabled the students to learn basic vocabulary necessary for everyday affairs. The extensive Old English gloss proves the success of Ælfric's *Colloquium*; and one of Ælfric's students, named (confusingly) Ælfric Bata, brought out in the early eleventh century an expanded redaction of his master's work, as well as two further *colloquia*. These texts introduce students to more complex Latin vocabulary and give a fascinating glimpse of the workings of an Anglo-Saxon school.[75] Such variety of literary activities underscores the vitality and effectiveness of Æthelwold's school at Winchester. Of particular interest in this connection is a group of lighthearted poems from Æthelwold's school, consisting of a vigorous debate between a pedantic master and a class of high-spirited students.[76]

The third proponent of the English reform movement, Oswald, bishop of Worcester and York (died 992), is not known to have left any writings, though he was certainly literate, and had been a student of Frithegod of Canterbury. However, Oswald ex-pended much energy in establishing monasteries, and principal among these was the fenland house of Ramsey (founded c. 970). It was to Ramsey that the great Frankish scholar Abbo of Fleury came at Oswald's invitation during the period 985–7, when Ab-bo's personal fortunes at Fleury were at a low ebb. The impact of this exceptionally learned man on English education, particularly in the fields of scientific and computistical studies, was enor-mous.[77] Abbo composed two works for his students at Ramsey: the *Passio S. Eadmundi*, an account of the martyrdom of the East Anglian king Eadmund, killed by Vikings in 869—an account soon rendered into Old English by Ælfric—and a series of *Quaestiones Grammaticales*, mainly on questions of Latin scansion.[78]

Some impression of the range of Abbo's teaching may be gleaned from the works of his English pupil, Byrhtferth of Ramsey, a ma-jor scholar and literary figure of the late Anglo-Saxon period. Lit-tle is known of Byrhtferth's life, save that he was a monk (or nov-ice?) at Ramsey during Abbo's brief stay, and seems to have spent the remainder of his days there. His writings consist of compu-tistical, hagiographical, and historical works. In the sphere of computus,[79] he assembled a collection of writings (993?) on this subject, including those of Bede, to serve as a computistical com-monplace book; to it he added a preface or *epilogus* describing his scholarly intentions. Byrhtferth's autograph of the commonplace book does not survive, but we have at least one accurate copy of it preserved in an early twelfth-century manuscript in Oxford, St. John's College 17. Near the beginning of this commonplace book is a series of computistical texts which was perhaps assembled by Abbo and which set out the principles on which the study of computus was based. In order to make these materials readily comprehensible to his students, Byrhtferth composed (1008–11) an introduction or *Enchiridion*, partly in Latin and partly in Old English (see chapter 4).

As hagiographer, Byrhtferth wrote two saints' lives.[80] The first of these (995–1005) is the lengthy *Vita S. Oswaldi*, the life of Oswald of Worcester and York, and founder of Ramsey. This *vita* contains firsthand accounts of several major events that occurred during Byrhtferth's lifetime, such as the murder of King Edward the Martyr in 978 and the death of Byrhtnoth, the latter commemorated in the Old English poem *The Battle of Maldon* (see chapter 6); the *vita* is an important source for tenth-century Anglo-Saxon history. At the invitation of the monks of Evesham, Byrhtferth subsequently wrote the *Vita S. Ecgwini* (1014–20); Ecgwine, an early eighth-century bishop of Worcester, was the founder of Evesham. Both these *vitae* reveal that Byrhtferth was deeply influenced by Aldhelm's prose style: like other compositions of the time, they abound in obscure, learned-sounding vocabulary, especially grecisms and neologisms. The same stylistic tendency appears in Byrhtferth's historical writing.[81] As with Bede, Byrhtferth's interest in computus led to an interest in chronology, and thus he compiled a miscellany of historical materials. This collection included excerpts from Bede, Asser, and an important but otherwise unknown set of annals apparently put together at York in the late eighth century. These annals provide our main source for this period of Northumbrian history. Byrhtferth's historical miscellany is preserved anonymously in the twelfth-century *Historia Regum*, which passes under the name of Symeon of Durham. But because of his unmistakable Latin prose style—with its predilection for learned words and numerology—the work is unquestionably his. In sum, these various writings reveal Byrhtferth as a man of substantial, if idiosyncratic, learning.

Byrhtferth was a native product of Anglo-Saxon schooling,

though he was trained by a continental master. Throughout its history, Anglo-Saxon learning owed much to European teachers. But the presence in England of foreign scholars was perhaps never so marked as during the eleventh century.[82] Even before the Norman Conquest, the reign of Edward the Confessor (1042–66), himself a product of continental education, was characterized by numbers of foreign ecclesiastics active in England; these men left an indelible impress on English learning. One such man, an anonymous Flemish monk, composed (1040–2) the *Encomium Emmae*,[83] a history of the Danish conquest of England and its aftermath under Sveinn and then Cnut (1016–35), and a laudatory account of Emma, Cnut's queen. The *Encomium* is written in a highly accomplished rhyming Latin prose, the first such prose to be written in England since Lantfred; it abounds in reminiscences of Vergil, Lucan, and Sallust. Some years later, in 1065 or 1066, another anonymous Fleming composed a life of Edward the Confessor (*Vita Ædwardi Regis*):[84] this work resembles its predecessor in its use of rhyming prose, though it also includes long passages of verse. Like the earlier work, it contains an encomium of the queen, in this case Edward the Confessor's queen, Edith.

We know the names of two Flemish monks who were active in England as hagiographers at this time, each of whom has some claim to be considered the author of the *Vita Ædwardi:* Folcard and Goscelin. Folcard, a monk of Saint-Bertin, acted as abbot of Thorney for nearly twenty years (1067–85) and during this time composed *vitae* of St. John of Beverley and of St. Botulf.[85] Goscelin, also a monk of Saint-Bertin, came to England in 1058 in the service of Herman, bishop of Salisbury. For the next forty years, Goscelin was active as a professional hagiographer, writing lives of saints apparently on commission from various houses. While living in Wessex, he wrote saints' lives for Wilton and Winchester; then after Herman's death (1078) he worked for various East Anglian houses, and finally, in the last decade of the eleventh century, seems to have resided at St. Augustine's, Canterbury, where he composed a good number of *vitae* of Canterbury saints. His literary estate is large indeed, but has never been properly assessed, collected, or edited.[86]

These Flemings were not the only hagiographers active in eleventh-century England: from approximately the same period, we have *vitae* of St. Kenelm, an early ninth-century Mercian martyr; of St. Indract, an Irish missionary martyred near Glastonbury; of St. Neot, a Cornish saint whose relics were translated to Huntingdonshire in the late tenth century; and of St. Rumwold, a prodigy who preached the gospel and then died at the young age of three days.[87] More saints' lives no doubt remain to be discovered; eleventh-century Anglo-Latin literature is the period least investigated by modern research.

The Norman Conquest had as profound an effect on the tradition of Anglo-Latin literature as it did on the literature written in the vernacular. The Latin learning cultivated so vigorously by Anglo-Saxons did not long survive it. In the years following 1066, native bishops and abbots were replaced by Normans, and these repudiated the learning and tradition of their predecessors. In the post-Conquest period, for example, many pre-Conquest Anglo-Latin saints' *vitae* were rewritten so as to eliminate the flamboyant phrasing and obscure vocabulary. William of Malmesbury was particularly scathing about the Latinity of Frithegod and Æthelweard. The writings of Aldhelm, copied and studied so intensively in the pre-Conquest period, were henceforth neglected. In lieu of Anglo-Latin authors, a new Norman curriculum was instituted, and Latin literature produced in England after the Conquest reflects the study of different stylistic models—in poetry, the "New School" of Latin poets from the Loire valley (such as Hildebert, Marbod, and Baudri) with their rhyming, leonine hexameters; in prose, the influence of Cicero is felt in England for the first time. With the exception of Bede's works, most pre-Conquest Anglo-Latin literature was forgotten. But during the four centuries which separate Aldhelm from the Norman Conquest, England produced some of the most articulate and learned men of Europe, men like Aldhelm, Bede, and Alcuin, who may justly be claimed as the preceptors of the early Middle Ages. These men, and the scholarly tradition which trained them, deserve our renewed attention, not only as background for Old English literature, but also for the interest they have in their own right.

NOTES

1. See Deanesly 1961; Godfrey 1962. For the early period, see Mayr-Harting 1972; for the later period, see Knowles 1963.

2. Gneuss 1968, pp. 194–206, 265–413.

3. See Law 1982, esp. pp. 53–80.

4. See Curtius 1953, pp. 48–54; Glauche 1970.

5. See Lapidge 1985, pp. 33–89.

6. On manuscripts, see Gneuss 1981; on manuscripts of curriculum authors and the way they were studied, see Lapidge 1982d; see also Wieland 1983.

7. *Disticha Catonis*, ed. in Duff 1934, trans. in Chase, W. 1922. See also Cox 1972. Prosper ed. in *PL* 51, 498–532; Juvencus ed. in Huemer 1891; Caelius Sedulius ed. Huemer 1885, trans. in Sigerson 1922; Prudentius ed. and trans. in Thomson 1949; Arator ed. in McKinlay 1951; Avitus ed. in Peiper 1883.

8. See Lapidge 1975a.

9. The earliest extant Latin writing from the A-S period (early sixth century?) is the historiographical *De Excidio Britanniae* (On the Fall of Britain), by a Romanized British clergyman called Gildas: a lamentation over Britain's vicissitudes from Roman times to his own, Gildas' account is the closest insular contemporary description of the arrival and first two-hundred-years' activities of the Germanic peoples destined to inherit the island. Since it was written by a Briton, the work is not, of course, Anglo-Latin. On Anglo-Latin literature, see Bolton 1967; Lapidge 1981a. The complete history of Anglo-Latin literature remains to be written.

10. Bede, *Historia Ecclesiastica* III. 18; see Jones, P. 1928.

11. The gospel-book is MS CCCC 286; see Wormald, F. 1948. On the charters, see Levison 1946, pp. 174–233; Chaplais 1973. A theological work has been attributed to Augustine by Machielsen 1961.

12. Bede, *Historia Ecclesiastica* IV. 2, trans. by Colgrave/Mynors 1969, pp. 333–5.

13. On Theodore's writings, see Brooks, N. 1984; on the penitential attributed to him, see Frantzen 1983a, pp. 61–9; on Theodore's exposition of the Bible, see Bischoff 1976, pp. 75–7.

14. Ed. in Ehwald 1919, trans. in Lapidge/Herren 1979 and Lapidge/Rosier 1985.

15. See Winterbottom 1977.

16. See Lapidge/Rosier 1985.

17. See Lapidge 1979a.

18. See Godman 1981.

19. Ed. in Glorie 1968, pp. 165–208.

20. Ed. in Glorie 1968, pp. 209–71.

21. Ed. in Ehwald 1919, pp. 528–37.

22. Ed. Porsia 1976; on the A-S origin of this work, see Lapidge 1982a.

23. Ed. De Marco 1968; see also Law 1982, pp. 64–7, and 1983, pp. 61–2.

24. Ed. Colgrave 1956.

25. The typical saint's life traces the saint's early days and vocation with conventional symbolic incidents, his path to the ascetic life, and his trials; as he gains experience and judgment, he performs miracles and physical healings, and later has the gift of prophecy; finally there is the death warning, farewell to the disciples, and miracles at the tomb. See Kurtz 1926 and Colgrave 1959.

26. See Levison 1946.

27. See Reuter 1980; the standard account of Boniface is Schieffer 1972; see also Wallace-Hadrill 1971a.

28. Ed. Gebauer/Löfstedt 1980.

29. Ed. in Glorie 1968, pp. 273–343.

30. The Bonifatian correspondence ed. in Tangl 1916; selections trans. by Kylie 1911 and Emerton 1940.

31. Willibald ed. in Levison 1905, pp. 1–57; Hygeburg ed. in Holder-Egger 1887, pp. 80–117; on this work, see also Gottschaller 1973. Willibald's *vita* and parts of Hygeburg's work trans. by Talbot 1954.

32. See Hunter Blair 1985.

33. On Northumbrian hagiography, see Jones, C. 1947. *Vita S. Gregorii* ed. Colgrave 1968; anonymous *Vita S. Cuthberti* ed. in Colgrave 1940, pp. 59–139; "Eddius" Stephanus, *Vita S. Wilfridi* ed. Colgrave 1927; see also Kirby 1983. Anonymous *Vita S. Ceolfridi* ed. in Plummer 1896, pp. 388–404.

34. On Bede, see Thompson 1935; Hunter Blair 1970; Bonner 1976.

35. On Bede's learning, see Laistner 1935 and Meyvaert 1976. The standard collected edition of Bede's writings is that in *PL* 90–95; this edition is slowly being replaced by more scholarly editions in the series *CCSL* 118–123 (ten volumes published to date); see Jones, C./*et al.* 1955.

36. Ed. in Colgrave/Mynors 1969, pp. 580–7.

37. Colgrave/Mynors 1969, p. 583.

38. All three works ed. Jones, C./*et al.* 1955, vol. 123A. On *De Orthographia*, see Dionisotti 1982; on *De Arte Metrica*, see Palmer 1959; for a trans. of the Appendix to the latter, on figures and tropes, see Tanenhaus 1962.

39. Both works ed. Jones, C. 1943. Jones's lengthy introduction to this book is still the best on medieval computus; text, but not the introduction, rpr. in *CCSL* 123B 1977.

40. Bede's exegetical works (excepting only the *Explanatio Apocalypsis*, which is ed. in *PL* 93, 129–206) have either been issued or are about to appear in *CCSL* 118–121. On Bede's exegetical methods, see Jenkins 1935.

41. *CCSL* 119A, p. 244.

42. On Bede's book of epigrams, see Lapidge 1975b. Probable remnants of the book of hymns ed. in Fraipont 1955, pp. 407–38; see also

Gneuss 1968, pp. 53–4. The poem *De Die Iudicii* ed. in Fraipont 1955, pp. 439–44; see also Whitbread 1944.

43. On Bede's *Martyrologium*, see Quentin 1908, pp. 17–119. The metrical *Vita S. Cuthberti* ed. by Jaager 1935. The *Vita S. Felicis* ed. in *PL* 94, 789–98; see also Mackay 1976. On the *Passio S. Anastasii*, see Franklin/ Meyvaert 1982. The prose *Vita S. Cuthberti* ed. in Colgrave 1940, pp. 142– 307; trans. in Webb/Farmer 1983, pp. 41–102.

44. On Bede as historian, see Levison 1935; Jones, C. 1947, pp. 80–93; Ray 1976; and various articles by Hunter Blair in Lapidge/Hunter Blair 1984.

45. Ed. Mommsen 1898; rpr. *CCSL* 123B 1977.

46. Ed. in Plummer 1896, pp. 364–87; trans. Webb/Farmer 1983, pp. 185–208.

47. Ed. Plummer 1896; trans. Colgrave/Mynors 1969 and Sherley-Price 1955.

48. For a critical analysis of the *HE*, suggesting that Bede has tight control of his narrative and owes some debt to Gildas (see n. 9, above), see Hanning 1966, pp. 63–90.

49. *Dialogus* ed. in Haddan/Stubbs 1869, vol. 3, pp. 403–13; Penitential, pp. 416–31. On the Penitential, see Frantzen 1983a, pp. 70–7.

50. Ed. Godman 1982.

51. There are general studies of Alcuin by Gaskoin 1904 and Duckett 1951. Neither is satisfactory.

52. Ed. in *PL* 100–101 (Migne's edition is a reprint of an early eighteenth-century edition; in many cases the texts reprinted by Migne have been surperseded).

53. Ed. in Dümmler 1881, pp. 160–351.

54. Ed. in Dümmler 1895, pp. 18–481; a selection of his letters trans. by Allott 1974.

55. See Wright, R. 1982, pp. 104–22.

56. See Marenbon 1981, pp. 30–2.

57. See Deug-Su 1983.

58. See Loewe 1969, pp. 133–40.

59. On Candidus, see Marenbon 1981, pp. 38–62 and Ineichen-Eder 1981. On Frithugils (whose name is usually given in corrupted form as Fredegis *vel sim.*), see Marenbon 1981, pp. 62–6. Frithugils' letter *De Nihilo et Tenebris* ed. in Dümmler 1895, pp. 552–5.

60. *Miracula S. Nyniae* ed. in Strecker 1923, pp. 943–61, trans. in MacQueen 1961.

61. Ed. Campbell, A. 1967.

62. See Brooks, N. 1984, pp. 170–4.

63. See Lapidge 1981b.

64. Ed. in Campbell, A. 1950, pp. 4–62; see also, Lapidge 1975a, pp. 78–81; Brooks, N. 1984, pp. 228–31.

65. Ed. Campbell, A. 1962a. See also Winterbottom 1967. Some notion

of the difficulty of Æthelweard's Latin as it has been transmitted may be gained from the commentary on a short passage of the *Chronicon* in Keynes/Lapidge 1983, pp. 334–8.

66. On the monastic reform in England, see Knowles 1963.

67. Ed. Symons 1953.

68. *Vita S. Dunstani* ed. in Stubbs 1874; see also Brooks, N. 1984, pp. 245–6. On Dunstan's Latin poetry, see Lapidge 1975a, pp. 95–7, 108–11 and Lapidge 1980. On Dunstan's handwriting, see Hunt 1961; and on Dunstan's administrative achievements in general, see Brooks, N. 1984, pp. 243–53.

69. See Biddle 1975; Sheerin 1978.

70. Ed. Sauvage 1885.

71. On Æthelwold's possible Latin writings, see Lapidge 1975a, pp. 88–90; on his work as an English translator, see Gretsch 1974; on his involvement in the development of Standard Old English, see Gneuss 1972.

72. Godeman's poem ed. in Lapidge 1975a, pp. 105–6; on the manuscript, see Wormald, F. 1959.

73. On Wulfstan's Latin writings, see Gneuss 1968, pp. 246–8. Wulfstan's *Vita S. Æthelwoldi* ed. in Winterbottom 1972, pp. 33–63, trans. Brearley/Goodfellow 1982. The *Narratio Metrica de S. Swithuno* ed. in Campbell, A. 1950, pp. 65–177. See also Planchart 1977, vol. 1, pp. 27–33.

74. Ælfric's *Vita S. Æthelwoldi* ed. in Winterbottom 1972, pp. 17–29; the *Grammar* and *Glossary* ed. Zupitza 1880; the *Colloquium* ed. Garmonsway 1978.

75. The colloquies of Ælfric Bata ed. in Stevenson, W. 1929, pp. 27–74 (nos. IV–V); Bata's expanded and revised version of Ælfric's *Colloquium* ed. in Stevenson, pp. 75–102 (no. VI).

76. See Lapidge 1972.

77. See Lutz 1977; van de Vyver 1935.

78. *Passio S. Eadmundi* ed. in Winterbottom 1972, pp. 67–87; *Quaestiones Grammaticales* ed. Guerreau-Jalabert 1982.

79. On Byrhtferth as computist, see Forsey 1928; *Enchiridion* ed. Crawford 1929; see also Baker 1982.

80. *Vita S. Oswaldi* ed. in Raine 1879, vol. 1, pp. 399–475; *Vita S. Ecgwini* ed. in Giles 1854, pp. 349–96. On the attribution of these two *vitae* (which are transmitted anonymously in manuscript) to Byrhtferth, see Lapidge 1975a, pp. 90–4 and Lapidge 1979b.

81. Byrhtferth's historical works ed. in Arnold 1885, vol. 2, pp. 3–91. See Lapidge 1982b; Hart 1982.

82. See Barlow 1979; Grierson 1941.

83. Ed. Campbell, A. 1949.

84. Ed. Barlow 1962.

85. On Folcard, see Barlow 1962, pp. li–lix. *Vita S. Botulfi* ed. in *Acta*

Sanctorum, Iun., 3, pp. 402–3. *Vita S. Iohannis Episcopi Eboracensis* ed. in Raine 1879, vol. 1, pp. 239–60.

86. On Goscelin, see Barlow 1962, pp. xlv–li and 91–111. The principal editions of works by Goscelin are as follows: Esposito 1913; Wilmart 1938, pp. 5–101, and 265–307; Talbot 1955; Talbot 1959. See also Wilmart 1934 and Rollason 1982, pp. 60–7.

87. St. Kenelm: see von Antropoff 1965; St. Indract: see Lapidge 1982c; St. Neot: see Dumville/Lapidge 1985; St. Rumwold: see *Acta Sanctorum*, Nov., 1, pp. 682–90.

CHAPTER 2

The Alfredian Translations and Related Ninth-Century Texts

The history of early English prose is a record of unprecedented decisions to compose in the vernacular. In many spheres of intellectual, religious, and practical life, the English, unlike their contemporaries on the Continent, chose their native tongue as the favored instrument of expression. England had a code of laws early in the seventh century, and it was written in the English of that day. Bede's eighth-century translation of the Gospel of St. John, now unfortunately lost, was the first rendering of the New Testament into a post-classical European language after Ulfilas's fourth-century Gothic version. In the tenth century Ælfric produced the first Latin grammar using a vernacular language (see chapters 1 and 3). Many more examples could be cited, for the tradition of native composition was deeply imbedded in English culture from the seventh to the eleventh centuries. Perhaps England's isolation intensified this attachment to Anglo-Saxon, but whatever the cause, the fact remains that England, almost alone in the early Middle Ages, created a national prose literature of astonishing scope and variety. This tradition formed at least the partial base on which later English prose built.[1]

Alfred, king of Wessex from 871–99,[2] played the central role in creating this literature. More than one historian and literary critic have called him simply: the father of English prose.[3] His achievement is all the more remarkable when set in its historical context. Grandson of the powerful Ecgberht of Wessex (802–39)—who returned from exile in Charlemagne's realm to establish the southwestern kingdom of Wessex as the dominant force in ninth-century England—Alfred faced overwhelming hardships throughout his life. His grandfather may have strengthened the hand of Wessex against the eighth-century hegemony of Mercia, but he left to the next four generations the problem of staving off the Vikings. When Alfred reached the throne in 871, Wessex alone of all the English kingdoms remained unconquered by the Danes, and its survival was by no means assured. Alfred spent his reign constantly devising defensive strategies to secure the peace and integrity of his kingdom against a horde bent on conquering the whole country and forcing it under pagan Danish rule.[4]

About this man, whom Stenton designates "the most effective ruler who had appeared in western Europe since the death of Charlemagne,"[5] we know a reasonable amount. Even when we dismiss the later medieval and Renaissance legends which grew up around him, a fair picture emerges. He was born at Wantage, a royal village in Berkshire, in the year 849. He died at the age of fifty. His father, Æthelwulf, who ruled from Ecgberht's death in 839 to 858, defended Wessex well against Danish and Welsh marauders and allied his house with Mercia by giving his daughter Æthelswith as a "peace-weaver" in marriage to its king, Burgred. According to Asser, Alfred's biographer, Æthelwulf and his wife Osburh cherished Alfred "more than all his brothers."[6] Alfred visited Rome twice, the first time in 853 when he was only four or five years old, and again in 855 accompanied by his father. Under the year 853, the Parker MS of the Anglo-Saxon Chronicles records Alfred's visit to the court of Pope Leo IV, and reports that the pope "hallowed him as king." As the youngest of six children and the last of five sons, it seems improbable that the pope would so consecrate him. A letter of the pope reveals that in fact he "decorated him as a spiritual son with the dignity of the belt and vestments of the consulate."[7] Some see in such confusions a later attempt by Alfred to slant history and influence his biographer for political (though honorable) ends; others deny any such propagandistic motive. But there is evidence that Alfred wished to stress the parallels between himself and Charlemagne and so create an "empire" that could withstand the ravages of the Danes and provide a lasting tradition of letters.[8]

Many of the well-known stories about Alfred are patent myths: the burning of the cakes, his appearance behind the Danish lines in the guise of a minstrel, his "inglorious youth," his founding of both the Royal Navy and the University of Oxford. But even without these romantic encrustations, Alfred remains a magnificent figure. Much like Hrothgar and Beowulf, Alfred became king only after several older brothers or nephews had died. He had served long and bravely in the Danish wars under their leadership and when his last remaining brother, Æthelred, died in 871, Alfred *secundarius* ascended the throne. Nearly annihilated by the Danes, he was forced to retreat with a small troop to the island of Athelney in the western marshes. From there he reconstituted an army which was eventually to defeat the Vikings under King Guthrum in 878. Guthrum agreed to accept Christianity, and Alfred was his sponsor at the baptism. Although he was never free from predatory attacks, Alfred now ruled over all England south of the Humber. The Danes occupied the northern and eastern sections of the island (later called the Danelaw) under a treaty established between Alfred and Guthrum sometime in the years 886–90.

Most of our knowledge about Alfred as a person comes from Asser's *De Vita et Rebus Gestis Alfredi.*[9] It is the first biography of an English layman, and also a literary and historical curiosity. Asser was a Welsh monk, summoned, as he himself tells us, by Alfred to help educate him. The *Life* was undoubtedly written for a Welsh audience and intended, perhaps, to convince the Welsh to put aside their ancient hostilities towards the English and join their fellow Christians against the heathen Danes. In compiling his work, Asser relied on two sources—annals from the Anglo-Saxon Chronicles (which he often misunderstood, since West Saxon was not Asser's native tongue) and his own personal knowledge of King Alfred. The result has struck many as bizarre, with its juxtaposition of a bare annalistic style and a full, digressive narration.

However barbarous his Latin, Asser did have a precise idea of his plan. His work fuses the two genres of historical writing into one—the annals and chronicles illustrate the fickleness of worldly affairs, and the saints' lives and martyrologies depict figures who are outside temporal history.[10] Asser thus placed Alfred both within and beyond time; he saw him as king and saint.

Einhard's *Life of Charlemagne* was the most important influence on Asser, though other Carolingian works such as the anonymous *Life of Alcuin* also made their imprint.[11] Yet the differences between Einhard's biography and the (perhaps unfinished) West Saxon *Life* should not be overlooked. Asser composed his work in 893 while Alfred was still alive; Charlemagne was over fifty when Einhard joined his court and he did not write the *Vita* until thirty years later. The *Life of Charlemagne* has a monumental character, whereas Asser's humbler piece reveals a personal view of the king, despite its hagiographical aura.[12] Asser, for example, details the mysterious illness which came upon Alfred at his wedding feast: "Certainly it was not known to any of those who were present on that occasion, nor to those up to the present day who have inquired how such an illness could arise and—worst of all, alas!—could continue so many years without remission, from his twentieth year up to his fortieth and beyond."[13]

Asser's portrait of Alfred shows a man possessed by the desire for a liberal education. Denied the proper training when he was of an age to learn, Alfred came to know Latin late in life. He seems to have been devoted to Anglo-Saxon poetry—the famous anecdote of his memorizing a whole book of native poems to win the codex from his mother would attest to that. Yet it was not until the king "first began through divine inspiration to read [Latin] and to translate at the same time, all on one and the same day"[14] that he began his *Handbook* or *Enchiridion*. In this *Handbook*, which has not survived, Alfred had Asser record the "many various flowers of Holy Scripture, with which he crams full the cells of his heart."[15] Alfred's predilection for the realms of thought and letters led him to inaugurate a radical plan to educate his people. Inspired again by certain elements in the Carolingian revival of the late eighth and early ninth centuries, Alfred's scheme was nonetheless quite different. He was not merely interested in spreading the circle of

Latin erudition, but instead envisioned a system that would make all free men of his kingdom literate in English and also raise the level of Latin literacy of his clergy. This instruction in both languages—Latin and English—was an extraordinary new path to have chosen.[16]

Like Charlemagne, Alfred turned to other countries for teachers. As the king remarks in the *Preface* to his translation of Gregory's *Pastoral Care*, learning in England has so declined that:

> we have to get them [wisdom and learning] from abroad, if we would have them [at all]. So completely had it [knowledge] fallen away among Englishmen that [when I ascended to the kingdom] there were very few on this side of the Humber who could understand their services in English, or even translate a letter [*ærendgewrit*] from Latin into English; and I think that there were not many beyond the Humber.[17]

From France came Grimbald, whose piety earned him sainthood, and from Saxony John, whom Alfred established as abbot of his new monastery at Athelney in the Somerset fens, site of his retreat in his darkest hour. Asser (later bishop of Sherborne) was among those foreigners brought to the court in Wessex, along with four Mercians: Plegmund, who became archbishop of Canterbury in 890, Wærferth, bishop of Worcester, and the priests Æthelstan and Werwulf. These were the men whom Alfred gathered to assist him in his ambitious project.

While the works surviving from the Alfredian period may not be the entire corpus of vernacular texts produced,[18] those which do survive were obviously chosen with great care. The earliest of the translations, Wærferth's version of Gregory's *Dialogues*, done at Alfred's behest sometime between his accession to the throne and the early 890s,[19] has a brief preface by the king, in which he states that "from time to time we should subdue and bend our minds to the divine and spiritual law in the midst of this earthly misery."[20] He then adds that he sought "trusty friends" to translate the work for him, so that "I through this admonition and love being strengthened in my mind, may now and then contemplate the heavenly things in the midst of these earthly troubles." In Wærferth's translation, intended for Alfred's own personal use and consolation, the king no doubt caught the parallel between his position as leader of a war-torn realm and Gregory's as pontiff, caught in a web of depressing secular affairs. The work itself is a succession of miracle stories told by Gregory to his deacon, including an entire book devoted to the virtues and miraculous deeds of St. Benedict, the founder of Western monasticism. The translation adheres quite strictly to the Latin and is a literal (though not error-free) rendering. A revision of Wærferth's late ninth-century text was made by an anonymous translator some one hundred or one hundred and fifty years later. The two versions offer a unique opportunity to trace the development of the language and style of Old English prose over a crucial span in Anglo-Saxon letters. The later version is a more controlled translation, both clearer and tighter in composition.[21]

Alfred's choice for the first of his own translations was a classic work by Pope Gregory.[22] Bede had recommended the *Pastoral Care* to Ecgberht of York in his Epistle of 734, Alcuin had recommended it to Eanbald of York in 796, and on the Continent Hincmar of Rheims insisted that his bishops hold copies during their consecration. Gregory composed the *Cura Pastoralis* (or *Liber Regulae Pastoralis*) in the late sixth century after John of Ravenna, one of his archbishops, had publicly rebuked him for his reluctance to assume the burdens of the papacy.[23] Gregory's work is an extended treatise on the qualities required of a bishop, the many types of character a bishop will encounter in his pastoral work, and the ways he should treat the varieties of mankind. Subtle in its psychology, warm in its humane understanding of the mode of applying Christian morals, the book is a teaching manual—Gregory called teaching (i.e., spiritual direction) "the art of all arts." In the manuscripts it is usually divided into four sections: (1) the motives which attract men to the office, (2) a description of the ideal bishop/ruler, (3) the actual "care of souls" in the world, and (4) a brief concluding chapter on "spiritual recollection," combined with a warning against pride. Both Gregory's original and Alfred's English version are often described as mediocre and tedious works,[24] but such comments betray a lack of sympathy for a text that medieval Christians found of great significance. Gregory's work had applications reaching far beyond the narrow confines of a bishop's duties, for it also spoke directly to the problems faced by secular rulers.

This wider applicability was not lost on King Alfred. While he ordered copies of the work to go to all English bishops for their use and instruction, he could not have helped making the connection between the seven rules Gregory laid down for bishops and the ideals for which he himself strove.[25] That Alfred saw this relation is implied in his decision to compose a *Preface* to the work, a foreword which was to serve not only as a specific set of instructions for the disposition and use of this singular piece, but also as an introduction to his whole program of spiritual and educational reform. In this remarkable document, mentioned above in connection with the decay of learning, Alfred embarked on something entirely new. Here he struggled, as Huppé writes, "to create an English prose style responsive to intellectual demands."[26] Apart from lamenting the state of learning in his kingdom, and outlining a restorative scheme, Alfred fashioned an independent English prose, using some of the techniques of classical rhetoric, but no direct model. His selection of works to be translated, he says, will include "those which are most useful for men to know," Englished because few can still read Latin. He worries about this decision momentarily, but then concludes that the history of Christian letters is the sequence of turning "originals" into "copies," from Hebrew through Greek, then through Latin to English. His method of translation—"sometimes word by word, sometimes sense for sense"—came out of a venerable tradition. Gregory and Jerome had described their translations similarly in Latin, and Asser also used the phrase to describe Wærferth's translation of Gregory.

The *Preface* itself reveals an ability to employ classical rhetorical figures with ease. Huppé sees the strong influence of Old English poetic techniques here as well, particularly in the use of enlacement and progression. Alfred's formal scheme illustrates a reliance on the early papal epistle with its five subdivisions: (1) Protocol, or Salutation, (2) Arenga or Proem, (3) Narration or Statement, (4) Disposition or Petition, and (5) Final Clause or

Codicil.[27] Balanced and elaborately structured, Alfred's *Preface* is a long-pondered and highly wrought piece of prose, all the more extraordinary because it seems to have been created in a stylistic vacuum.

Morrish believes that the document should not be considered a "preface" at all, but "an independent letter which stands before the translation something like a covering form-letter."[28] Whatever its genre, this introduction manifests Alfred's constant concerns, those which were to form the basis both of his selections and interpretations of works to come later. Alfred did not wish merely to promote literacy and education; the corpus of translations, with the *Pastoral Care* as the first installment, was meant to inculcate wisdom in the souls of his own "flock." Paul Szarmach writes persuasively that "Alfred's *Preface* to the *Pastoral Care* is a fundamental statement about Christian culture that receives its full meaning when read in the light of the Augustinian distinction between *sapientia* and *scientia*,"[29] that is, between divine wisdom and earthly knowledge. This wisdom is God-given, and in two later works, his translations of Boethius and Augustine's *Soliloquies*, Alfred was to identify it "not only with the highest good, but with God."[30]

The translation of the *Cura Pastoralis*, dating from somewhere between 890 and 895,[31] resembles the "Mercian" translations of Wærferth and the Old English Bede (see below) in its relative closeness to the original. The work survives in two contemporary manuscripts, although one was twice badly burned and is readable only in a seventeenth-century transcription by Junius. The full ninth-century text is a major source for our knowledge of Early West Saxon.[32] Alfred follows Gregory's order faithfully and omits very little, but he does not try to duplicate Gregory's logic, his elaborate *figurae*, or his terse and compact statements. Complicated Latin syntax dissolves into a series of short English clauses, and single Latin words often turn into alliterating English doublets. Alfred's purpose was to insure that his readers understood the meaning clearly, even at the expense of literal accuracy.[33] A section of the warning against unlearned teachers illustrates some of these traits:

Forðæm hi swæ mid on ofermettum and mid upahæfennesse becumað to ðære are ðære hirdelecan gemenne, hi ne magon meðumlice ðenian þa ðenunga, and ðære eaðmodnesse lareowas bion.[34]

(Since with pride and vainglory they come to the honor of pastoral care, they cannot worthily fulfill their ministry and be teachers of humility.)

The rendering has often been pejoratively described as: "clumsy," "slavish," and "mediocre." But in its fidelity to the sense of Gregory's book and in its sincere attempt to convey this to an unlettered English audience, it seems a worthy prologue to Alfred's educational plan.

Though the chronology of Alfred's works is uncertain, many scholars reason that sometime after completing his version of the *Pastoral Care*, Alfred turned to his philosophical translations, those of Boethius' *Consolation of Philosophy* and St. Augustine's *Soliloquies*. Boethius' Latin work was written in 524, while the author, presumably an orthodox Catholic, was in prison, accused of treason by the Ostrogoth King Theodoric, an Arian "heretic." After nine months of isolation and uncertainty, Boethius was tortured and savagely executed. He quickly became one of the martyrs for the faith. Under the name St. Severinus he is included in the encyclopedic Bollandist collection of saints' lives, the *Acta Sanctorum*. To Boethius, scion of an aristocratic family and a highly placed figure in Theodoric's court, his sudden turn of fortune seemed at first inexplicable. The *De Consolatione Philosophiae* was his reasoned answer to undeserved misfortune.[35]

Its philosophy is imbued with neo-Platonism overlaid with late classical Stoicism. Unlike his polemical theological treatises, the *Consolation* studiously avoids any specific Christian reference, but it draws on Greek philosophy in a way that is wholly compatible with Christianity. Yet in its stronger emphasis on a personal God, it deviates from neo-Platonism. The *Consolation of Philosophy* fits under several different literary headings: *consolatio*,[36] Platonic dialogue, prison literature, personification allegory, Menippean satire (the alternation of prose and verse), and theodicy. It was as a theodicy that the work had its most powerful effect: Boethius' attempt to "justify" God's ways to man proceeds by means of a dialogue between an allegorical Lady Philosophy, who appears in

Boethius' cell, and the author. Lady Philosophy reviews the vagaries of Fortune and the false, unstable happiness that the fickle goddess brings. It moves on through a discussion of the nature of good and evil (which Boethius believes does not exist as such), God's perfect ordering of the universe, His omniscience and man's free will, and Providence and Fate, to a Platonic conclusion which locates the source of true felicity in the one, true, and immutable Good. Despite the absence of specific Christian doctrine, the *Consolation* became one of the most popular books in the later Middle Ages. Well over four hundred manuscripts survive. Some critics have claimed that the treatise influenced Anglo-Saxon poetry, *Beowulf, The Wanderer,* and *Deor* especially, though this cannot be proved.[37]

Alfred had no native precedent for his interest in the *Consolation.* Malcolm Godden reminds us that the work "seems to have been little known, if at all, among the Anglo-Saxons before the time of Alfred . . . [and] it may well have been the king's Welsh adviser Asser who introduced him to the text."[38] But once acquainted with it, Alfred found many parallels between Boethius' predicament and his own situation. This translation has justly been called Alfred's "most personal" work.[39] Alfred had faced both the vicissitudes of war and wracking bodily pain and could well understand how the experience of life leads to doubting God's goodness and power.

In sharp contrast to Wærferth's *Dialogues,* and even his own *Pastoral Care,* Alfred's Boethius is a radical adaptation of the Latin original. He changed the five books of Latin prose with alternating *metra* into forty-two chapters of Old English prose, with a proem and epilogue; later, from this prose, he made another version, translating all but nine of the Boethian meters into verse (see chapter 10). He omitted large chunks, collapsed material, added a great deal of his own, and nearly abandoned the final book—on divine Providence and man's free will—altogether. Two related explanations for Alfred's extreme revisions have enjoyed currency among scholars. The first holds that the simple English king was not intellectually capable of dealing with the *Consolation's* complexities; this notion derives from William of Malmesbury's statement that Asser explained the sense of Boethius' text in "clearer words" to Alfred, who then turned it into English. The second attempts to account for the many divergences by reference to one or another of the Latin commentaries on Boethius.[40] Debate has centered on whether a commentary by Remigius of Auxerre, one by an anonymous author of St. Gall, or even an unknown one by Asser might have been the document Alfred consulted.[41] Wittig has challenged this line of inquiry and argued that Alfred did not depend on any Latin commentary. He maintains that the differences between Alfred and Boethius are the result of the common Christian background Alfred shared with the commentators, or perhaps simply of the king's own concerns.[42]

Critics now grant more willingly that Alfred had both a specific purpose and clear vision in making his many alterations. While he may not have been perfectly successful at grafting his views onto Boethius, he can be acquitted of the charge of ineptitude. He saw in the Boethian Good the Christian God, and his whole perspective was filtered through the writings of Augustine and Gregory:[43] *se wæg is God.* He may have replaced the logic of philosophical speculation with a zealous Christian dogmatism, but he did so deliberately. The emphasis Alfred thus achieved was more on man's almost terrifying freedom to act than on God's ordered and universal control.[44] Alfred's version concentrated on earthly activity and the operation of the human mind; he was more interested in Christian psychology than in the nearly mathematical clarity of Boethius' metaphysics. It is not that Alfred rejected Boethius' ideas, but that he often presented them in an emotional fashion.

Everywhere Alfred personalizes his material by the addition of illustrations, comments, metaphors, and similes. In Alfred's Christian universe, references to God, Christ, Christians, angels, and the devil abound. The hymn to the universal obedience of the Creation to the Creator, for example, reminds Alfred of the outstanding exception of the rebellious angels; and his expanded retelling of the Orpheus and Eurydice story, found in Boethius III, meter 12, makes the moral allegory explicitly Christian. For the pious Alfred, Orpheus represents the penitent turning toward the light who looks back at his old sins and so forfeits all he had hoped to gain. The two central characters, Lady Philosophy and Boethius, are changed into Wisdom and (frequently) Mind, and the encounter between them often drifts towards an interior dialogue. Wisdom, the loftiest of all the virtues, incorporating within itself the four cardinal virtues of Prudence, Temperance, Courage, and Justice, is ultimately equated with God. And Mind is led from despair to faith and heroic resignation, a process quite different from Boethius' progress from a resentful incomprehension to a jubilant understanding. Alfred and Boethius began, in fact, with widely varying dramatic situations. In the Latin, Boethius cannot understand how God can permit him, a good and just man, to be so unjustly accused; in the Old English, Boethius is "guilty" of the charge that he conspired against Theodoric, but he is tormented by the question of why God permits the evil king to triumph. For Boethius the central issue is the nature of order and justice; for Alfred it is the question of power and goodness.

The king's "realistic" worldview caused an occasional rough fit between his adaptation and the Boethian original. Thus Boethius' confident assertion that evil does not exist brings the Alfredian insistence that nonetheless evil men indeed do wicked things. And Boethius' strong Platonism with its antimaterialism is (awkwardly) balanced by Alfred's insistence that the things of the world are to be *used* for good ends. Alfred's duties as king are frequently reflected. In a famous passage he has Mind say, "O Philosophy, lo, you know that I never greatly took pleasure in greed and the possession of earthly power, nor yearned at all for this earthly kingdom, but I desired instruments and materials to carry out the work I was commanded to do, which was that I should virtuously and fittingly guide and take care of the authority committed to me." The king's "material and instruments of rule," Mind continues, "are that he have his land well peopled, . . . [and] men of prayer, men of war, and men of work," together with "land to dwell in, gifts, weapons, meat, ale, clothing."[45] In the worldly kingdom, of course, all must be ruled by Wisdom in a service which is freedom, not slavery. As Alfred avers, God created angels and men so they could freely serve Him, for what profit would be gained "if there were a very powerful king and he had no free men in all his kingdom, but all were slaves?"[46] Alfred's notion of freedom, as has often been observed, had none of the metaphysical complexity of Boethius'. His truncated version of Book V, in which Boethius explains the relationship of Divine Foreknowledge and man's freedom, becomes an Augustinian assertion, albeit a simple one, that man *is* free. Alfred may thereby escape the determinism that is always present as a submerged threat to Boethius' system, but in the process he also radically simplifies the idea. He replaces Boethius' intricate discussion of necessity with the famous simile of the wheel of destiny:

> Just as on the axle of a wagon the wheels turn and the axle stands still and yet bears all the wagon and controls all the motion, so that the wheel turns around and the nave next to the axle moves more firmly and securely than the rim does. So the axle is the highest good, which we call God; and the best men move next to God, just as the nave moves next to the axle . . . [The simile continues, comparing the middle sort of men to the spokes, one end in the nave, and the other in the rim, now thinking of this life below, now looking upward toward the Divine, etc.] [47]

Finally, Alfred himself emerges from this work as a highly moral and attractive person. He is his own best apologist with Mind speaking for him: "I have wanted to live honorably while I was alive, and after my life to leave to those men who come after me my memory in good works." [48] The fusion of Germanic and Christian elements in this moving passage is reflected again by his well-known substitution in Boethius' *ubi sunt* lament: "Where now are the bones of Fabricius?" which becomes, "Where now are the bones of the famous and wise goldsmith, Weland?" [49]

Both Alfred and Boethius were creators, in their separate contexts, of a philosophical language. It may be difficult to conceive of an intellectual world in which the words *philosophia, fatum,* and *fortuna* did not exist, but Boethius coined them. Alfred found the same semantic vacuum when he was forced to turn these Latin terms into English equivalents. Conventional wisdom has it that Boethius achieved far greater success than Alfred. Where Boethius expressed abstract relationships, general laws, and indefinite statements with ease, Alfred relied on particular instances, similes, and circumstantial detail. Boethius' style is nominal and abstract, Alfred's is verbal and concrete, a contrast not unexpected given their very different orientations toward the worlds of thought and action. Alfred consistently simplified the hypotactic sentences of his source and turned them into paratactic constructions. But these new renderings do not lack balance and structure, nor richness of expression, as we see in this passage:

> Swa eac þa mennisce mod bið underetan and aweged of his stede þonne hit se wind strongra geswinca astyroð oððe se ren ungemetlices ymbhogan.[50]

(So too, man's soul is undermined and moved from its place when the wind of sore hardship beats it or the rain of great care.)

Alfred made his translation more than either a "word by word, or sense by sense" version of the *Consolation;* he made it a fine literary and philosophical document in its own right.

Scholars assume that Alfred's free adaptation of Augustine's *Soliloquies* followed closely upon the translation of Boethius,[51] for this work develops in predictable ways out of the *Consolation.* The sporadic interiority of the *Consolation* now becomes the all-embracing internal debate of the *Soliloquies.* It has all the qualities of a mature piece, one in which Alfred not only adapted his main source with even greater freedom, but also one in which he created an amalgam out of widely diverse texts, personal ancedote, and speculation. Not all the sources of this effort have been identified, but Alfred did draw upon Augustine's *De Videndo Deo,* Gregory's *Dialogues, Moralia, Cura Pastoralis,* and *Homily on Luke,* and Jerome's translation of the Bible (the Vulgate) and his *Commentary on Luke*—in addition to the *Soliloquies.*

It was as one of his last endeavors that Alfred turned to this early and incomplete dialogue by Augustine, one composed during his *Christianae vitae otium* ("Christian retirement") at Cassiciacum in the winter of 386–7.[52] Written shortly before Augustine's long-postponed baptism, the *Soliloquies* is a passionate inner searching for wisdom, a quest which could only be ended through acceptance of Catholic authority. The catechumen Augustine had not yet purged all of his Academic Skepticism nor his neo-Platonism by the time he wrote the *Soliloquies;* later in his life he was to return to it, as well as to other early writings, and "reconsider" the errors of logic and doctrine they contained. But such heterodoxy posed no problem for Alfred, who, once again, substituted clear Christian dogma for much of Augustine's classical metaphysics.

Alfred's *Soliloquies* survives in a twelfth-century manuscript, the first of the two codices bound together in Cotton Vitellius A.xv (see chapter 6).[53] No medieval commentator—not Asser, Æthelweard, nor even William of Malmesbury—mentions it, but it is assigned to Alfred in the sole manuscript. The many similarities in subject and style between the *Soliloquies*, the Boethius, and the *Pastoral Care*, reaffirm an Alfredian authorship. Here too, the king added a *Preface* to his translation, one in which he developed a complex extended metaphor.[54] Alfred depicts his life's work, the pursuit of wisdom and his translation of books, as a journey into the forest to gather wood from the finest trees for the making of tools and his "rare house," a "transitory cottage by the road while [he is] on this world-pilgrimage." He sees himself as a "wayfarer" (*homo viator*) yearning for his "everlasting home."[55] He exhorts others who are capable and "who have many wagons" to go into that forest and collect beams wherewith to build "many a fair wall, to set up many a peerless house, and to build a fair town" where they may dwell happily and easily in winter and in summer, "as I have not yet done."[56] Alfred recognizes that his grand scheme for his unstable nation has only just begun, and he urges his subjects to continue their pursuit of both temporal and spiritual wisdom. This last *Preface* echoes and realizes the hopes Alfred had expressed for a revival of English learning in his *Preface* to Gregory's *Pastoral Care*.

Augustine's dialogue, an exchange between himself and Reason in two books, is a difficult text. In this attempt to know God, and to affirm His and the soul's immortality, Augustine encountered no small amount of frustration; he left the work unfinished and refers Reason to another of his works—*De Videndo Deo* (*On Seeing God*)—for an answer to his questions about what men know after death. Alfred, with his passion for knowledge and his belief in the temporal efficacy of wisdom, was apparently unsatisfied by Augustine's inconclusive ending. And so he turned to *De Videndo Deo* (and other texts) to make a third book, describing the life of the soul after death—the good soul in glory and the wicked damned, according to the merits of each while they inhabited bodies on this earth. He also included arguments for the eternal value of wisdom attained on earth in the growth of the intellect, and its contribution to happiness in heaven.

In these three books Alfred becomes progressively more detached from his prototype, until in the short third segment he seems almost to be writing on his own, and his characterization of the whole as a gathering of blooms or flowers is a distinctive medieval touch not at all suggested by Augustine's austere dialogue. Out of a desire for historical neatness, some scholars have tried to associate this chrestomathy, as the genre is called, with the *Enchiridion*, or *Handbook*, the genesis of which Asser records. But such an attempt is based solely on sentiment and the *Soliloquies* cannot be this lost miscellany. Much of Augustine's intricate epistemological debate remains in Alfred's version, as the thirty-three-year-old character "Augustine" struggles for answers about the nature of God, the soul, and goodness. But one also recognizes typical Alfredian touches—his fondness for concrete examples manifests itself everywhere in the *Soliloquies*. Among these are his elaboration, in Augustine's long prayer to God near the opening, of the passage on God's rule through a cyclical alternation. Augustine talks about the seasons and the stars, but Alfred adds the seas and the rivers, and then comments that some things in their cycles become not exactly what they were:

> Ac cumað oðre for hy, swa swa leaf on treowum; and aepla, (and) gears, and wyrtan, and treowu foraldiað and forseriað; and cumað oððer, grenu wexað, and gearwað, and ripað, for þat hy eft onginnað searian.[57]

(But others come in their place, as leaves on trees; and apples, and grass, and plants and trees grow old and become sere and others come, wax green, and bloom, and ripen; wherefore they in turn begin to wither.)

There is also the cleverly wrought metaphor contained in this picture of the ship (man) anchored in his virtues:

> Therefore you need to look rightly with the eyes of the mind to God, just as the ship's anchor-cable is stretched in a straight direction from the ship to the anchor, and fasten the eyes of your mind on God, just as the anchor is fastened in the earth.[58]

Other instances include the description of the ship's master (the mind) steering the storm-tossed vessel through to calm weather, the desire for wisdom compared to the passion for kissing "on the bare body," mankind's various ways of finding truth likened to the many roads to the king's palace (wisdom), and the seeing of wisdom with the mind's eyes portrayed as the climbing of a sea-cliff by ladder. These images establish the *Soliloquies* as an authentic Alfredian creation.[59]

Also attributed to Alfred are the ninth-century prose psalms (nos. 1–50) contained in the unique manuscript of the Paris Psalter.[60] William of Malmesbury records that Alfred's death interrupted his translation of the Psalter. Though this evidence alone does not establish Alfred's authorship, investigations into the vocabulary, phraseology, and syntax of the prose psalms reveal so many similarities between them, the Boethius, and the *Pastoral Care* that the case for Alfred as their translator seems plausible.[61] From the Anglo-Saxon perspective, this prose version of the psalms may also have been a complete translation, for it was common practice to divide the Psalter as a whole into three sections of fifty.[62] Alfred's choice of the first group was especially appropriate to his own circumstances, for they contain King David's lamentations in the face of oppression by hostile foreigners and his declarations of the need for learning and faith in God.[63]

Alfred, if indeed he is the author, translated the psalms from a Latin text based on the Roman Psalter, occasionally consulting glosses derived from the Gallican Psalter.[64] His renderings vary from reasonably close translation to expansions incorporating exegetical commentary. He employed no single treatise on the psalms, though several were available, including the *Exegesis* ascribed to Bede. To each of the psalms (except *Ps.* 1) Alfred prefixed a short explanatory "Introduction," giving the historical occasion for the verse and either a threefold or a fourfold interpretation. These "Introductions" are modelled on the Latin *titulus*, which outlines the circumstances of composition, and the *argumentum* (an exegetical term), which describes the psalm's main theme. For this arrangement, Alfred depended upon an Irish model, although he made extensive modifications.[65] He seems to have conceived his psalm translations as a combination of text and gloss which would

give the uninformed reader all he needed to know on a first encounter with such obscure lyrics. In themselves they are important creations, making the abstract concrete, as was Alfred's habit,
and often more successful in their literary effect than their Latin
counterparts.[66]

Three historical works are closely associated with Alfred's plan
for intellectual reform in his kingdom. Together they cover, in one
fashion or another, the history of the world up to Alfred's own
time as it was conceived by men of the early Middle Ages. The
first, Paulus Orosius' *Historiarum adversum Paganos Libri Septem*
(Seven Books of History against the Pagans), was long included among
the king's own translations; William of Malmesbury identifies it as
Alfredian. But definitive arguments have placed it outside the accepted canon.[67] Augustine commissioned Orosius (c. 385–420), an
Iberian priest, to write the work as a historical supplement to his
own theological tract, *The City of God*. In this "universal" or "compendious" history Orosius provided an overview of world history
from the creation of Adam to the year of its composition (417–8).
His polemic aimed to answer the charges that the sack of Rome
resulted from the acceptance of Christianity; throughout the *Seven*
Books he rails against the pagans and accentuates the greater evils
of pre-Christian times. Despite his admiration for Augustine,
however, Orosius' history is not an illustration of the philosophy
of history expressed in *The City of God*. There, Augustine insisted
that man would be presumptuous to pretend he could decode
God's plan in the unfolding of history; but Orosius thought of Rome
as God's new-chosen nation and maintained that the imperial city,
now united to the Church, was progressing triumphantly toward
the Last Judgment.[68]

The Old English *Orosius*, dated sometime between 889 and 899,
is much more of a paraphrase than a strict translation. It reduces
Orosius' seven books (of 236 chapters) to six (of 84 sections); the
cutting is especially severe in Books 5 and 6. The translators, or
translator, also add much original material, and at times the final
product bears only a slight resemblance to the Latin text.[69] These
extensive alterations have more than a quantitative effect; the entire perspective on world history is likewise changed. The Old
English author seems less interested in Orosius' polemical side,

and even finds such ancient Romans as Scipio (Africanus Major) and Julius Caesar praiseworthy.[70] He may accept, indeed emphasize, Orosius' belief that history reveals God's purpose: the four universal empires have been Babylon, Macedon, Carthage, and Rome—the last paving the way for the universal Church. But he does not go out of his way to find examples of pagan barbarity, and he judiciously omits all Orosius' references to the heinousness of the Germanic tribes.

Orosius' history begins with a geographical survey, and the translator follows his tripartite division of the world into Asia, Europe, and Africa (also called the "second" Europe). The account of Europe calls forth a ninth-century description of Northern Europe and Scandinavia, which leads in turn to the insertion of the famous voyages of the Norwegian Ohthere and the Anglian (or Danish) Wulfstan. They had visited Alfred's court and reported respectively on their journeys into the White and Baltic Seas. The two sea captains' voyages are first-rate narrative. From Ohthere we learn about the far North and about the existence and subsistence of the Lapps (Finns), of whale and walrus hunting (the walruses being highly valued for the very fine "bone [ivory] in their teeth"), and of friendly and hostile inhabitants of the Arctic waste. From Wulfstan we hear a tale of the Estonians' strange burial custom: of their "refrigerating' of the dead man for as long as six months, of the feasting and carousing around the bier, of the final cremation of the body, of the placing of the man's treasure at spaced distances from the village, and of the horse race which follows to sweep up that treasure. The story concludes with the laconic remark that "for that reason swift horses are very dear there." These first-hand reports are couched in an economical and suggestive prose; as R. W. Chambers comments, in the space of two or three pages,

> we get a shrewd idea of the traveller's [Ohthere's] character: the mixture of curiosity and more practical ends which prompted his exploration; the caution which led him to stop it; a caution which also prevented him dwelling on the many tales which he heard of the lands beyond, "but which he knew not the truth of it, for he saw it not himself."[71]

We can credit the men themselves for these personal accounts, but the sources of the other geographical additions are obscure. Some argue that the translator used a *mappa mundi*, the traditional map of the classical geographer depicting the "whole earth"; but this cannot be proved and the Old English writer may well have had access to a glossed Latin manuscript or a commentary on Orosius.[72]

Most of the additions involve explanations for names, events, and customs that would have been unfamiliar to an Anglo-Saxon audience, and often ancient habits appear in Anglo-Saxon dress: Roman cohorts are what "we now call *truman* ['troops']," and a certain Roman maiden devoting herself to Diana "is said to have been a nun." The translation is littered with misinterpretations and mistakes of various kinds, but many are not without interest. For example, the translation of the passage describing the first elephants brought against the Romans by Pyrrhus contains the sentence, "He [Minutius, a Roman] ventured under an elephant so that he stabbed it in the navel." The Latin reads to the effect that "With his sword he sliced off the beast's trunk stretched out against him." There was obviously some confusion in the Anglo-Saxon translator's mind about the unusual Latin *manus* for "trunk" and about elephantine physiognomy.[73]

The style of the Old English *Orosius* is much more paratactic than that of Alfred's attested translations, resembling instead the native historical prose of the Anglo-Saxon Chronicles.[74] But the work possesses a rhythm and a balance that easily allow the translator to change roles from recorder of history to moralizing orator.[75] One well-known addition, the lament of Babylon, shows a fine use of prosopopoeia (personification) and hyperbole: "Now that I am thus fallen and passed away, lo, you can perceive and understand in me that you have nothing fast or strong in your possession which can endure."[76] This is a fitting emblem for an Anglo-Saxon work. A further item of interest in this unusual translation: for the historian of the language, the Tollemache (or Lauderdale) MS is one of the three basic sources of our knowledge of Early West Saxon.[77]

Although both Ælfric and William of Malmesbury identified Alfred as the translator of Bede's *Ecclesiastical History*, most scholars have for some time discounted this attribution.[78] The strong presence of Mercian dialect points to another author, one perhaps connected with the Mercian group of scholars Alfred gathered at his court.[79] Stylistically, the Old English Bede most closely resembles Wærferth's translation of Gregory's *Dialogues*, with its over-literalness and its excessive use of tautology—doublets translating single Latin words;[80] but Wærferth himself cannot have produced the work. Bede completed his *Historia Ecclesiastica Gentis Anglorum* in 731 and it has remained a monument to eighth-century Northumbrian scholarship (see chapter 1). For Bede, Anglo-Saxon history revealed that the English were God's new "chosen" nation, elected to replace the sin-stained Britons in the promised land of Britain.[81] The adaptor of Bede's work kept this racial perspective, although he narrowed it, thereby making the history even more parochial. This new Bede is thoroughly "English" history; it omits most details which do not contribute to the record of the Anglo-Saxons and the demonstration of their superior orthodoxy.

Over one-quarter of the Latin original is missing: papal letters, poems in honor of saints, and the long sections on the Easter controversy. Presumably epistolary documents would not interest a wider lay audience, and the date of Easter was no longer an issue during Alfred's time. In a prose that is somewhat tortured and hardly idiomatic, but still at times inspired, the Old English translator concentrated on the miraculous side of Bede's *History*: the accounts of the religious conversion of the English, all the saints' miracles except one, and the coming of the divine gift of poetry to Caedmon. He made his selections judiciously and in an orderly fashion—he knew what he wanted to create. But Bede's interest in precision, his care for the authenticity of sources, and his respect for authority are not present, nor is his concern with geography, chronology, or etymology. Bede was above all a patristic writer, still passionately involved with the doctrinal disputes of the early Church;[82] the translator was a more plainly chauvinistic writer. He had, however, something of a poetic turn of mind, exhibited in a rich poetic vocabulary and in metaphoric creativity. His retelling of the conversion of Edwin is far more concrete in its images than Bede's cool and abstract Latin: he transforms, for instance, the bald *paruissimo spatio* 'in the littlest space' of the sparrow simile into *an eagan bryhtm* 'in the twinkling of an eye'. The translation cannot be dated precisely, though external evidence suggests that it was done in the same decade as the other Alfredian pieces.

It has always been tempting to view the Anglo-Saxon Chronicles not only as a part of the larger Alfredian plan, but also as a specific conclusion to the historical works. Along with the Orosius and the Bede, they would create a useful trilogy, providing Alfred's subjects with all they needed to know of ancient, British, and English history. But these sentimental notions do not stand scrutiny. First, any connection of the Chronicles with Alfred's court is highly dubious; they have, as Stenton points out, "the character of private work."[83] Stenton postulates that some West Saxon nobleman, in imitation of the King, commissioned their compilation and then had them distributed.[84] Few accept Plummer's enthusiastic ascription of the originals to Alfred himself; even fewer would subscribe to the idea that Alfred intended them as nationalistic propaganda to unite his kingdom against the Danes.[85] But it is not unlikely that the king's own program may have created the milieu which made them possible.

The Anglo-Saxon Chronicles are sets of annalistic writings stretching from the time of Julius Caesar to (in the case of the Peterborough Chronicle) 1154, the year infamous King Stephen died. In the late 880s or early 890s, at least two West Saxon compilers produced the prototype, which was then distributed throughout the kingdom.[86] Subsequent bulletins were dispatched for inclusion, not all of which were incorporated into every version. Local additions were also frequent. Consequently, the Chronicles developed out of the common stock in quite divergent ways. None of the extant seven versions, which form four distinct groups, is closer to the prototype than two removes, and much late copying, interpolation, and collation of texts occurred.[87] It is thus erroneous to speak of a unitary *Anglo-Saxon Chronicle*, for the recensions differ so markedly.

On paleographic, stylistic, and historical grounds, the completion date for the prototype has been variously set at 890, 891, and 892.[88] The oldest manuscript, the Parker, or Winchester MS (the "A" version of the editions), is written in one late ninth-century or early tenth-century hand nearly up to the end of the 891 entry. Presumably, this recension drew upon an earlier West Saxon set of annals (perhaps in Latin), as well as upon the epitome at the end of Bede's *Ecclesiastical History*, an epitome of an unidentified "universal" history, some genealogies, and several classical sources.[89] Influenced by the great Frankish collections of annals, this initial compilation must have required extensive research and could not have been completed within a short period.

Since annalistic writing grew out of the practice of jotting down brief notices in the tables used to calculate the date of Easter, the style of the first block is terse, objective, and colorless: "671: In this year there was the great mortality of birds"; "777: In this year Cynewulf and Offa fought around Benson, and Offa captured the village"; "806: In this year there was an eclipse of the moon on 1 September. And Eardwulf, king of Northumbria, was driven from his kingdom, and Eanberht, bishop of Hexham, passed away." The syntax is mainly coordinate and there is no sense of cause and effect, of motivation, or of personality. Early commentators on the Chronicles found this style rudimentary and hopelessly crude, but Cecily Clark has demonstrated that this artificial manner was deliberately cultivated. Not all ninth-century prose is written in this way, and the fact that the first Chronicle purposely adopts this style indicates the compilers' desire to underscore the truth of their entries through a vehicle deemed stylistically appropriate.[90] Against this nearly formulaic mode, the expansive and dramatic narrative of the Cynewulf-Cyneheard feud (annal 755) stands out in high relief. Clearly an interpolation, the story is detailed in a prose that suggests an oral tradition or an even earlier written source.[91] Resembling the structure and ethos of the later Icelandic sagas, this brief episode depicts with political overtones the irresolvable conflicts between *comitatus* loyalty and blood relationships.

Alfred's wars against the Danes after the resumption of hostilities (893–6) are written in a different hand and constitute the "first continuation." Stylistically they also reflect a change in perspective. They are longer, fuller, and show a marked increase in subordinate constructions. Some rhetorical patterning also appears, giving the effect of an interpretative report rather than of a factual account. Once these stylistic possibilities have been admitted, the

Chronicles move even further in this "literary" direction, though they never entirely abandon the original voice: the "E" Chronicle's version of the Conquest "recaptures the lapidary dignity of the earliest annals."[92] But before this event, biased reporting and an emotional style developed significantly. Striking examples are the "D" and "E" renditions of the difficulties Edward the Confessor had in 1051 with Godwine and his sons over Eustace of Boulogne (Edward's brother-in-law) and the actions of his men in Dover. Both texts are "northern recensions" till 1031, but after that date the two part company: "D" continues to be northern (probably compiled at York), and "E" seems to have found its way to Canterbury. As a result, the "D" text shows a decided partisanship for Edward, while the "E" is more favorably disposed to Godwine, who held the earldom of Kent, Sussex, and Wessex. In spite of these factional loyalties, English nationalism comes to the fore in both accounts,[93] a nationalism emphasized in six poems inserted in the Chronicles (see chapters 6 and 10). The presence of these poems indicates further the heterogeneity of tastes and styles incorporated in the Chronicles by their many contributory hands over two and a half centuries.

One last work may be mentioned as possibly connected with the Alfredian circle—the Old English *Martyrology*, of which five fragments survive.[94] This collection from the second half of the ninth century may have been translated from an earlier Latin martyrology, or it may have been a text composed originally in Old English using a variety of Latin sources.[95] Günter Kotzor has shown that the Old English *Martyrology* is quite independent of the entire Latin martyrological tradition, remaining distinct even from the first of the narrative or "historical" martyrologies, that compiled by Bede.[96] The Old English exemplar drew upon longer hagiographical texts, homilies, liturgical texts, and literary works such as Bede's *Ecclesiastical History*, Felix of Crowland's *Vita Guthlaci*, Eddius Stephanus' *Vita Wilfridi*, and the Irishman Adamnan's *De Locis Sanctis*. Other Irish religious writings seem to lie behind certain details that do not appear in more conventional specimens.[97] Most unusual are the sections narrating the six days of creation, the signs and portents marking Christ's birth, His descent into hell, His ascension, and the Pentecost, as well as entries for Rogation Days, and the consecration of St. Michael's church.

The dialect of the Old English text is clearly Mercian, though the translation may have been carried out as part of Alfred's plans. Possibly one of Alfred's imported Mercian scholars was responsible for it. Many English saints are represented, but Mercian saints are especially plentiful: Chad of Lichfield and his brother Cedd, Guthlac of Crowland and his sister Pega, and Abbot Hygebald of Lindsey.[98]

Both the *Martyrology* and the Mercian *Life of St. Chad* (c. 850) have been described as forerunners of the alliterative prose which flourished in the late tenth and early eleventh centuries (see chapter 3).[99] The *Life of St. Chad* is extant only in the twelfth-century MS Hatton 116, transcribed in Worcester, the last important stronghold of Anglo-Saxon learning and culture in Norman England.[100] Ultimately translated from the account of the bishop of Mercia from 669–72 in Bede's *History*, this homily uses certain hagiographical stereotypes, and takes its introductory and concluding lines from Sulpicius Severus' *Life of St. Martin*.

A final twelfth-century work should be mentioned and removed from the Alfredian canon. The *Proverbs of Alfred* are a later compilation ascribed to the king who, like Solomon in religious tradition, embodied the high ideal of wisdom. The proverbs seem to be drawn from Old Testament Books of Wisdom and the popular Latin *Distichs of Cato* (see chapters 1 and 3).[101]

The vigorous activity of translation and vernacular writing in the latter part of the ninth century, associated with Alfred's name in one way or another, suggests the king's right to the title "the father of English prose." This prose, as represented in the Hatton MS of the *Pastoral Care,* the Parker MS of the Chronicles, and the Tollemache MS of the Orosius—all contemporaneous or early-tenth-century—has been used to establish Early West Saxon as "standard" Old English for many an Old English grammar.[102] But valid objections have been raised to accepting Alfred's West Saxon as a norm for Old English. Alfred's dialect is anything but "pure" West Saxon—the earlier political ascendancy of Mercia, along with the amanuenses from various locales employed by Alfred, may in part account for the admixture of Anglian forms in Alfred's language. Further, Alfred was no grammarian, unlike his literary heir Ælfric a century later; and many linguists prefer Ælfric's language (Late West Saxon) as the norm for the study of the language.[103] There were, of course, translations into English before Alfred's time: Bede undertook several, though none of them survives, and his efforts were not as programmatic as Alfred's. The great king's importation of many Mercian scholars, however, does not necessarily mean that a Mercian "school" of translation existed earlier in the ninth century. The *Martyrology* and *Chad* seem to come from Mercia, as do Wærferth's translation of Gregory's *Dialogues*, and the Tanner MS of the Old English Bede. Mercian originals may lie behind such pieces as the prose *Guthlac*, *The Blickling Homilies*, and the prose texts in the *Beowulf* MS.[104] But we need not posit a whole Mercian school of translation such as Alfred later created. As important as Alfred's Mercian scholars were for the implementation of his grand program, they do not seem to have had any significant literary influence on Alfred's translations; for the Mercian texts manifest great differences in dialect, vocabulary, and style from those that are definitely associated with Alfred. Particularly noticeable in the former is a consciously rhythmic phrasing and extensive use of alliteration, a style that was to find its most refined use in the works of Ælfric and Wulfstan.

NOTES

1. Chambers 1932, pp. lviii–lix. Chambers here responds to the many who insisted that OE prose was a rude and isolated phenomenon. But see Wilson 1959, who questions Chambers' conclusions. See also Gordon, I. A. 1966. For a discussion of OE prose studies, see Gatch 1976.

2. For a recent summary of Alfred's career, see the "Introduction" to Keynes/Lapidge 1983. This book, which contains translations of Asser's *Life* of the king, of extracts from the king's writings, and of other sources pertinent to Alfred's reign, also provides a useful bibliography.

3. See Chambers 1932, p. lvi; Stenton 1971, p. 270.

4. Barraclough 1976 reminds us that it was only England which the Danes attempted to subdue as a whole (p. 124).

5. Stenton 1971, p. 269.

6. Keynes/Lapidge 1983, p. 74; for the Latin text, see Stevenson 1904. Portions of Asser's *Life* are also translated in Whitelock 1979, pp. 289–303.

7. Davis 1971, p. 176; see also Whitelock 1979, pp. 879–80.

8. See Nelson, J. 1967; Brooke 1970; Davis 1971. Cf. Whitelock 1979, p. 123, and especially Whitelock 1978.

9. The only MS of Asser's *Life* known to modern times, Brit. Lib. Cott. Otho A. xii, burned in the fire of 1731 (see chapter 6); Stevenson 1904 is based on Archbishop Parker's transcripts (not his edition of 1574) and on extracts recorded by Florence of Worcester, Simeon of Durham, and the compiler of the *Annals of St. Neots*. On the authenticity of Asser's *Life*, see Whitelock 1968a; see also Gransden 1974, pp. 46–53 and Keynes/Lapidge 1983, pp. 50–1.

10. Schütt 1957, p. 219.

11. Brooke 1970, p. 232; Keynes/Lapidge 1983, p. 55.

12. See Schütt 1957, pp. 212–8.

13. Keynes/Lapidge 1983, pp. 88–9.

14. Ibid., p. 99.

15. Ibid., p. 100.

16. Bullough 1972, p. 460.

17. Text: Sweet 1871, p. 3.

18. Whitelock 1979, p. 92.

19. See Yerkes 1982, p. 9; Yerkes 1985.

20. Text: Hecht 1900, p. 1.

21. See Yerkes 1979 and 1982.

22. There is some question about the chronology of Alfred's works, since all postdate Asser's *Life* or at least are not mentioned therein—see Anderson, G. 1966, p. 264; also Bromwich 1950, p. 302. For text and translation of the OE *Pastoral Care*, see Sweet 1871. A more modern edition of one manuscript is Carlson 1975 (Part I); Part II completed by Hallander/ *et al.* (see Carlson 1978). On textual transmission and authority, see Sisam, K. 1953, pp. 140–7. For sympathetic critical treatment of this and most of the Alfredian translations, see Duckett 1956, pp. 142 ff.; Whitelock 1966. The MSS have been reproduced in Ker 1956. See also Clement 1985.

23. See Potter 1947, p. 114.

24. See, for example, Brown, W. 1969, p. 684.

25. See Duckett 1956, p. 133; Wallace-Hadrill 1971b, pp. 141–51 stresses the importance of Alfred's role as king in all his works.

26. Huppé 1978, p. 119. The classical study of the *Preface* is Klaeber 1923; see also Gneuss 1986.

27. Huppé 1978, p. 120.

28. See Morrish 1985.

29. Szarmach 1980, pp. 80–1. But cf. Shippey 1979, who does not believe Alfred intended anything so "over-pious" (p. 353). See also Orton 1983b, who claims that the syntactic indirectness in the *Preface* may stem from Alfred's belief that some of his bishops were to blame for the decay of learning.

30. Bately 1980a, p. 8.

31. See ibid., p. 5; Whitelock 1966, p. 74.

32. See Sisam, K. 1953, p. 140. See also Sweet 1871, pp. xix–xlii.

33. See Brown, W. 1969, p. 679.

34. Text: Sweet 1871, p. 26.

35. For material on Boethius, see Patch 1935; Chadwick, H. 1981; Gibson 1981. For a modern translation, see Green, R. 1962.

36. Cross 1961b.

37. See Markland 1968; Whitbread 1970; Bolton 1971; Kiernan 1978; but see Roper 1962, who discounts such influence.

38. Godden 1981, p. 419.

39. Sedgefield 1899, p. vii. Two MSS, a fragment, and a seventeenth-century transcription by Junius survive: Bodleian 180 is of twelfth-century origin and is entirely in prose; Cotton Otho A. vi is an early-tenth-century copy and contains the OE *Meters* (see chapter 10). Sedgefield's edition is a composite of the two MSS, and was translated by him in 1900.

40. The seminal article is Schepss 1895.

41. See Schmidt 1934; Otten 1964; Donaghey 1964; Courcelle 1967, pp. 241–97.

42. Wittig 1983, p. 166.

43. See Otten 1964, p. 281.

44. This is the major thesis of Payne, F. 1968. But Payne's ideas have received some sharp rebuttals: see Proppe 1973; Fischer 1979; Bolton 1985.

45. Text: Sedgefield 1899, p. 40.

46. Text: ibid., p. 142.

47. Text: ibid., p. 129.

48. Text: ibid., p. 41.

49. Text: ibid., p. 46.

50. See Otten 1964, p. 287; text: Sedgefield 1899, p. 27.

51. See Whitelock 1966, pp. 75–7.

52. See Brown, P. 1969, pp. 115–27; Duckett 1956, pp. 155–7.

53. Ed., with a Latin text, in Hargrove 1902; trans. in Hargrove 1904. For other editions, see Endter 1922; Carnicelli 1969.

54. See Potter 1949.

55. On this theme in medieval thought, see Ladner 1967.

56. Text: Carnicelli 1969, pp. 47–8.

57. Text: ibid., p. 53.

58. Text: ibid., pp. 61–2.

59. See Waterhouse 1985; Gatch 1985.

60. The eleventh-century text is Paris, Bibliothèque Nationale, MS latin 8824. The text of the prose psalms has been edited by Bright/Ramsay 1907; however, this edition is not reliable. The entire *Paris Psalter* has been reproduced in Colgrave 1958.

61. See Sisam, C./K. 1958; Bromwich 1950; Bately 1982.

62. Whitelock 1966, p. 71.

63. Keynes/Lapidge 1983, p. 32.

64. With the tenth-century Benedictine reform, the Gallican Psalter, used in France and Ireland, gradually supplanted the Roman in English churches. The change, however, was not complete; see, for example, the *Eadwine Psalter*, c. 1150.

65. See O'Neill 1981.

66. See Bately 1980a, pp. 14–5.

67. See Liggins 1970. This opinion is shared by Bately 1980b, pp. lxxiii–lxxxvii. Bately's edition is based on the Lauderdale MS; the older edition by Sweet 1883 has the Latin original. Bosworth 1859 is based on the Cotton MS and contains a translation, as does Thorpe 1873.

68. For an examination of Orosius' place in the development of a Christian philosophy of history, see Hanning 1966, pp. 37–43.

69. See Liggins 1985, who argues for more than one translator.

70. See Whitelock 1966, pp. 90–1.

71. Chambers 1932, p. lx. On the navigational problems involved in Ohthere's voyage, see Binns 1961; note, p. 43, gives further bibliography. Geographical problems are discussed by Ekblom 1960; Derolez 1971; Korhammer 1985.

72. See Linderski 1964; Bately 1980b, p. lxvii.

73. Text: Bately 1980b, p. 84, lines 18–9. For further examples, see Potter 1953.

74. Potter 1939, p. 49; see also Liggins 1985.

75. Bately 1980b, p. ciii.

76. Text: ibid., p. 44.

77. Reproduced in Campbell, A. 1953.

78. Ælfric (*Catholic Homilies* II, 116–8) and William of Malmesbury (*De Gestis Regum Anglorum*); but Alfred's reputation may have been responsible for the attribution, just as it was for the ascription to him of the later *Proverbs of Alfred*. Some scholars still argue that Alfred was the translator: see Kuhn 1947 and 1972a.

79. Miller 1890, editor of the standard text with translation, was the first to point out the work's Mercian qualities; another edition of the text alone is by Schipper 1899. On the dialect, see van Draat 1916; Campbell, J. 1951; Vleeskruyer 1953.

80. See Whitelock 1962 and 1966, pp. 77–8; see also Fry 1985.

81. See Hanning 1966, pp. 63–90.

82. See Bonner 1973.

83. Stenton 1971, pp. 692–3.

84. Stenton 1925.

85. Davis 1971; but see Whitelock 1978.

86. Bately 1978, p. 129.

87. Ed. and trans. in Thorpe 1861. The most useful edition is Plummer 1892. For separate editions of the different MSS, see Whitelock 1961, p. xxv; the portions up to 1042 are also translated in Whitelock 1979. In ad-

dition, see Garmonsway 1953. For a general commentary, see Gransden 1974, pp. 29–41.

88. See Whitelock 1979; Bately 1978; and Keynes/Lapidge 1983, pp. 278–9.

89. For the sources, see Plummer 1892, pp. cxiv ff.; Garmonsway 1953, pp. xliii–xliv; Bately 1978 and 1979; see also Waterhouse 1980.

90. See Clark, C. 1971; on the style and changes in source, see Waterhouse 1980.

91. On the possibility of an oral prose saga, see Wright, C. 1939; Wrenn 1940. Whitelock 1961 describes the prose as "archaic" (p. xxii); Towers 1963 describes it as "vigorous and living." For general interpretations of the Cynewulf-Cyneheard episode, see Waterhouse 1969; Turville-Petre 1974; McTurk 1981.

92. Clark, C. 1971, p. 234.

93. See Chambers 1932.

94. Ed. Kotzor 1981; see also Sisam, C. 1953.

95. See Cross 1985a and 1985b for evidence of the OE writer's expertise in Latin.

96. See Kotzor 1985.

97. See Cross 1977; 1981; 1982.

98. See Sisam, C. 1953.

99. See Funke 1962b.

100. Ed. Vleeskruyer 1953; this includes the parallel texts of the Tanner MS of the OE Bede and the Moore MS of the Latin Bede.

101. Ed. Arngart 1942; see also Arngart 1951.

102. E. g., Moore/Knott 1955.

103. E. g., Quirk/Wrenn 1958. See also Wrenn 1933, pp. 65–88; Gneuss 1972.

104. Menner 1949, pp. 56–64; Vleeskruyer 1953, esp. pp. 39–71; Funke 1962b. For some reservations about Vleeskruyer's Mercian and early-dating enthusiasm, see Sisam, C. 1955.

CHAPTER 3

Ælfric, Wulfstan, and Other Late Prose

Alfred's immediate political heirs consolidated and expanded his territorial gains, but though they made gifts to the Church and tried to maintain the standards of literacy Alfred had envisioned, their success was less dramatic than his (see chapter 1). Edward the Elder (d. 924) united the whole kingdom as far north as the Humber under his rule, though it cost him unceasing vigilance and campaigning to do so, first against some of his own rebellious subjects and then against the Danes. Edward's son Æthelstan (d. 939) won the greatest English victory of the century when he defeated a combined force of Scots and Danes at the Battle of "Brunanburh" in 937. But monasteries observing the Benedictine Rule scarcely existed—Alfred's own foundation at Athelney vanished for want of recruits. Entries in the Chronicles became very thin and, with the exception of *The Battle of Brunanburh*, no outstanding pieces of Anglo-Saxon literature can be assigned to this time.[1] It was not till the peaceful reign of Edgar (959–75), Alfred's great-grandson, that religious reform laid the foundation for a cultural renascence, a quickening that produced at least two outstanding scholars and writers in the vernacular, Ælfric, monk of Cerne (or Cernel) and Abbot of Eynsham (c. 995–c. 1012),[2] and Wulfstan, archbishop of York and bishop of Worcester (d. 1023).

To this same period also belong works of literature (see chapter 1) and art of the highest quality: the "Winchester" style in manuscript illumination, sculpture in ivory, and metalwork all outshone continental production.[3] And in this period, too, nearly all the Anglo-Saxon poetry extant today was collected and transcribed.

The monastic (or "Benedictine") reform of the later tenth century was long overdue. Since the "golden age" of Wearmouth-Jarrow and York had departed with the onslaught of the Danish invasions at the end of the eighth century, the moral and cultural force of regular monastic discipline had languished in England.[4] The extent to which spiritual dissolution had set in may be seen in Ælfric's perhaps somewhat exaggerated account of conditions at Winchester in 963: "At that time in the Old Minster, where the bishop's seat is situated, there were clerics living badly, possessed by pride, arrogance, and wantonness to such an extent that some of them refused to celebrate mass in their turn; they repudiated the wives whom they had taken unlawfully and married others, and continually devoted themselves to gluttony and drunkenness."[5] The Benedictine revival began in France (see chapter 1), but the appointment of Dunstan as abbot of Glastonbury (c. 940) conventionally marks its start in England.[6] With the accession of Edgar and his raising of Dunstan to the post of archbishop of Canterbury in 960, the monastic revival was firmly established. Besides Duncan (d. 988), two other English monks were prominent in this new period of reform: Æthelwold, abbot of Abingdon and bishop of Winchester (d. 984), who had been a pupil of Dunstan's, and Oswald, bishop of Worcester and archbishop of York (d. 992), a member of an aristocratic Danish family. While Dunstan may have provided the initial impetus for the reform, the most powerful personality in this trinity was Æthelwold. A man of extreme discipline and austerity—he drove the dissolute canons out of Winchester cathedral and replaced them with his monks—he was a forceful organizer who laid the groundwork for the development of late Old English prose and perhaps established West Saxon as the standard literary dialect.[7]

Latin *vitae* of all three founders of the Benedictine reform were composed shortly after their deaths. Two *vitae* of Æthelwold survive, one written by Wulfstan, precentor at Winchester, in 996, and one by Ælfric in 1006 (see chapter 1).[8] Ælfric's is the shorter, sparer *Life*, and it is evidently an abbreviation of Wulfstan's longer, stylistically elaborate version. The hallmarks of hagiography are evident in these two works: Æthelwold's mother has a prophetic dream of a golden eagle issuing from her mouth, a dream of the saint who was to become the standard-bearer of God's army. Miracles are attributed to Æthelwold from the time of his infancy to the period after his death. One should especially note in this "unrealistic" context one factual detail: Æthelwold is felled by a post during his inspection of a building under construction. This part of his activity was of major importance for the full restoration of monastic life in England, and his rescue is providential. An anonymous Anglo-Saxon priest, who identified himself only as .B. and who claimed to have witnessed the events he recorded, composed an account of Dunstan's life. Written in an obscure and artificial style typical of late tenth- and early eleventh-century Latin, this *vita* (c. 1000) dwells more on Dunstan's sanctity than on his actions as an ecclesiastical reformer.[9] A second early *Life* (c. 1005–12), by Adelard, a monk of Ghent, increases the amount of miraculous detail. St. Oswald is commemorated in a *Life* written by Byrhtferth of Ramsey between 995 and 1005.[10] As in the *Lives* of St. Dunstan, the wonder-working aspects of Oswald's career receive the greatest attention, though this *Life* remains an important source for information on the state of monastic affairs just before the revival; it exhibits the traits of Byrhtferth's florid and verbose style (see chapter 1).

One of the first problems for the reform movement was to ensure uniform liturgical and disciplinary practices; diversity in such matters had become widespread because the number of monasteries had increased rapidly as a result of King Edgar's personal commitment to the cause and his many gifts of land. Thus about 973 a Synodal Council was held at Winchester.[11] This Council issued a Latin customary known as the *Regularis Concordia* 'The Agreement Concerning the Rule' (see also chapter 1). Intended as a supplement to the Benedictine *Rule*, it had a profound effect on the English church and its liturgy.[12] Although drawn mainly from European sources—representatives from the reformed monaster-

ies of Ghent and Fleury-sur-Loire were present at the Council—
the *Regularis Concordia* contains some uniquely English references:
for example, Edgar's support of the monks is rewarded by re-
minders that they should pray constantly for the king.

Æthelwold is usually credited with the major role in compiling
the *Concordia*. But at least two works in Old English came from his
pen. He translated the Benedictine *Rule* into a clear and rhetorically heightened Anglo-Saxon. Two versions exist, one for monks
and one for nuns, both showing that Æthelwold was conscious of
the need for a detailed explanation of St. Benedict's orders to unlettered novices.[13] A fragment in Old English describing Edgar's
reestablishment of the monasteries is also attributed to Æthelwold.[14] Closely connected with these Æthelwoldian translations are
the Lambeth Psalter gloss, the glosses to the *Expositio Hymnorum*
and the Old English translation of the *Rule of Chrodegang*.[15] The
fragmentary *Life of Machutus*, which relates the miracles of a Bre-
ton saint who was a disciple of St. Brendan, may also be connected to this "Winchester" school.[16]

While the full flowering of the Benedictine revival came in the
works of Ælfric and Wulfstan, it would be misleading to suppose
that they were the only writers of vernacular prose in the late tenth
and early eleventh centuries. In fact Ælfric and Wulfstan are preceded by a significant body of prose, comprising mainly anonymous homilies and homiletic fragments, a few saints' lives, and
some penitential texts. Many of the surviving homilies from this
period appear in more than one manuscript and overlap with one
another.[17] Two good-sized collections (homiliaries) are of special
importance—the *Blickling* and the *Vercelli Homilies*.[18] They represent the synthetic tradition of vernacular preaching before the wa-
tershed of the monastic revival, although that rebirth may have
inspired their transcription.

The dates of these two homiliaries are hard to set. An internal
reference to 971 (Homily XI on "Holy Thursday") in the Blickling
collection sets a *terminus post quem* for the compilation of the manuscript; scholars date the Vercelli codex at the turn of the tenth
and the eleventh centuries. Gatch believes that both codices are
"at least a generation earlier than Ælfric's earliest publication of
his work around 990."[19] Each collection draws on antecedent ver-

nacular homiliaries which could have been extant even in pre-Alfredian times, and it should be noted that the Latin tradition behind the anonymous homilies is the Gallican-Celtic tradition which prevailed on the Continent before the Carolingian reforms. This ascetic strain also provided the spiritual background for much of Old English religious poetry. However, the later homilies of Ælfric and Wulfstan are more dependent on reformed Carolingian materials.[20]

The *Blickling Homilies* (named after the former residence of the manuscript in Blickling Hall, Norfolk) consist of eighteen homilies and a fragment, arranged, with two exceptions, to follow the Temporale, that part of the breviary or missal which contains the daily offices in the order of the ecclesiastical year. The homilies begin with "The Annunciation of Saint Mary" and include the important Sundays, Lent, and Rogation Days, but the cycle is not complete. The last five full homilies are *vitae*, treating, most importantly, the deaths of Peter and Paul after their encounter with Simon Magus, the miracles of St. Martin, and the life of St. Andrew, a narrative which parallels the poetic *Andreas*. These lives follow the order of the Sanctorale, that part of the breviary or missal which contains the offices proper for saints' days.

Both theological and literary criticism have often characterized all the anonymous homilies as crude; but although they draw heavily upon fragments of Latin originals, they do create coherent orations. And while the Blickling collection may not be entirely consistent in its theology, particularly in its explanations of what happens to the soul between death and the Last Judgment, it nevertheless reveals an informed idea of confession and penance.[21] As Dalbey has shown, the compiler had a special interest in gathering homilies that stress gentleness and compassion: they are parenetic (that is, hortatory) in tone, rather than stern and didactic. While their emphasis is on repentance, it is also on the possibility of living a virtuous Christian life and achieving redemption. To this end the various authors in the Blickling group devote considerable attention to stylistic effects which will make their pleadings psychologically effective. These homilies may be theologically conservative, but they are not without some intelligent awareness of the human predicament seen from a benevolent Christian perspective.[22]

Although some of the Blickling texts begin with a reference to the Gospel pericope (reading of the day's mass), they do not proceed with an exegesis of that biblical selection, a procedure Ælfric favored in many of his homilies. Instead, they remain discursive exhortations.[23] A strong millenarial sense pervades them; one monitory sermon Morris entitles "The End of the World is Near." And they, like most anonymous homilies, are rich compendia of common Christian *topoi*, many of them drawn from the Apocrypha.[24] From the Apocalypse of Thomas come the signs of the impending Judgment for each of the preceding six days; the *ubi sunt* motif appears in several homilies; in Homily X the "dry bones speak," warning the living of the transitoriness of life; and the conflict between soul and body occurs repeatedly.[25] Most famous is the seventeenth selection, on the "Dedication of St. Michael's Church," because it incorporates a portion of the *Visio Pauli* which is remarkably similar to the description of the haunted mere in *Beowulf*:

> As St. Paul was looking towards the earth's northern region, from where all waters flow down, he saw there above the water a certain hoary stone; and north of the stone had grown very rimy groves. And there were dark mists, and under the stone was the dwelling place of water beasts and monsters. And hanging on the cliff in the icy groves he saw many black souls bound by their hands; and devils in the likeness of vile creatures were gripping them like greedy wolves. And the water was black down beneath the cliff. And between the cliff and the water were about twelve miles; and when the twigs broke, then down went the souls who hung on the twigs, and the water beasts seized them.[26]

In general, the theology of the *Blickling Homilies* is sober and cautious, not given to the miraculous. The prose often has a lyrical quality and is usually more metaphorical than any of its sources: Christ, for instance, is called *se goldbloma* 'the golden-blossom.' However, as we shall see, it does not rise to Wulfstan's impassioned heights, nor does it possess the rational clarity of Ælfric's writings.

The homilies in the *Vercelli Book* are intermingled with the Old English Christian epics *Elene* and *Andreas* and other poems, including the exquisite *Dream of the Rood*. There are twenty-three homiletic pieces in the collection[27] for such Church seasons or feasts as Lent, Rogationtide, Good Friday, and Epiphany, but these are not arranged in any order which corresponds to the Temporale. Many feasts have no homilies, and some are represented by two or more. Unlike the Blickling series, they do not serve a liturgical purpose, but seem to have been collected by someone in a monastic setting to illustrate his personal interest in penitential and eschatological themes and to glorify the ascetic way of life.[28] All the pieces are thus unified by these concerns. The emphasis here is also on provoking an emotional response in the audience (or reader), but the *Vercelli Homilies* do not show the same compassion as their Blickling counterparts. Instead the compiler selected sermons with a harsher and more strident tone, pieces that would indeed strike genuine terror into the hearts of his listeners.

Many of the Vercelli texts are a type of sermon known as the *Kompilationspredigt*, that is, a collection of religious themes for a hortatory purpose.[29] And most of these fall into the particular genre called "concentric homilies," which, as Szarmach illustrates, feature some central narrative, dramatic, or expository section surrounded at the beginning and end with generally conventional *topoi*.[30] Given his inclination, the collector provides monitory homilies on themes like the Eight Capital Sins (*ehta heafodleahtras* in Homily XX), derived mainly from Alcuin's *Liber de Virtutibus et Vitiis*, and the Last Judgment. As in the *Blickling Homilies*, there is some confusion in eschatological doctrines, for both rely more on authority than on logical analysis of sources and traditions. Interestingly, the millenarian urgency which so strongly characterizes the *Blickling Homilies* is not present here. Many of the subjects we noted in Blickling reappear, however, but the horrors of death occupy a far greater space in the Vercelli series. The *topos* of the conflict between the soul and the body receives special attention and development: Homily IV is the "most fully developed description of the actual judgment of the soul at the Last Day that we have in Old English."[31] Extensive descriptions of infernal punishments abound; so much so that the homilists' interest in the colorful and the dramatic often leaves the reader with an impression of crassness or moral insensitivity—or even of lapses in taste.[32] Yet the sense of a prose verging on poetry is to be remarked.[33]

Besides the poetic saints' lives of *Elene* and *Andreas* (see chapter 7), the *Vercelli Book* also contains some hagiography in prose: a life of St. Martin and a homily on the life of St. Guthlac. The latter, actually chapters four and five of the Old English translation of Felix of Crowland's *Vita Guthlaci*,[34] concludes the whole codex.

The penitential nature of the homilies is reflected in other vernacular documents—including handbooks of penance or "penitentials," various liturgical texts (among them instructions for confessors), prayers for penitents, and rites of public penance.[35] These diverse items derive from continental sources, themselves based on seventh- and eighth-century Irish and English penitentials. The most significant is the "Pseudo-Egbert Penitential," which divides into the "Confessional" (or *Scrift Boc*) and the "Penitential."[36] A third text, "The Handbook for the Use of a Confessor," represents the tenth-century culmination of such collections.[37] As Frantzen writes, "the three vernacular handbooks show increasing mastery of the form of the penitential, moving from the relative disorder of the 'Scrift Boc' to the simplicity and clarity of the 'Handbook'."[38] Such penitential materials were far more plentiful in England than in Europe, and they served as important sources for Ælfric and Wulfstan.

Abbot Ælfric, the greatest prose writer of the Anglo-Saxon period, received his first instructions in Latin from an ignorant country priest. In the early 970s Ælfric went to Winchester and studied there at the Old Minster under Æthelwold. His own writings began after his move to the monastery at Cernel in 987; he ended his religious career as Abbot of Eynsham. Sometime between 989 and 995, Ælfric wrote his first works, the two series of *Catholic Homilies*.[39] To this period, which concludes with a third series of homilies on the *Lives of Saints*, also belong his *Grammar*, *Glossary*, and *Colloquy* for the oblates in monasteries, his version of Bede's *De Temporibus Anni* (see chapter 4) and his contributions to the so-called *Old English Heptateuch*.

Ælfric's *Catholic Homilies* are a unique achievement in medieval

Europe. No other author or country produced such an extended collection of vernacular, exegetical homilies arranged according to the liturgical year.[40] They stand as a magnificent prologue to Ælfric's whole program of religious education in both Latin and Old English. Ælfric labored to strengthen his people through learning against the horrors and temptations of the chaos produced by the renewed Viking attacks in the late tenth century, attacks that were to lead to the Danish conquest of England in the eleventh. The political situation he faced strongly resembled that under which Alfred had struggled, and the homilist may even have based the idea of his educational scheme on the king's. His works reveal a knowledge of most of Alfred's translations and he himself made reference to them. A digression in the mid-Lent homily from the *Lives of Saints* echoes some of the king's laments:

> Well may we think how well it fared with us when this island was dwelling in peace, and the monastic orders were held in honor, and laymen were ready against their enemies, so that our word spread widely throughout the earth. How was it then afterward when men cast off monastic life and held God's services in contempt, but that pestilence and hunger came upon us, and afterward the heathen army held us in contempt?[41]

Finally, in using the vernacular as a medium for theology and the discussion of religious doctrine, he clearly followed the Alfredian precedent.[42] But Ælfric extended the scope of the undertaking and systematized it. He gave his enterprise a much more religious focus, perhaps because he was also concerned to help those in the present clergy who did not know Latin well enough to understand the basic points of Christian theology—the sweep of Christian history embracing the Creation, Fall, Redemption, and Last Judgment.

The two series of *Catholic Homilies* and the collection of the *Lives of Saints* may be discussed together for at least two reasons. First, they were viewed by Ælfric as something of a continuum, whereby he first made accessible in English an account of and commentary on the major tenets of Christianity, including the Scriptures, the origins and spread of Christianity, and the stories of its martyrs. Many of the "homilies" are actually saints' lives and many of the hagiographic pieces incorporate homilies. Second, they reveal a development in Ælfric's celebrated style. These three series consist of approximately forty sermons each, and for the *Catholic Homilies* the first serves as an introductory discourse: CH I, "On the Beginning of Creation," CH II, "On the Testimonies of the Prophets"; for the *Lives of Saints,* the "Memory of the Saints" seems similarly intended, although this *spel* 'homily' comes well into the middle of the series.

Ælfric gave his sources: mainly Gregory the Great, Augustine, Jerome, and Bede—though he may have found the homilies of these forerunners conveniently collected in some version of the popular homiliary of Paul the Deacon.[43] But Ælfric, though no innovative philosopher or theologian, was also no mere translator, despite his characterization of himself as such: he expanded, condensed, clarified, and embroidered in the light of his specific purpose to expound to his countrymen the universal truths of Christianity. Orthodoxy was his main concern. Ælfric gave each of the series a Latin and an English preface, and in the Anglo-Saxon one to the first volume of the *Catholic Homilies* he outlined his rationale for his ambitious undertaking:

> Then it came to my mind, I trust through God's grace, that I would turn this book from the Latin language into the English tongue; not from confidence of great learning, but because I have seen and heard much heresy [*or* folly] in many English books, which unlearned men in their simplicity esteemed as great wisdom.[44]

Ælfric was undoubtedly here referring to many of the apocryphal selections in the *Blickling* and *Vercelli Homilies.* He was extremely conservative and careful in his teachings, never asserting as dogma (for instance the Assumption of the Virgin—see *Blickling Homily* XIII) anything that he questioned. And, compared with that of the two anonymous anthologies, Ælfric's eschatology is considerably more advanced. By understanding that the historical Church participates in the eternal order of God's kingdom, he was able to avoid the confusion which pervades their speculations on the soul's fate between death and Judgment.[45] But not all of Ælfric's beliefs were uncontroversial: he preached the Eucharistic doctrine of Ratramnus that the bread and wine were mystically symbolic of the body and blood of Christ, a view that was to be condemned, ultimately, at the Synod of Vercelli in 1050 in favor of the doctrine of transubstantiation. It is one of the ironies of history that Ælfric later became the favorite of Protestant reformers in the Renaissance precisely because of this "heretical" stance.[46]

The First Series of *Catholic Homilies* is largely scriptural and exegetical in content, while the Second is more legendary, less didactic, and more concerned with the development of Christianity in England. Godden has demonstrated that in the First Series Ælfric speaks directly to the lay congregation, using the preacher only as his voice, whereas in the Second Series he provides a collection of homiletic material designed for the preachers themselves.[47] These homilies were distributed for delivery in churches—probably during the Prone, that section of the Mass following the Gospel which developed in Carolingian times as an appropriate interlude for catechetical instruction.[48] The *Lives of Saints*, however, seems to have been intended primarily for a reading audience. This series contains the passions and lives of those saints whom the monks themselves honor by special services,[49] not those celebrated in the general Sanctorale.

Like Alfred before him, Ælfric translated not "word for word, but sense for sense."[50] And like the poets, he used Old English social, political, and legal terms to portray biblical relationships and even the smallest features of daily life. He used similes from spheres of human activity, as had Alfred, though his sources were more likely the Fathers than "life." His style is characterized by the absence of complex metaphors and an insistent simplicty of diction, yet he could compare the joys in heaven over the conversion of a sinner to "the greater love which a chieftain feels in battle for the soldier who after flight boldly [ðegenlice] overcomes his adversary, than for him who never took to flight, nor yet in any conflict performed any deed of valor [ðegenlices]."[51]

For a rich poetic language, Ælfric substituted allegory and classification. Usually his allegory involves the simple dichotomy of the literal and the spiritual (*þæt anfealde andgit* as opposed to *þæt gastlice andgit*).[52] So the eighth day of Christ's life, on which He was circumcised, signifies the eighth age of this world, in which we will arise from death, cut off from every corruption.[53] But Ælfric could also give more complex, if standard, interpretations. In an Easter sermon from the Second Series he explains the crossing of the Red Sea on a fourfold level of meaning: literally, the crossing of the Israelites from servitude to the promised land; allegorically, the passage of Christ from "middle-earth" to the heavenly Father; tropologically, the moving in this present life from sin to virtue; and anagogically, the crossing in the next life after our resurrection to eternal life in Christ.[54] Classification abounds: there are the two forms of the Holy Ghost, the three laws of the world, the four beasts of the Evangelists, the six ages of this present world, the eight capital sins, and the ten orders of angels, to list only a few. Various sorts of wordplay substitute for intricate metaphors, and onomastic interpretations are of special interest to Ælfric.

His sermons are indeed a web of subtle repetitions and variations on words, phrases, and sounds—conscious literary acts.[55] Out of this web he creates a remarkable style, one which encapsulates his allegorical perspective and establishes a correspondence between doctrine and expression. Homily XIX in the First Series, *De Dominica Oratione*, offers a fine example of Ælfric's technique.[56] This catechetical homily on the Lord's Prayer divides the Prayer's seven petitions into two categories—the first three are begun by us in this world, but they will last eternally; the second four begin and end in this life. Each of these petitions is explained and moralized within the pedagogical context of what makes men either children of God or of the devil. Towards the end of the homily Ælfric makes an important doctrinal point, and in reviewing the progress of the piece we come to realize that this idea has governed his stylistic choices from the outset:

> He does not say in that prayer, "My Father . . . ," but He says, "Our Father". . . . In that is revealed how greatly God loves unity and concord among His people. According to God's book all Christian men should be united as if they were one man: therefore, woe to the man who breaks that unity apart.[57]

The moralizations Ælfric has derived from each of the prayer's seven petitions are not just exhortations to do good. For Ælfric, action in this world and its moral consequences lead to metaphysical propositions. He sees the Christian endeavor in abstract terms: to reduce (or elevate) the diversity of sinful human life to unity. The process has three steps—from complete separateness, which is a dangerous state *(min)*, through commonality and mutality *(ure, gemænlice)*, to unity *(annysse)*. This progress requires an absolute transformation of being, and the style of Ælfric's homily embodies and reenacts that transformation. Ælfric's style not only depicts a correspondence between the cosmic and the earthly,[58] it also strives to transmute the sublunar into the divine. To use an alchemical metaphor: Ælfric attempts to turn base words into doctrinal gold. Sin is division, and redemption, therefore, is the process by which this division is made perfect unity. Ælfric effects this unity through his style, and thus he makes his style redemptive. It is the act by which unity is both portrayed and achieved.

Returning to the beginning of the homily, we see how this doctrine and its stylistic enactments work. After Ælfric describes the gospel setting of the Prayer, and quotes it, he writes:

> God Fæder Ælmihtig hæfð ænne Sunu gecyndelice and menige gewiscendlice. Crist is Godes Sunu, swa þæt se Fæder hine gestrynde of him sylfum, butan ælcere meder. Næfð se Fæder nænne lichaman, ne he on ða wisan his Bearn ne gestrynde þe menn doð: ac his Wisdom, þe he mid ealle gesceafta geworhte, se is his Sunu, se is æfre of ðam Fæder, and mid þam Fæder, God of Gode, ealswa mihtig swa se Fæder. We men sind Godes bearn, forðon þe he us geworhte.[59]

> (God, the Father Almighty, has one Son naturally, and many by adoption. Christ is God's Son, in that the Father begot Him of Himself without any mother. The Father has no body, nor did He beget His Son in the way that men do: but His Wisdom, with which He wrought all creatures, is His Son, who is ever of the Father and with the Father, God of God, as mighty as the Father. We men are children of God, because he made us.)

The one and the many are an important consideration from the start, with accompanying, paradoxical notions of community. Christ is God's *one* natural Son and good Christians are his sons adoptively—children alienated, but brought back into union with the Father by other than natural means. And in the long, balanced sentence which follows, Ælfric explains what he means by "natural" generation, which, from a human point of view, is not natural at all. The sentence breaks clearly in two: *ac* is the fulcrum. In the first part the order is Father/Son, the statement negative, the topic human creation, the verbs active and transitive, and the perspective temporal. In the second part, all is reversed: the order is Son (Wisdom)/Father, the statement positive, the topic spiritual creation, the verb "to be" is ontological, and the perspective eternal. Chiasmus is prominent, with the second clause reversing and so "uncreating" the first, which describes human creation. And the theme of unity and division is restated, but in a negative paradox. Particularity is associated with the body and thus is not an attribute of divinity; divinity does not act, but *is*, and so can create all and be all. The quotation ends with a balanced return to the topic sentence: in contrast to God's one Son, we are God's many sons.

If we examine other sections of this homily, we see that Ælfric's concerns remain the same, though his strategies become more complex. This becomes evident in a longer, more intricate portion:

> *Witodlice se man þe deofle geefenlæcð, se bið deofles bearn, na þurh gecyne oððe þurh gesceapenysse, ac ðurh þa geefenlæcunge and yfele geearnunga. And se man ðe Gode gecwemð, he bið Godes bearn, na gecyndelice, ac þurh gesceapenysse and ðurh gode geearnunga. . . . Forði nu ealle cristene men, ægðer ge rice ge heane, ge æðelborene ge unæðelborene, and se hlaford, and se ðeowa, ealle hi sind gebroðra, and ealle hi habbað ænne Fæder on heofonum. Nis se welega na betera on ðisum naman þonne se ðearfa. Eallswa bealdlice mot se ðeowa clypigan God him to Fæder ealswa se cyning. Ealle we sind gelice ætforan Gode. . . .*[60]

(Truly the man who imitates the devil is a child of the devil, not by nature nor by creation, but by that imitation and (by his) evil merits. And the man who makes himself acceptable to God is God's child, not naturally, but by creation and (by his) good merits. . . . Now therefore all Christian men, whether high or low, noble or ignoble, and the lord and the slave, are all brothers, and have all one Father in heaven. The wealthy man is not better on that account than the needy. The slave may call God his father as boldly as the king. We are all alike before God.)

Here we notice that two singular men—one the devil's, one God's—are stylistically almost identical. Little in the ordering of words distinguishes one from the other. The substitution of *gesceapenysse* 'creation' for *geefenlæcunge* 'imitation' and good for evil is all— however important—that separates them. But the paragraph does not leave us there. For we move from *se man* (whether sinner or good Christian) to *all*. And Ælfric's syntactic strategies likewise alter: they go from antithetical balance to a series of connected, cumulative phrases, thus mirroring the sense of the Christian community, the *ealle cristene men* being described. The entire effect is much more significant than simply repetition with variation. The concatenation of *ealle*'s, merging with the two *ealswa*'s and then recurring transformed in the direct statement *ealle we sind*, is a forceful reenactment of the themes Ælfric has in mind. God is unity, the *ænne Fæder;* we are manifold, but we can be brought into a collective body, transformed into a oneness before God. The important issue here is not the doctrine *per se;* what Ælfric says is a standard Christian notion. What is most impressive are the stylistic choices by which Ælfric conveys that doctrine, the various ways he makes the style enact the meaning. And with regard to the *Lives of Saints*, Tandy has shown a similar process at work. In the "Life of St. Eugenia" he proves that pagans and Christians are distinguished by a different use of verbal aspect. The former are "characterized as active, punctual, imperative, nondurative; the latter are virtually nontemporal, all their actions having moral goals and contexts." He concludes that these patterns create a subtle narrative structure, delineating the opposing characters and marking out the spiritual values of the narrative.[61] Thus Ælfric's style is more than rational, clear, balanced, and logical. While these terms may accurately describe its surface, they do not take into account that for Ælfric even the grammatical forms, the placement of clauses, and the rhythmic patterning of words are a devotional exercise.

The technical questions concerning Ælfric's style have received much attention. In these three series of homilies he moves from a prose heightened occasionally by alliteration and other rhetorical effects to an almost regularly metrical style—the shift comes in the middle of the Second Series and is complete by the time of the *Lives of Saints*. The latter are so rhythmical and alliterative that earlier critics disputed whether they were not meant to be poetry; Skeat printed many of the *Lives*, or portions of them, as such, and Jost reverted to this practice in his edition of Wulfstan's *Institutes of Polity* (see below). Ælfric could have derived this style from older prose writings in English—it occurs to some extent in the Alfredian translations. But some have wondered whether this distinctive mode which Ælfric perfected was not his conscious imitation of the contemporary rhymed Latin prose (such as that practised by his Winchester colleague, Lantfred: see chapter 1), with a substitution of alliteration for the rhyme and even an attempt to capture Latin rhythm, particularly the *cursus*, the rhythmical final clause in medieval Latin prose whose three types had two stresses and a fixed number of unstressed syllables. The alliterative measure of Old English poetry must also have made a strong impression on this sensitive stylist's mind.

Whatever the exact mixture of influences, most scholars now agree that the predominant force behind Ælfric's rhythmical prose was his native English heritage—with some Latin coloring in rhetorical effects.[62] The prose is characterized by a certain looseness in rhythm and great freedom in the rules for alliteration and its relation to the stress patterns of the line. It is an ordered prose rather than a debased poetry, but one can hear faint echoes of classical Old English poetry behind it. Here is a brief example from Ælfric's "Life of St. Oswald, King and Martyr":

> *Hwæt þa oswold cyning his cynedom geheold*
> *hlisfullice for worulde and mid micclum geleafan*
> *and on eallum dædum his drihten arwurðode*
> *oð þæt he ofslagen wearð for his folces ware*
> *on þam nigoðan geare þe he rices geweold*
> *þa þa he sylf wæs on ylde eahta and þrittig geara.*[63]

(Lo, then Oswald the king held his kingdom, gloriously before the world and with great faith, and in all his deeds honored his Lord, until he was slain in defence of his people, in the ninth year that he ruled the kingdom, when he himself was thirty-eight years old.)

Throughout his active career, Ælfric continued to revise and expand these homilies, and many different versions of them exist. However, it is still debatable whether Ælfric intended eventually to produce a complete set of homilies for the Temporale.[64]

Ælfric is usually considered the first important translator of the

Bible into English,[65] but his efforts are not all of one piece. They fall into three categories: (1) Paraphrases and epitomes of several books of the Bible. These include his homiletic epitome on the Book of Job (CH II. XXXV), and a series of paraphrases from the Old Testament—Kings, the Maccabees (LS XVIII and XXV), Esther, Judith, Judges, and Joshua. Ælfric's technique here is customarily one of radical compression. (2) Translations of individual passages. These comprise mainly his renderings of the gospel pericopes and other biblical passages in his homilies. Here Ælfric can be termed "faithful" to the biblical source, though he often altered and simplified to fit the context. (3) An extended literal translation of parts of Genesis (1–3, 6–9, 11–24) and Numbers (13–26). Ælfric undertook these projects with some hesitation, though he had precedents to follow: tradition held that Bede translated the Gospel of St. John, and there existed mid-tenth-century versions of the Gospels in West Saxon.[66] He nevertheless felt reluctant to turn God's sacred word into English. He commented on this subject more than once—in a closing prayer at the end of Catholic Homilies II, at the close of the Latin Preface to the Lives of Saints, and in the Preface to his translation of Genesis.

The Genesis translation forms, naturally, the first part of what has been called the Old English Heptateuch (so designated by Thwaite, its first editor, in 1698); it consists of a translation of and a commentary on the Pentateuch, Joshua, and Judges.[67] To Ælfric had once been attributed the entire work, but his contributions now seem more limited. In the Preface he agrees to translate what his powerful patron Æthelweard had requested, that portion of Genesis up to the section on Isaac. Another man, Ælfric notes, had already completed the book from there to the end.[68] He is genuinely afraid of translating the Old Testament, because he fears that

gif sum dysig man þas boc ræt oððe rædan gehyrþ, þæt he wille wenan þæt he mote lybban nu on þære niwan æ, swa swa þa ealdan fæderas leofodon þa on þære tide, ær þan þe seo ealde æ gesett wære, oþþe swa swa men leofodon under Moyses æ.[69]

(if some foolish man reads this book, or hears it read, that he will think he may live now under the new law as the ancient fathers lived in that time before the old law was established, or as men lived under Moses' law).

Polygamy and the marriage of priests are the specific items which cause Ælfric alarm, but his larger concern is his audience's inability to comprehend the *spiritual* meaning underlying the "naked," i.e., literal narrative *(nacedan gerecednisse)*.[70] Much of the Preface, therefore, is devoted to an explanation of the spiritual interpretation of the Bible, a clear and basic elucidation for which Ælfric has justly been praised.

Following Jerome's dictate that in Holy Scripture even the very order of the words is a mystery not to be tampered with, Ælfric warns that he did not dare change the *endebyrdnysse* 'order, arrangement,' even though English and Latin do not have the same idiom.[71] Ælfric was so conservative on this point that he was willing to translate an occasionally incomprehensible passage from Jerome's Latin (itself based on an impenetrable Hebrew) into a "nonsense" Old English in order to keep the deep spiritual meaning intact, something he had avoided in his looser homiletic paraphrases.[72] The Genesis remains, in fact, Ælfric's only literal translation, although even here he omitted "catalogs" and abstruse passages.

Contemporary allusions also intrude upon Ælfric's versions of biblical history. At the end of his paraphrase of Judges, which treats mainly of Samson, Ælfric updates his material by expounding the figural meaning of Samson, commenting on the consuls and Caesars of Rome, especially on Constantine and the elder and younger Theodosius, and concluding with a paean of praise for Alfred, Æthelstan, and Edgar, the three "victorious" kings of Wessex.

Another work on the Bible, alternately called the *Letter to Sigeweard* and *On the Old and New Testament*, is an epitome of the entire Scriptures clearly composed for an untutored man, summarizing the major events in sacred history under the six ages of the world—the seventh being continuous with these six ages but concerned with the departed souls, and the eighth being "the one everlasting day after our resurrection."[73] It should also be noted that Ælfric treated the six days of creation at greater length in his adaptation of St. Basil's *Hexameron*.[74]

Three works, the *Grammar*, *Glossary*, and *Colloquy*, form a special group of Ælfric's writings. They are pedagogical efforts, created to help the oblates at Eynsham learn to speak, write, and dispute in Latin. Ælfric's *Grammar*, while not the first grammar written in England, was nonetheless the first in any European vernacular language (see chapter 1). Prefacing, as usual, by both Latin and English, Ælfric states in the English Preface that he turned to the *Grammar* after completing the eighty *Catholic Homilies*. His purpose is to educate monks in the teachings of the Church, and his tone once again is recognizably Alfredian:

> so that holy learning may not grow cold or cease, as it had happened among the English for a few years now, so that no English priest could compose or interpret a letter in Latin, until Archbishop Dunstan and Bishop Æthelwold again established that learning in monastic life.[75]

His *Grammar* draws upon the standard works of two Latin grammarians—the *Ars Grammatica (Maior)* and *Ars Minor* of Donatus (fl. 350) and the *Institutiones Grammaticae* of Priscian (fl. 510). It is a thorough treatment of the Latin language, with much attention also paid to Ælfric's native English. Having no models, Ælfric faced a difficult task in translating technical terms. Many he simply carried over from Latin ("case," "part"). However, he also created a large number of calques, loan translations which were exact renderings of the Latin. None of these terms has survived, and some must have been tongue twisters even in Ælfric's own time: *interjectio* becomes *betwuxaworpennys* 'between-throwing,' *subjunctivus* becomes *underðeodendlic* 'under-joining.'[76] A *Glossary* of several hundred words—and probably by Ælfric—is appended to seven of the extant manuscripts of the *Grammar*. Arranged topically (heaven, angels, earth, sea, man, birds, fish, animals, plants, etc.) rather than alphabetically, the *Glossary* stresses words in everyday use, a fact which again underscores the pedagogical nature of Ælfric's endeavors.

The *Colloquy* is, perhaps, the most famous prose text from the Anglo-Saxon period; most students become acquainted with it early in their study of the language. The continuous Old English gloss found in one of the four complete manuscripts is not, however,

Ælfric's, but presumably the work of a cleric a generation or two later. Written as a supplement to the Latin *Grammar* and *Glossary*, the *Colloquy* exhibits the "direct method" of language instruction. It is the most engaging and literarily effective example of a type of medieval dialogue that "became the drudge of monastic pedagogues, and in the role of a literary Cinderella laboured in obscurity in monastic classrooms to help boys with their lessons."[77] The realism of this work has often been noted, as has its inclusive picture of the social strata of Anglo-Saxon England. A short extract conveys the idea:

> [Master]:
> "What do you say, plowman? How do you carry out your work?"
> [Plowman]:
> "Oh, dear lord, I work very hard. I go out at dawn driving the oxen to the field, and yoke them to the plow. There is no winter so severe that I dare hide at home—for fear of my lord. But after the oxen have been yoked, and the share and coulter fastened to the plow, I must plow a full acre or more every day."[78]

It must be emphasized that the "occupations" in the *Colloquy* are mere "roles" in a fictive situation to introduce certain kinds of vocabulary, and not a reflection of a broad basis of education among the classes of Anglo-Saxon society.[79]

Less noted has been its fine organization and structure, dramatic in effect, with its pairing and contrasting, for example, of the king's bold hunter and the independent, timid fisherman who would rather catch fish he can kill than hunt those (whales) which can destroy him and his companions; and with its lively disputation toward the end about which occupation is the most essential. Ælfric's work is a good illustration of how even the most unpromising material, from a modern point of view, can become "literature" in the hands of a master.

Finally, Ælfric composed a number of important, mostly pastoral letters at various times throughout his life. The *Letter for Wulfsige* outlines the duties of the clergy, which include such topics as the requirement of celibacy and instructions about the Eucharist.[80] The *Letter to Wulfgeat*, written to a prominent landowner who had been stripped of his honors and estates by the king, gives a brief summary of the Christian view of history and then advises Wulfgeat to "agree with thine adversary" (Matthew 5:25).[81] In the *Letter to Sigefyrd*, which consists of a list of examples, Ælfric returns to the question of clerical celibacy.[82] The *Letters for Wulfstan* were composed in response to a request from Wulfstan, archbishop of York.[83] Again on clerical duties, they were first written in Latin, but translated, upon Wulfstan's request, into Old English a year later. The letters deal with familiar subjects: the ages of the world, the history of the early Church, the priest's duties and obligations, directions for the order of the Mass (in general and on specific occasions), expositions of the Ten Commandments and the eight capital sins. A version of the second letter is actually Wulfstan's rewriting of Ælfric's original, and the stylistic alterations are of special interest.

Although Humphrey Wanley made the identification of Archbishop Wulfstan with the Latin *nom de plume* "Lupus" very early in the eighteenth century,[84] Wulfstan's reputation has grown at a much slower pace than that of Ælfric. In part this may be because Wulfstan's writings are not so encyclopedic; or, it may be because Wulfstan frequently used Ælfric for source material. The archbishop absorbed, adapted, and rewrote many of the abbot's compositions. Yet the interests and styles of these two major Anglo-Saxon prose writers could not be more different. In contrast to the private, speculative, and intellectual Ælfric, Wulfstan stands out as an energetic public man imbued with a crusading spirit. He is appropriately described as both a homilist and statesman,[85] for he composed as many laws, both secular and ecclesiastical, as he did sermons (see chapter 4).

Wulfstan first appears in the historical records as bishop of London from 966 to 1002; from 1002 to his death in 1023 he was archbishop of York and bishop of Worcester, though he relinquished the latter see in 1016, or, perhaps, appointed a suffragan. While he was at York, he instituted reforms in the northern Church, which had suffered severely from Danish depredations, and probably helped rebuild the York library by encouraging the collection of manuscripts. Though there is no record of his belonging to any of the eleventh-century monastic houses, Wulfstan was a

Benedictine. He died at York, but was buried at Ely, as the one medieval account of his life, the twelfth-century *Historia Eliensis*, informs us.[86]

During his tenure as bishop of London he established his reputation as a preacher, probably with his eschatological sermons, five texts on the coming of Antichrist. The approach of the millennium and the incursions of the Danes gave rise to a rash of such works—as we saw in the *Blickling Homilies*. Wulfstan related the end of world history to the political and social evils of his day. In so doing, he reveals a passionate desire to maintain Christian orthodoxy against the works of treacherous ministers, so that at times he gives the impression of straining to imitate the voice and tone of an Old Testament prophet. His approach is hortatory and topical, and his sermons minimize doctrinal and intellectual concerns. Wulfstan also seems uninterested in the historical and personal details about the Antichrist to be found in his source—Adso's *Libellus Antichristi*. Instead he shifts the focus to a more legalistic perspective. His use of sources is likewise radical, for he strips them down to the barest outline. But, as Gatch remarks, "he invests [this scheme] with a sense of urgency of moral or legal rigorism in a time of great danger."[87] After these five early sermons, Wulfstan dropped the Antichrist theme and made only generalized references to the Last Judgment in later works. With his famous *Sermo Lupi ad Anglos* he returned to discuss the Antichrist, but by that time a good deal of other work had intervened.

Wulfstan's second period produced the *Canons of Edgar* and six catechetical sermons on the Christian Life. While the sermons include two that have been translated from Ælfric, it must be stressed that Wulfstan's ultimate purpose and Ælfric's are in no way related. Wulfstan made no connection between his preaching texts and either the Temporale or the Sanctorale. His sermons are few in number and were written for the clergy to use when they felt the greatest need—without reference to a liturgical setting. Wulfstan saw Baptism as the central sacrament of the Christian religion, and three versions of a sermon on Baptism occur in this group. Others include expositions of the Creed, the Pater Noster, the Gifts of the Holy Spirit, and an exhortation on the Christian life. The final sermon, a rendering of Ælfric's work on False Gods

(De Falsis Diis), inveighs against both the classical pantheon and their equivalents among the Scandinavians. But it is in the *Canons of Edgar* that Wulfstan created one of his most powerful harangues against paganism:

> 16. And it is right that every priest eagerly teach Christianity and completely suppress everything [connected with] heathendom; and that he forbid worship of (*or* at) wells, necromancy, and auguries, and spells, and tree-worship, and stone-worship, and the devil's craft which one performs when one drags a child through the earth.[88]

The *Canons of Edgar* is "a document designed to combat the immorality and laziness of the secular clergy and to give them practical guidance on the carrying out of their duties."[89] Because he believed that with the reforms accompanying the Benedictine revival the *regular* clergy were now reasonably under control, Wulfstan turned his attention to the *secular* clergy. They had improved little since the days when Æthelwold had forcibly removed them from the Old Minster at Winchester. Wulfstan's inspiration for the *Canons* may well have come from Ælfric's *Pastoral Letters*, though he relied on several continental texts as well.

Two other groupings complete Wulfstan's twenty-one sermons, Archiepiscopal Functions and Evil Days. In this final section, the *Sermo Lupi ad Anglos* 'Sermon of the Wolf to the English' finds its appropriate place. Five manuscripts of this sermon survive, revealing three significant versions. Earlier editors had supposed that the briefest text represented the first draft, and that the fullest text represented the last. But it seems likely that the longest version, rubricated *Quando Dani Maxime Persecuti Sunt Eos Quod Fuit Anno Millesimo .XIIII.* 'when the Danes greatly persecuted them which was in the year 1014,' stands closest to Wulfstan's original composition. It was preached in the troublesome times between Æthelred's expulsion in 1013 and his death in 1016, probably in the year given. The textual history of the sermon is, then, one of excision, and the shorter versions lack the references to the Danish attacks, since these would no longer be relevant after Cnut's accession to the throne.[90]

Returning to the theme of the Antichrist, Wulfstan here reveals a change in perspective. No longer does he view the tribulation of the last days as simply a punishment for sin, but instead he sees the retributive process dynamically. Hollis defines this as follows: "Antichrist's reign is presented not as the ultimate horror foreshadowed by manifold tribulations but as the climax of a progressive growth of afflictions which is proportionate to the increasing quantity of sin."[91] The pulpit orator is nowhere more thunderous than in this denunciation of the English for such sins, sins which had occasioned the Danish "persecutions." Toward the end of his sermon, Wulfstan makes specific reference to Gildas' earlier excoriation of the Britons for their justified punishment at the hands of the Anglo-Saxons. The actual source of the reference is Alcuin, who had used it to point the same moral to the monks at Lindisfarne after the Viking raids of 793.[92] Wulfstan begins:

Leofan men, gecnawað þæt soð is: ðeos worold is on ofste, and hit nealæcð þam ende, and þy hit is on worolde aa swa leng swa wyrse; and swa hit sceal nyde for folces synnan ær Antecristes tocyme yfelian swyþe, and huru hit wyrð þænne egeslic and grimlic wide on worolde.[93]

(Beloved men, know what is true: this world is in haste, and its end approaches; and therefore things go from bad to worse in the world, and so it must of necessity greatly deteriorate because of the people's sins before the coming of Antichrist, and indeed it will then be dreadful and terrible far and wide throughout the world.)

He repeatedly calls attention to treachery and disloyalty as the cardinal sins: "There has been little loyalty among men, though they spoke fair enough"; "For now for many years, as it may seem, there have been many injustices in this country and fickle loyalties among men everywhere"; "Nor had anyone had loyal intentions toward another as justly he should, but almost everyone has deceived and injured another by word or deed"; "For here in the country, there are great disloyalties both in matter of Church and State . . . [he proceeds to give examples, including the death of Edward the Martyr and the expulsion of Æthelred]"; "Many are forsworn and greatly perjured, and pledges are broken again and again." He paints a brutally realistic picture: "And often ten or a dozen, one after another, insult disgracefully the thane's wife, and sometimes his daughter or near kinswoman, while he looks on, he who considered himself brave and mighty and strong enough before that happened." While Wulfstan usually eschewed this kind of detail, in this context it clearly serves his overriding moral purpose.[94] Whatever his task, Wulfstan's method of composition was always careful and painstaking: he selected quotations from Latin authorities on the topic, then translated and expanded them into his own creation. The hallmarks of his style are so readily identifiable, that the presence of any one is nearly sufficient to assign the work to him.[95]

Wulfstan indulges in many kinds of figures of sound, especially alliteration and rhyme, but figures of thought, such as metaphor and simile, are almost entirely absent. He works with a varied palette of acoustical colors; yet none of the sharp images, the analogical interpretations of Scripture, or the realistic detail which appealed to Ælfric, have importance for him. His work is characterized by a greater dependence on parallelism of word and clause than Ælfric's, as well as an ironic point of view—perhaps not unexpected in such a moralist. And one authentic mark of his writing is a pause that comes in the progression of a sermon, most often in the second half, to reflect upon some ethical or religious truth. The form of this pause is usually a rhetorical question or an exclamation. Wulfstan reveals definite preferences in vocabulary, favoring, for example, the ON *lagu* over the OE *æ* 'law,' and *dryhten* 'Lord' where Ælfric has *hælend* 'Savior.' He is fond of intensifying compounds made with *worold* or *þeod*—*woroldscamu* 'great disgrace'—and he has a stock of adverbial phrases which concentrate the force of his passionate oratory—*ealles to swyþe* 'all too greatly.' Wulfstan also had acquaintance with the classical idea of levels of style, the classical (and Augustinian) division of rhetoric into low, middle, and high in order to teach, delight and move.[96] His sermons show a conscious manipulation of stylistic levels for different ends, and he is as capabale of composing in an appropriately low or plain style (Homilies II and IV) as he is in the high or impassioned style (Homilies V and XX) for which he is renowned.[97]

His use of paired opposites illustrates both his binary view of the world and also the rhythmic structure of his prose. A passage from the *Sermo ad Anglos* demonstrates this clearly:

ac wæs here ond hunger, bryne ond blodgite on gewelhwylcum ende oft ond gelome; ond us stalu ond cwalu, stric ond steorfa, orfcwealm ond uncoðu, hol ond hete ond ripera reaflac derede swiðe þearle . . .[98]

(but there has been devastation and hunger, burning and bloodshed in every district again and again; and stealing and murder, sedition and pestilence, murrain and disease, malice and hate and robbery by plunderers have harmed us very badly.)

Wulfstan's prosodic devices are easily discernible here, and have been defined by McIntosh as "a continuous series of two-stress phrases related in structure to the classical half-line, and severely restricted in somewhat the same fashion to certain rhythmical patterns."[99] His line is tighter and shorter than Ælfric's, something which emerges at once when comparisons are made. A selection from Ælfric's *De Falsis Diis,* and Wulfstan's rewriting of it for *his* sermon, will bring out various of these differences:

Ælfric:

An man wæs eardiende/ on þam ilande Creta,// Saturnus gehaten,/ swiðlic and wælhreow,// swa þæt he abat hys suna,/ þa þa hi geborene wæron,//and unfæderlice macode/ heora flæsc him to mete.// He læfde swaþeah/ ænne to life,// þeah þe he abite/ his gebroðra on ær.[100]

(There was a man dwelling on the Island Crete, called Saturn, cruel and bloodthirsty, so that he ate his sons as soon as they were born, and in an unfatherly way made their flesh his meat; he left, nevertheless, one alive, though he had before eaten his brothers.)

Wulfstan:

An man wæs on geardagum// eardiende on þam iglande/ þe Creata hatte// se wæs Saturnus gehaten;// ond se wæs swa wælhreow// þæt he fordyde/ his agene bearn// ealle butan anum//ond unfæderlice macode// heora lif to lyre// sona on geogoðe.// He læfde swaþeah uneaðe// ænne to life,// þeah ðe he fordyde/ þa broðra elles.[101]

(There was a man in days of yore, dwelling on the island which is called Crete, who was called Saturn; and he was so bloodthirsty that he destroyed his own children all except one, and in an unfatherly way brought their life to loss straightway in youth. He left, however, unwillingly one alive, though he had otherwise destroyed the brothers.)

The markings of the above passages attempt to indicate the difference in breath groups, phrasing, and alliterative patterns in the two writers: Ælfric's phrasing is longer, and its two halves are often bound by alliteration, whereas Wulfstan's are shorter (two-stress) with alliteration predominantly within the two-stress phrasings. Wulfstan's characteristic softening of realistic detail appears, moreover, in the handling of Saturn's eating of his children. One should note, though, that the intensifying adjectives and adverbs are not present in this passage.

The difference between Ælfric's and Wulfstan's rhythms and Alfred's may be seen by viewing the above lines side by side with this brief portion from Alfred's *Soliloquies:*

Gyf ðu enigne godne heorde hæbbe, þe wel cunne healdan þæt þæt ðu gestreone and him befæste, sceawa hyne me. Gyf þu þonne nanne swa geradne næbbe, sec hyne oð þu hyne finde.[102]

(If you have any good steward, who can keep well that which you acquire and entrust to him, show him to me. If you have none so prudent, look for him until you find him.)

Alliteration and phrasing in the Alfredian sentences have not been marked; they can be parsed rhythmically in several ways. But the style exhibits a simplicity and periodicity that is most attractive.

Of Wulfstan's other minor works, the prose portions of *The Benedictine Office* are of some significance. The *Office* is non-liturgical, intended only for teaching purposes, with introductory material from Hrabanus Maurus, the Carolingian expositor, and metrical paraphrases in the native Caedmonian tradition (see chapter 9). Ure believes that Wulfstan rewrote an existing vernacular text, which he postulates was Ælfric's translation;[103] but the attribution of such a hypothetical text to Ælfric is dubious, and much still remains to be clarified about their literary relationship.[104]

Wulfstan's last work is also his greatest accomplishment in the field of political theory. The *Institutes of Polity* is the most complete vernacular statement on the organization of Christian society to his time. An example of estates literature, it survives in three main manuscripts, indicating a first (I Polity) form and a greatly expanded revision (II Polity). The Institutes defines the duties of all classes of men, though it does not include the specific lay obligations of thegns, ceorlas, and slaves except as they impinge upon their religious duties. Beginning with the responsibilities of the king, Wulfstan moves to the doctrine of the three supports of the throne—preachers, workers, and warriors—a division he took from Ælfric's Letter to Sigeweard and which had earlier appeared in Alfred's Boethius. He then considers the duties of those in authority, starting with the highest ecclesiastics, and moving to secular government where he discusses such persons as earls, reeves, judges, and lawyers. By defining the limits of power, Wulfstan tries to clarify the interrelationship of the Church and the secular state. The work contains strong statements about the duties of secular leaders and a lament about the decay of honesty since the death of Edgar, but for the main part Polity deals with the Church and its expectation of protection and reverence from all Christian men.[105] Probably also by Wulfstan, at least as a rewriting, is the Rectitudines Singularum Personarum and its second part Gerefa.[106] If the attribution is correct, the work would nicely complement the Institutes, for it treats the lay duties of tenants of a great fief to their temporal lord and in more detail the reeve's manorial duties. As archbishop of York and bishop of Worcester, Wulfstan would have had direct and intimate knowledge of the operations of large estates and he would have been especially concerned with their proper management.

The Norman Conquest greatly curbed the influence which Ælfric and Wulfstan might have had on the development of English theology and prose style. While their rigorous approach to sources and their absolute commitment to orthodoxy contributed to the work of later, more systematic theologians,[107] and while their native styles did not completely disappear, their lasting effect was minimal. This does not, however, lessen their importance as the two most eminent writers of prose in any vernacular before the twelfth century.

At this point, mention should be made of some other religious texts—glossed psalters and other biblical translations. Fourteen glossed psalters appeared between 975 and 1075, six of them based primarily on the Gallican text and eight on the Roman.[108] Of linguistic interest especially, as exhibiting the later tenth-century Northumbrian dialect, is the gloss of the famous late seventh-century *Lindisfarne Gospels* made by Aldred of Chester-le-Street. With Ælfric's biblical translations, the anonymous translations of the other books of the Heptateuch, the West Saxon Gospels, and Bede's (lost?) version of the Gospel of St. John, these comprise the major scriptual texts rendered into prose in the native tongue during the Anglo-Saxon period. A translation of the Gospel of Nicodemus, which details Christ's Harrowing of Hell, appeared in the early or mid-eleventh century; a rendering of the *Visio Pauli*, in the ninth century.[109]

Perhaps the most interesting feature of the classical period in Old English prose is the introduction of Oriental themes and stories in translations. Of the works showing Eastern influence, by far the most attractive is the Old English version of the Greek-Latin romance *Apollonius of Tyre*.[110] This translation survives in one manuscript, the mid-eleventh-century CCCC MS 201, along with some of Wulfstan's homilies, and presumably was composed in the first quarter of that century. The story's continuing popularity is attested to by the many earlier manuscripts of the Latin text, by two Middle English versions (one of which is John Gower's, in his *Confessio Amantis*), and of course by Shakespeare's *Pericles, Prince of Tyre*. The hero endures adventures typical of the romance hero: his wooing of the tyrant Antiochus' daughter and his solving of the incest riddle that makes him an exile from his own land; his shipwreck and regaining of fortune; the "death" of his wife at sea after giving birth to a girl; his daughter's later adventures in a brothel, with her chastity miraculously preserved; and the final reunion of Apollonius, Arcestrate (now a priestess of Diana) and daughter Thasia. But the tale is more than a romance-adventure; and the Old English version—the central part seems unfortunately to be missing—translates the Latin characters with sensitivity and understanding and the human relationships with a humor

unique in Old English prose literature. As a sample, we may observe the passage where first Apollonius, now friend to Arcestrates and tutor to his daughter, and then the king, who is con-
fronted by three suitors for Arcestrate's hand, perceive from the
young girl's letter that she loves Apollonius. The king asks Apollonius if he understands whom his daughter means by her statement that she loves "the shipwrecked man":

*Apollonius cwæð: "Ðu goda cyning, gif þin willa bið, ic hine wat." Ða geseah se
cyngc þæt Apollonius mid rosan rude wæs eal oferbræded, þa ongeat he þone
cwyde and þus cwæð to him: "Blissa, blissa, Apolloni, for ðam ðe min dohtor
gewilnað þæs ðe min willa is. Ne mæg soðlice on þillicon þingon nan þinc
gewurðan buton Godes willan." Arcestrates beseah to ðam þrym cnihtum and
cwæð: "Soð is þæt ic eow ær sæde þæt ge ne comon on gedafenlicre tide mynre
dohtor to biddanne, ac þonne heo mæg hi fram hyre lare geæmtigan, þonne
sænde ic eow word." Ða gewændon hie ham mid þissere andsware.[111]*

(Apollonius said: "You good king, if it is your desire, I know him."
When the king saw that Apollonius was all suffused with the redness
of the rose, he understood the words [his daughter had written] and
so said to him: "Rejoice, Apollonius, because my daughter desires that
which is my desire. Truly nothing in such matters can take place without God's will." Arcestrates turned to the three young noblemen and
said: "It is true what I said to you earlier, that you have not come at a
suitable time to ask for my daughter['s hand], but when she can free
herself from her studies, then I shall send word to you." Then they
went home with this answer.)

The smooth Old English prose, so suitable for narrative and so
different from anything by Alfred, Ælfric, or Wulfstan, is a glimpse
of a native style that might have developed if English had not been
replaced by French after the Norman Conquest. We may notice
particularly the wordplay on *þin willa, min dohtor gewilnað, min willa,*
and *Godes willan,* and the humor (in the implicit identification of
the *lar* with the *lareow*—of the studies with the instructor) in the
king's dismissal of the three suitors; neither of these felicities is
present in the Latin. But in spite of these verbal pleasures, the
Apollonius shares with other Anglo-Saxon romances a marked ret-
icence about sexual matters which their Latin sources can treat directly and in some detail. It has even been suggested that the Old

English version is complete as we have it, the translator having deliberately suppressed material which would have offended his Christian audience.[112]

The interest of the Anglo-Saxons in the strange and marvelous, and especially in Oriental wonders,[113] manifested itself in three additional prose texts: the *Prose Solomon and Saturn*, *The Wonders of the East*, and *The Letter of Alexander to Aristotle*. These works appear in MS Cotton Vitellius A. xv. The collection consists of two parts, and the last two works, along with a *Life of St. Christopher*,[114] are part of the second, or *Beowulf* codex. These three texts are in the same hand (c. 1000) that transcribed the first 1939 lines of the Old English epic. Sisam has argued[115] that the *Beowulf* codex was compiled as a book about monsters—an English *Liber monstrorum*—though this suggestion has not met with universal acceptance. In his view, *St. Christopher*, a late accretion (c. 950) to the earlier works, found its place in the collection by virtue of its presentation of the saint as a giant—twelve fathoms tall in the Old English as compared to twelve cubits in the Latin; but "fathom" and "cubit" may refer to the same measurement and St. Christopher may be only a slightly exaggerated figure. *The Wonders of the East* is found additionally in MS Tiberius B. v. (c. 1000), where each section is preceded by the Latin text;[116] illustrations in oil colors adorn this manuscript. This description of marvels traces its ancestry to a compilation made in England probably in the eighth century, though the Old English version of the fictitious Latin *Letter of Fermes* to the Emperor Hadrian may be no earlier than the first quarter of the tenth century, and of Mercian provenience. The author may also have known *The Letter of Alexander to Aristotle*. Among the wonders indiscriminately detailed is an account of hirsute women thirteen feet tall, with boars' tusks, asses' teeth, and oxen's tails, who are the color of marble and who possess eleven feet. Alexander destroyed them.

Alexander's Eastern conquests became popularized in the Middle Ages through Julius Valerius' Latin translation (and through the *Epitome* of this translation) of the Greek Pseudo-Callisthenes. *The Letter of Alexander to Aristotle*, as it is called, is a fictitious epistle in which Alexander purportedly greets his mentor from India, reciting the many wonders he has encountered on his military expeditions to the East: the magnificent palaces, elephants, water-monsters, two-headed snakes, flying mice as big as pigeons, three-horned rhinoceros, hairy people who live on whales, talking trees, and a ten-foot bishop three hundred years old, to cite a few examples.

Among the more straightforward narrative accounts are the campaigns against Darius and Porrus. Of greatest interest to the Old English translator is a passage in which Alexander recounts with relish his meeting, disguised as a servant, with the tyrant Porrus, and of his tricking Porrus by telling him that his "master" Alexander is so old that he cannot warm himself anywhere save by the fire—a narrative visitation that has analogues in William of Malmesbury's accounts of King Alfred's similar visit to the Danish camp and of the Dane Anlaf's to Æthelred's before the Battle of "Brunanburh." The Old English translator abruptly concludes his version after the prophecy of Alexander's early death by the speaking tree, though the Latin continues with more of the marvels encountered by the Greek potentate. *The Letter* does not measure up to the Old English *Apollonius*, being heavy and ponderous in its somewhat shaky translation and in its excessive use of doublets for single Latin words. Both in style and in spirit this translation may well go back to the late ninth century, though it is common to speak of it and the other "Oriental" pieces as appearing on the scene only as the Anglo-Saxon period drew to its close.[117]

The *Prose Solomon and Saturn*—there is also a poetic version (see chapter 11)—is part of the mid-twelfth-century manuscript which was bound with the *Beowulf* codex sometime in the sixteenth or seventeenth century.[118] Among other pieces, this manuscript contains Alfred's translation of Augustine's *Soliloquies* (see chapter 2). The *Prose Solomon and Saturn* is a catechistic dialogue, dependent, it would seem, on the same source(s) which later resulted in the Middle English version known as *The Maister of Oxford's Catechism*. It falls into the genre of the Latin *Joca monachorum*, of which examples exist in many languages, and consists of exchanges between two disputants, representing Eastern and Western wisdom. Questions are asked by Saturnus, and answered by Solomon. Of the total of fifty-nine questions, twenty are common to another

Old English question-and-answer series, *Adrian and Ritheus.*[119] Subjects covered are manifold and diverse: the creation of man and the universe, the life (and weight and height) of Adam, the nature of flowers and of the stars. The arcane and the trivial make frequent appearances; we learn, for instance, that St. Peter was the first man to talk with a dog and that stones are not fruitful because Abel's blood fell on a stone when he was killed by Cain. These lists consist of a miscellaneous body of biblical, rabbinic, and apocryphal lore, a good part of which had filtered through Irish tradition before reappearing in Old English. As witnesses to aspects of medieval popular—and heterodox—religious culture, they are of great value.

The somewhat esoteric biblical and scientific lore represented in such dialogues had a complement in collections of popular proverbial wisdom, the two most important being the *Dicts (or Distichs) of Cato* and the *Durham Proverbs.* The old English *Dicts,*[120] which translate sixty-eight of the collection of Latin proverbs dating back to the third or fourth century, concern themselves with such gnomic items as the seizing of opportunity by the forelock, the guarding against praise going to one's head, the teaching of one's son a trade if one cannot leave him wealth, and the accepting of responsiblity for one's own poor judgment rather than blaming fortune. Despite the obviousness of much of the content, the translations themselves are clever variations on the Latin, often exhibiting a sophisticated sense of rhetorical possibility in Anglo-Saxon. The *Durham Proverbs,*[121] an eleventh-century collection of forty-six Latin and Anglo-Saxon apothegms, show some dependence upon the *Distichs;* but on the whole the sources and age of the maxims vary within wide limits. They bridge the gap between the oldest Anglo-Saxon gnomic verses and later Middle English specimens. Most of the Old English lines are alliterative and approach verse form, though some do not. Reminiscences of Old English poetry occur, particularly hints of *The Wanderer.* They employ some of the formulas of the *Cotton* and *Exeter Gnomes,* the *sceal* and *byþ* formulas especially: "A man *shall* not be too soon afraid, nor too soon pleased": "A friend avails whether far or near, but *is* the nearer more useful." A few of these proverbs reveal more of a sense of humor than the gnomes: "Those do not quarrel who are not together," and, "It is far from well, said he who heard wailing in hell." These, then, are some of the last words from a genuine Anglo-Saxon culture, except for the late laws and scientific texts—which bear scrutiny in and of themselves.

NOTES

1. See Gneuss 1972, p. 69; this assumes, of course, that *Beowulf* was not written during this period (see chapter 6).

2. On Ælfric's dates, see Clemoes 1959b.

3. See the essays on tenth-century culture in Parsons 1975.

4. See Knowles 1963, pp. 24, 31–6. For a view that the Church itself, as distinct from monasticism, was firmly rooted in the English social order, and of not-inconsequent moral force in these times, see Fisher 1952. A general political account of the revival can be found in Stafford 1978.

5. Text: Winterbottom 1972, pp. 22–3. A parallel dissolution had occurred on the Continent; the English clergy were not alone in their iniquity.

6. See Duckett 1955. A facsimile of Dunstan's Glastonbury classbook has been edited by Hunt 1961; it contains the well-known picture of Dunstan kneeling at Christ's feet, a drawing perhaps by the saint himself. See further chapter 1.

7. Gneuss 1972. See further chapter 1.

8. Both ed. in Winterbottom 1972; Wulfstan's *Life* trans. in Brearley/Goodfellow 1982; Ælfric's *Life* trans. in Gem 1912, pp. 166–80; Whitelock 1979, pp. 903–11.

9. Ed. in Stubbs 1874; portions trans. in Whitelock 1979, pp. 897–903.

10. Ed. in Raine 1879; portions trans. in Whitelock 1979, pp. 911–7. For the identification of Byrhtferth as the author, see Lapidge 1975a, pp. 90–5.

11. The date is conjectural; for a discussion of this question, see Symons 1975.

12. For the Latin text and English translation of the *Concordia,* see Symons 1953.

13. Ed. Schröer 1885. See also Bullough 1972; Gretsch 1973 and 1974; Oetgen 1975.

14. Ed. in Cockayne 1864, vol. 3, pp. 433–44; a portion is trans. in Whitelock 1979, pp. 920–3. For attribution, see Whitelock 1970.

15. See Gneuss 1972; ed. in Napier 1916.

16. Ed. Yerkes 1984.

17. See tables in Scragg 1979, pp. 270–7; Gatch 1965, pp. 119–22 for *Blickling Homilies* and pp. 138–42 for *Vercelli Homilies*. Important editions of the uncollected anonymous homilies are Assmann 1889; Belfour 1909; Bazire/Cross 1982; Fadda 1977; Napier 1883; Tristram 1970.

18. *Blickling Homilies* ed. Morris 1874; for a facsimile edition, see Willard 1960. *Vercelli Homilies* ed. Förster 1932; Szarmach 1981b; for a facsimile edition, see Sisam, C. 1976.

19. Gatch 1977, p. 8; see also Menner 1949 and Vleeskruyer 1953, pp. 38 ff.

20. See Gatch 1977, pp. 120–8. For a discussion of the influence of Caesarius of Arles on these and other homiletic texts, including Ælfric, see Trahern 1976.

21. See Gatch 1965, pp. 124–36; and Frantzen 1983a, pp. 152–7.

22. See Dalbey 1969, 1973, 1978, 1980; and Letson 1978.

23. Letson 1979a.

24. For some remarks on the apocalyptic OE literature, see Förster 1955 and Gatch 1964. Although the Gospel of Nicodemus, which narrates the Harrowing of Hell, has been thought to exert a strong influence on Anglo-Saxon texts, Campbell, J. 1982 argues that early English authors depended entirely on biblical and patristic sources for their knowledge of this central event in Christian history.

25. See Cross 1956 and 1957.

26. Text: Morris 1874, pp. 209–11.

27. The Vercelli MS was deposited in Vercelli, Italy, probably in the eleventh century, where it remains to this day; for conjectures about its arrival in this northern Italian town, see Sisam, K. 1953, pp. 116–8 and Boenig 1980. Scragg 1973 identifies the MS as a Kentish compilation.

28. Gatch 1965, pp. 136–65.

29. Szarmach 1978, p. 241.

30. Szarmach 1981a, pp. 104–5. For a discussion of the influence of the catechetical *narratio*, the recitation of redemptive history, on homiletic literature, see Day 1974.

31. Willard 1935, p. 982; see also Gatch 1964,p. 384–8.

32. Gatch 1965, pp. 158 ff.

33. See Szarmach 1978 and Letson 1978.

34. Felix's *Vita* ed. and trans. by Colgrave 1956, trans. in Jones, C. 1947; see further chapter 1. The OE prose is edited by Gonser 1909; see also Roberts 1985.

35. Frantzen 1983b, p. 23; see also Frantzen 1983a.

36. Ed. Raith 1933 and Spindler 1934.

37. Ed. in Fowler, R. 1965. For translation of the OE penitentials, see McNeill/Gamer 1938, pp. 179–248.

38. Frantzen 1983b, p. 55.

39. Scholars do not agree on the exact dates: see Clemoes 1959b and Godden 1979. The standard edition of the *Catholic Homilies* is Thorpe 1844, although Godden 1979 replaces Thorpe's second volume. For a facsimile of the First Series, see Eliason/Clemoes 1966. General studies of Ælfric's life and writings are White 1898; Dubois 1943; Clemoes 1966; Hurt 1972.

40. See Gatch 1978.

41. Ed. Skeat 1881; quotation from vol. 1, p. 294. Homilies XXIII, XXIIIB, XXX, and XXXIII in Skeat were not composed by Ælfric, and XXXVII is not from the main MS and may not have been intended as part of the collection. Three final items, *Interrogationes Sigewulfi*, *De Falsis Deis*, and *De Duodecim Abusivis*, have been lost from the MS and were not printed by Skeat. They do survive in other MSS (see Godden 1980, p. 208, n. 10).

42. See Godden 1978.

43. See Smetana 1959 and 1961; see also Cross 1961a. Father Smetana observes that Ælfric does not maintain a strict distinction between *sermon* (a discourse on a dogmatic or moral issue for instructional purposes) and *homily* (a commentary and exegesis on scriptual text). Of the eighty-five actual homilies in the *CH*, he further observes, fifty-six may properly be termed exegetical; twelve are topical sermons and expanded Gospel texts; seventeen are saints' lives.

44. Text: Thorpe 1844, vol. 1, p. 2.

45. See Gatch 1977, pp. 66–104.

46. See Leinbaugh 1982.

47. Godden 1973.

48. See Gatch 1977, pp. 37–8.

49. See the Latin Preface in Skeat 1881, vol. 1, p. 2.

50. Latin Preface to *CH* I; Thorpe 1844, vol. 1, p. 1.

51. Text: Thorpe 1844, vol. 1, p. 343.

52. See Clemoes 1966, pp. 188 ff.

53. Thorpe 1844, vol. 1, p. 98.

54. Thorpe 1844, vol. 2, p. 282. See Schelp 1960; on the fourfold method of interpretation, see Smalley 1983; Huppé 1959; Robertson, D. 1951.

55. See Clemoes 1966, p. 182. Pope 1967 (vol. 1, pp. 105–36) gives an extended technical description of Ælfric's rhythmical prose.

56. Thorpe 1844, vol. 1, pp. 258–74.

57. Text: ibid., p. 272.

58. See Clemoes 1970.

59. Text: Thorpe 1844, vol. 1, pp. 258–60.

60. Text: ibid., p. 260. This same theme also appears in the poem *Vainglory*; see chapter 11, n. 37.

61. Tandy 1978, p. 199. See also Clark, C. 1968; Waterhouse 1976, 1978, and 1982; Moloney 1982 (a reply to Waterhouse 1976); Gaites 1982.

62. For the view that Ælfric was influenced by Latin rhymed prose, see Gerould 1924; for the view that he was influenced by OE poetry, see Bethurum 1932a. Vleeskruyer 1953 stresses the use of OE poetic formulas and alliteration as the basis of all OE prose style. Pope 1967 and Lipp 1969 favor the native influence. For further discussion of these and other aspects of Ælfric's style, see Nichols 1971; Middleton 1973; Kuhn 1972b and 1973. A study of Ælfric's vocabulary, with some remarks on its relation to style, is Godden 1980; see also Cross 1969a.

63. Text: Skeat 1881, vol. 2, p. 134.

64. See Clemoes 1959b and Pope 1967 for opposing views.

65. For a summary of Ælfric's work as a biblical translator, see Hurt 1972, pp. 84–103.

66. For texts of the West Saxon Gospels, see Grünberg 1967.

67. Ed. Crawford 1922.

68. There has been a great deal of controversy about the "anonymous" author of the non-Ælfrician parts of the translation. Clemoes 1974 proposed that Byrhtferth was responsible for these sections and also for the *Pseudo-Egbert Penitential;* though he does not believe that Ælfric's reference to "another man" is of any importance for the compilation of the *Hexateuch.* (No single MS contains the *seven* texts which make up Thwaites' *Heptateuch;* Cotton Claudius B. iv contains only the five books of the Pentateuch plus Joshua, and thus is referred to as the *Hexateuch.*) Baker 1980 refutes Clemoes, but admits that all three texts may have been products "of Ramsey Abbey, or some nearby center" (p. 32).

69. Text: Crawford 1922, p. 76.

70. Ibid., p. 77.

71. Ibid., p. 79.

72. See Minkoff 1976. On the different meanings of Ælfric's "refusals" to translate more from the Bible and their rhetorical antecedents, see Nichols 1968.

73. Text: Crawford 1922, p. 70. It has long been assumed that Ælfric was indebted to Augustine's *De Doctrina Christiana.* But see Reinsma 1977, who questions whether the Anglo-Saxons were directly acquainted with this famous work.

74. Ed. Crawford 1921.

75. Text: Zupitza 1880, p. 3.

76. See Williams, E. 1958.

77. Garmonsway 1959, p. 249.

78. Text: Garmonsway 1978, p. 20.

79. See Anderson, E. 1974.

80. For general summaries of the pastoral letters, see Hurt 1972, pp. 36–40. The *Letter for Wulfsige* is ed. in Fehr 1914, pp. 1–34.

81. Ed. in Assmann 1889, pp. 1–12.

82. Ed. ibid., pp. 13–23.

83. Ed. in Fehr 1914, pp. 35 ff.

84. Wanley 1705, pp. 140 ff; quoted in Bethurum 1957, p. 25.

85. Whitelock 1942; see also Bethurum 1966.

86. Wulfstan the homiletic writer (Wulfstan II of York), should not be confused with St. Wulfstan, a later bishop of Worcester (Wulfstan II of Worcester, d. 1095) and the last of the Anglo-Saxon bishops in Norman England.

87. Gatch 1977, pp. 102–16; quotation p. 108.

88. Text: Fowler, R. 1972, p. 5.

89. Ibid., p. 1.

90. Dien 1975.

91. Hollis 1977, p. 178.

92. Alcuin's *On the Sack of the Monastery at Lindisfarne* is trans. in Calder/Allen 1976, pp. 141–6.

93. Text: Bethurum 1957, p. 267. A separate edition with a valuable introduction and commentary is Whitelock 1963; trans. in Whitelock 1979, pp. 929–34.

94. See Jurovics 1978.

95. See Jost 1950, esp. pp. 110–68.

96. See Bethurum 1957, pp. 87–98; Bethurum 1966, pp. 229–35; Whitelock 1963, pp. 17–28.

97. Hollowell 1977.

98. Text: Bethurum 1957, pp. 262–3; on "paired opposites" in Wulfstan, see Cummings 1980.

99. See McIntosh 1950. For expansion and modification, see Funke 1962a. Jost 1959 edits major portions of the *Institutes* in two-stress lines to give reality to McIntosh's findings; his decision has not met with universal acceptance. Hollowell 1982 has called McIntosh's whole theory into question.

100. Text: Pope 1967, vol. 2, p. 682.

101. Text: Bethurum 1957, p. 222.

102. Text: Carnicelli 1969, p. 49.

103. Ure 1957.

104. See Clemoes 1960.

105. Bethurum 1966, pp. 227–8.

106. Bethurum 1963; ed. in Liebermann 1903, vol. 1, pp. 444–55 with notes in vol. 3, pp. 244–55.

107. Gatch 1977, pp. 127–8.

108. For editions of these, see Rosier 1962, pp. xii–xiii.

109. On biblical materials, see Morrell 1965 and Fowler, D. 1976. The Gospel of Nicodemus, ed. Crawford 1927; see also Campbell, J. 1982. The OE translation of the *Visio Pauli*, ed. Healey 1978.

110. Ed. Goolden 1958; see also Raith 1956.

111. Text: Goolden 1958, pp. 33–4.

112. See Donner 1972; Kobayashi 1979.

113. Non-Oriental interest in monsters may be found in *Beowulf* and in the eighth-century Latin *Liber monstrorum*, which was compiled in England; see chapter 1. The work has been ascribed (wrongly) to Aldhelm; see Kelly 1971, esp. p. 321, and Lapidge 1982a.

114. Ed. Rypins 1924.

115. Sisam, K. 1953, pp. 65–96.

116. Knappe 1906 collates both OE texts and the Latin. For facsimiles, see James 1929.

117. See Sisam, K. 1953, p. 63.

118. Ed. in Cross/Hill 1982; ed. with Italian trans. in Cilluffo 1981. See also Cilluffo 1980.

119. Ed. in Cross/Hill 1982.

120. *Distichs* ed. Cox 1972.

121. *Proverbs* ed. Arngart 1981.

CHAPTER 4

Legal and
Scientific Prose

While little of the prose we have examined is intentionally "literary," there is yet a separate corpus of texts which must be put into its own category called "practical." A greater amount of this kind of prose in the vernacular survives from Anglo-Saxon England than from any other Western European country. Shortly after Augustine's conversion of Kent, Æthelberht (560–617), a newly baptized Christian king, began the long tradition of legal writing in English. Æthelberht's Laws antedate by more than five hundred years similar codes in continental Germanic languages. But his decrees (602–3?) are not only the first legal documents using a native tongue, they are also the first piece of extant Old English prose. Thus the corpus of Anglo-Saxon laws, stretching from these brief, early seventh-century dooms to the extensive codes of Æthelred and Cnut compiled by Wulfstan in the eleventh century, may illustrate the development of Anglo-Saxon prose style in miniature.

To approach the Old English laws only in a chronological fashion is, however, to falsify the actual records; for the several texts do not always come down to us in manuscripts contemporary with the promulgation of the laws themselves. For example, Alfred's Laws were committed to vellum not long after their creation, but his code is also the single witness for the earlier Laws of Ine, king

of Wessex from 688–725; and Æthelberht's Laws, somewhat revised and "modernized," survive only in the early twelfth-century Norman codex known as the *Textus Roffensis*.[1] A proper study
of the laws, then, must address both the development of the legal
and stylistic traditions and the use succeeding generations made
of earlier compilations. For the Anglo-Saxon king did not so much
frame new laws as declare ones that already existed; he was the
conveyer and interpreter of the received codes and customs to his
own time. The entire body of Anglo-Saxon law thus became, to
some extent, an aggregate that could be pressed into service at a
later date.[2]

The Germanic legal code was originally oral; the impulse to write
down parts of the law resulted from the Latin influence following
the conversion of England to Christianity in the seventh century.
Certain qualities of an oral style still remain in the written texts—
alliteration, assonance, parallelism—which show an affinity between the speaking of the law and the recitation of poetry. Under
the influence of the homiletic style, these qualities became more
marked as the centuries progressed. But the earliest entries are curt
and elliptical.[3] Decrees 4 and 5 of Æthelberht's Laws give a sense
of this terse manner:

> *Gif frigman cynige stele, IX gylde forgylde. Gif in cyniges tune man mannan
> ofslea, L scill' gebete.*

> (If a freeman should rob the king, he must pay back nine-fold. If one
> man should slay another in the king's enclosure, he must pay 50 shill-
> ings in compensation.)[4]

Before less than a century passed, a fuller style emerges in the
Kentish Laws of Hlothere and Eadric (673–85?); and by the end of
the seventh century the Laws of Wihtred (695) have both a prologue and a more complex syntax:

> *Gif þæs geweorþe gesiþcundne mannan ofer þis gemot, þæt he unriht hæmed
> genime ofer cyngæs bebod ond biscopes ond boca dom, se þæt gebete his dryhtne
> C scll' an ald reht.*

> (If after this meeting, any nobleborn man chooses to enter into an illicit
> union despite the command of the king and the bishop and the decree

of the books, he must pay his lord 100 shillings according to ancient law.)[5]

The chief task of the new codes was to integrate the body of customary law with the dictates of the Christian religion. In this respect, the Laws of Alfred are the first great achievement of Anglo-Saxon jurisprudence. They join a detailed series of compensations for various offenses to an overriding view of the law as God's eternal ordinance. Quoting extensively from Moses, Alfred traces the law's progress through the Apostles and the Church synods. His own code is thus generally based on Hebraic, Roman, and Germanic precedents and specifically dependent on the existing ones of Kent, Mercia, and Wessex. He concludes the Introduction so:

> Now I, King Alfred, have gathered together these laws and I have ordered that many of those which our ancestors obeyed should be written out—those which seemed good to me. But many—those which did not seem good—I have rejected by the advice of my councillors; and in other cases I have ordered changes to be made. I dared not be so bold as to set down many of my own in writing, for I did not know which of these would please those who came after me. But of those laws dating from the time of Ine, my kinsman, or of Offa, king of the Mercians, or of Æthelberht, the first [king] to be baptised among the English, I gathered together here such as seemed to me best, and the others I rejected.[6]

This passage reveals the conservative sense of law as an ancient and continuing force, as well as Alfred's dynastic ambitions. The code itself is a model of Christian legal philosophy. Alfred's successors, Edward, Æthelstan, Edmund, and Edgar, also left collections of varying importance, those of Æthelstan and Edgar being the most significant. They deal with problems connected with the settling of the Danelaw and a number of matters concerning obligations to the Church.

The fusion of ecclesiastical and secular law reached its highest state in the many legal pieces composed, compiled, or supervised by Wulfstan. His easily recognizable homiletic style can be spotted in a number of texts written in the early eleventh century. He authored the "Laws of Edward" and the "Laws of Guthrum," ascribing them to those earlier rulers so as to increase the laws' authority, and he was responsible for all the later edicts (V–X) of Æthelred's troubled reign. His belief, passionately held, that corruption in a kingdom brings God's retribution, led him to legislate in such a way that "sins and crimes [were] dealt with indifferently and [were] equally offensive to the Church and to the State."[7] He became the chief legal adviser to Cnut, the Danish king of England (1016–35), and evidently was in charge of the creation of I and II Cnut—the culmination of Anglo-Saxon law. For after the chaos of Æthelred's reign, Wulfstan tried to reestablish the laws of the West Saxon kings, especially those of Edgar. Much of what he had written for Æthelred he incorporated into them, increasing the specificity of punishments for a great many misdemeanors, but evincing a humane concern for mercy as well as justice: he warns that capital punishment should not be imposed for minor breaches.

A single example will demonstrate Wulfstan's rhythmic homiletic style as it reappears in his legal drafts (see chapter 3). The opening sections of Cnut's code of 1018 reveal Wulfstan's preference, as Kennedy remarks, for the general over the particular and the statement of large principles over any specific explanation of their practical application; they are exhortations to conduct lives of Christian virtue:

> Þonne is þæt ærest þæt witan geræddan. þæt hi ofer ealle oðre þingc ænne god æfre wurðodon. ond ænne cristendom anrædlice healdan. ond cnut cyngc. lufian. mid rihtan. ond mid trywðan. ond eadgares lagan. geornlice folgian.
>
> And hig gecwædan þæt hi furðor on æmtan smeagan woldan. þeode þearfe mid godes filste. swa hi betst mihton.
>
> Nu wille we swutelian. hwæt us mæg to ræde for gode. ond for worlde. gime se þe wille.
>
> Uton swiðe georne fram sinnan acirran. ond ure misdæda geornlice betan. ond ænne god rihtlice lufian ond wurðian. ond ænne cristendom anrædlice healdan. ond ælcne hæðendom georne forbugan.

(First, the councillors decreed that, above all other other things, they would always honor one God and resolutely hold one Christian faith, and rightly and with loyalty love King Cnut, and zealously observe the laws of Edgar.

And they declared that they would further consider at leisure, with God's help, the people's needs, as best they could.

Now we wish to reveal what may be for our benefit in divine and worldly matters, let him who will, take heed.

Let us turn very zealously from sins, and earnestly atone for our misdeeds, and rightly love and honor one God, and resolutely hold one Christian faith, and zealously turn away from every heathen practice.)[8]

One might note that the code begins with *hig gecwædan*, 'they declared,' illustrating as late as the early eleventh century the oral basis of Anglo-Saxon law.[9]

A number of anonymous codes also seem to be Wulfstan's work; others, including a set of laws for Northumbrian priests (1020–3), which draws heavily on Wulfstan's earlier *Canons of Edgar* (see chapter 3), are connected with his circle. Yet not all the legal materials from the Anglo-Saxon era need be classified as royal codes. In addition to the serial decrees left by kings, there also exist treaties (Alfred and Guthrum), various ordinances, a set of instructions for conducting the "ordeal," and the procedure to be followed in the betrothal of a woman.[10]

The codes of the early English kings were not meant to be inclusive; they did not represent the full body of law as it was known and enforced. Kings issued laws when certain aspects of Anglo-Saxon social organization—either secular or religious—needed special emphasis, clarification, or restatement. Much of Anglo-Saxon law, then, has not come down to us, particularly not through the medium of the royal codes. But the nearly 2,000 legal and quasi-legal documents which do survive and which pass under the general rubric of "charters" provide a more detailed picture of Anglo-Saxon law in action.

The term "charter" is a confusing one, and is often used to refer to any document that had a legal purpose—land-charters, wills, leases, manumissions (freeing of slaves), writs, *notitiae*, declarations, or *talu*, i.e., narrative accounts giving the history of estates or of litigations.[11] A stricter classification is that provided by Dorothy Whitelock: "Charters can be . . . divided into two classes, royal and private, and the first of these groups subdivided into the 'diploma' and the 'writ'."[12] The solemn royal diploma is the original of all such legal documents in England, and was evidently imported from the Continent by ecclesiastics who wished to provide a means of assuring title to their lands. Some scholars would date the introduction of the diploma into England from the arrival of the earliest missionaries; others maintain that, while certainly ecclesiastical in origin, it stems from the late seventh century, the period of Theodore and Wilfrid.[13] Throughout its history in Anglo-Saxon times the diploma remained an exclusively Latin document, and diplomas in English, with one possible ninth-century exception, are translations. Most of them survive in later medieval cartularies, books of charters recopied by monks to preserve their rights to specific estates. Charters are evidentiary items, and they record the new creation or the voluntary transfer of "bookland," a much-debated term, but one which probably describes land free of royal dues and capable of being alienated by the possessor. The earliest surviving charter in contemporary form is one dated 679 and issued by Hlothhere of Kent.

Much controversy has raged as to whether the Anglo-Saxon diploma or charter was written by scribes employed by the king in a "royal secretariat," or whether the beneficiary, usually a religious establishment, was responsible for producing it.[14] Whoever drafted these Latin instruments, they are important in the history of Old English literature because they influenced other, vernacular documents, such as leases and wills. They were modeled on the late Roman private deed, and their form, with some variation, was established from the outset. They consisted of an invocation, a proem praising God, a dispositive section, immunity and reservation clauses, blessing and sanction (anathema), boundary and dating clauses, witness list and endorsement.[15] By the tenth century, boundary clauses were always written in English.

Diplomas survive from the entire Anglo-Saxon period, though the mid-tenth century seems to have been the era of their greatest circulation. While not replaced, they were superseded by a less formal document composed entirely in English—the writ. The Anglo-Saxon writ, which developed independently from the diploma, was patterned on epistolary models. It is "a letter on administrative business to which a seal was appended, and the protocol (or opening clauses) of which named the sender of the letter and the person or persons to whom it was addressed and contained a greeting."[16] From Alfred's mentioning of an *ærendgewrit* and *insegel* a 'writ' and 'seal' in his translation of Augustine's *So-liloquies* (and the former also in the *Pastoral Care*), we can tell that writs were in common use by the late ninth century; but the first surviving genuine ones date from Æthelred's reign. The great majority, however, are from the time of Edward the Confessor. While the writ shares some features with the diploma, on the whole it differs markedly from that earlier deed. It was intended to be read by a royal emissary in a public assembly, and its general structure follows this outline: protocol, main announcement, prohibition clauses, perhaps a statement of the religious motive, and occasionally a sanction or penal clause. It has certain stylistic traits of other late tenth- and early eleventh-century prose: the two-stress pattern, and a reliance on alliteration, assonance, and rhyme. Eleventh-century writs are especially rich in the variety of their formulaic linkings: in their use of two different words alliterating (*sacu and socu, mid lande ond mid læse* 'feud and right,' 'with land and with pasture'), of two contrasting words alliterating (*binnan byrig ond butan* 'within the city and without'), of rhyme (*be lande and be strande* 'by land and by strand'), and of assonance (*mid mæde ond mid læse* 'with mead and with pasture'). A simple writ from Æthelred's troubled reign will give an example of this indigenous Anglo-Saxon creation:

> *Æþelred kinc grete mine [beres] ond mine eorles. ond ealla mine þeinas of þam sciram þær mine preostas on Pales mynstre habbað land inne freondlice. Ond ic cyþe eow þæt ic wille þæt hig beon heora saca ond heora socna weorða æiþer ge binnan burh ond butan. Ond swa godera laga wyrþe nu swa ful ond swa forð swa hig betste wæron on æniges kinges dæge. Oþþe on æniges beres on eallum þingan.*

> (King Æthelred sends friendly greetings to my bishops and my earls and all my thegns of the shires where my priests in Paul's minster have land. And I make known to you that I will that they be entitled to their sake and their soke, both within the borough and without, and entitled now to as good laws—as fully and completely—as ever they were in all things in the days of any king or bishop.)[17]

The Latin diploma was more elaborate and more solemn than the writ, but the latter's seal of authentication and its direct address to responsible individuals made it emerge as the more popular and convenient of the two. It was the writ which the Normans adopted when they began to administer affairs in England, probably because this uniquely English document had proven itself most efficient and business-like.[18]

Wills in Old English seem to go back at least to the first half of the ninth century.[19] Certainly by the end of that century they were common, King Alfred's being the most famous example. His is of particular interest for its long *talu*, or narrative, which precedes the will itself and which details the story of how Alfred came to own the lands he includes in his testament. The narrative refers to the deaths of Alfred's older brothers, the history of his inheritance, and the disruption caused by the Danish invasions; it also describes a court hearing held to judge the authenticity of a previous will. The will proper signals its beginning by restating the name of its maker:

> Ic Ælfred Westseaxena cingc mid Godes gyfe ond mid þisse gewitnesse, gecweðe hu ic ymbe min yrfe wille æfter minum dæge. Ærest ic an Eadwearde minum yldran suna þæs landes æt . . .

> (I Alfred, King of the West Saxons, with God's grace and with these witnesses, declare what I wish done concerning my inheritance after my lifetime. First, I [give] to Edward, my elder son, the land at . . .)[20]

Like other Anglo-Saxon legal documents, wills were mainly evidentiary—testaments to a promise made by the maker in the presence of witnesses. And like the diploma, the will was ecclesiastical in origin: "it was not only developed under clerical influence for the material benefit of Anglo-Saxon churches and convents, but it was ultimately brought . . . within the scope of the jurisdiction of ecclesiastical courts."[21] Wills assumed diverse forms: some opened with a solemn invocation reminiscent of the diploma; some began in the manner of writs; others simply stated that "this is the will of X." However various in pattern, nearly all of them contain a notification of the circumstance, a disposition of the property, and a sanction meant to bind the survivors to the will's terms. From a modern point of view, the most distinctive legal aspect of the Anglo-Saxon will is its contractual nature. Dispositions were neither gratuitous nor unilateral; in keeping with

Germanic customary law, they required counter-gifts or counter-performances. This contractual basis of Anglo-Saxon law provides a key to many aspects of their life and society; it may even affect a poet's attitude toward his own creations (see discussion of Cynewulf's epilogue to *The Ascension* in chapter 8).

Whatever the provenance of a specific legal form, the diplomas, writs, leases, manumissions, and wills carry, to some degree, that sense of ceremonial language that official articles always do. It is only in the purely narrative examples that we find an Old English prose at least partially free from legal formulas. Here in translation is an especially vivid example from the late Anglo-Saxon period:

A HEREFORDSHIRE LAWSUIT

It is shown in this document that a shire-meeting was held at Aylton in the time of King Cnut. There Bishop Æthelstan and Alderman Ranig sat, and Edwin, the alderman's son, and Leofwine, Wulfsige's son and Thurkil the White. And Tofig the Proud came there on the king's errand, and Bryning the sheriff was there and Ægelweard of Frome and Leofwine of Frome and Godric of Stoke and all the thegns of Herefordshire. Then Edwin, Eanneawn's son, came travelling to the meeting and there spoke against his mother concerning a certain piece of land, which was Wellington and Cradley. Then the bishop asked who was to answer for his mother. Then answered Thurkil the White and said he was, if he knew the claim. When he did not know the claim, then three men were chosen from the meeting [to go] to the place where she was—and that was at Fawley. They were Leofwine of Frome and Ægelsign the Red and Thinsig the seaman, and when those three came to her they asked what claim she had concerning the lands which her son spoke for. She then said that she had no land which in any way belonged to him, and she was very angry against her son, and summoned her kinswoman Leofflæd, Thurkil's wife, and before them all spoke to her in this way: "Here sits Leofflæd, my kinswoman, to whom, after my death, I grant my land, my gold, my clothing and my raiment, and all I possess." And after that she said to the thegns: "Behave like thegns, and clearly proclaim my message to the meeting before all the good men, and make it known to them to whom I have granted my land and all my possessions, and never a thing to my own son, and ask them to be witnesses to this." And they did so; they rode to the meeting and told all the good men about the charge that she had laid upon them. Then Thurkil the White stood up in the meeting and asked all the thegns to give his wife the lands unencumbered which her kinswoman had granted her, and they did so. Then, with the consent and knowledge of all the people, Thurkil rode to St. Æthelbert's minster, and had it recorded in a gospel book.[22]

The great variety of Anglo-Saxon legal instruments has been amply served by modern scholarship. When we turn to the period's scientific prose, however, we find a different situation. Perhaps in no other area of Anglo-Saxon studies has the denigratory attitude of past scholars held on so tenaciously. While we acknowledge that these texts do not resemble what we would call "scientific" today, still they constitute a large corpus of writings—far beyond anything produced contemporaneously on the Continent. For heuristic purposes we classify as scientific any Anglo-Saxon text which attempts either to describe or to control the world. Validity is not an appropriate criterion to apply, but the mere fact that Anglo-Saxon science is in many ways rudimentary and awkward does not mean it is contemptible.

The most significant body of surviving scientific prose is medical, or magico-medical, as it is often characterized.[23] Indeed we can draw no clear line between a purely rational science and a ritualistic magic in the documents. Empiricism blends with prayer and incantation at every turn; recipes for herbal medicaments become charms and spells in seamless units. Four major collections of medieval prescriptions have come down to us: the *Læcboc* 'Leechbook' associated with Bald; *Lacnunga* 'Healings,' 'Cures'; the *Peri Didaxeon* 'Concerning Schools of Medicine'; and the *Herbarium Apuleii*, which is completed by a treatise on betony (an especially prized herb) and some recipes from pseudo-Dioscorides. All of these medical anthologies concern themselves with plant remedies, but animal remedies follow the *Herbarium* in the translation of the *Medicina de Quadrupedibus* attributed to Sextus Placitus.[24]

Criticism of these pieces as scientific endeavors has been less than generous; they have usually been described as the final degradation of rational classical medicine into superstition. Most commentators have claimed that these compilations were not meant for the Anglo-Saxon medical practitioner, but were mainly exercises in literary copying. The listing of many plants grown only in southern Mediterranean areas became strong evidence in support of this view.[25] But Talbot defends the Anglo-Saxon medical treatises against the charge of irrationality; he maintains that they are in fact quite sophisticated for their time and that they perpetuated the classical traditions of medicine in a far more responsible manner than had hitherto been allowed.[26] And Voigts asserts that the Anglo-Saxon works on herbal medicine have been ignorantly maligned. She shows that the texts were used and improved by succeeding generations of practising leeches (or doctors); that many of the recipes have been found effective; and that in the milder climate of Anglo-Saxon England it would have been both possible and probable for southern plants to be cultivated in monastic gardens.[27]

The oldest of these manuals is Bald's *Læcboc*, in three books, so called because a colophon near the end of Book II states that the leech Bald is the owner of the book.[28] The unique manuscript is dated from the mid-tenth century, but we have reason to believe that the original gathering of the materials was done in Alfred's time. Near the end of Book II a number of prescriptions are said to have been ordered given to King Alfred by Elias, Patriarch of Jerusalem from about 879 to 907—and we know from contemporary sources that Alfred received gifts from Elias and may have had other communications with him. The first thirty chapters of Book I give prescriptions for infections of the body in descending order, from head to feet; the rest of the chapters deal with various ailments, one whole chapter being devoted to bloodletting. Book II is more learned than I, containing symptoms and diagnoses as well as prescriptions for internal disorders. Book III, largely repeating the first, contains many more charms or magic incantations, including Christian invocations (on these, see chapter 11). The *Læcboc* is a plain but elegant remnant of Anglo-Saxon culture. Intended for practical use, it does not contain a great deal of literary interest. But one of its most famous passages—a wry medical comment—deserves quoting:

Wið nædran slite: gif he beget and yt rinde sio þe
cymð of neorxna wonge, ne derað him nan atter. Þonne cwæþ
se þe þas boc wrat þæt hio wære torbegete. (Chap. xlv)

(Against an adder's bite: If he finds and eats the rind which comes out of paradise, no poison will harm him. He who wrote this book said that it was hard to get.)

Lacnunga also survives in a unique manuscript, one from the mid-eleventh century.[29] While a few passages parallel the *Læcboc*, *Lacnunga* is a rambling collection of about two hundred prescriptions, remedies, and charms derived from Greek, Roman, Byzantine, Celtic, and Teutonic sources; it stands at a much greater distance from its classical antecedents than the *Læcboc*. Although the work contains a good admixture of Latin Christianity, the predominance of pagan Germanic material has earned this work much scorn. *Lacnunga* beautifully illustrates the four Germanic ideas on the cause of disease: from 1) flying venoms, 2) the evil nines, 3) the worm, and 4) the power of elf-shot. If Anglo-Saxon medicine can in any way be called magico-medicine, then the *Lacnunga* would provide the best example. It is also the repository of several of the most well-known poetic charms (see chapter 11).

The single manuscript of *Peri Didaxeon* may be as late as 1200[30] and there is considerable debate as to whether its language is Late Old English or Early Middle English. It represents the more rational aspect of Anglo-Saxon medicine and derives from the same fundamental texts as the *Læcboc*, although the sections chosen do not correspond with those of the Alfredian work.

In contrast to the preceding three items, the Old English translation of the *Herbarium* of pseudo-Apuleius survives in four manuscripts, including the brilliantly illustrated Cotton Vitellius C. iii, dating from sometime shortly after 1050.[31] The collection, usually known as the *Anglo-Saxon Herbal*, contains descriptions of 132 plants; another 33 from Dioscorides are appended. The herbs are described individually and then followed by the various medical uses to which they can be put. This contrasts with the order in the *Medicina de Quadrupedibis*, which places the disease first and then recommends an animal cure. A fairly large number of individual recipes and charms exist in odd fragments, but the collections mentioned contain the majority of Anglo-Saxon medical lore. They embody—the *Læcboc* in particular—"some of the best medical literature available to the West at that time."[32]

In connection with these medical treatises, we might mention the existence of the Old English *Lapidary* (early eleventh century). A scientific work in the broadest sense, it is the earliest known vernacular lapidary of Western Europe. Derived from Isidore and

Bede, it describes the twelve apocalyptic stones, and is notable for the absence of magical properties attributed to the gems. The last stone, Agate, is, however, said to avail against poison and dust.[33]

Two Old English works on time and nature offer a somewhat different perspective on Anglo-Saxon science. Ælfric's *De Temporibus Anni*,[34] written after the compilation of his *Catholic Homilies* sometime between 992 and 1012,[35] is a brief series of extracts on the sun, the moon, the progress of the year, and the calculation of the date of Easter drawn mainly from Bede's three scientific works: *De Temporum Ratione*, *De Temporibus*, and *De Natura Rerum* (see chapter 1). While Ælfric knew the works of Bede well, he had little patience with Bede's ideas of scientific experiment. Ælfric's treatise is doctrinaire; he sees science as essentially a branch of theology.

A longer—and more idiosyncratic work, one which uses Ælfric's *De Temporibus* as a source—is the *Enchiridion* (or *Manual* or *Handboc*) by Byrhtferth of Ramsey, written in 1011.[36] The *Enchiridion* was composed by this Benedictine monk to teach his (often inattentive) students about the *computus*, the astronomical science that grew up around the ecclesiastical calendar.[37] Byrhtferth's work is a mélange of Latin and Old English, varying about equally at the start, moving almost exclusively to the vernacular in the middle, and returning to Latin again at the end. The hallmarks of the monk's flamboyant Latin style are present, even in the Anglo-Saxon portions. Any clear principles of organization are hard to discern, though the *Enchiridion* is divided into four parts. Part I begins with a prologue which describes the solar and lunar years and the Roman calendar. Further into Part I, an excursus on the material underlying Byrhtferth's "Diagram of the Physical and Physiological Fours" interrupts the calendrical discussion. Reflecting the late Old English view of man as the microcosm of the macrocosm,[38] his "Diagram" is an example of diagrammatical representation of allegorical concepts—Byrhtferth's major contribution to the history of Western ideas. Here he makes something of an attempt at a cosmic philosophy based on science. Part II treats the months and the seasons; it also contains an excursus on poetical meter. Part III splits into two sections, one dealing with the calculation of the date of Easter, and the other with rules of grammar and literary composition. This short dissertation on "figures" Byrhtferth translated from the first part of Bede's *De Schematibus et Tropis.* He supplies seventeen *schemata* or "figures of words"—the first such treatment of figures in the English language.[39] Part IV consists of a long discourse on number symbolism, the systematic treatment of which is remarkably original.[40] While it would be an exaggeration to compare his achievement favorably with Bede's, nevertheless his work contains a body of knowledge not unworthy of the last period of Anglo-Saxon culture.

NOTES

1. For a facsimile, see Sawyer 1957. The great edition of the A–S laws is Liebermann 1903. Convenient digests and translations can be found in Thorpe 1840; Attenborough 1922; Robertson, A. 1925; Whitelock 1979, pp. 357–478. For a bibliography on the law and legal prose in general during the Middle Ages, see Alford/Seniff 1984.

2. Helm 1963, p. 111; Richards 1985.

3. Bethurum 1932b.

4. Text: Attenborough 1922, p. 4.

5. Text: ibid., p. 24.

6. Text: ibid., p. 62.

7. Bethurum 1966, p. 224.

8. Text: Kennedy, A. 1983, p. 72; for Kennedy's remark, above, see p. 67.

9. Wormald, P. 1978, pp. 48ff.

10. See Whitelock 1979.

11. See Carlton 1970, p. 18; Harmer 1914, p. vi.

12. Whitelock 1979, p. 376; her essay on the charters is the best introduction to the subject. See also Robertson, A. 1939.

13. See Stenton 1955, p. 31.

14. For a summary of the arguments, see Keynes 1980, pp. 14–83.

15. Keynes 1980, p. xiv; see also Stenton 1955, p. 55.

16. Harmer 1952, p. 1.

17. Text: ibid., p. 241.

18. Barraclough 1976, p. 140.

19. Whitelock 1968b, p. 19.

20. Text: Harmer 1914, p. 17. See also Keynes/Lapidge 1983, pp. 173–8 and 313–26.

21. Hazeltine in Whitelock 1930, p. xii.

22. Text: Robertson, A. 1939, pp. 150–2.

23. See Grattan/Singer 1952; see also Grendon 1909 and Storms 1948.

24. All these texts are in Vol. 1 of the three-volume compilation done by Cockayne 1864. A separate edition of the *Herbarium* and *Medicina De Quadrupedibus* is De Vriend 1984.

25. See especially Grattan/Singer 1952, pp. 3–94 and Bonser 1963, pp. 3–33.

26. Talbot 1967, pp. 9–23.

27. Voigts 1979; see also Cameron 1982.

28. Ed. in Vol. 2 of Cockayne 1864; for a facsimile, see Wright, C. 1955. See also Cameron 1983 and Meaney 1984.

29. Ed. in Vol. 3 of Cockayne 1864, pp. 1–80; also in Grattan/Singer 1952.

30. Ed. in Vol. 3 of Cockayne 1864, pp. 81–145.

31. Ed. in Vol. 1 of Cockayne 1864, pp. 1–325, including the continuation from Dioscorides.

32. Talbot 1967, p. 19.

33. Ed. in Evans/Serjeantson 1933, pp. 13–5; also in Kitson 1978, pp. 32–3.

34. Ed. Henel 1942.

35. Clemoes 1959b, p. 34.

36. Ed. Crawford 1929; see also Henel 1942 and 1943.

37. Baker 1982, p. 124. See also Henel 1934 for an edition of an OE prose Menologium (or calendar) from MS Harley 3271, collated with MS CCCC 422, p. 48.

38. See Cross 1963.

39. See Murphy 1970.

40. See Hart 1972 and Bullough 1972.

CHAPTER 5

Some Remarks on the Nature and Quality of Old English Poetry

Old English, Old Icelandic, Old Saxon, and Old High German poetry all derive from a common verse form still clearly discernible behind the separate developments of the surviving poetic corpora.[1] That form is keyed to a dominant linguistic fact: the Germanic fixing of stress upon the initial syllable of a word, exclusive of most prefixes. A concomitant of such stress was the tendency to aid continuity of discourse—not to mention continuity of hereditary lineage—by the use of alliteration, or initial rhyme. It is these two features, intensified, that contributed to the stabilized Germanic verse pattern, one we find as early as the fourth- or fifth-century runic declaration of pride in craftsmanship inscribed on the golden horn of Gallehus:[2]

Ek HlewagastiR HoltijaR   horna tawido

(I, Hlewagast, Holt's son,   made [this] horn.)

Difference in the verse forms of the individual Germanic languages may be attributed to, among other things, differing degrees of retention of initial stress, with consequent loss of or increase in the number of short syllables in the poetic line. The earliest Icelandic poetry, with its tightly packed line, exhibits the result of strong initial stress, the looser Old Saxon and Old High German lines the result of weakened initial stress. Old English poetry seems to stand somewhere between these alliterative verse extremes.[3]

The Germanic poetic line, as the Gallehus inscription suggests, consists of two half-lines, or verses, divided by a caesura, with two major stresses, or lifts, in each verse: *Ek HlēwăgăstiR HóltijaR hŏrnă tăwidŏ.*[4] The *a*-verse, or on-verse as it is sometimes called, may have its two lifts alliterating, as in the inscription, or only one; but the important consideration is the binding of the *b*-verse, or off-verse, to its antecedent half-line by alliteration of its first lift. The number of weak or secondary stresses (dips) in each of the two feet (measures) of the half-line is variable within certain limits; there is even the possibility of anacrusis, that is, of dips before the first measure begins.[5] In Old English poetry the accepted pattern of alliteration demanded that an initial consonant alliterate with itself, whatever the following vowel or consonant, except that the paired consonants *sc*, *sp*, and *st* could alliterate only each with itself. A vowel commonly alliterated with any other vowel, less commonly with itself. Verse-binding alliteration was recognized only as it coincided with major stresses; and such stress was most likely to fall upon nouns and adjectives. The phonetic quantity of syllables was also significant, lifts normally being reserved for long syllables, though light verses, with the stress on short syllables, were permissible in the first foot; and resolution of two short syllables was common, as in line 2425a of *Beowulf*, where we find *Bēowŭlf mă∂elăde.*[6] Occasionally we find verses, especially *a*-verses, that seem to have only one stressed syllable, as in *The Wanderer*, line 11a: *þæt biþ in ēorle;*[7] and there are others that are hypermetric, with more than two stresses, as in *Beowulf*, line 1168a: *ărfæst æt ēcgă gelăcŭm.*[8]

The recognition of stress and alliteration in Old English poetry is one thing; the actual reading of the verses is another.[9] Basically, there are two schools of thought on the latter: the isochronous and the nonisochronous. Eduard Sievers formulated the latter, with his hypothesis of five basic kinds of poetic verses containing at least four syllables and consisting of two feet with a major stress in each. He based his categories upon observable lift-dip patterns, categories which even dissidents from his theory refer to: Type A: ⌐x/⌐x; Type B: x⌐/x⌐; Type C: x⌐/⌐x; Type D: either ⌐/⌐x̀x or ⌐/⌐x̀x; Type E: ⌐x̀x/⌐.[10] Even in these basic patterns, without introducing allowable extra dips, there is obvious inequality of duration between some feet in the verse unless one goes to exaggerated lengths to draw out or hurry through the feet in the D and E types. This difficulty led to various assaults on Sievers' hypothesis, and the resort to musical analogy of equal time per measure. John Pope in particular, with his brilliant theorizing about the use of the harp as a musical "rest" to eke out measures not superficially conforming to the $4/8$ time he postulates for normal and the $4/4$ time for hypermetric verses, revolutionized our ideas about Old English meter.[11] A. J. Bliss, however, has attacked isochronous theories as unwarranted impositions upon an era unfamiliar with the concept, suggesting a somewhat modified Sievers position.[12] A number of other hypotheses about Old English metrics have been advanced, but their subtleties are beyond the scope of this volume.[13]

Whether the harp (or lyre) was a formal accompaniment to the recitation of the oldest English verse is unclear. In *Widsith*, ll. 103–5, the fictitious scop (or singer) who is the persona declares that "We two, Scilling and I, with clear voice/delivered song before our liege-lord,/loud to the harp the voice resounded"; in *Beowulf*, ll. 89–90, the poet describes the sound of revelry in the hall Heorot as "There was the sound of the harp,/clear the song of the scop"; and Bede's story of Caedmon (see chapter 10) informs us of the illiterate cowherd's embarrassment when he saw the harp, that should accompany his own verse-making, approach him at the dinner table. Opland would distinguish such accompanied performances as *songs*, differentiating them from *poems*.[14] If the harp was actually used to accompany verse recitation, lyric or narrative, was it plucked only during "rests"? How was the instrument played—with fingers or with a plectrum? Despite such uncertainty, some admirable attempts to reconstruct the harp or lyre have been made on the basis of the Sutton Hoo and Taplow Barrow fragments.[15]

In addition to investigating the rhythmic and phonemic principles and practices of Old English poetry,[16] scholars have devoted considerable attention to the nature of its diction and to aspects of its style. Despite the limited number of extant writings in Old English, it seems certain that poetry utilized not only the language of prose, but also a specialized vocabulary of its own.[17] Some archaic words evidently acquired poetic status by their perpetuation only in verse: *mece* 'sword' and *guð* 'battle' are two such words. But more important were metaphoric, especially metonymic, words like *ceol* 'keel' for 'ship' and *lind* 'linden-wood' for 'shield.' The poets also invented compounds or combinations of basic nouns plus limiting genitives to designate periphrastically persons or objects by one of their attributes. Such compounds as *hæðstapa* 'heath-stepper' for the referent 'stag' and *garbeam* 'spear-tree' for 'warrior,' and *yða ful* 'cup of waves' for 'sea,' illustrate this last concept. These compounds and combinations are usually referred to as *kennings*, though it is perhaps better to distinguish the first as a *kent heiti* (pl. *kend heiti*)—a more direct periphrasis identifying the referent with something it *is* (the stag is, of course, a 'stepper')— and the last two as true *kennings*, wherein the referent is identified with something it is *not*, except in a very special metaphoric sense: a warrior is not a 'tree' except as both stand tall, straight, and unshrinking under blows; nor is the sea literally a 'cup.'[18]

The Old English poets utilized their word-hoard formulaically. Originally of oral composition, Anglo-Saxon poetry was fashioned from a stock of verse or verse-pair formulas and formulaic systems; that is, from stylized syntactically related collocations of words in regular rhythmic patterns.[19] The poet could find among his formulaic resources almost any semantic values he needed for the immediate sense or ornamentation of the poem he was creating. Conveniently, he could substitute individual words within the grammatical and rhythmic patterns either for contextual or alliterative purposes.[20] Thus we find the *Beowulf* poet at l. 2765a talking about *gold on grunde* and again, in l. 3167a, about *gold on greote*. In the former the "ground" or "earth" occurs in a context condemning gold as overpowering men's souls, even when buried; in the latter, the more specific "dust" suggests Beowulf's grave barrow, in which the useless gold he gained in killing the dragon is being reburied with the hero. Or we find the exiled Adam in *Genesis A*, l. 930a, *dugeðum bedæled* 'deprived of joys' and Satan similarly deprived in *Christ and Satan*, l. 121a; while the Wanderer is *eðle bidæled* 'deprived of native land' in *The Wanderer*, l. 20b, and Adam and Eve have caused mankind to be *eðle bescierede* 'cut off from native land' (Paradise) in *Christ I*, l. 32b. These formulas and formulaic systems were, moreover, useful in combination to present fixed themes, such as that of the beasts of battle, which appears in twelve passages in nine poems, or that of exile, which appears not only in the "elegies" but in some unexpected contexts.[21] We can readily recognize the convenience of these systems for oral composition, but the formulaic-thematic habit also carried over into written composition, and was easily absorbed into sophisticated rhetorical devices learned from Latin poets and rhetoricians.[22]

We might expect that a poetry so constructed, so formulated, would become dull and conventional in the pejorative sense of the term; and so it did in the hands of lesser poets (see comment on *Death of Edgar* in chapter 10). Yet the better scops used their stocks of words, formulas, formulaic systems, and themes individualistically.[23] One of the methods whereby the Old English poets achieved originality was coining compounds, as the *Beowulf* poet's immense wealth of apparently new-minted compound words attests. In a larger way, originality in the use of formulas and themes depended upon the degree of tension created between the traditional associations evoked by these stylizations and the unique applicability they had in their specific contexts.[24] The *Beowulf* poet, for example, hoards the "beast of battle" theme, not using it in the traditional way in scenes describing battles, but reserving it uniquely and climactically for the end of the Messenger's speech prophesying doom to all of the dead hero's people (see chapter 6).[25] Or the poet, working on the degree of expectancy set up by the traditional collocations, or by his own creation of habitual patterns within his poem, could deliberately extend or frustrate that expectancy in several ways.[26] In *The Wanderer*, for example, the opening line temporarily suspends the conventional association of "wretchedness" and "lone-dwelling" (*earm anhaga* is the traditional pattern) when the poet says: *Oft him anhaga are gebideþ* 'Often the lone-dweller experiences mercy,' suggesting by the syntactic and alliterative-metrical pattern the possibility that God's mercy may be extended to an exile, a key idea that is brought to a resolution in the poem's concluding lines. It is not till line 2b that the traditional collocation with wretchedness is made through the adjective *modcearig* 'weary in spirit.' In a somewhat different way the poet could achieve semantic linking via the metrical pattern despite an absence of syntactic dependency, as when the *Beowulf* poet comments of the Danes that

> Swylc wæs þeaw hyra,
> *hæþenra hyht;*   *helle gemundon*
> *in modsefan,*   *Metod hie ne cuþon.* . . .   (ll. 178b–80)

> (Such was their custom,
> the hope of heathens: it was hell that
> governed in their thoughts, not knowing God. . . .)

Here the hope of heathens is equated, through alliterations and stress, with hell, their ultimate destination.[27]

This brief sampling of the possibilities of individuality within the Old English formulaic convention verges on the subject of style.[28] Of various Anglo-Saxon stylistic elements, none has received more attention than the device called *variation*.[29] This device may be seen at its simplest in such a line as *Beowulf maðelode, bearn Ecgðeowes*, where 'son of Ecgtheow' *varies* the noun *Beowulf*. More complexly (and arguably) we find it in the opening lines of the epic:

> *Hwæt, we Gar-Dena*   *in geardagum,*
> *þeodcyninga*   *þrym gefrunon,*
> *hu þa æþelingas*   *ellen fremedon.*

> (Indeed, we have heard of the Spear-Danes'
> glory, and their kings', in days gone by,
> how princes displayed their courage then.)

Here both *þeodcyninga þrym* and the following line-clause are variational objects of the verb *gefrunon*. *Variation*, then, may be defined as a double or multiple statement of the same idea within a clause or in contiguous clauses (and sentences), each restatement suggesting through its choice of words either a general or more specific quality, or a different attribute, of that concept; and such statements may, as in the first example, or may not, as in the second, be grammatically parallel.[30] The importance of this stylistic device in Old English poetry, its potentialities and limitations, have been well-summarized by Brodeur:

> Variation is . . . the chief characteristic of the poetic mode of expression. . . . [It] restrains the pace of Old English poetic narrative, gives to dialogue or monologue its leisurely or stately character, raises into high relief those concepts which the poet wishes to emphasize, and permits him to exhibit the object of his thought in all its aspects. But it could be a dangerous instrument in the hands of an inferior poet: it could impart on the one hand an effect of sheer redundancy, on the other an unpleasing jerkiness of pace; it could stiffen the flow of style, and clog the stream of thought.[31]

One interesting illustration of the effectiveness that could be achieved through variation is in lines 129b–31 of *Beowulf*, where King Hrothgar laments Grendel's ravages:

> Mære þeoden,
> æþeling ærgod, unbliðe sæt,
> þolode ðryðswyð, þegnsorge dreah.

> (The illustrious
> prince, deserving good, sat dejected,
> the mighty lord mourned the loss of thanes.)

These lines present both substantive and verbal variation. The latter

> moves from understatement (*unbliðe sæt*) to strong statement of suffering in *þolode* to an intensive kind of specific suffering in 'he suffered sorrow for his thanes.' Yet concurrently, the variations for 'Hrothgar' intensify from 'famous prince' to 'prince good-of-old' (or 'immeasurably good') to 'the very powerful one', *ðryðswyð* being all the more notable for its being an adjective used substantivally.[32]

The *th* and *d* sounds in this passage further contribute to its emotional intensity.

The sound pattern in the above passage seems no more than ornamental; but Anglo-Saxon poets could also "play" sound meaningfully against sense, as in the famous "Swan" riddle (emphasis added):

Hrægl min **swigað**   þonne ic hrusan trede,
oþþe þa wic buge,   oþþe wado drefe.
. . .   Frætwe mine
swogað hlude   ond **swinsiað**,
torhte singað,   þonne ic getenge ne beom
flode ond foldan,   ferende gæst.

(My garment is still when I settle on earth,
or abide at home or beat the waters.
. . .   My adornments
sound loudly and make melody,
brightly sing when I am not touching
water and land, [am] a wide-faring spirit.)

In this lovely poem the sound similarity of *swigað* and *swogað* (along with *swinsiað*) play against their contrary meanings, emphasizing the riddle's central paradox: the swan's feathers are silent when the bird is not flying, but make music when it is in flight. That *hrægl/hrusan* are the alliterating syllables in the first line, and *hlude* the non-alliterating second stress in its line, contributes further to the poem's sound richness.[33] The variation "brightly sings" suggests the fusion of sight and sound in a synesthetic image,[34] and the parallel syntax of the *þonne* clauses, with their differences, provides a kind of envelope rhetorical pattern for the poem as well as illustrates the "play" of syntax and sense.[35]

Other facets of Old English poetic style have received critical attention. The scops seem to have used paronomasia and "etymological" wordplay more widely than previously thought.[36] Interlace patterns, such as those found in Anglo-Saxon seventh- and eighth-century art, have been connected with the nonrepresentational impulse of the Old English literary aesthetic.[37] Matters of style, it has been argued, should be considered in the editing of poetic texts.[38] At the same time, we have been made aware how precarious is our knowledge of Old English linguistic and semantic "facts," facts upon which we base stylistic and interpretive studies.[39]

We shall encounter these matters again and again in the individual poems discussed in the following chapters.[40] But before turning to specifics, it might be best to say a few words here about the dating of Old English poetry, about the poetic subject matters and genres, and about the manuscripts containing the poems.

Almost all of the surviving Old English poetry has been preserved in four manuscripts, known as the *Beowulf* MS (Cotton Vitellius A.xv), the Exeter Book, the Junius MS (Junius 11), and the Vercelli MS.[41] The first three reside in England—in the British Library, the Chapter Library of Exeter Cathedral, and the Bodleian Library at Oxford University respectively; the fourth (as stated earlier) somehow crossed the Alps during the Middle Ages and ended up in the Cathedral Library at Vercelli, Italy, where it remains to this day. All four manuscripts date from around the year 1000; their dialect is mainly Late West Saxon, the language of Ælfric, with an admixture of Anglian and Northumbrian forms that undoubtedly survived as part of the common poetic vocabulary from the earlier centuries.[42] The dates of composition of the poems in these manuscripts, whether of oral or written provenience, cannot be determined with precision. Amos has shown, for example, that few linguistic criteria—especially syntactic, grammatical, and stylistic ones—used for dating literary texts are reliable.[43] It must be stressed, moreover, that there is strong critical disagreement about the dating of individual poems. The elegies, for example, have been located in every century from the seventh to the tenth by one critic or another. And *Beowulf* has both early and late dating enthusiasts.[44]

The four Old English manuscripts collections, and other manuscripts containing one to several poems, offer a variety of poetic genres, from lyric through epic and allegory, from riddles to didactic verse. Some of the poems are exclusively secular in thought and content, others are devotionally or doctrinally oriented. Some have their roots in Germanic pagan antiquity, some in Christian Latinity.[45] Mostly, as we shall see, there was a fusion, both ideationally and stylistically. Because of the difficulty of dating, and for other reasons, it has seemed best in the following chapters to consider the poems according to subject matter. We shall begin with the secular hero, proceed to the Christian saint, then to poems about Christ himself, poems about Old Testament figures, verse dealing with miscellaneous Christian and secular subjects, lore and wisdom in verse, and finally elegiac poetry.

NOTES

1. On prosodic terms used in discussions of OE poetry, see Burchfield 1974.
2. On runes, see chapter 11.
3. On the importance of linguistic features in the patterning of the poetic line, see Lehmann, W. 1956.
4. $\bar{}$ indicates a long, heavily stressed syllable, $\bar{}$ or $\grave{x}$ a secondarily stressed long or short syllable respectively, and x an unstressed syllable. Resolved stress, where a short stressed syllable is rhythmically yoked with a following unstressed one, is marked $\overset{\frown}{}x$. A long syllable contains either a long vowel or diphthong, or a short vowel or diphthong closed by a final consonant or by two medial consonants immediately following; otherwise, the syllable is short. Thus *God* 'God,' *gōd* 'good,' and the first syllable of *gōdes* (gen. sg.) are long, but the first syllable of *Godes* 'God's' is short.
5. See Cable 1971 on constraints on anacrusis.
6. See note 4.
7. For some observations on A3 verses, as they are called, see Stanley 1974.
8. On the origin and structure of these expanded verses, see Bliss 1972.
9. See Cable 1984.
10. See Sievers 1893. A cogent outline of Sievers' main points is in Cassidy/Ringler 1971, pp. 274–88; see also Pope 1981a, pp. 105–16.
11. Pope 1966; see also Pope 1981a, pp. 116–38.
12. Bliss 1967.
13. For bibliography on OE prosody, see Greenfield/Robinson 1980, pp. 103–9 and 195–6; further Renoir/Hernández 1982, pp. 47–58.
14. Opland 1980, who also discusses possible distinctions between *scop*, *gleoman*, *woðbora*, and *leoðwyrhta*—OE terms for singers and narrators; see further Hollowell 1978.
15. Among the artifacts unearthed in the royal burial mound at Sutton Hoo in southeastern Suffolk, England, in 1939 were the remains of a small harp or lyre. For discussion of this instrument's nature and its possible use in connection with the recitation of OE poetry, see, in addition to Opland 1980, Bessinger 1958 and 1967; see also Wrenn 1962. The defini-

tive work on Sutton Hoo is Bruce-Mitford 1975; see also Bruce-Mitford 1979. On the relationship of *Beowulf* to Sutton Hoo, see Chambers 1959, pp. 508–23.

16. For a possible relationship between OE alliterative meter and the A-S world view, see Clemoes 1970.

17. On its prosaic vocabulary, see Stanley 1971.

18. On the kenning, see Marquardt 1938; Gardner, T. 1969 and 1972. On poetic diction, including the kenning, see Brodeur 1959, pp. 1–38; see also Stanley 1955 and Whallon 1969.

19. The seminal article on OE formulas is Magoun 1953; on formulaic systems, see Fry 1967 and 1968b.

20. See Cassidy 1965 on the poet's freedom and syntactic formulas.

21. On the beasts-of-battle theme, see Magoun 1955b; on exile, Green-field 1955. Among other themes which have been identified are "the hero on the beach" (Crowne 1960) and "the traveller recognizes his goal" (Clark, G. 1965). On formulaic themes and type-scenes, see Fry 1968a. See further Foley 1976a.

22. Great controversy has raged over the oral vs. written provenience of extant OE poetry—see chapter 6, n. 5. An annotated bibliography on oral-formulaic scholarship is Foley 1983b. On the use of Latin rhetorical figures in OE poetry, see Campbell, J. 1965 and 1978.

23. See Foley 1983a.

24. Greenfield 1955.

25. Bonjour 1962, pp. 135–49.

26. See Quirk 1963 and Greenfield 1972, pp. 30–59.

27. Quirk 1963, p. 159.

28. For a survey of studies of OE style, see Calder 1979b.

29. See Paetzel 1913; Brodeur 1959, pp. 39–70; Greenfield 1972, pp. 60–83; Robinson 1979b.

30. Paetzel 1913 and Robinson 1979b feel syntactic parallelism is necessary for true variation; Brodeur 1959 and Leslie 1959 do not.

31. Brodeur 1959, p. 39.

32. Greenfield 1972, p. 75; on the use of variation to achieve shifts in perspective, see pp. 68–72. Robinson 1979b suggests other ways in which OE poetry used "artful synonymy" (e.g., to clarify a metaphor) *and* exact repetition to achieve nuances of meaning, relating the latter especially to other echoic patterns in the poetry; see further Robinson 1985.

33. On the play of sound and sense, see Greenfield 1972, pp. 84–108.

34. Cf. Robinson 1970, who cautions us about lexicographers' tendencies to eliminate the possibilities of such images by their reductive definitions.

35. On "envelope" and other larger rhetorical patterns in OE poetry, the seminal work is Bartlett 1935. Various essays by Hieatt (see Bibliog-

raphy) explore further the envelope pattern in individual poems. On syntax and sense, see Greenfield 1972, pp. 109–32.

36. Frank 1972; see also items by Robinson in the Bibliography, especially Robinson 1975.

37. Leyerle 1967 and Schroeder 1974.

38. Leslie 1979.

39. See Mitchell 1975 and Stanley 1979.

40. For other surveys of OE verse, see Kennedy, C. 1943 and Shippey 1972. Some wide-ranging discussions of the poetry from particular critical stances are Huppé 1959, Isaacs 1968, Lee, A. A. 1972. A collection of previously published essential articles on the poetry is Bessinger/Kahrl 1968.

41. The names given to the Exeter and Vercelli MSS need no comment. On Cotton Vitellius A.xv, see chapter 6. The Junius MS (Junius 11) is named for the Dutch scholar Franciscus Junius, who in 1654 first published the poems it contains; it was also known as the Caedmon MS— see chapter 9. Facsimile editions of the four are, respectively, Malone 1963; Chambers/et al. 1933; Gollancz 1927; Förster 1913. The poetic corpus is edited in six volumes in ASPR. A concordance to the poetry based on ASPR is Bessinger/Smith 1978. The Exeter Book has been edited by Gollancz/Mackie 1895, with facing translations. Prose translations of most of the poems will be found in Bradley 1982; see also Gordon, R. 1954. Editions of individual poems, and some translations, are cited in notes to the following chapters.

42. On the dialect of the poetic vocabulary, see Sisam, K. 1953, chapter 8.

43. Amos 1980.

44. See chapter 6, n. 6.

45. For Germanic and Celtic analogues, see Calder/et al. 1983; for Latin analogues, see Calder/Allen 1976. On the excesses in the search for Germanic pagan roots, see Stanley 1975.

Secular Heroic Poetry

Old English poetry amply demonstrates that the fund of common narrative material associated with the Teutonic Migration Period (fourth to sixth centuries) survived in the songs of the Germanic tribes who settled in Britain. Through allusions to these stories and their characters, poems like *Widsith* and *Deor* attest to the vitality that tales about continental heroes like Ermanaric, Theodoric, and Ingeld must have had in the early English oral tradition, in songs now lost to us. Perhaps more important for Old English poetry as a whole than the particular Migration Period figures were the spirit and code of conduct they embodied, for these were to endure or be resurrected in the poetry down to the Norman Conquest. This heroic spirit manifested itself most strongly in the desire for fame and glory, now and after death. The code of conduct stressed the reciprocal obligations of lord and thegns: protection and generosity on the part of the former, loyalty and service on that of the latter—a mutuality that was the core of the *comitatus* relationship described as early as A.D. 98 by the Latin historian Tacitus in his *Germania*, and incorporated as late as the tenth century in the Old English poem on a historical military defeat of 991, *The Battle of Maldon*. Interestingly enough, this spirit and code, suitably transformed, found accommodation in Old English poetic paraphrases

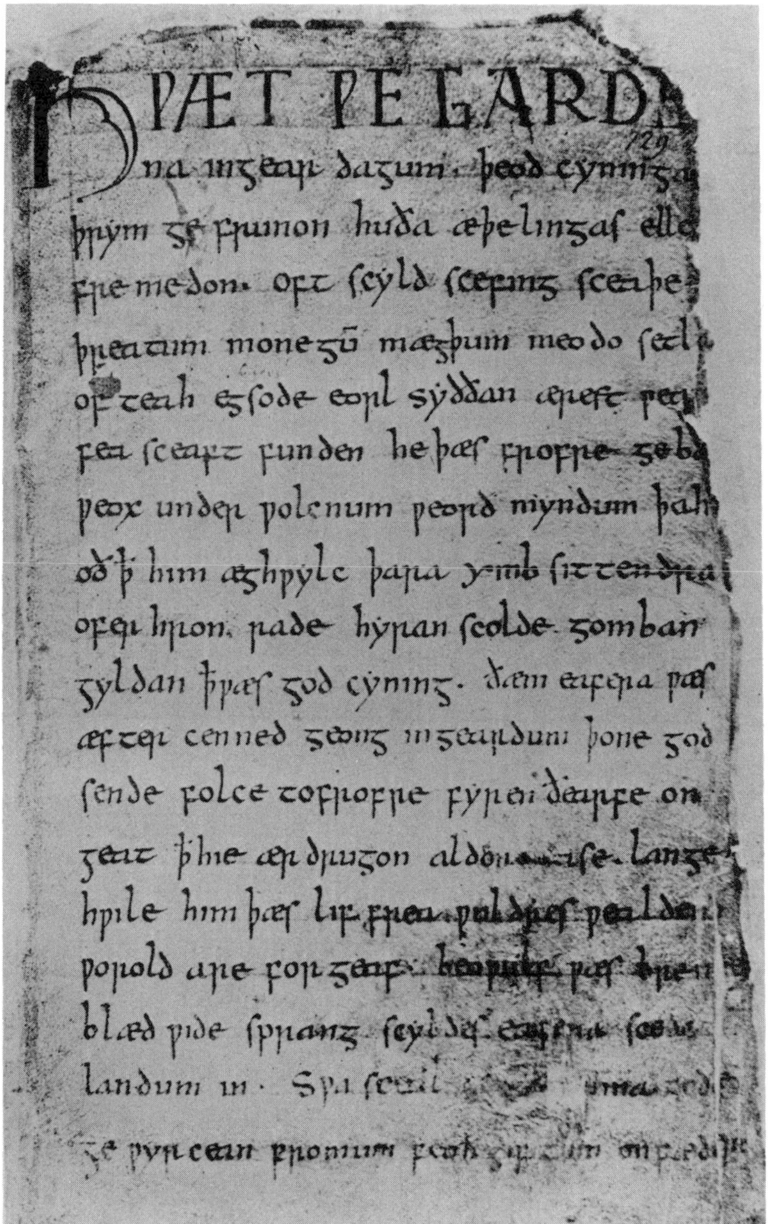

Cotton Vitellius A.XV, fol. 129ʳ
Ll. 1–21 of *Beowulf*

of Old Testament narrative, in saints' lives, and in the figure of Christ Himself.

For the moment our concern is with the Germanic secular hero as he appears in Old English poetry; and preeminent stands Beowulf. Though he has his analogues in such Scandinavian heroes as Boðvarr Bjarki and Grettir the Strong,[1] Beowulf is unique and gives his name to modern editions of the Old English epic. His origins, along with those of the monsters he fights, are to be found in folktale and legend more than in heroic story.[2] But in the Anglo-Saxon poet's hands Beowulf has become epically proportioned like the Homeric and Vergilian heroes of an earlier age, and been given a historical setting (the first quarter of the sixth century) involving him with the fates of two dynasties, the Danish Scyldings and Geatish Hrethlings.[3] There may have been Germanic pagan songs or lays about Beowulf, but the only form in which the story is extant, in British Library MS Cotton Vitellius A. xv, was clearly the work of a Christian poet. The extent to which Christianity permeates the poem, the poet's relative debts to the art of the Germanic scop and Latin Christian letters, and the validity of Christian allegorical or mythic interpretations, are questions which have been widely debated.[4] But whatever the critical stance, Beowulf is universally recognized as the richest jewel in the treasure-hoard of Anglo-Saxon poetry.

Before we discuss the poem itself, some account of its history and manuscript transmission may serve to indicate the still-precarious state of our knowledge about the poem's composition and the perils Anglo-Saxon manuscripts faced through the centuries. Critics dispute the method and the date of Beowulf's composition. Those who pursue oral-formulaic studies, comparing Beowulf with the rest of Old English poetry and with Greek, Yugoslavian, and even Bantu poetry, have been unable to prove that Beowulf—or any other English poem—is of oral provenience.[5] The early consensus on dating, that Beowulf, a poem of Mercian or Northumbrian origin, was fixed in its present form by the eighth century and then transmitted through one or more scribal copies to its present manuscript, has crumbled. Various linguistic, historical, and esthetic arguments suggest dates of composition from the late eighth through the early eleventh century.[6] If, however, a manu-

script existed in the eighth century, it must have somehow survived the later Danish invasions to have been copied into the extant codex. And the language of *Beowulf* is that same Late West
Saxon *koiné*, or artificial literary dialect, that includes some Anglian and other non-West Saxon forms, in which the other three
chief codices of Old English poetry are also written.

The manuscript is transcribed in two hands: the first copyist did
the three prose pieces preceding *Beowulf* (see chapter 3) and *Beowulf* up to line 1939; the second copied out the remainder of the
epic, as well as the fragmentary poem *Judith*. In the course of the
centuries, the codex survived the sixteenth-century dissolution of
the monastaries,[7] became bound in the early seventeenth century
with the twelfth-century manuscript containing Alfred's *Soliloquies*
(see chapter 2), and came to rest on the first shelf beneath the bust
of the Emperor Vitellius in the famous library of the antiquarian
Sir Robert Cotton (d. 1631). Fate kindly spared it when in 1731 fire
swept the library and destroyed or badly mutilated many of the
Cottonian collection, though the scorching it received caused some
deterioration around the edges of the vellum leaves and some
fading and crumbling elsewhere. Fortunately, the Icelander Grí-
mur Thorkelin had procured two copies of the text while he was
in England (c. 1786–7), one made by an unknown copyist who
knew no Old English (Thorkelin Transcript "A"), and one by
himself (Thorkelin Transcript "B"),[8] before further deterioration
occurred.

Whatever the disagreements about details and the interpretation of small passages and large sections, or about ultimate poetic
unity and *significatio*, the narrative movement of the 3,182-line
Beowulf is clear enough. It pits the "marvelous" hero, who has the
strength of thirty men and more than ordinary endurance in aquatic
feats,[9] against two troll-like descendants of Cain, the monsters
Grendel and his mother, and finally against a fire-breathing dragon.
The setting of the first two interrelated engagements is Denmark.
Beowulf, nephew to King Hygelac of the Geats, a nation existing
then in what is now southeastern Sweden, sails across the sea to
offer his aid to the Danish King Hrothgar. The cannibalistic Grendel, roused to fury by the sounds of joy and The Song of Creation
in the hall Heorot, has nightly ravaged Hrothgar's hall for twelve

years. After Beowulf meets three verbal challenges—by the Danish coastguard, by the hall warden, Wulfgar, and climactically by Unferth the *þyle*,[10] confrontations in which he displays his quickness of mind and self-assurance—he fights Grendel hand to hand in Heorot's dark night. The hero's physical prowess is equal to his impressive appearance and verbal acumen.[11] Grendel is forced to flee, despairing of life, having left his arm as "life-ransom" in Beowulf's grasp. The following night, unexpectedly, Grendel's mother materializes to avenge her son, devouring Hrothgar's dearest counselor, Æschere. At Hrothgar's plea, Beowulf agrees to avenge Æschere's death; this time he must seek out his antagonist in her underwater lair. In a memorable passage, similar to one in *Blickling Homily* XVII (see chapter 3), Hrothgar describes the lake or mere in which she lurks:

> They live in land unknown,
> on wolf-haunted hills, windy headlands,
> perilous fen-paths where the mountain stream
> plunges down into the headlands' mists,
> flows beneath the earth. It is not far
> from here in miles to where the mere stands;
> frost-bound groves, woods firmly rooted, lean
> over it, shadowing its waters.
> There one can see a fearful wonder
> every night: fire on the flood. No man
> breathes so wise as to know its bottom.
> Though the heath-stalker, the full-horned hart,
> put to flight and far pursued by hounds,
> may seek the woods, sooner will he yield
> his life up on the shore than leap in
> to save his head—hardly a pleasant place! (ll. 1357b–72)

In the ensuing battle beneath the water, strength of arm is not enough to assure the hero victory; nor does the peerless sword Hrunting, lent him by a chastened Unferth, avail. Only an old sword, the work of giants, which the hero spies on the wall of the monster's cave, enables him to kill Grendel's mother, thus finally cleansing the Danish kingdom of the external evil manifested in these descendants of Cain.

The third confrontation takes place in Beowulf's old age. King of the Geats for fifty years, the hero must now avenge a dragon's fiery ravaging of his homeland and his own throne, a catastrophe occasioned by a thief's stealing a cup from the hoard the dragon had guarded for three hundred years. Not without foreboding, Beowulf challenges the monster at the entrance to its barrow, and battle ensues. To kill the dragon, the hero ultimately needs the aid of his retainer and kinsman, Wiglaf; but even with that aid he receives his death wound. He is given a hero's funeral pyre; his ashes, along with the dragon's hard-won hoard, are placed in a splendid tumulus atop a seaside cliff; and twelve chieftains ride around Beowulf's Barrow, lamenting and praising their fallen lord.

Such a bare outline of the major action tells little about the poem's magnificence. Even so, we have tried to suggest something of the poet's structural sense in the "movements" of the three contests: in the differing natures and motivations of the antagonists; in the progressive difficulties Beowulf has conquering his foes; in the shift of locales from the human confines of Heorot to the submerged cavern and to the barrow on the headland.[12] Paralleling these movements is a sense of the hero's progressive isolation: in the Grendel fight his retainers draw their swords attempting to help their leader—they fail because Grendel's skin is charmed against weapons; in the second contest this band can only sit and wait on the mere's shore; and in the dragon fight Beowulf's *comitatus*, with the exception of Wiglaf, abandons him to the ultimate isolation of death. This last variation embodies the theme of loyalty vs. disloyalty that pervades the poem's ethos. As the ethical norm we have Beowulf's fealty to his uncle and lord, Hygelac, in his refusal to accept the crown after the king is killed in Friesland; and as one of several contrasts the poet suggests latent treachery in Heorot through the character of Unferth, who has killed his kinsmen in battle, and through Hrothulf, Hrothgar's nephew and co-ruler, who will usurp the Danish throne.[13]

The poem's complexity and richness may perhaps be best summarized by the notion of *contrast*. Contrasts and parallels, interfacing in the poem, unify the larger structural elements, character presentations, themes, and even the most detailed stylistic matters. This unifying technique allows the poet to introduce the many apparent digressions, whether they be legendary—as they largely are in the first part of the poem—or historical—as in the second. And it permits the Christian and pagan elements to coexist meaningfully within the poem's framework.[14]

The two major structural divisions (ll.1–2199 and 2200–3182) provide an overall contrast between youth and age: with youth in Part I is connected the ideal of the perfect retainer, exhibited in Beowulf's strengths of mind, body, and character, and his conception of service to both Hrothgar (who had once aided Beowulf's father Ecgtheow) and his own lord, Hygelac; with old age in Part II is represented the ideal of the Germanic king, as Beowulf attempts not only to protect his people but to provide them with treasure. Critics have disagreed, however, about Beowulf's "perfection." A few have seen the young warrior as brash, maturing only after he has killed Grendel's mother.[15] Many more have seen King Beowulf "flawed" in his eagerness for treasure, overreliance on his own strength, and imprudence in fighting the dragon; they see him thus exemplifying the degeneration and sinful pride which Hrothgar had warned him against in his sermon after his conquest of Grendel's mother (ll. 1735 ff.). Others have seen King Beowulf as admirable by the secular standards of the heroic world, but falling short from the poet's Christian perspective, subject to the curse and damnation laid upon the dragon's hoard by those princes who had first buried it.[16]

The structural contrast of youth and age is also related to success and failure and, in a widening sense, to the rise and fall of nations.[17] In Part I, the rise of the Scylding dynasty in Denmark introduces the story proper, and then the glory of Hrothgar's hall and court at its opulent peak is set scenically before our ears and eyes: the Germanic aura of singing, feasting, and drinking, giftgiving and magnanimity of spirit. The many allusions to and "digressions" on stories from the whole realm of Germania suggest the panorama of heroic life. In Part II, the focus is on the end of the Geatish nation, on barrow rather than hall. The panorama now is historical rather than legendary, unfolding in flashbacks by the poet himself, then by Beowulf, and finally by Wiglaf's messenger. We discover the progressive elimination of King Hrethel's sons: the eldest accidentally slain by bowshot at his brother Haethcyn's hands, Haethcyn killed in attacking the Swedes, and the last brother, Hygelac, humbled in Friesland when he "asked for woe"; then Hygelac's son Heardred killed by the Swedes. Beowulf, the last survivor of the dynasty, is childless.[18] The messenger prophesies the final defeat and dispersal of the Geats:

> No warrior shall wear
> ornament in memory, nor maiden
> aid her beauty with bright necklaces,
> but sad of mind, stripped of gold, they shall
> walk on foreign ground, not once but often,
> now that our leader has laid down laughter,
> joy, and mirth. Therefore many a spear,
> morning-cold, shall be grasped in hands
> and raised on high; no sound of the harp
> shall wake warriors, but the dark raven,
> eager for doomed men, shall speak much, telling
> the eagle how he fared at eating
> when he plundered the slain with the wolf. (ll.   3015b–27)[19]

The rise and fall of nations is emphasized further in the contrast between the tones of the poem's two parts. The heroic dominates Part I, with the evocation of "the good king," the resolution with which Beowulf faces Wyrd or Fate, and in Beowulf's advice to Hrothgar upon Æschere's death that

> It is better
> to avenge one's friend than mourn too much.
> Each of us must one day reach the end
> of worldly life; let him who can win
> glory before he dies: that lives on
> after him, when he lifeless lies. (ll.   1384b–9)

The elegiac dominates the second part: there is the elegy of the last survivor (ll. 2247 ff.) who buried the hoard the dragon finds and guards; King Hrethel's lament for his son, Herebeald, and the elegy of the old man whose son hangs on the gallows; the final lamentation around Beowulf's funeral mound.

The larger contrasts are modified by such matters as Scyld's arrival and ship burial, a prologue to the whole poem (ll. 1–52), which contains both the heroic and elegiac within itself and affords a larger parallel to the burial of Beowulf at the poem's conclusion; seeds of downfall in the Danish dynasty sown in significant allusions to future treachery and the burning of Heorot; age in the figure of King Hrothgar himself; and the helplessness of the Danes, their futile prayers to the *gastbona* 'soul-slayer' (or devil) under the attacks of Grendel. Further, there is the *historical* allusion in Part I to the death of Hygelac, made at the moment Queen Wealhtheow bestows upon Beowulf the valuable necklace which, the allusion points out, Hygelac will be wearing when killed.[20] Such movement back and forth in time from the historical present of the poem's action—to mythic and legendary past, to historical future unknown to the poem's characters, to the poet's own day, to eschatological adumbrations—is a prominent feature of the poem's narrative style.[21] While tragic overtones qualify the heroic temper of Part I, heroic actions recounted qualify the elegiac in Part II. Wiglaf's behavior in coming to Beowulf's rescue is a pointed example, but though his aid is not too little it is too late, serving only to heighten the central theme—*lif is læne* 'life is transitory.'[22]

The failures of heroic society in *Beowulf* have led some critics to perceive the Christian poet as suggesting flaws in, and limits to, not only the hero, but the social fabric itself. One sees the poet condemning that society because it lacks Christ's redeeming grace; another criticizes the socioeconomic foundation of gift-giving, because it leads to wars of plunder and creates social instability.[23] Nevertheless, the poet seems to emphasize through gnomic wisdom a continuity in God's governance of man's life and actions from *geardagum* 'days of yore' to *þyssum windagum* 'these days of strife,' a reasonable recognition by a Christian poet that no secular age or society has a monopoly on imperfectibility. The heroic ideals —loyalty, courage, generosity—may not always be achieved; but the poem's perspective seems more universal than specifically Christian, suggesting it is *life* which has its limits rather than heroism or the heroic world.[24]

Perspective, continuity, and larger structural contrasts have their counterparts in smaller details of the poem: character contrasts, as in Hrothgar's scop's allusions to Sigemund (good) and Heremod (bad) in his improvised lay about Beowulf's conquest of Grendel; the niggardly, wicked Thryth versus the liberal, gentle Hgyd of the Offa-Thryth digression. There are, furthermore, symbolic contrasts, good and evil finding their correspondences in light and darkness, joy and sorrow.[25] And, on the most detailed stylistic level, we find such moments as that in which Beowulf comes, the morning after the celebration of Grendel's death, to ask whether Hrothgar has spent the night pleasantly. *"Ne frin þu æfter sælum! Sorh is geniwod/Denigum leodum. Dead is Æschere,"* replies the king. ('Ask not of joy! Sorrow is renewed/among the Danes. Dead is Ashere.') The opposition of joy and sorrow is suggested by the syntactic break at the caesura, yet the alliterative connection of *sælum* and *sorh* underlies the confluence of the emotions.[26] Similarly, when Grendel stalks Heorot: *Com on wanre niht/scriðan sceadugenga. Sceotend swæfon* 'Out of dark night/swept death's shadow forward. The warders slept,' the moving Grendel and the sleeping warriors are effectively contrasted through syntactic severance and chiastic use of the verbs, yet ironically associated by the alliterative and metrical pattern.[27]

These are but samples of the range of the *Beowulf* poet's accomplishments in drawing together, by what has been called the "interlace pattern" from its resemblance to Anglo-Saxon art, the many disparate elements of his poem into one of the triumphs of English poetry.[28] One further example of structural interlace is of particular interest.

The Finn Episode (ll. 1068–1159), a sample of the entertainment provided by the scop in Heorot after the defeat of Grendel, is an excellent tragedy in itself, focusing as it does on the conflicting claims imposed upon Hengest: to revenge his dead leader Hnaef, on the one hand, and to keep the peace he has been forced by circumstance to make with Hnaef's slayer, King Finn of Friesland, on the other.[29] The final resolution, with Hengest and the Danes slaughtering Finn and his retainers in their hall to exact revenge, is presented by Hrothgar's scop as a Danish victory, and on this level alone would have its *raison d'être* in the context of *Beowulf*.[30] But the Episode contributes more subtly to the overall unity of the poem. For though the scop concentrates on Hengest, the *Beowulf* poet himself gives another perspective through Hildeburh's wretchedness: her loss of brother (Hnaef), son, and finally of husband (Finn), so that this story reflects the heroic-elegiac pattern in miniature. On another level, the theme of treachery is emphasized at the beginning, in the litotical comment that Hildeburh had "little reason to speak well of the loyalty of the Jutes (or giants)";[31] and the theme of treachery runs throughout the piece, to be echoed after the scop finishes his song, when the poet alludes to the future treachery in Heorot itself. The Episode also reveals the failure of human efforts to achieve peaceful compromise, another recurrent theme; and the unenviable position of Queen Hildeburh has its immediate parallel in Queen Wealhtheow, whose son will lose the throne to the usurping nephew Hrothulf, and a more distant parallel in Wealhtheow's daughter Freawaru, whose future suffering Beowulf will prophesy in his report to Hygelac. Finally, the Finn Episode is balanced by that of Ingeld in Beowulf's report, for the former treats of past triumph within the framework of disaster, while the latter foretells disaster within the framework of triumph. We know from *Widsith* that Ingeld, though he probably burned Heorot, was defeated by Hrothgar and Hrothulf.[32] In this balanced presentation of past and future, we see an additional way the poet has gained epic scope for the folktale contests that are the narrative basis upon which he so expertly built.[33]

The Finn Episode in *Beowulf* presents a part of what must have been a series of stories about the Danish-Frisian conflict. Another segment is preserved in the fragmentary *Fight at Finnsburh*, now extant only in Hickes's transcription, the manuscript having been subsequently lost.[34] Only some forty-seven lines of this probably early oral poem remain, lines which recount a previous stage in the hostilities, when the Frisians began their attack on Hnaef. From what can be pieced together from Fragment and Episode, Hnaef and his band of sixty Danes had been visiting Hnaef's sister Queen Hildeburh and her husband King Finn when, through treachery by some part of Finn's retainers,[35] Hnaef's party was attacked in the hall. The Fragment's beginning is missing, but clearly a sentinel for the Danes spots moonlight (or torchlight) glittering on swords as the treacherous attack is about to be launched. The Danes, after positioning warriors at the two doors, hold out against the besiegers for five days without losing a man. As the Fragment ends, a Dane (some say a Frisian) is wounded severely and queried by Hnaef (or Finn?)[36] as to how well the warriors are surviving their wounds. From the Episode we know that in the continuation of the battle Hnaef died and was succeeded by Hengest, who ultimately made a truce with Finn when both forces were decimated.

The emphasis and style of the Fragment differ considerably from those of the Episode, and from the epic *Beowulf*. The *Fight at Finnsburh* is no curtailed epic, but a bona fide *lay*, a brief narrative with compressed description and rapid conversation.[37] Perhaps the fragmentary poem opened with the sentry's question about the meaning of the light he sees, for Hnaef replies:

Not day dawns eastward, nor dragon flies,
nor are this hall's horned gables burning;
but they bring forth bright arms, war-birds sing,
the grey-coat howls,[38] wood war-spear hisses,
shield answers thrown shaft. Now shines the moon
breaking from clouds: now woeful deeds burst
forth, incited by this folk's enmity. (ll. 3–9)

The narrative progresses in a series of *then* announcements, jerking the movement along powerfully as the poet commends the small band for their courage and devotion in repaying their leader's generosity in more propitious days. Although the *Fight* is mainly valued for the light it throws on the Episode in *Beowulf*, it is nonetheless a moving account of stark, unvarnished heroic action in the best spirit of ancient Germanic poetry, such a lay as might well have moved the audience in a Germanic chieftain's hall.

Among other fragments shored against the ruins of extant Germanic heroic poetry are two manuscript leaves, discovered in 1860 in the Royal Library of Copenhagen, containing portions of the Walter of Aquitaine story. The legend itself, varied in its surviving forms in different languages,[39] recounts the history of Hagen, Walter, and Hildegund (-gyth), hostages at the court of Attila the Hun. When Gunther becomes the Burgundian king and refuses to continue payments for his countryman Hagen, the latter escapes, as do the betrothed Walter and Hildegund. Loaded with treasure taken from Attila, the lovers are accosted on their way to safety by Gunther, covetous of the treasure, and his unwilling vassal

Hagen, who had become a brother-in-arms to Walter in the Hunnish court. The Burgundians attack Walter; and, protected in a narrow defile, he defeats them one by one till only Gunther and Hagen, who has hitherto refused to fight, remain. In the Latin *Waltharius*, the conflict ends after Gunther and Hagen, finally drawn into the fight by Gunther's shame and by the earlier death of his own nephew, attack Walter in the open. Each of the heroes is maimed but not killed in the encounter, and they are reconciled.

The fragments, consisting of sixty-odd lines which modern editors entitle *Waldere*,[40] include three speeches evidently connected with the final combat. Only the speaker of lines 11 ff. of Fragment II, in which the Burgundian king is taunted, has been identified (Waldere); and there is no agreement over the attribution of the other two speeches. That of Fragment I, urging Waldere on to combat, is most likely Hildegyth's; the first speech of Fragment II (ll. 1–10), praising a sword, has been assigned to Hildegyth, Hagen, and Guthhere (Gunther). Uncertainty also exists as to the order of the fragments.[41] The relationship of *Waldere* to the Latin epic *Waltharius* has likewise been a problem, though the consensus now sees the Anglo-Saxon lines as the remnants of an earlier independent version, since the poem is more heroic than the Latin and Hildegyth is more important than the Latin Hildegund.[42] Even the nature of the original poem has been called into question: was it an epic, or a shorter lay? It is a pity that we do not possess more of *Waldere*; what survives is largely interesting only as it relates, however puzzlingly, to the Walter saga as a whole, and as it exemplifies common traits of Anglo-Saxon heroic conduct and poetic style.

Of much greater interest among early verse reflecting the Germanic heroic tradition is the allusive *Widsith*, a poetic *tour de force*. The text is preserved only in the tenth-century Exeter Book MS.[43] The lay or epic material is embodied in three *thulas* or mnemonic poetic lists, which comprise the main body of the poem, around and through which is woven the lyric-narrative "history" of the fictitious Widsith 'Far-journey(er),' a scop or poet-singer by trade.[44] "Widsith spoke up, unlocked his word-hoard," the poet begins. He then interposes some eight lines to characterize his widely-traveled hero as one with some status among his native tribe, the

Myrgings—his first trip abroad was with the lady Ealhhild to the court of Ermanaric, a historically attested figure of the Migration Period.[45] The fictitious Widsith then speaks for himself in lines 10–134, describing a career of travel whose geographical and chronological boundaries are realistically impossible.[46] In the first thula Widsith says he has heard about many great rulers: "A ruled B" is the normative verse pattern here. The scop emphasizes their power, the establishment and keeping of a prosperous realm, culminating in praise for the prowess of the Anglian ruler Offa and for the long peace between Hrothulf and Hrothgar after they defeated Ingeld (see *Beowulf*, above). In lines 50–6, he talks about his personal affairs in a somewhat elegiac strain, but ends stressing the rewards he achieved by his singing. In the second thula Widsith mentions the various tribes he had been *with*, rather than rulers he has heard *about:* the normative verse pattern is "With C-tribe I was." In this section he praises the liberality of the Burgundian King Guthhere and the Lombard Ælfwine (Alboin), but most highly Ermanaric's gift of a precious ring, a treasure which he then gave to his own lord, the Myrging Eadgils, in return for the regranting of his ancestral estate; he also lauds Ealhhild's similar gift, for which he acclaimed her in song throughout many lands. The third thula's basic verse pattern is "So-and-so *sought* I," where once again Widsith stresses the importance of those who gain glory in battle and sway over men, as God grants them such power and rule. The poet resumes speaking at line 135 in a nine-line epilogue paralleling the nine-line prologue. Now the poet's concern is not with the individual, idealized scop, Widsith, but with all gleemen who wander the earth till they find discriminating and generous lords, those who wish to win fame on earth through poetic praise for their noble deeds, "till all pass away,/light and life together."

Though many details of *Widsith* are problematic, the larger form and structure seem clear enough. The poet's intention, and the Anglo-Saxon audience's response, are not. The emphasis on kings' liberality in rewarding scops' endeavors has suggested to some that *Widsith* was a "begging" poem, a real scop's plea for patronage.[47] One critic sees two moral visions juxtaposed in the poet's and in the scop's voices, with the poet's voice undercutting his fictitious character's "giddy enthusiasm for earthly rulers," and thus implying the higher value of the heavenly kingdom.[48] Still another believes the poem celebrates the power of poetry itself, the three thulas corresponding to the functions of poetry as didactic, experiential, and immortalizing.[49] However the poem was interpreted in Anglo-Saxon times, it can still stimulate our human, or at least scholarly, imaginations.

Although *Deor*, like *Widsith*, employs a fictitious scop as narrator and also alludes to Germanic heroic story, since its tone is overridingly elegiac, we shall consider it in chapter 12. Two poems of the tenth century, however, deserve consideration here, for, though they do not concern themselves with Germanic story, they nevertheless reflect the continuing vitality of the secular heroic ethos in the later literature. These are the two historical pieces, *The Battle of Brunanburh* and *The Battle of Maldon*. The former is a chronicle poem; that is, it appears in four of the manuscripts of the Anglo-Saxon Chronicles as the entry for 937—there are five other such poems (see chapter 10). The latter is extant only in a transcript (c. 1724) made by David Casley, because the manuscript (which also included the unique text of Asser's *Life of Alfred*—see chapter 2) perished in the Cottonian fire.[50]

Brunanburh is a panegyric on the heroism of King Æthelstan and his younger brother Eadmund, who was but sixteen at the time of the battle celebrated. These grandsons of Alfred the Great defeated and put to flight near Brunanburh the combined forces of King Constantine II of Scotland, King Eugenius (Owen) of the Strathclyde Britons, and Anlaf (Olaf), son of the Viking king of Dublin. The precise location of the historic battle site is a matter of conjecture.[51] To the late Old English poet this victory was the most glorious occasion in English history

> since from the east
> Angles and Saxons came over here,
> sought out Britain across the broad seas,
> proud war-forgers subdued the Welsh folk,
> brave warriors seized and won the land. (ll. 69b–73)

The poem is a tissue of heroic formulaic cliché, themes, and stylistic variation: *Her Æthelstan cyning, eorla drihten,/beorna beahgifa*

. . . 'In this year King Æthelstan, lord of earls,/ring-giver to men,' it begins, echoing the diction of a typical annal in the Chronicles. And toward the end it introduces the conventional "beasts of battle" to whom the victorious English leave the bloodstained field. Yet stylistically the poet can produce some striking effects. He seems to use synesthesia in line 12: *feld dennode/secga swate* 'the field resounded with warriors' blood';[52] and he can make multiple variation suggest the movement of battle (ll. 48–51). He can use a cluster of weapons images "to associate the skill with which a weapon is wielded to the skill with which it was welded, to equate carving ornaments with carving up battle formations, shields, or bodies."[53] Conventional heroic epithets and stylistic mannerisms are infused with a nationalistic fervor. The poet describes the English slaughter of the invaders

> since the sun,
> that glorious star, rose up and glided
> across the earth (bright candle of God,
> eternal Lord), till that noble creature
> sank to rest. (ll. 13b–7a)

This passage, whose "since" clause parallels the final lines (69b–73) cited above, hints at "progression and circularity, kinesis and stasis, in historical events, so that the victory of the royal brothers in A.D. 937 is given a retrospective quality associated with their forebears and, simultaneously, a glorious, even celestial dignity associated with the sun."[54] This panoramic sweep may not bring us face to face with individual heroes like Beowulf and Hnaef, but it reflects the heroic virtues embodied in their actions.

Maldon is in the more scenic style of the older epics, and its heroes-in-defeat, especially Ealdorman Byrhtnoth, seem to have historic reality. Many earlier scholars felt that the poet must have been an eyewitness to the battle, or at least that he was giving an accurate account of the English defeat by Viking invaders, a defeat laconically reported as follows in the "A" version of the Chronicles for 993 [=991]:

In this year Olaf came with 93 ships to Folkestone, and ravaged round about it, and then from there went to Sandwich, and so from there to

Ipswich, and overran it all, and so to Maldon. And Ealdorman Bryht-
noth came against them there with his army and fought against them;
and they killed the ealdorman there and gained control of the field.[55]

But Bessinger cautions against "equation of poetic verisimilitude
to historical verity";[56] and though the historicity of certain aspects
need not be denied, under the poet's handling of traditional heroic formulas *Maldon*'s historical heroes-in-defeat merge with legendary ones.[57] Their conduct reflects the heroic code embodied in
the old Germanic *comitatus* as described by Tacitus: obedience,
loyalty, fortitude, self-sacrifice in repayment for the lord's prior
generosity[58]—with the addition of the Christian virtues of trust-
ing in God and submitting to His will.[59]

Unfortunately, the beginning and ending of the *Battle of Maldon*
(now only 325 lines) are missing, though it seems unlikely that
much has been lost at either point. The poem presents the English army or *fyrd*, specifically that of Essex under the leadership
of the old *eorl* Byrhtnoth, taking up defensive positions along the
bank of the Panta (now called the Blackwater) against the Vikings,
who are on an island in the estuary (the nearby town of Maldon
is not actually named in the extant poem). A Viking messenger
calls across the water asking for a payment of tribute in exchange
for peace, an exchange the English leader spiritedly refuses. When
the invaders try to reach the mainland by the only available foot-
access, a causeway or bridge, accessible when the tide ebbs,
Byrhtnoth's men easily withstand them. Resorting to deceit (*ly-
tegian*), the Vikings then ask that they be allowed to cross the
causeway unmolested to engage in full combat; and *for ofermode*
'excessive pride,' the poet says, the *eorl* accedes to this request.
His action leads, with the inevitability of tragedy, to the moving
denouement. Though wounded by a Viking spear, Byrhtnoth drives
his own through the neck of his assailant and pierces another
through the heart. But when he (prematurely) exults for "the day's
work the Lord had granted him" (ll. 146b–8), he is fatally struck
down. His death proves too much for some of his trusted retainers: Godric, forgetting his lord's gifts of "many a horse," mounts
Byrhtnoth's steed, all others having been previously driven away
to the nearby woods, and flees with his two brothers to the safety

of those woods. Others follow, thinking it is Byrhtnoth whom they see in flight. The English army is thus divided, its doom sealed. But the heart of the poem lies in the hearts of those who remain, in their loyalty exhorting themselves and each other to avenge their lord and/or die with him (ll. 202–325). One by one they fall. The final exhortation, by the old retainer Byrhtwold, sums up the heroic mode for all readers of Old English literature:

"Hige sceal þe heardra, heorte þe cenre,
mod sceal þe mare, þe ure mægen lytlað." (ll. 312–3)

("Mind must be firmer, heart the keener,
courage the greater, as our might fails".)

In its fragmented form, the poem ends with another Godric (*not* the coward, the poet stresses) dying valiantly.

The poet's attitudes toward his subject and characters, especially toward Byrhtnoth, have been the subject of some heated scholarly argument. Is *ofermod*, a word elsewhere in Old English used only in religious contexts with a pejorative sense, "magnificent, perhaps, but certainly wrong," purely adversative as in the Christian *superbia*, or magnificent and right?[60] Some have suggested that Byrhtnoth's behavior reflects the pattern of a saint's life; others have vigorously rejected such a notion.[61] One critic can interpret the theme as the poet setting "the noble desire for honor against the base impulse toward survival"; another can see the heroic in the poem as delusive fantasy, with the poet advocating "careful thought and moderate action rather than marvellous feats performed in impetuous haste, and since [the poem] places great emphasis on the destruction of war, one may interpret it as antiheroic."[62] But the antiheroic view seems more a modern projection *onto* the poem than an Anglo-Saxon attitude *in* it:

Byrhtnoth's heroism is not diminished by his *ofermod* or by his hubris . . . . The poet makes a moral comment on Byrhtnoth's decision to allow the Vikings too much land, and he makes another, through his structure, as the tragedy of a man cut down at the moment of his triumph. But ultimately the audience is called upon to admire the hero, commanding, fighting, and dying bravely with God on his lips. . . .

Loyalty is the poet's theme, and in their devotion to their leader the men who died at Maldon were victorious.[63]

Though the poet may not have used Old English metrical types with great versatility, nor his poetic diction and formulas with great originality or imagination, and though he used considerable formulaic repetition, he nevertheless produced a spirited and esthetically effective poem. In his structural patterning, for example, he carefully manipulates the ordering and length of the speeches the loyal retainers give after Byrhtnoth has died, suggesting rank and significance. First, the ealdorman's kinsman Ælfwine has thirteen lines of direct discourse; then Offa, his officer, speaks the same number of lines; then the warrior Leofsunu has seven and a half, and the *ceorl* Dunnere only two. Edward the tall has two lines of indirect discourse following, and after Offa and others have been slain, Oswold and Eadwold likewise have two lines of indirect speech. Finally the old companion, *Byrhtwold maþelode, bord hafenode* 'Byrhtwold spoke, raised his shield'; and he is given eight lines, including the two quoted above.[64]

Byrhtnoth's early ironic response to the Viking messenger is a powerful display of style and language:

"Gehyrst þu, sælida,   hwæt þis folc segeð?
Hi willað eow to gafole   garas syllan,
ætrynne ord   and ealde swurd,
þa heregeatu   þe eow æt hilde ne deah.
Brimmanna boda,   abeod eft ongean,
sege þinum leodum   miccle laþre spell,
þæt her stynt unforcuð   eorl mid his werode,
þe wile gealgean   eþel þysne,
Æþelredes eard,   ealdres mines
folc and foldan.   Feallan sceolon
hæþene æt hilde.   To heanlic me þinceð
þæt ge mid urum sceattum   to scype gangon
unbefohtene,   nu ge þus feor hider
on urne eard   in becomon.
Ne sceole ge swa softe   sinc gegangan:
us sceal ord and ecg   ær geseman,
grim guðplega,   ær [w]e gofol syllon."   (ll. 45–61)

("Hear you, Viking, what this folk responds?
As tribute they wish to send you spears,

deadly darts and ancestral swords,
armor to tax and test your mettle.
Sea-men's messenger, make this reply,
tell your people more distasteful news:
that here stands a noble earl with his troop,
who will defend this homeland dear,
Ethelred's—my own lord's—dominion,
his folk and their homes. Heathens shall fall
in battle. Too shameful would it be
for you to take ship with our treasures
unfought for, now that you have so far
made entry here in our dominion.
Not so softly won the wealth you seek:
the sword's point and blade, fierce battle-play,
must arbitrate ere we pay tribute.")

Part of this speech directly echoes, with a difference, the messenger's. For example, the Viking says, *"Eow betere is/þæt ge þisne garræs mid gafole forgyldon"* (ll. 31b-2)—'it will be better for you that you buy off this spear-rush with tribute.'Byrhtnoth's line 46 gives a chiastic twist to *garræs-gafole* in *gafole-garas*, as well as plays off the sound of the compound *garræs* against the simplex *garas*.[65] The pun in Byrhtnoth's use of the word *heregeatu* in line 48—the word means both 'war equipment' and a 'tax (heriot) due to a lord on the death of his tenant'—is doubly ironic. Elsewhere, the poet's calling the Vikings *wælwulfas* 'slaughter-wolves' when they finally cross the Panta (l. 95) is noteworthy, since a few lines further on the raven and eagle, "beasts of battle," are mentioned, but not their grey-coated forest companion, the wolf, who seems to have been "humanized" in the de-"humanized" invaders.

Maldon is a poem worthy of its epic precursors. Though by the late tenth century, or early eleventh, ealdormen like Byrhtnoth certainly did not live in the manner of earlier tribal chieftains, an English poet could still find the old ethos and mode worth incorporating into a traditional verse narrative to make a historic defeat into a poetic victory. That he could have done so without the heroic spirit's still having some resonance for his late Anglo-Saxon audience is doubtful, whether he wished to applaud or depreciate it. Anglo-Saxon paraphrases of the Old Testament, such as the earlier "Caedmonian" poetry and the late *Judith*, poetic saints' lives, and even the poetic depictions of Christ Himself contain elements of the heroic: that these poems were copied into manuscripts during the late tenth century suggests a positive rather than a negative resonance.

NOTES

1. Bjarki appears in the Norse saga of Hrolf Kraki: for trans., see Jones, G. 1961, pp. 221–318; for trans. of *Grettissaga*, see Fox/Pálsson 1974. For bibliography of translations of Old Norse sagas, see Fry 1980a. On Celtic analogues, see Puhvel 1979. On the "Bear's Son Tale" and its relationship to *Beowulf*, see Panzer 1910. For general essays on the hero in medieval literature, see Jones, G. 1972; Huppé 1975; Swanton 1977.

2. See Niles 1983, chapter 1.

3. On *Beowulf* as epic tragedy, see Greenfield 1962. On heroic aspects, see Chadwick, H. M. 1912, esp. chapter 15. On Vergilian parallels, see Haber 1931; Andersson 1976, chapter 4. For historical and nonhistorical elements and translation of analogues, see Chambers 1959; Garmonsway/Simpson 1968. A judicious account of *Beowulf*'s relation to history, religion, and culture is Robinson 1984.

4. Cherniss 1972 and Niles 1983, chapters 2 and 3, see a heavier debt to Germanic than to Christian tradition; Goldsmith 1970 sees the reverse, and reads the poem allegorically; Lee, A. A. 1972, chapter 4, reads the poem mythically. An essay summarizing *Beowulf* criticism is Short 1980a. Specialized *Beowulf* bibliographies are Fry 1969; Short 1980b.

5. For arguments in favor of oral composition, see Magoun 1953; Creed 1959; Lord 1960. For arguments against, see Schaar 1956; Brodeur 1959; Benson 1966; Watts 1969; Russom 1978a. Opland 1980 makes comparisons with South African oral poetry. For a *Beowulf* concordance, see Bessinger/Smith 1969.

6. On the dating of *Beowulf*, see Chase, C. 1981; also Kiernan 1981 and Lapidge 1982a. On the poem's audience, see Whitelock 1951.

7. The sixteenth-century A-S antiquary Laurence Nowell apparently had something to do with the MS at this time: his name appears on the first page of the *Beowulf* codex.

8. These transcripts, plus Zupitza's facsimile edition and ultra-violet light readings, have been invaluable in establishing the poem's present text. For facsimiles of the Thorkelin transcripts, see Malone 1951; of the Nowell Codex, Malone 1963; of *Beowulf*, Zupitza 1959. A study of Thorkelin's actual working on the transcripts is Kiernan 1983. Some editions of the poem are Wyatt/Chambers 1920; Klaeber 1950; Dobbie 1953 (see ASPR 4); Wrenn/Bolton 1973; Heyne/von Schaubert 1958. Translations from *Beowulf* in this *History* are from Greenfield 1982a; a brief survey of *Beowulf* translations is Short 1984.

9. See Greenfield 1982b.

10. On the controversy over Unferth—the form and meaning of his name, the meaning of þyle, and his role in the poem—see Greenfield 1972, pp. 101–7 and Clover 1980.

11. On the theme of *sapientia et fortitudo*, see Kaske 1958; on action-agent identification, see Clemoes 1979.

12. Cf. Calder 1972a.

13. Not all critics accept these suggestions of treachery: see Sisam, K. 1965; Niles 1983.

14. Cf. Bonjour 1950. A reading stressing contrasts and irony is Irving 1968. On the Cain-descended Grendel-kin, see Osborn 1978a; Mellinkoff 1979. On the contrast between the dragon and the Grendel-kin, see Haarder 1975, pp. 152–6, 109–18. On dragons in general, see Brown, A. 1980.

15. See Renoir 1978a.

16. A seminal essay for viewing King Beowulf negatively is Leyerle 1965; for a summary of such negative views, see Short 1980a. For positive views, see Niles 1983, chapter 13; also Greenfield 1985. Hrothgar's "sermon" is a locus for allegorical interpretations.

17. See Tolkien 1936.

18. See Greenfield 1963a.

19. On the "beasts of battle" theme—eagle, raven, wolf—see Bonjour 1957; for other themes and motifs, see Short 1980a.

20. The historicity of this incident (521) is attested by Gregory of Tours in his *Liber Historiae Francorum;* on this and other references to Hygelac, see Chambers 1959, pp. 2–4, 381–7 and Garmonsway/Simpson 1968, pp. 112–5.

21. Cf. Niles 1983, pp. 179–96.

22. For proposed unifying themes (not the same as the theme-motifs mentioned in n. 19), see Short 1980a, pp. 8–9.

23. See Hanning 1974 and Berger/Leicester 1974.

24. See Greenfield 1976 and 1985.

25. Cf. Wright, H. 1957.

26. This connection is difficult to make in Modern English; on such difficulties of translation, see Renoir 1978b, and cf. Greenfield 1979.

27. Cf. Quirk 1963; Greenfield 1967; Dieterich 1983.

28. See Leyerle 1967; further, Nicholson 1980. Not all inconsistencies in the poem can be harmonized: Magoun 1958 and 1963 suggests that *Beowulf* is a pastiche of three separate poems; Sisam, K. 1965 sees the poem as loosely unified in the person of the hero, having "enough high qualities without the claim to structural elegance" (p. 66). Most critics, however, defend its structural unity (and elegance)—e.g., Brodeur 1970.

29. The theme of conflicting loyalties was first proposed by Ayres 1917, challenged by Fry 1974b, pp. 5–25, and reasserted by Moore 1976.

30. For a symbolic-literal reading, see Vickrey 1977.

31. The OE term *eotenas* has usually been taken as 'Jutes,' referring either to the Frisians or to a tribal band serving with the Frisians under King Finn; but Kaske 1967a argues that the term must mean 'giants,' and is a hostile eipthet for the Frisians. Tolkien/Bliss 1982 suggests that 'Jutes' were serving both Hnaef and Finn.

32. Fry 1974b summarizes interpretations of the Finn Episode. Camargo 1981 suggests further interrelationships between the Episode and its context. On Wealhtheow, see Damico 1984. For opposing views on the Ingeld Episode, see Malone 1959 and Brodeur 1959, pp. 157–81.

33. Other kinds of balance have been proposed—see Short 1980a, pp. 7–8. On the pitfalls of interpretation, see Shippey 1978. On the poet's compositional methods, see Brodeur 1959 and Bonjour 1962. Chickering 1977 weighs arguments over the poem's *gestalt* and individual cruxes. Book-length interpretations are provided by Irving 1968; Goldsmith 1970; Niles 1983.

34. Hickes 1703. Text ed. in most editions of *Beowulf* and in ASPR 6; separately by Fry 1974b. See also Hill, J. 1983.

35. See Tolkien/Bliss 1982.

36. See Greenfield 1972, pp. 45–51.

37. On stylistic and verse differences between OE *epic* and *lay*, see Campbell, A. 1962b; on differences between Episode and Fragment, see Fry 1974b, pp. 25–9.

38. On the "beasts of battle," see n. 19; *grey-coat* is the wolf.

39. For ed. and trans. of these MS survivals, see Magoun/Smyser 1950.

40. Ed. in ASPR 6; separately by Norman 1949; Schwab 1967; Zettersten 1979. See also Hill, J. 1983.

41. See Carroll 1952; Eis 1960; and editions.

42. Cf. Schwab 1979.

43. Ed. in ASPR 3; separately by Chambers 1912 and Malone 1962b. See also Hill, J. 1983. Most scholars date the poem late seventh century; but see Reynolds 1953 and Langenfelt 1959, who date it tenth century.

44. Critics usually refer to this poet-singer by the OE term *scop*; Anderson, L. 1903 uses the term to cover variously designated poet-singers. On distinctions between *scop, gleoman, leoðwyrhta,* and *woðbora,* see Hollowell 1978 and 1980; Opland 1980.

45. On legends about Ermanaric, see Brady 1943.

46. For Icelandic and Celtic analogues to this kind of figure, see Schlauch 1931.

47. See French 1945; Meindl 1964; Eliason 1966.

48. Fry 1980b; but see Creed 1975, esp. p. 384.

49. Rollman 1982.

50. Both poems are ed. in ASPR 6; *Brunanburh* separately by Campbell, A. 1938, *Maldon* separately by Scragg 1981. Thomas Hearne had printed

Maldon in prose form in 1726; his printing formed the basis of early editions, since Casley's transcript remained lost till N. R. Ker discovered it in MS Rawlinson B. 203 in the early 1930s. The transcript was formerly believed to be by John Elphinston(e)—but see Rogers 1985. Gordon, E. 1937 was the first edition to use the transcript.

51. The thirteenth-century *Egill's Saga* describes a tenth-century battle between Æthelstan and a force of Norse and Scots at *Vinheiðr*, probably to be identified with Brunanburh. This identification does not help locate the site, however; see further Page 1982.

52. See Robinson 1970, pp. 106–7 and Berkhout 1974.

53. Lawler 1973, p. 55.

54. Greenfield 1972, p. 78; see also Bolton 1968.

55. Text: Plummer 1892, vol. 1, p. 126. On the errors in this entry— among others it is marked as 993—see Scragg 1981, p. 10. Most scholars would date the poem shortly after the battle, but McKinnell 1975 and Blake 1978 argue for a date as late as 1020–3.

56. Bessinger 1962, p. 31.

57. See Irving 1961.

58. The closest literary parallel containing the idea of dying with one's lord seems to be the *Bjarkamál*—extant mainly in the twelfth-century summary of Saxo Grammaticus. It has been suggested as the source for the poet's inspiration, and thus the poem exhibits a deliberate antiquarianism rather than an ongoing live tradition—see Phillpotts 1929 and Woolf 1976.

59. Other accounts of the English defeat at Maldon, with embellishments of the marvelous, are in Byrhtferth of Ramsey's *Vita Oswaldi* (c. 1000) and in the *Liber Eliensis* (c. 1170)—see Gneuss 1976a.

60. Arguments for a positive sense are Elliott 1962 and Clark, G. 1968. Cross 1974 and Gneuss 1976b argue for a pejorative meeting. The quotation is from Tolkien 1953, p. 15.

61. For the former, see Blake 1965; for the latter, Cross 1965. Doane 1978b argues that "the mode of action is secular . . . but its end is sacramental" (p. 55).

62. Clark, G. 1968, p. 58; Stuart 1982, p. 137—cf. Swanton 1968.

63. Scragg 1981, pp. 39–40. For similar but not identical views, see Clark, G. 1979 and Robinson 1979a.

64. On formulaic introductions to the speeches in the poem, see Greenfield 1972, pp. 55–8.

65. For stylistic analysis of other parts of the passage, see Shippey 1972, pp. 108–12; see further Robinson 1976.

CHAPTER 7

The Christian Saint as Hero

For many years scholars and critics oversimplified the relation between the Germanic secular hero and the Anglo-Saxon "epic" saint. Because religious writers adopted Old English poetic diction, their Christian heroes and heroines seemed ill-fitted in the borrowed robes (or armor) of their secular counterparts, especially since their spiritual battles against evil and the forces of Satan demand, for the most part, a kind of passive resistance. On the Old English saints' lives, therefore, even sensitive critics pronounced adverse judgments, finding them poetically inferior and doctrinally naive.[1] But the Anglo-Saxon writers may have had patristic as well as scriptural precedent for their use of martial imagery in the figure of the *miles Christi*. To a great extent they self-consciously adapted *this* imagery for their purposes and subordinated that associated with the secular hero.[2] Even more important, the Old English poetic saints' lives are not just Christian themes decked out in the trappings of secular heroic poetry, but typological or figural constructs in the best tradition of medieval hagiography.[3] The individual saint's life is a pattern of Christ's. Its moral or tropological teaching leads to what Earl calls an "iconographic" or flat style, for ideologically and stylistically it eschews realism and thus needs to be interpreted in its own generic terms.[4] Each "life," however, has its own distinctive properties; and even Cynewulf's, though having stylistic traits that mark them as *his*, are "a radical exercise in perspective and . . . traditional formulas to create a singular work of poetic art."[5]

Andreas, a late ninth-century (?) poetic version of the life of St. Andrew, illustrates the complexities involved in assessing an Old English poetic saint's life. This 1722-line text, inscribed in the Vercelli Book, is based on a nonextant Latin recension of the Greek apocryphal *Acts of St. Andrew and St. Matthew*.[6] It narrates the story of Andrew's journey to Mermedonia to free his fellow apostle Matthew from the cannibalistic Anthropophagi. Andrew's sea voyage with a band of "thegns," the rescue from man-eating fiends, and other features of the story are reminiscent of Beowulf's mission to Denmark. Certain locutions, strikingly resembling some in *Beowulf*, seem awkward and even ungrammatical in their contexts in *Andreas*, suggesting direct and ill-advised "plagiarism." But Andrew's journey *is* a fact of the Greek and Latin accounts; and the nature of composition by theme and formula is such that the *Andreas* poet may simply have chosen his formulas on occasion neither wisely nor too well.[7] Even where there are more extended resemblances to Old English heroic or elegiac situations in general, one cannot assume the undiluted influence of those situations. For example, a poignant passage in which Andrew's followers refuse to be put ashore despite the rigors and terrors of their ocean voyage, *does* reflect the *comitatus* arrangement:

"Where shall we turn to, lacking our lord,
sad in heart and without sustenance,
wounded with sins if we desert you?
We shall be loathed in every land,
despised by the people when brave men
deliberate in council as to
which of them has always served his lord
best in war when on the battle-plain
hand and shield, hard pressed by hacking swords,
endured great distress in hostile strife." (ll. 405–14)

But the opening elegiac question, though characteristically Anglo-Saxon in its turn of phrase ("*Hwider hweorfað we hlafordlease . . .*")

is based upon its Latin-Greek apocryphal original and has scriptural echoes.[8] Still, the battle vocabulary hardly correlates objectively with their circumstances; and what is most noteworthy about Andrew's martial prowess in the poem is his patience in adversity. The *Andreas* poet may well be the least successful among the composers of Old English poetic lives in avoiding vocabulary directly associated with secular heroic diction: that diction, Joyce Hill comments, "inevitably arouses the wrong set of expectations with the result that, when inaction follows, . . . we experience a strong sense of incongruity." But whether *Andreas*, "for all its vigor . . . [is] naive and unsatisfactory as a Christian poem,"[9] remains debatable.

That *Andreas* is not equal to *Beowulf* as poetry is hardly surprising—little in *all* of English literature is. Nevertheless, *Andreas* is a fine poem. The poet establishes the cannibalistic scene on the island where Matthew's lot is ordained (ll. 14–39): the devilish Mermedonians eat the flesh and drink the blood of all foreigners who come to their land, first putting out their eyes ('head-gems') and giving them a potion that makes them lose their senses and graze on hay and grass. By line 160 Matthew is taken 'in the fray.' Incarcerated, blinded, compelled to behave like a dumb beast, he still bows to God's will and loves Him. God heeds his prayer for mercy, sending a sun-like 'token of glory' into his cell, healing his wounds, and promising to send Andrew to rescue him before the time his *hellfuse* 'hell-bent' foes have scheduled him for their feast.

In addition to the physical setting and motivation for the story, the poet here has introduced themes, figural images, and paradoxical contrasts that he will develop further. For one, a physical blindness through which one can still see God's light versus spiritual blindness which leads to damnation; closely connected is the theme of bondage versus freedom. A perverted Eucharistic ritual is indicated—God calls the Mermedonians *sylfætan* 'self-eaters.'[10] And in his *imitatio Christi* Andrew is given a hellish setting to harrow. The action continues with God's calling upon Andrew in Achaia to rescue Matthew. Andrew's dismayed reply is a tissue of Anglo-Saxon formulas and kennings appropriate to the themes of exile and sea-voyaging, replete with variation:

"Hu mæg ic, dryhten min,   ofer deop gelad
fore gefremman   on feorne weg
swa hrædlice,   heofona scyppend,
wuldres waldend,   swa ðu worde becwist?
Ðæt mæg engel þin   eað geferan,
halig of heofenum;   con him holma begang,
sealte sæstreamas   ond swanrade,
waroðfaruða gewinn   ond wæterbrogan,
wegas ofer widland.   Ne synt me winas cuðe,
eorlas elþeodige,   ne þær æniges wat
hæleða gehygðo,   ne me herestræta
ofer cald wæter   cuðe sindon." (ll.   190–201)

("How can I, my Lord, on a far course
over the deep water find my way
so quickly, Creator of heaven,
Master of glory, as you command?
Your holy angel from heaven can do that
more easily: he knows the ocean's realm,
the salt sea-currents where the swan rides,
the sound and terror of pounding surf,
paths in far-flung lands. No friends know me
among those aliens, nor am I familiar
with men's thoughts there, nor known to me are
the coursing ways over the cold water.")

There is excess here, but it suggests the enormity of the task Andrew sees before him. The difference from the closest Latin version is striking:

"I am ready, Lord. I pray you, do not be angry with your servant if I dare to speak a word in the ears of my Lord. How can I accomplish this in three days, when it will take me three days to get there? For, Lord, you know all things, and you know I am a man of flesh and I don't know the way. So, Lord, if it is your will, send your angel there; he can quickly cross over the sea and speedily rescue your apostle Matthew from prison."[11]

Among other differences, there is a kind of psychological realism in the Old English Andrew's added sentence, which simultaneously provides a rhetorical envelope for his speech: "How can I do it? Your angel can. There's no one there who knows me." That sentence is a retrospective rationalization for what is, of course, a denial of his Lord's command; there is no "I am ready, Lord" here. That denial, triply emphasized by the anaphoric *ne* series, is a sin more grievous (as God will later point out) than his not recognizing God as his Helmsman when he does make the ship journey. It prefigures, too, the Jews' denial of Christ's miracles and ministry, related at length by Andrew in his conversation with the Helmsman; and, in a reverse configuration, the Mermedonians finally *accept* Christ. The formulaic terms for the sea in the passage move and vary from emphasis on the "depths" to "space" to "terror," with the climax of the "cold" or threatening and fatal water.[12] This last formula, *ofer cald wæter*, is thrust back at Andrew by God: you *shall* go on this errand, *"ond on cald wæter/brecan ofer bæðweg"* (ll. 223b–4a) 'and on the cold water/churn across the sea'; it appears a third time describing Christ and his angels as sailors who drive their ship "upon the cold water" (l. 253a). Finally, in somewhat different form in l. 310a—*ofer cald cleofu*—the Helmsman tempts Andrew before giving him and his thegns passage on the ship, with words to the effect "How could you think of taking such a journey over cold cliffs without money or provisions?" Much more could be observed about the *Andreas* poet's artistry in such matters,[13] but we must return to its larger thematic, structural, and figural features.

Not until after the journey, when Andrew recognizes that Christ had been his Captain, does He explain that Andrew's mission is not only to free Matthew but also to convert the Mermedonians. In the Latin, *this* mission is given at the outset. Further, he will have to imitate Christ's passion on the Cross (ll. 950–76). Andrew now fully accepts his lot. After rescuing Matthew and the other prisoners, who disappear under a cloud cover reminiscent of that in Exodus,[14] Andrew suffers his passion for more than three days, ultimately 'fighting' and putting to flight the devil himself. Though his body has been broken, his hair torn out, and his blood spilled over the pathways, God heals all, and flowering Edenic groves spring up in the tracks of his blood. The narrative and thematic climax comes when Andrew looses the watery flood from the stone column, a "baptism" which soon converts the Mermedonians.

Andrew then resurrects the young cannibals who were drowned, though not the fourteen worst.[15]

Structurally the poem has many virtues, however much some of them inhere in the original *Acts*. For example, the first part focuses on Andrew's talk with the Helmsman, in which the saint answers the Pilot's questions about Christ's life on earth (ironically not knowing to Whom he is talking) while the rough seas counterpoint the calmness of this discourse; the second part balances the first by pitting Andrew against Satan and his cohorts, where Andrew's patience and calm under tortures counterpoint the furious raging of the Mermedonians and the devil. In the first part Andrew relates how God commanded the Temple's stone image to speak and convert the Jews, and, failing this conversion, to travel to Canaan and bring people elsewhere to see the Light; in the second part the waters of the stone column at last convert the cannibals. Earl comments on the figural nature of the story of "the living stone":

> If we see this story in its context, we see that it is the capstone of a long argument about the Jews' refusal to recognize Christ. The whole episode fits into our poem because Andrew's mission itself is a sub-fulfillment of Christ's mission to the Jews; and within the typological framework of the poem the conversion of the Mermedonians is a prefiguration of the final gathering of the Jews into the faith. The relationship of the allegory of the living stone to the conversion of the Mermedonians is strengthened by Andrew's use of the stone at the end of the poem. As Christ addresses the *stan* of the Temple wall, so Andrew addresses the *stan* of the Old Law; both stones bear witness to Christ, and as stubbornly as the Jews disbelieved the evidence before their eyes, the Mermedonians hasten to accept it.[16]

Andreas is indeed neither a naive Christian poem nor without literary merit.

Of less merit, but more carefully crafted and rich in expressive irony than critics long thought, is the short poem usually coupled with it, the *Fates of the Apostles*.[17] Though this piece follows *Andreas* in the Vercelli Book and was once believed to be part of that Christian epic, it is now considered on stylistic and other grounds a separate poem.

The *Fates*, in fact, bears the runic signature of Cynewulf; and it is to this one Anglo-Saxon poet who left his name on four poems that we now turn. This name, spelled "Cynewulf," appears near the end of *Juliana* and *Elene;* spelled without the *e*, it is woven into the conclusion of *Christ II* and the *Fates.*[18] Although other poems were long thought to be part of the Cynewulf canon, the stylistic studies of S. K. Das and Claes Schaar convincingly demonstrated that only the four "signed" poems can be so attributed.[19] The *Dream of the Rood*, *Guthlac B*, and *Christ I* bear certain stylistic resemblances to these poems, but there are also enough differences to suggest that although their authors may have been influenced by Cynewulf, they could not have *been* Cynewulf; *Christ III*, *Phoenix*, *Guthlac A*, and *Andreas*, other poems once considered Cynewulfian, seem definitely outside the canonical pale. Of the signed poems, three are martyrological in nature; the fourth, *Christ II*, is a special exposition of a devotional subject, the Ascension of Christ (see chapter 8).

But who was Cynewulf? Apart from the signatures and the four poems, we know nothing. It was once fashionable to think that the "autobiographical" lines toward the end of *Elene* might be taken as a literal confession. In these lines the poet professes to speak of himself as having led a sinful life until God through His grace had enlightened him and conferred upon him the gift of song. The conventionality of the *topoi* or motifs therein, however, tend to discount the element of personal revelation.[20] Attempts to identify the poet with Cenwulf, Abbot of Peterborough (d. 1006), Cynewulf, bishop of Lindisfarne (d. about 782), and Cynwulf, a priest of Dunwich (fl. 803), have proved inconclusive. Nevertheless, from the subject matter that he chose, from his style, from the dialect rhymes in *Elene* that underlie the Late West Saxon of the manuscripts, and from the two spellings of his runic name, certain deductions can be made. Cynewulf was undoubtedly a literate man who lived in the first half of the ninth century, a cleric, whose native dialect was Anglian (probably West Mercian). Not a great scholar, he nonetheless knew Latin well; he had knowledge of the Bible, the liturgy, and ecclesiastical literature, of doctrine and dogma: but his "attitude toward patristic exegesis and the body of Latin commentary seems more an acceptance of a perspective than a devotion to a rigid scheme. . . ."[21] His work reflects a long tradition of Latin Christian poetry fused with the vernacular formulaic verse system.[22]

Unlike the *Andreas* poet, Cynewulf was not dominated by the traditional heroic conception, though he certainly utilized it, particularly in *Elene;* nor did he have the taste for violence and the fantastic which that author had. Though he composed the famous sea-voyage metaphor at the end of *Christ II* and elaborated upon Elene's sea voyage beyond his Latin source, he was not much given to nature or scenic description such as delighted the *Andreas* and *Beowulf* poets. Whereas the *Beowulf* poet deals with narrative facts and their immediate development, Cynewulf wraps his *narratio* in abstractions; he subdues the sense of martial vigor (except in *Elene*) and emphasizes the spiritual conflict between the eternally opposed forces of good and evil. His poetic mission, like that of the apostles in *Fates* and *Christ II,* was clearly evangelical. Stylistically, he lingers through an abundance of clauses upon the impression of each separate idea, and is generally reflective in his reconsideration of concepts. He is fond of grammatical chiasmus and of sound patterns, both of which he uses to link his sequential thoughts. He has an architectonic sense of structure which, through juxtaposition and mirror-imaging of disparates, imbues his poems with sometimes subtle, sometimes heavy irony.[23]

The difference between the heroic mood of *Andreas* and the Cynewulfian reflective mode may be seen by comparing the epic-formulaic introduction of the former with that of *Fates:*

Indeed, we have heard in distant days
of twelve stalwart men beneath the stars,
thegns of the Prince. Their power and glory
did not fail in battle when banners clashed
after they went their own ways as God,
heaven's high King, himself prescribed their lots.
These were famous men throughout this earth,
bold leaders of the people and brave
in the stress of war, when shield and hand
defended helmet on battlefields,
fate-measured plains. (*Andreas,* ll. 1–11a)

Indeed, I made this song travel-sore
and sick at heart, here gathered widely
how noble ones made known their courage:
twelve they were, bright and glorious,
in deeds illustrious, dear in life
to the Lord who chose them; lauded were
the might and fame of the Prince's thegns—
no little glory gained throughout this world.
Their lots led this holy band to where
they were destined to preach the Gospel,
expound it to men. (*Fates*, ll. 1–11a)

Even in translation, the difference is obvious: the first-person opening of the latter is elegiac in tone, and the emphasis is upon the fame, praise, and glory of the twelve in abstract terms rather than as concomitants of warfare.[24] While *Andreas*, after its heroic beginning, focuses in turn upon Matthew and Andrew, *Fates* briefly enumerates how each of the twelve met his death; then the poet returns to the elegiac mood, asking for prayers for himself when he must make his long journey (i.e., die). In riddle fashion, he says that a shrewd man can discover who wrote this poem: he entwines his runic signature—in the order F, W, U, L, C, Y, N— into a general reflection of the transitoriness of life. What the word meanings of *all* the runic characters are in context has been much debated,[25] but it is clear there is a pun on the F-rune (=*feoh* 'wealth'). It "stands last," the poet says, indicating that F is the last letter of his anagrammatic name and that, while it outlasts man, wealth is ephemeral. There follows another solicitation of prayers for the poet, and a final hymn to heaven's everlasting glory and joy.

This 122-line poem has richly repaid the close scrutiny critics have given it.[26] Through his opening lines and double epilogue Cynewulf establishes an analogical relationship between the apostles and himself, between their preaching and his art, at the same time creating an ironic distance between their past heroic deaths and heavenly rewards, and his fearful lone journey. Lexical, syntactic, and sound parallels and mirror images point up this analogical conjunction and disjunction. For example, ll. 119–20a: *þær cyning engla clænum glideð/lean unhwilen* 'where the King of angels gilds the pure/with eternal reward' reflects back upon ll. 101b–2: *æfter tohweorfan/ læne lices frætewa efne swa lagu toglideð* 'afterwards will separate/the body's fleeting ornaments even as water glides away.' Calder comments:

> [T]hese ornaments and wealth that *glide* away are reversed in heaven as Christ *gilds* (the word's associations with wealth are clearly intended) the pure with eternal reward; the eternal rewards *(lean)* supplant the fleeting *(læne)* ornaments of the body. Inverted word order, repetition, and variation first create a symmetrical analogy between the two sections and then reveal the awesome contrast that exists within this symmetry; the world of man and time remains absolutely distinct from God and eternity.[27]

Even Cynewulf's breaking apart of his name in giving his runic signature may reflect his spiritual anguish. *Fates* may not be a great poem, but it is well crafted.

The apostles as saintly heroes receive no more than catalog treatment in the *Fates. Juliana* and *Elene*, on the other hand, go at length into the spiritual struggles of female saints.[28] As poetry, *Juliana* is the least impressive of the Cynewulf group, its diction being rather prosaic and repetitive, its syntax rather loose. For this reason it has been considered (by different critics) the first and the last of his four signed poems,[29] though certainty about the chronology continues to elude us.

Juliana, preserved in the Exeter Book, consists of 731 lines as it stands, but two passages are missing, between lines 288–9, and between 558–9. The poem is clearly based on a Latin prose Life, perhaps the one printed in the Bollandist *Acta Sanctorum* for February 16. Before Cynewulf's time, Juliana had made her appearance in several martyrologies, notably the one ascribed to Bede. Various redactions of her Life appear in other medieval languages, but Cynewulf's is the earliest extant vernacular version. Her "passion" follows a typical hagiographical route. In the reign of Maximianus (308–14), the young Juliana had been betrothed by her father Affricanus to Eleusius, a senator and prefect. But the girl, having been converted to Christianity and wishing to preserve her chastity as a bride of Christ, demanded that her suitor be baptized and forsake his false gods. For her temerity, her father turned her over to Eleusius, who had her scourged, hung by the hair from a tree and beaten for six hours, cast into prison, engulfed in flame, spitted on a sword wheel, and immersed in molten lead. Cheerfully and without bodily harm the saint endured all, until she received the palm of martyrdom by beheading.

Cynewulf's treatment of his material deserves respect. Though the subject may be a poor one to modern taste, the poet does a workmanlike job with it, changing, condensing, and expanding to concentrate on the great spiritual struggle that is both his theological center and poetic concern. The Latin *Vita* opens with a simple factual statement: "In the days of the Emperor Maximianus, a persecutor of the Christian religion, there was a senator in the city of Nicodemia named Eleusius. He was a friend of the emperor and was betrothed to a girl from a noble family named Juliana." Cynewulf, however, begins with a 25½-line expansion, ironically establishing the counter-themes he will oppose in the saint's person and figure: the wealth and breadth of the emperor's worldly kingdom and of his thegn's (Heliseus') dominion, idol-worship, and the persecution of Christian saints.[30] Though the last-mentioned foreshadows Juliana's specific passion, its obverse is to be her discursive "persecution" and routing of the devil who comes to tempt her. The vanity of the world will be shown by the "wealth" of conversions the saint obtains as God's power exalts her and by the deprivation of treasures in the *dryht* of hell, which Heliseus joins at his death.[31]

In terms of character, the Latin Juliana is at the beginning somewhat deceitful, demanding first that Heliseus become a prefect before she will marry him and then, when he gains the prefecture, changing her ground to demand his conversion. Cynewulf whitens her character by omitting the first request. At the same time he blackens Heliseus' portrait by transforming his somewhat tolerant attitude toward Christianity into a zeal in the service of devil-inspired idols. His zeal matches Juliana's fervid Christianity; and thus Cynewulf sets the stage for the conflict.

The struggle that ensues cannot be read realistically. For one thing, Juliana's attitude, in her initial rejection of Heliseus' marriage bid, suggests a prior knowledge of her coming torture:

"Never can you prepare so much pain
of vile torments through violent hate
that you will turn me from these words." (ll. 55–7)

Her dramatic perspective as an already canonized saint, and the narrative one of her becoming such, are thus superimposed; she may also be a figure of *ecclesia* suffering and triumphing over her worldly tormentors.[32] Her *imitatio Christi* seems specifically reflected in at least two ways: (1) the punishments her father and suitor inflict on her have their parallels in Christ's Passion; for Africanus interrogates, beats, and hands Juliana over to Heliseus for judgment, while Heliseus has her scourged again and hung on a high cross for six hours; and (2) her besting of the devil in her prison cell resembles the Harrowing of Hell.[33] There is also a suggestion that Affricanus-Heliseus-devil are ironically opposed as father, prospective son-in-law, and unholy spirit to the Holy Trinity.[34]

Cynewulf expands considerably the role of the devil who, in the guise of an angel, attempts to make the saint avoid future tortures by forsaking God. This spiritual counterpart of Heliseus is himself forced to reveal his true nature when Juliana, appealing for God's help, is told to seize him and demand what she would know. In a long recitation the devil admits the torments and persecutions he has inflicted on mankind since the beginning, tortures which parallel on a mass scale those the human antagonist inflicts on the saint. The devil's quick collapse and betrayal of *his* lord contrasts with *her* steadfast faith under much greater duress. The devil's depressed feelings and lamentations, in the fashion of an elegiac exile, also contrast with the tone and spirit of the patient and exultant Juliana. Cynewulf's expansion upon his source in the exilic fashion and in his use of a subdued but potent martial imagery (perhaps suggested by Ephesians vi. 11–17) may best be seen in lines 382–409a, crystallizing the conflict between good and evil. The Latin has the devil say at one point:

"But if one of them [those he tempts] can overcome us, and withdraws from his idle thoughts, begins to pray, to listen to Holy Scriptures and to receive the Divine Mystery, headlong we flee from him. For where

Christians receive the Divine Mystery, at that very hour we retreat from them. We care only about the ruination of men who live well. And if we see them do anything good, we afflict them with bitter thoughts so they may follow our wishes."

The Old English devil says:

"When I find some bold and battle-fierce
champion of God firm against the storm
of arrows, who will not flee far thence
from war but in wisdom raises
the holy shield, spiritual armor,
against me—who will not betray God
but strong in prayer will take his stand
firmly with the troops—then I must far thence
depart dejected, deprived of joys,
in the flames' grip to bemoan my grief:
that I could not overcome him in war
by my strength; but sadly I must seek
another, a weaker warrior
less bold where banners clash together,
whom I can tempt with my enticement,
impede in war. Though he may purpose
some good in spirit, I am straightway
ready to read his innermost thoughts,
to find how his mind is fortified,
its entrance barred; I breach the wall's gate
through iniquity: when the tower's
pierced and entry-way lies open, then
first I send by the flight of arrows
bitter, wicked thoughts into his breast,
inflaming various fleshly sparks,
so that it seems to him far better
to indulge in sins, the body's lusts,
than in the praise of God."[35]

Heliseus and his thegns drown on the "swanroad" and descend to hell, where they are ever to be deprived of beer-drinking and the receiving of treasures; in contrast, the saint's body is fittingly buried within the city by a large crowd.

The poet ends on the note of his own salvation, weaving his runic signature into a generalized reflection of man's destiny. Here, unlike in the *Fates*, he stresses requital of deeds on the Judgment

Day rather than the transience of life. And he utilizes the letters of his name uniquely in groups: the first two being CYN and EWU, the third LF. There has been considerable controversy over how those runes are meant to be read. One commentator simply does not translate them.[36] But if we take them in their context—where Cynewulf is stressing the *separation* of the "dearest of all," that "united pair" (body and soul) whose "relationship" will be "severed" at his death (ll. 697–8)—we can read each of the three runic groups as standing for Cynewulf himself, his own name torn apart through his sins, in contrast to the Trinity-in-Unity (ll. 726–7), Whose grace he craves.[37] Such a reading consorts well not only with the unholy/Holy Trinity conflict in the poem, but also with the observation that "Cynewulf clearly intends that he himself [in the epilogue] should fit midway between the poles of the cosmic scheme [saint vs. devil] he has wrought from the bare legend."[38] The structure of the epilogue reinforces this sense of a triple division: (1) ll. 695b–718a, which include the runic signature, are enveloped in a prayer to Juliana to help him in his great need: "*Is me þearf micel/þæt seo halge me helpe gefremme . . . þæt me seo halge wið þone hystan Cyning/geþingige; mec þæs þearf monaþ*' ' "I have great need that the holy one help me . . . that the holy one intercede for me with the highest King; need so moves me" '; (2) ll. 718b–29a are a prayer to every man who recites the poem to remember him by name and to pray to God to help him *in þa frecnan tid* 'in that dangerous hour'; and (3) ll. 729b–31 end the poem with a prayer to the God of Hosts Himself that *we*—all of us—may find him merciful *on þa mæran tid* 'in that glorious time.'

Juliana is Cynewulf's foray into narrating a saint's martyrdom: *Elene* is an epic celebration of an apocryphal event in Christian history. The 1321-line poem is preserved in the Vercelli Book; the ultimate source is the *Acta Cyriaci*, a version of which may be found in the *Acta Sanctorum* for May 4. Cynewulf's model was undoubtedly a Latin prose recension, the closest parallel being in St. Gall MS 225.[39] The legend combines the story of the finding of the true Cross on May 3 with that of the anti-Christian Jew Judas, who finally repents, is converted, and renamed Cyriacus. Section one describes the vision of the Cross which came to the Emperor Constantine as his small force lay encamped waiting for battle against

the Huns. This scene lent itself naturally to epic-formulaic dilata-
tion, as did the subsequent sea voyage of his mother Queen Elene
(Helen) to discover the Cross.

Cynewulf's poem proceeds through a series of revelations, outer
miracles being matched by inner illuminations. One may see, in
fact, the struggle between good and evil that preoccupied Cynewulf here presented thematically as a contrast between light and
darkness, both on a physical and a spiritual level.[40] The narrative
opens in the sixth year of Constantine's reign—the poem kalei-
doscopes the events of 306, 312, and 322 when the Franks threatened the empire, when Constantine received his vision of the Cross,
and when he achieved this martial victory. Almost immediately
we find ourselves in an epic environment. Constantine is a Germanic chieftain, and the traditional beasts of battle clamor for their
prey, the wolf and eagle following the Huns, the raven the Romans. At this literal and figurative darkest hour for the pagan emperor, he is granted the splendid vision of the Cross, dispelling
the veil of darkness with its radiance (ll. 69–98). Rejoicing, Constantine has a replica of the visionary Cross made and carried into
the fight, an engagement described in the conventional formulas
of the attack on the shield wall. The beasts of battle are closer now,
all together behind the Romans, who triumphantly pursue their
routed foes in a manner nor dissimilar to the pursuit depicted in
Brunanburh:

> The trumpets sang
> loud in the host to the raven's delight;
> the dewy-winged eagle watched the trial
> of cruel-minded warriors; the wolf wailed
> at the forest's edge: battle-fear arose.
> There shields loudly crashed and men were crushed,
> hard blow answered blow and foe felled foe
> when once arrows wound among them all.
> . . . . Then headlong fled
> the host of Huns when the Holy Tree
> was raised aloft as the Roman king,
> fighting hard, commanded. . . .
> Then that army exulted in their hearts,
> pursued the foreigners from first dawn
> till evening came: ash-made arrows flew,

battle-adders biting hard the backs
of hostile foes. Of that Hunnish force
few remained to find their homes again. (ll. 109b–43)

After Constantine's conversion to Christianity as a result of his
victory,[41] he sends his mother Elene to search out the Cross. Cynewulf's famous sea-voyage passage follows, with its many images of "sea-horses" breasting the waves—a passage that has no
counterpart in the Latin. Arriving in Jerusalem, Elene tries to as-
certain from the Jews the location of the buried Cross (ll. 276–708,
fitts [Sections] 4–8 in the MS). Her first speech, to 3,000 assembled Jews, calls attention to the darkness-light dichotomy and ini-
tiates the theme of the transference of power from the former
chosen race to the new[42]—themes which *are* present in the Latin:

"I have readily recognized
through mystic sayings of sage prophets
in God's books that you in days of yore
were precious to the Prince of Glory,
dear to the Lord and bold in your deeds.
Indeed you unwisely spurned that wisdom,
perversely, when you reviled Him who
thought to free you from fiery torment,
from damnation and needful bondage,
through His power and glory. You spat your filth
upon that face which lifted the veil
of blindness from your eyes, brought them light
anew through his noble spittle
. . . .
But blind in spirit, you thought to blend
lies with the truth, the light with darkness,
envy with honor. . . .
. . . . That bright power
you dared condemn, and dwelt in error
with dark thoughts until this very day." (ll. 288–312)

The mourning, fearful Jews select 1,000 of their most learned men
to confront the queen; this time Elene asks for information by invoking learning herself, citing David, Isaiah, and Moses. Of the
thousand, 500 are now chosen, whom the queen excoriates in a
short, pithy speech. In council by themselves, (though evidently

Elene knows what they are saying, from a remark she later makes, 664b–6), the Jews focus upon one man, Judas, who knows through his father's teaching the answer Elene wants. Pictured unhistorically, both in the Latin and the poem, as the brother of the protomartyr Stephen, he knows the truth about the Cross and Christianity but is unwilling to embrace them or to satisfy Elene's questioning lest the Hebrews' might dwindle, as his father predicted. In informing the council of Jews about the Cross, Judas contrasts the darkness of Christ in the grave for three days and His resurrection as "Light of all light." He also mentions Saul's stoning of Stephen and his subsequent conversion to St. Paul, a foreshadowing of Judas's own hardheartedness toward Elene and later conversion to Bishop Cyriacus. At the end of the council, the Jews, threatened by the queen with death by fire, offer Judas up as their knowledgeable scapegoat. Elene asks him to choose between life and death. Who, he asks, starving in the wilderness, would choose a stone rather than bread? But he will not yield to her heart's desire for knowledge of the Cross's location, and Elene has him cast in a pit, chained, to starve until he "sees the light" and repents.[43]

In lines 708 ff. Judas takes Elene's men to Calvary, where he prays for a miracle to reveal the exact spot where the Cross lies buried. Smoke arises, Judas digs, and twenty feet deep he finds three crosses. Another miracle, the raising of one from the dead at the ninth hour of the day, identifies the true Cross. All else having failed to keep the true Light in darkness, the devil dramatically appears, prophesying the martyrdom of Judas under, presumably, Julian the Apostate. But Judas bests the devil in this "flyting," promising that the devil himself will be cast down by the "brightest of beacons" into eternal damnation.[44] Of interest in the remainder of the poem is the search for and discovery of the nails from the Cross, a miracle which converts the Jews in both the Latin and the poem. Elene is advised to shape them into a bridle for her son's horse by a wise counsellor, who reintroduces the martial note of the "vision" scene when he states that thereby Constantine

> shall have luck in battle,
> victory in war and peace everywhere,

fortune in hard strife, he who shall lead
that bridled horse where battle-brave ones,
splendid warriors, bear shield and sword
amid the press of spears. (ll. 1181b–6a)[45]

With Elene's departure (there is a *finit* in the MS at the end of
fitt xiv), the poem proper ends. There follows another "autobiographical" passage, in which Cynewulf uses heavily rhymed verses
for his "personal" situation (ll. 1236–51a), to stress that God "unlocked the art of poetry" in him, an art which he has used joyfully
and willingly in this world (cf. end of the discussion of the *Ascension* in chapter 8). Then comes the passage with his runic signature:

> Until then the man had always been buffeted with surging cares, (he
> was like) a drowsing torch [C], although he had received treasures in
> the mead-hall, apple-shaped gold. The (disused) bow [Y], his compan-
> ion in need [N], mourned, suffered oppressive sorrow, an anxious se-
> cret, where formerly the horse [E] had measured for him the mile-paths,
> galloped proudly, decked with wire ornaments. Joy [W] is diminished,
> and pleasure, after the passing of years; youth is gone, the glory of
> old. Manly strength [U] was once the pleasure of youth. Now the for-
> mer days have departed after the passage of time, the joys of life gone,
> just as the flood [L] ebbs away, the rushing tides. Wealth [F] is transi-
> tory to every man beneath the heaven. (ll. 1256b–70a)

By using rune names in this fashion, Cynewulf presents "a coherent picture of the day of judgment with its inherent contrast
between man's earlier state and the elemental upheaval of
doomsday itself, while at the same time weaving into the narrative the runes that spell his name, so that prayers might be offered for his salvation."[46] The appropriateness of this runic passage to the poem as a whole is particularly noteworthy: the heroic
imagery of the mead hall and the battle horse recall the Constantine episode, the "flood" hints at the sea voyage of Elene, and the
suggestion of the Judgment Day reflects various references to
eternal punishments made by speakers throughout. This relevance has prompted many critics to find a threefold structure in
the poem, with three conversions (Constantine, Judas, Cynewulf)
related in three narrative modes (historical, dramatic, confessional).[47]

The achronological conversion of the Jews at the discovery of the nails prepares for the intense focus on the Judgment Day at the poem's end, for that conversion was a standard sign of the approach of the Apocalypse. The poem fittingly concludes with a threefold division of the adjudged souls into the faithful, the sinful, and the accursed transgressors: the third group will be cast down from the fierce fire into the depths of hell, while the first two groups, in the upper and middle reaches of the purgatorial flame, will be cleansed and come into everlasting bliss.

The struggle between good and evil that we have seen in the three Cynewulf poems, the *Fates*, *Juliana*, and *Elene*, is presented at a more elemental and unsophisticated level in *Guthlac A*, the first of two consecutive poems in the Exeter Book on the native English saint (c. 674–714).[48] Here the narrative focuses on the conflict between devils and the hero, the latter abetted by angels and finally by the apostle Bartholomew. The body of the poem concerns itself with the attempts of the devils in the (Crowland) wastes to regain their unblissful seats, the *beorgseþel*, of which Guthlac has deprived them in his eremitic zeal. They make a number of threats, but the poet focuses on two: (1) a temptation to vainglory, in which the devils show Guthlac the corruption of youth in the monasteries (ll. 412 ff.), and (2) a threat of torture and damnation, when they carry him to hell's gates (ll. 557 ff.).[49] The saint resists the first by observing, in effect, that even in monasteries youth will be served, and is not necessarily unsalvageable. Guthlac himself, when young, had followed worldly pursuits and pleasures. He counters the second by placing his trust in God, reminding the devils of their own rebellion and falseness, and declaring their permanent damnation. God's messenger, St. Bartholomew, then orders the devils to return the saint unharmed to his *beorg*, and in something of an idyllic, and probably symbolic, passage (ll. 733b ff.), Guthlac is welcomed "home" by the birds and beasts of the forest wasteland. The Life then comes to an end quickly, describing how angels led Guthlac's soul into the eternal joys of heaven.

Guthlac A receives scant notice in most surveys of Old English poetry,[50] but despite its lack of poetic charm and repetitiveness, it does have a unity and coherence.[51] Set in an aging world, when God's laws are fading (ll. 37–47; 54–8), it presents an aging hero[52] who demonstrates by his words and deeds what we may call "Holy Living." From beginning to end the poem emphasizes the virtuous individual vs. the sinful crowd, earthly transient joys vs. heavenly permanent ones, ineffectual words vs. significant words *and* deeds. In addition, angelology-demonology plays a role, with the struggle of a good and bad angel over Guthlac's earthly conduct (the latter finally routed by God's command) foreshadowing the major conflict and resolution.[53] Most important is the centrality of the *beorg*: the word can mean 'hill, mountain' or 'barrow, tumulus'; and its meaning in *Guthlac A* has been much disputed.[54] Perhaps the poet used it in both senses, to signify the burial of the old (the physical) and the growth of the new (the spiritual). Burial mounds are, after all, hills, and they become in time overgrown with vegetation. Not only is the *beorg* the geographic center of conflict between the saint and the devils, but in the course of the poem it also comes to symbolize the life of the good Christian.[55] Further, as it appears progressively more desirable, less fearful and treacherous as the *bytla* (ll. 148; 783) or 'builder' conquers threats and temptations, the dedicated and burgeoning *beorg* prefigures the New Jerusalem, to which all blissful souls will turn after their going hence (ll. 811–end). This ending is foreshadowed in the Prologue, where we are shown an angel greeting a departed good soul and assuring it of a safe journey to the Heavenly City.

According to the testimony of the poem itself, *Guthlac A* was composed within the living memory of the English saint, who died in 714–5. The question of its source in oral tradition or a written Life focuses upon its relation to Felix of Crowland's prose *Vita*, c. 730–40 (see chapters 1 and 3). The relationship is much disputed; most modern scholars feel there is none.[56] But the 561-line *Guthlac B* definitely depends upon the *Vita*, mainly its fiftieth chapter.[57] This second Guthlac poem is quite different from its predecessor, emphasizing time rather than place, "Holy Dying" rather than "Holy Living," the Fall and Redemption rather than saintly apotheosis.[58] The poem begins with a long prologue recounting death's entrance into the world through Adam and Eve's

transgressions: "never since," says the poet, "could any man escape the bitter drink that Eve gave Adam" (ll. 868–9).[59] The narrative then focuses on Guthlac, passing quickly over his life and
reputation, his succor to beasts and people, to concentrate on his
fatal illness and dying. Holy as his life has been, he must bow to
the decree our progenitors brought about by their deeds (ll. 967–
75). The *poculum mortis* 'cup of death, bitter drink' image is repeated and developed in ll. 980–91a, fusing the individual saint's
fate with that of Adam and Eve. The figure then modulates into
that of death's door opening, then into Death as a *wiga wælgifre*
'slaughter-greedy warrior' and an *enge anhoga* 'a cruel solitary' who
rushes upon Guthlac *gifrum grapum* 'with greedy grasps,' somewhat as Grendel attacks his victims.[60]

The central sections of the poem are mainly a dialogue between
the dying saint and his servant (unnamed in the poem, Beccel in
the *Vita*). Guthlac, though sorely afflicted by his illness, comforts
his sorrowing attendant-thegn: Be not sad-hearted; I am going to
my heavenly reward because I have done well on earth. At this
point the poet emphasizes that the time is Easter, when Christ rose
from death and harrowed hell. Simultaneously, Guthlac rises from
his bed of pain and preaches the Lord's mysteries to his servant
so wondrously that the words seem an angel's rather than a mortal's: the saint is thus identified with the risen Christ.

Once again the poet reverts to the figure of Death as the ravaging warrior, both shooting arrows at his victim and unlocking
the "treasure-hoard of life with treacherous keys." Guthlac's servant, a sorrowing exile figure, beseeches his master to speak.
Guthlac reminds him of his compact with him, and orders him to
tell his sister (named Pega in the *Vita*) of his death, and request
her to bury his body. The servant then questions Guthlac about
the mysterious visitor the saint has had these many years, about
whom he had been told nothing; and Guthlac reveals that he has
had a guardian angel. Once more the saint sinks back, exhausted
from his great struggle with death. In anticipation of his soul's
translation, a great light shines over men's dwellings. Death's last
effort is to "sting" Guthlac with "death-darts" *wælstrælum* (l. 1286a);
but Death's "victory" is, of course, paradoxically Guthlac's who,
refreshed with the Eucharist, opens the "gems of his head" one

last time and sends forth his spirit "beautified by its deeds into the joy of glory" (l. 1304). The transfiguration is accompanied by light, melody, and sweet fragrances (ll. 1308–24).[61]

The poem does not end on this note, however. As with Christ's death (cf. *The Dream of the Rood*), the earth itself shudders; and Guthlac's disciple, sorrowing, flees to a ship to seek the saint's sister with his late-lamented master's message. Like other Old English poetic exiles (see chapter 12), he uses traditional gnomes:

> "Courage is best for him who confronts
> too often his lord's demise, laments
> that separation decreed by time
> and fate: well he knows who must feel it,
> sorrowing in soul; he knows earth holds
> his kind gold-lord, and he must grieving
> thence depart depressed." (ll. 1348–54a)

Perhaps, as Olsen suggests, this ending—though we cannot be sure it *is* the ending, since a gathering has been lost in the manu- script—indicates a cyclic pattern in man's life, with Beccel repre- senting, in his yet unredeemed state of sorrow and lack of under- standing, the need for every man who wishes salvation to reenact not only the Fall but the Redemption.[62]

Guthlac A and *B* are different not only in sources, content, sym- bolic modes, and structures, but in diction, metrical, and syntactic patterns.[63] Nevertheless, the Exeter Book scribe evidently felt they complemented each other, even as the *Christ* poems make some- thing of a "fit."[64] In them, too, we shall find a mixture of the he- roic vernacular and Christian traditions, but a greater orientation toward contemplation in the treatments of their subjects.

NOTES

1. E.g., "It is best . . . to enjoy *Andreas* as a good story, without too much solemnity of judgment either from the religious or literary point of view"—Woolf 1966, p. 53.

2. See Hill, J. 1981. Some argue that poetic context often indicates that the heroic formulas had lost their original referential and connotative force—see Cherniss 1972 and Schneider, C. 1978.

3. See Hill, T. 1969 and notes throughout this chapter.

4. Earl 1975; see also Bridges 1984 and Bjork 1985, who treat the problem of genre at length.

5. Calder 1981, p. 144. Cf. Anderson, E. 1983, pp. 176–8.

6. Ed. in ASPR 2; separately by Brooks, K. 1961. There are two OE prose versions of the *Life*, one in the *Blickling Homilies*, one in MS CCCC 198— see chapter 3.

7. On similar locutions, see Brooks, K. 1961, pp. xxiv–xxv. Shippey 1972, pp. 92–6 argues that the resemblances are the product of a general formularity in OE verse; Stanley 1966a, pp. 110–4 finds that *Andreas* borrowed directly but clumsily from *Beowulf*. Brodeur 1968, pp. 98–105 sees *Andreas* influenced by *Beowulf* but stylistically fine in its own ways; cf. Hamilton 1975. The uncertainty about the extant *Beowulf*'s date of composition (see chapter 6, n. 6) complicates the issue of "borrowing" or "influence"; of course an even earlier version of *Beowulf* may have existed.

8. See Walsh 1981.

9. Hill, J. 1981, pp. 72–3; cf. Cherniss 1972, pp. 171–93. Irving 1983 finds the heroic in *Andreas* not at all incongruous.

10. Earl 1980, p. 79; see further Boenig 1980. On "diet" imagery as a sign of spiritual hunger, see Hamilton 1972. On figural narrative in *Andreas*, see Hill, T. 1969. On the Harrowing of Hell typology in the poem, see Hieatt 1976.

11. This and translations of other Latin sources and analogues throughout the volume are taken from Calder/Allen 1976.

12. See Brooks, K. 1961, Glossary, on this meaning of *cald*.

13. See Irving 1983.

14. For explanation of this sudden disappearance, see Earl 1980, pp. 88–9.

15. On *Andreas*'s use of such themes as conversion and baptism, see Walsh 1977 and 1981.

16. Earl 1980, p. 85.

17. For editions, see n. 6.

18. Though there was great scholarly interest in A-S studies from the sixteenth century on, ironically enough Cynewulf's runic "identity" was not discovered until the poems and poetic manuscripts began to be edited in the 1840s. Because of damage to the Vercelli MS, the runic signature in the *Fates* was not found until 1888. See Calder 1981, pp. 12–5.

19. Das 1942; Schaar 1949.

20. See Anderson, E. 1983, pp. 17–9.

21. Calder 1981, p. 26.

22. The seminal essay for modern studies of Cynewulf is Sisam, K. 1932. On dating, dialect, and other textual matters, see Gradon 1958, pp. 9–15, 21–3. For some differences of opinion on these matters, see Storms 1956; Rogers 1971.

23. See Das 1942, chapter 2; Schaar 1949, pp. 323–6; Calder 1981; Anderson, E. 1983. The last two provide analyses of the whole Cynewulf canon; Anderson contains an extensive bibliogrpahy, including dissertations.

24. For analysis of the opening passages of *Andreas, Elene, Guthlac A* and *B*, see Bridges 1979.

25. See Elliott 1953b and Page 1973, pp. 105–7.

26. See Boren 1969; Hieatt 1974; Frese 1975; Howlett 1975; Rice 1977; Calder 1981, pp. 29–41, 144–8; Anderson, E. 1983, pp. 68–83.

27. Calder 1981, p. 39.

28. On women in OE literature, see Hansen 1976; Nitzsche 1981. Fell 1984 uses the literature, among other evidence, to provide an account of women's roles in A-S England.

29. See respectively Elliott 1953b and Woolf 1955a. Ed. in ASPR 3; separately by Strunk 1904, which contains the Latin *Vita*, and by Woolf 1955a.

30. See further Calder 1981, pp. 82–4.

31. See Lee, A. A. 1972, pp. 99–103.

32. See Wittig 1975 and Calder 1981, pp. 79, 86.

33. Wittig 1975, pp. 42–7.

34. Anderson, E. 1983, pp. 94–7.

35. Schneider, C. 1978 feels that in *Juliana* Cynewulf associates traditional heroic vocabulary (as in this passage) with the devil and evil men, whereas the diction he applies to the saint is quite unheroic; cf. Cherniss 1972, pp. 194–207. Anderson, E. 1983, pp. 90–2, finds this dichotomy too simplistic.

36. Page 1973, pp. 210–2.

37. Sisam, K. 1953, pp. 21–2 makes this suggestion, but without relating the separation of the name to its context.

38. Calder 1981, p. 102; see also Frese 1975, pp. 315–9.

39. The poem is ed. in ASPR 2 and Cook 1919; separately by Gradon 1958.

40. Cf. Stepsis/Rand 1969.

41. On Constantine's figurative role and unifying presence, see Whatley 1981.

42. On the *translatio imperii,* see Anderson, E. 1983, pp. 121–6.

43. Hill, T. 1971 sees Elene as a figure of the Church Militant and Judas as Synagogue, their "contest" being one between the Old Law and the New, between the letter and the spirit. Anderson, E. 1983, pp. 160–75 sees Cynewulf's theology embracing first penitence, then desire for God. On the "bread and stone" imagery, see Whatley 1975 and Hill, T. 1980a.

44. On the "devil's rights" theory, see Anderson, E. 1983, pp. 134–45.

45. Anderson, E. 1983, pp. 103–25 finds a dichotomous symmetrical structure in the fitt divisions; others see a tripartite structure—see below.

46. Elliott 1953a, p. 56; the translation of this difficult passage is El-

liott's. Cf. Page 1973, pp. 207–8. Cynewulf does not explicitly ask others to pray for him here, in contrast to his requests in the epilogues to *Fates* and *Juliana*.

47. See Campbell, J. 1972 and Fish 1975.

48. Ed. in ASPR 3; separately (with *Guthlac B*) by Roberts 1979. *A* contains 818 lines, though a folio of about 70 lines is missing between ll. 368–9. Earlier scholars considered the Prologue, ll. 1–29, to be the end of *Christ III* (see chapter 8); but see Roberts 1979, pp. 30–1; Calder 1975, pp. 66–9; Shook 1961.

49. Cf. Hill, T. 1979. If there is a third temptation in ll. 266 ff., where the devils ask Guthlac how he expects to live in the wasteland, hungry and thirsty, there might be a pattern of Christ's temptations in the wilderness.

50. Pearsall 1977, pp. 43–44 dismisses it in two sentences.

51. For an extended analysis, see Olsen 1981.

52. See Hill, T. 1981.

53. The poem is not quite a *psychomachia*, though the devils seem to be something of a projection of Guthlac's doubts and fears; see Calder 1975.

54. Olsen 1981, pp. 34–5 provides a brief summary of the controversy.

55. See Shook 1960 and Wentersdorf 1978; for a different reading, see Reichardt 1974.

56. Roberts 1979, pp. 19–29 thoroughly discusses the problem. *Vita*: ed. and trans. by Colgrave 1956.

57. On source relationships, see Roberts 1979, pp. 36–43. Chapter 50 of the *Vita* is trans. in Calder/Allen 1976.

58. See Calder 1975 and Olsen 1981.

59. All editions number the lines of the two Guthlac poems consecutively, despite recognition that they are by different authors and from different time periods; but see n. 64.

60. See Rosier 1970a.

61. See Calder 1972b.

62. See Olsen 1981, pp. 69–109, who sees *Guthlac B* as doctrinally based on the Orosian view of history. On Orosius, see chapter 2.

63. On these differences, see Roberts 1979, pp. 48–63 and 1971; Calder 1975.

64. Olsen 1981, pp. 111–39 argues that for the Exeter Book scribe and his audience there were *three* poems: *Guthlac A, B,* and a composite *Guthlac,* the last presenting in its overall configuration "a balance of opposing but related themes: saintly apotheosis and human grief, the other-worldly view of human history and the human view, and joy and sorrow" (p. 133).

CHAPTER 8

Christ as Poetic Hero

Christ as hero—in various aspects, from His co-eternality with God the Father, through His descent as Savior, to His Second Coming as Judge of mankind—makes several appearances in Old English poetry. Three of these are in the rather different poems which open the Exeter Book, depicting His Advent, Ascension, and Second Coming. Though Cook considered these poems a unified triptych *(Christ)* by Cynewulf, whose runic signature comes near the end of the *Ascension (Christ II)*,[1] modern scholars separate them on stylistic grounds.[2] Paleographic evidence likewise points in this direction;[3] but a few critics have invoked iconographic or liturgical rationales for an "intentional" yoking of the poems, even if they are by different authors.[4] Still, they are best considered and treated individually.

The *Advent (Christ I)* consists of twelve lyrics ranging from 21 to 73 lines in length (the first, beheaded in manuscript transmission, has only 17 lines), for a total of 439 lines.[5] Whether other lyrics preceded the first is open to question. The antiphons chanted in the office during the Advent season, specifically between December 17 and 23, provide sources for all but the eleventh lyric. Originally there were but seven antiphons, called the "Great O's" because they begin with the apostrophic *O* (OE *Eala*): of these the poet used four in his lyrical thematic variations (Lyrics I, II, V, and VI). Early in the Middle Ages other antiphons were modelled on the Great *O's*: and the *Advent* poet based his Lyrics III, IV, VII, VIII, IX, X, and XII on these Additional or Monastic *O's*.[6]

The Great *O's* consist of an invocation to Christ: Wisdom, Lord, Root of Jesse, Key of David, Sun, King of nations, Emmanuel; and of a petition: come to teach us, redeem us, deliver us, etc. The Additional *O's* may or may not be addressed to Christ: those which are not, replace the petition with some doctrinal statement or paradox. For example, the antiphonal source of Lyric IX, addressed to Mary, reads "O Lady of the world, born from a kingly seed, Christ has now come forth from your womb like the groom from the bridal chamber; He lies in a manger who also rules the stars." The *Advent* poet's use of such antiphonal material is masterful. Though some have questioned the structural unity of the twelve lyrics, suggesting that only a loose association through sources and subject binds them together, a number of features seem to indicate the poet's sense of a tight cohesion.[7] He has, indeed, woven a finely textured tapestry of religious concepts and images, rich in figures and diction; or, to change the analogy, he has composed a poetic equivalent of Bach's B-Minor Mass.

Despite its decapitation, the first lyric is clearly based on *O Rex gentium et desideratus earum, lapisque angularis qui facis utraque unum: veni, et salva hominem quem de limo formasti* 'O King of the Nations and the One they long for and the cornerstone; you who make both things one, come and save man whom you fashioned out of clay'. The poet chose to develop the *lapis angularis* image, conflating it with that of Ps. 117:22: "the stone which the builders rejected has become the head of the corner." He further introduced patristic overtones from St. Paul's interpretation of that psalm in Ephesians 2:20–22. Under his pen the rejected stone brings together the walls (Gentiles and Jews?) and becomes the head of a great hall (the founding of the universal Church):[8]

> . . . to the King.
> You are the wall-stone the workers once
> rejected from the work. Well it suits
> you now to be head of that great hall

5 and draw together the wide walls,
  flint unbreakable, in firm embrace,
  so throughout earth's cities all who see
  may marvel endlessly. Lord of glory,
  true and bright with victory, reveal
10 now your skill mysterious, making
  wall straight join with wall. Now that work needs
  the Craftsman and the King Himself to come
  and then repair what now is ruined:
  house under high roof. He shaped the whole body,
15 limbs from clay; now must the Lord of life
  free from the wrathful that wretched band,
  helpless ones from fear, as He often has.

The intricacies of this lyric, even apart from its concatenation of images and ideas with the rest of the poem, are such that one "may marvel endlessly." The poet refrains from explaining the wall-stone, the walls, the head of the great hall, the house in disrepair; but the typological significance of the Church as the spiritual body of Christ, and of humanity's sinful condition, emerge from the architectural images even if we are unaware of Pauline or other patristic interpretations which point to those meanings. Line 13, *ond þonne gebete nu gebrosnad is,* suggests not only making physical repair, but also making amends or atonement, and thus perhaps alludes to the Crucifixion; *gebrosnad* 'ruined' has overtones of "decay," portending the end of the individual sinner's body. That *hra* 'body' is also the *hus under hrofe* 'house under roof'—alliteratively linked across the caesura and syntactic break of l. 14. Burlin remarks:

> The individual body of man is not to be dissociated from the figure of the Church. . . . [T]he central image of building and reconstruction applies equally to each, for the ultimate significance of one is inseparable from that of the other. The reduplication of figural referents is an illusion which the typological imagination dispels, for it, like the Redeemer, 'facit utraque unum.'[9]

In Lyric I, the poet uses time as he does throughout the *Advent,* alternating between biblical past, historic present, and eternal present. The last verse, "as He often has," indicates that Christ repeatedly saves mankind in a perpetual advent. The reference to

Christ as Craftsman and King briefly suggests the co-eternity of
the Son with the Father, a theme more fully developed later.[10] The
epithet "Lord of life" is reserved for the climax of the lyric, alliterating with His creation, the "limbs from clay." The directness
of the Latin antiphon's petition, *veni et salva*, is only obliquely expressed in ll. 11–12 and 15–16: "Now that work needs . . . to
come" and "now must the Lord of life free. . . ." Not till Lyric
VI, at the poem's center, does the *veni* of the antiphon become a
direct *cum* (l. 149) in the mouths of the patriarchs waiting in hell.

Such detailed, yet still not exhaustive, analysis of all the *Advent*
lyrics cannot be attempted here, but we may glance briefly at a
few. The second is based on *O Clavis David:* "O Key of David and
Scepter of the house of Israel; you who open and no one closes;
you who close and no one opens; come and lead out the prisoner
from the prison-house, where he sits in darkness and the shadow
of death." It begins:

> O you Ruler and you rightful King,
> He who guards the locks and opens life,
> heaven's path, to the blessed, but bars him
> whose work fails from that fair desired way.[11]

Moving from the key image to that of the prison, the poet elaborates thereon, weaving together the concepts of life, lord, and light
with the idea of unlocking. The first half of the lyric ends with an
historical reference to the expulsion from Eden: "make us worthy
whom he admitted to the heavenly glory/when we abjectly had to
turn/to this narrow land, deprived of our homeland" (ll. 30–2).
The *eðel* 'homeland' of which the sinner speaks is both the earthly
Eden and the heavenly heritage we lost through Adam and Eve's
sin, and the promise of "admission" alludes to God's statement
in Genesis 3:15 that Eve's seed shall bruise the serpent's head, a
typological foreshadowing of the Redemption. This reference in
turn leads into a poetic exaltation of the virgin birth as the means
by which the promised Redemption was fulfilled and by which
the light of knowledge, through the sprouting of spiritual seeds/
gifts, opened the prison of spiritual ignorance (ll. 33–49).

After a 21-line invocation to the heavenly and earthly Jerusalem in Lyric III, Lyric IV presents a dialogue between Mary and the citizens of Salem; the latter ask Mary to explain how she was able to conceive and remain a virgin. Mary replies that this paradox must remain a mystery, but that by it, Eve's sin has been absolved. Lyric VII, the *Passus*, is another dialogue, based on the conventional "Doubting of Mary" motif. It has attracted much critical attention, partly for its pseudo-psychological realism and partly for the difficulty of fixing its speech boundaries.[12] One reasonable definition of these boundaries takes the first lines (164–74a), beginning *"Eala Joseph min,"* as a speech of Mary's. In it she expresses her grief that Joseph will reject her love, concluding "God can easily/heal the grievous sorrow of my heart,/comfort the disconsolate." Joseph's reply begins *"Eala fæmne geong,/mægð Maria"*; he says he has found no fault with her even though troubled by her "virgin" pregnancy. He is a prideful man, torn and hurt, and in a dilemma as to whether he should deliver Mary, whom he loves, to death by stoning, or conceal the crime, living himself as a perjurer (ll. 174b–94a). Mary's final speech, made in her full knowledge of the *ryhtgeryno* 'rightful mystery,' reveals that mystery to Joseph; Joseph, she says, will be acknowledged His father in the worldly way, while prophecy is simultaneously fulfilled. Despite the vast differences between this "human" Lyric and the "architectural" Lyric I, one can see a patterned repetition: rejection of a "cornerstone," the rejected reuniting the "walls" (Gentiles-Jews/Old Law-New Law), and the "mysterious skill"/"rightful mystery" which "repairs" and brings salvation.

Mary makes her final *Advent* appearance in Lyric IX, which is based on *O mundi Domina*. Here she is no longer the earthly lady but the Queen of Heaven, the Bride of Christ. Linked to Ezekiel's (Isaiah's, in the poem) vision of the "closed gate," she is also the *wealldor* (l. 328) through which Christ journeyed out to this earth. At the same time Mary is paradoxically most humanized, for "Now we beam at the Child upon your breast," the petitioners exclaim (l. 341), in the poem's only such mother–child image. Lyric X then moves far back "chronologically," invoking Christ as coeternal splendor with the Father before even the angels were created, and apostrophizing the third member of the Holy Trinity. We recognize our outcast state and oppression by accursed hellish spirits

as the result *sylfra gewill* 'of our own will' (l. 362b). In a final petition, mankind asks the King of men that He *Cym nu* (l. 372b),
endow us with the gift of salvation, so that henceforth we may
forever fulfill *þinne willan* 'Your will' (l. 377b). Lyric XI tells us "to
join the angelic chorus of praise." Lyric XII is a 24-line coda—a
quiet recapitulation of the poem's central themes, ending with the
"excellent counsel" for every man to praise God in deeds and
words, so that God will bestow His gift of everlasting life and joy.

Some of the binding forces among the twelve lyrics are revealed
in the above summary. Mary's "progress" is one such force. Various architectural and light/darkness figures weave in and out, as
do such motifs as the coexistence of Father and Son, man's inability to understand God's mysteries, man's misery and need of
grace, the doctrine of the Trinity, and the call to praise God. In
addition, the recurrence of exile images creates a narrative sub-
structure, taking us chronologically from the expulsion from Eden
(Lyric II) down through the poet's own time of man's spiritual exile and need for grace (Lyric X), a grace which will bring us to that
unknown *eðel*, the Heavenly Eden (l. 436).[13] The *Advent* clearly
shows a beautiful confluence of Christian doctrine and configuration with Old English poetic techniques. But its mode and manner are quite different from the equally powerful poem that follows it in the Exeter Book.

The *Ascension (Christ II)*, ll. 440–866 of *Christ*,[14] is by Cynewulf, as
the runic signature in ll. 797–807b indicates; and it bears the unmistakable stamp of this poet's ruminative or reflective style. The
poem's major source is the last three sections (9–11) of Gregory
the Great's 29th homily on the Gospels, but it also incorporates
material from Bede's Ascension Hymn, portions of Scripture
(mainly Psalm 23, Matthew 28:16–20, Luke 24:36–53, and Acts 1:1–
14), some patristic texts, and iconographic representations.[15] Cynewulf's poetic vision focuses on God's gifts to men, not only
through His Ascension, but also through the Incarnation and other
"leaps" (see below). These gifts assure God's continuing presence
among mankind, and His guidance and protection for those who
use these talents well in accord with His distribution of them. Man
has an obligation to so use them for his "soul's need," since deeds

performed while he lives will be judged severely when He comes again.[16]

What prompts Cynewulf's poetic meditation is the question Gregory asks in his homily as to why the angels appeared in white at the Ascension, but not so dressed at the Nativity. Cynewulf exhorts an "illustrious man" to seek "through his mind's wisdom" to know why this was so. Where Gregory proceeds directly to answer his question in abstract terms of the humbling of Divinity on the latter occasion and the exaltation of humanity on the former, the poet sets the problem aside for the moment and presents the scene of the Ascension, with Christ as *sincgiefa* 'treasure-giver' (l. 460a) summoning his *þegna gedryht* 'band of thegns,' (l. 457b)[17] to Bethany; there, in direct discourse, He tells them to go out among the heathen and preach the saving word. Then, amidst a troop of radiant angels, He rises through the temple's roof while the disciples remain behind lamenting His departure. They are admonished by two of the angels not to stand there in a circle: they can clearly see the true Lord ascending into the heavens; but He will return, the angels warn, with a great army to judge all men's deeds (through l. 526). After contrasting the sorrowing apostles, who return to the earthly Jerusalem, with the joy of the angels at Christ's return to the heavenly city, Cynewulf finally comes back to part of the opening conundrum: writings say, and that is well said, that angels came in white, radiant, brightly clothed at the Ascension as befitted that blissful occasion when the *folca feorhgiefa* 'the people's life-giver' (l. 556a) came to His high seat. Not till near the end, however, does Cynewulf, again with a reference to books, suggest the other half of Gregory's answer: how at first *eaðmod* 'humbly' the *mægna goldhord* 'Treasury of virtues' descended into a virgin's womb. Cynewulf exploits the meaning of the verb, *astigan*, meaning both 'ascend' and 'descend,' to equate Christ's Advent and Ascension.[18] But other doctrinal material and meditational flights come between these "answers" to the initial question.

A leaf is missing from the manuscript in the middle of l. 556,[19] and the text continues with an angelic herald's account of the Harrowing of Hell as Christ waits for heaven's gates to open (ll. 556b–85). *That* ascent is followed by a reference to Christ's *hider-*

cyme 'hither-coming' (descent into the Incarnation) as the means by which He *hals eft forgeaf* 'gave in turn salvation' to mankind, so that man now has the freedom to choose his path. Indeed, he *must* choose

> hell's infamy or heaven's glory,
> the brightest light or the baleful night,
> majestic fullness or murky dullness,
> joys with the Father or noise with fiends,
> grief with devils or glory with angels,
> life or death as his free will elects
> while flesh and spirit in fast embrace
> dwell in the world. (ll. 591–8a)[20]

After further manifestations of the ascent-descent motif, Cynewulf elaborates on God's gifts to men, going far beyond the spiritual endowments Gregory mentions in his homily. Again we have a rhetorically amplified passage, this time with two five-part anaphoric *sum*-series, one on the spiritual or intellectual gifts, the other on physical endowments:

> To one He sends wise eloquence,
> memory and a mouth to utter
> noble understanding: he can sing
> and tell all things well with such wisdom
> in his heart. One can play the harp
> skillfully, loudly strike the strings
> before a gathering. One can grasp
> the divine law. One can learn the stars'
> course, the wide creation. One can write
> speeches gracefully. To one He gives
> success in war, when archers send
> showers of darts over the shield wall,
> flying arrows. One can fearlessly
> drive his ship over the salty sea,
> stir up the foam. One can climb the steep,
> high tree. One can make a tempered sword,
> a weapon. One knows the wide-open plains,
> far-reaching paths. (ll. 664–81a)[21]

The passage ends with the comment that God will not give all gifts of the spirit to any one person lest he become presumptuous.

Continuing his meditation on Gregory's homily, Cynewulf expounds on the sun and the moon, the former symbolizing the Lord, the latter the Church which, strengthened by His Ascension, has been able to endure oppression in this world. Then follows the characterization of Christ's ministry as six symbolic "leaps," based on Solomon's statement: "Behold, He comes leaping upon the mountains and springing across the hills" (Canticles 2:8). Gregory mentions only five "leaps": the Incarnation, the Nativity, the Crucifixion, the Deposition and Burial, and the Ascension; Cynewulf adds, between the last two, the Harrowing of Hell.[22] The *Ascension* suggests that we have no need to be sorrowing as the disciples did on the occasion of the sixth leap, for God's gifts now include not only the physical ones of this transient life but also the spiritual salvation of those who had been bound in Hell and our own redemption, if we have the wisdom to meditate and understand. The "illustrious man" addressed at the beginning of the poem thus becomes in effect "each of [my] beloved ones" whom the poet exhorts in ll. 814 ff. to think of his soul's welfare.

In the midst of his concluding peroration, Cynewulf, as he does most particularly in *Elene*, turns to the Judgment Day motif, with his runic signature emphasizing God's righteous punishment of sinners and the transitoriness of the time-and-tide bound wealth of this world.[23] The poem concludes with the great sea-voyage metaphor, a spiritual enlargement upon the stock poetic metaphor, only hinted at in Gregory's "Although your soul may have floated hither and thither with the confusion of things so far, now fasten the anchor of your hope in the eternal homeland":

Now it is as if we sail with the tide,
across the cold water of the wide sea
in our ships, our sea-steeds, urging on
prowed vessels. Perilous the current,
tempestuous the waves we toss on
here in this frail world, windy the seas
upon the deep. Difficult that course
before we had sailed safely to land
over the rough sea-ridge. Help arrived
when God's Spirit-Son piloted us
to salvation's port and gave us grace
to perceive where, over the ship's side,

we can surely secure our sea-steeds,
our old ocean-stallions, fast at anchor. (ll. 850–63)

We may note l. 860b: *ond us giefe sealde,* a formula used earlier in
l. 660b in connection with the most elaborate statement of the "gifts
of men" theme. Though God has given us many gifts, from the
natural ones of food and dew and rain, of the sun and the moon
(ll. 604–11a), to the individual spiritual and physical ones described in ll. 664–81a, his greatest gift is this last, to be able to
recognize where the true port of salvation lies. And we may also
note that the very last verse of the poem (l. 866b): *þa he heofonum
astag,* usually translated "when He ascended to heaven," is highly
ambiguous (cf. l. 737b: *þa he to heofonum astag,* where the *to* clearly
signals the Ascension); the last verse could as well be interpreted
as "when He *from* heaven descended," that is, into the Incarnation. Since the poem's Ascent-Descent motif has dwelt on both
Christ's *hidercyme* and going hence as giving us the means to salvation, it is not unreasonable to see the double reference here.[24]

The *Ascension's* style is quite different from that of the *Advent.*
Anderson makes a nice distinction between the two:

> "Illumination" is supported in the Advent Lyrics by the use of seman-
> tic depth and dense texture as characteristics of diction, and by the use
> of interweaving rhetorical patterns such as chiasmus, sometimes com-
> bined with wordplay. In contrast with the Advent Lyrics, the straight-
> forward exposition of events and ideas in *Ascension* is supported by a
> "reflective" style, characterized by thematic repetition and confirma-
> tion of ideas, by sequentializing rhetorical patterns such as anaphora
> and parallelism, by higher frequency of phonological repetition, and by
> the use of envelope patterns that identify individual units of thought
> without detracting from the large form as the basic structural concep-
> tion.[25]

But Cynewulf's style, especially his use of the runic signatures,
illustrates something more about this poet: a self-consciousness
about his craft and his creations, a self-consciousness seen in his
Elene epilogue in particular. With his emphasis on Christ the gift-
giver in the *Ascension,* it is not hard to imagine Cynewulf viewing
his poems as his "contractual" offering to God, even as heroic gift-
giving between lord and retainer was a contractual arrangement,

one still manifesting itself in late Anglo-Saxon Christian wills (see chapter 4). Man must not only *use* his God-given talent well, but is obligated to *give* a *quid pro quo*. It seems not unlikely that Cynewulf's *quid*, in his eyes, was his poetry.

The final part of the *Christ* triptych, *Christ III*, consists of 798 lines on the Judgment Day.[26] From our modern perspective, it may be less satisfying than the *Advent* or the *Ascension*. But though utilizing many sources—an alphabetic hymn attributed to Bede, material from Gregory the Great, Augustine, Caesarius of Arles, and other Christian writers on the great theme of Judgment—it nevertheless blends vision imagery on the one hand and narrative voice on the other. These synthesize respectively the eternal and internal revelation of the Second Coming with the temporal and external account of events traditionally accompanying that apocalyptic event—a synthesis thematically centered around a call to immediate penance in the reader.[27]

The poem opens with the swift terror of the world's end:

Then at midnight the mighty Lord's
great day shall forcefully grip with fear
all earth's inhabitants and that fair
creation itself, just as an assassin,
a bold thief who threads the shadows
of the dark night, suddenly assails
care-less men caught fast in their sleep,
wickedly attacks mortals unaware. (ll. 868–74)

The angels trumpet their call to Judgment, and with Christ's appearance the poet sounds a major theme of his poem: that He appears *eadgum and earmum ungelice* 'differently to the blessed and the wretched' (l. 909). To the former, a glorious sight, to the latter, a fearful one. There follows an account of the devastation of the universe as the refleshed souls rise to Judgment (through l. 1080). A long passage on the Cross and Crucifixion focuses the sinners' attention on Christ's darkest hour, when the dumb universe sympathized but the sinners remained unmoved by the bloody event. The poet then describes the rewards of the virtuous and the punishment of transgressors at the Judgment, and exhorts his readers *now* to repent, to search out their sins by the eyes within since the "gems of the head" are useless for discovering that inner evil which will be all too clearly visible *then* (at the Last Judgment). The focus then switches to Christ in that future time, in which He welcomes the blessed to heaven and reminds the wicked of the love He showed them through the Incarnation and Crucifixion. In a poignant passage Christ rebukes the latter for their willful neglect of His Passion, for the greater suffering they have caused Him through the cross of their sins:

> "Why did you hang me on your hands' cross
> more heavily than I hung of old?
> Your sin's cross, which crucifies me now
> against my will, seems worse, more bitter,
> than that other which I ascended
> by My will when your misery grieved
> My heart so, when I drew you out of Hell,
> where you would dwell ever afterwards.
> In the world I was poor that you might be wealthy in heaven,
> in your land I was abased that you might be blessed in mine."
> (ll. 1487–96)

After Christ dooms the wicked to hell and its horrors, the poem concludes on a rhapsodic note describing the bliss of the saved in the heavenly paradise where "there is neither hunger nor thirst,/sleep nor terrible sickness, nor sun's heat,/nor cold nor care. . . ." (ll. 1660–2).

Two other poems on Judgment Day will be considered in chapter 10, since they do not focus on Christ. But Christ is prominent, by the nature of His Passion, in *The Dream of the Rood*, perhaps the finest Old English religious poem.[28] This 156-line lyrical narrative in adoration of the Cross survives in the Vercelli Book, and part of it appears in Northumbrian runic inscription on the east- and west-face margins of the late seventh- or early eighth-century Ruthwell Cross in Dumfriesshire, Scotland. Two lines reminiscent of the poem also appear on the late-tenth century Brussels Cross.[29] The relation between the Ruthwell inscription and the Vercelli text is not clear, but scholars assume that the former condenses an original Anglian poem (c. 700), preserved in West Saxon tenth-century form in the latter. The most likely place and time of the poem's composition is King Aldfrith's Northumbria (685–704).[30] Though some have felt that ll. 78 ff. were so different in style as to be the work of a later redactor, the *Dream* is coherent and uni-fied, compact and intense in its emotional effect.

> Listen! I will tell the sweetest dream
> which came to me in middle of the night
> when all who speak rest in peaceful sleep.
>   It seemed I saw the most stately tree
> stretched aloft, enveloped in light—
> the brightest cross. Covered with gold was
> all that sign. . . .
>   Stately that victory-Cross, and I sin-stained,
> wounded by sins. I saw the wondrous tree
> glorified by its garments, gold-adorned
> shining joyously: jewels had clothed
> illustriously the tree of the Lord.
> Yet I could perceive seeping through that gold
> former wretched strife, where it before
> bled on its right side. I trembled with sorrows,
> at the fair sight I was afraid. I saw that sign
> transformed in garments and hues: now flushed with moisture,
> drenched with flowing blood, and now adorned with treasure.
> (ll. 1–7a, 13–23)

This beginning, with its possible allusion to the Last Judgment, with its image of the double-visaged Cross gemmed and blood-drenched, and with its fearful, sin-stained persona, is a symbolic prelude to the poem's major interlocking subjects and themes: Christ's suffering and triumph through His Crucifixion; the abasement and exaltation of the Cross itself; the persona's penit-ence and hope for heavenly bliss through his worship of the Cross.[31] In lines 28–121 the poet uses the rhetorical device of *prosopopoeia* to have the Cross itself describe the Crucifixion from its particular point of view.[32] Speaking in riddle fashion (see chapter 11), the Cross succinctly narrates its origin as a tree and tells of its being felled, shaped into a rood, and fastened on a hill as a gallows for criminals. Then:

> "I saw mankind's Lord
> rush willfully: he wished to climb me.
> Standing there, I dared not bend or break
> against God's word, though I saw the ground
> quake and tremble. Easily I could
> have felled all foes, yet I stood firm." (ll. 33b–8)

This advance of Christ upon the Cross is not the usual depiction of Christ carrying the Cross to Calvary, but it has traditional sanction. It shows Christ freely willing His own Crucifixion, heightening this "leap's" heroic and voluntary nature. Stripping Himself for battle—again an unusual feature, but one within patristic tradition—Christ mounts the Cross, an admirable symbol of His divinity and of the earlier Middle Age's conception of the Redemption.

The Cross continues:

> "I quaked when the Hero clasped me, yet dared not
> bend or fall to earth: for I had to stand fast.
> A rood was I reared: I raised the King,
> Heaven's mighty Lord; nor dared I bow low.
> They pierced me with dark nails; on me the wounds are plain,
> visible hostile scars. I dared hurt no one.
> They mocked us both together. I was drenched with blood
> poured from the Man's side when He'd sent His spirit forth.
> Much cruel and painful I experienced
> on that hill: I saw the God of hosts
> dreadfully stretched; darkness had
> covered with clouds the Ruler's corpse,
> the shining splendor: a black shadow
> overcast the sky. All creation wept,
> bewailed the King's death: Christ was on the Cross." (ll. 42–56)

Crist wæs on rode: the breathtaking account of the Crucifixion ends on this simply stated yet highly emotional note. The Cross has presented itself as a loyal retainer in the epic mode, with the ironic reversal that it must acquiesce and even assist in its Lord's death, unable through His own command to aid or avenge Him. In its trembling and suffering, the Cross has also taken upon itself Christ's Passion. Thus it has become a surrogate for Christ, representing that other aspect of the Crucifixion which was to predominate in the doctrine and art of the later Middle Ages, His humanity.

By presenting a Christ heroically ascending the Cross and a Cross undergoing His human Passion, the poet threaded his way among the Christological disputes of the seventh and eighth centuries about the paradox of the Savior's dual nature. This tension between His divinity and humanity is highlighted stylistically in the following passage where the Cross describes the deposition and burial:

> "They carried away almighty God,
> raised Him from that heavy torment. Men left me there
> standing spattered with blood, badly wounded with darts.
> They laid down the weary-limbed One, stood and watched
> at the head of Heaven's Lord; a while He rested there,
> weary from that great struggle. Then from bright stone
> they hewed Him a tomb in view of His slayer,
> set therein the Lord of victories." (ll. 60b–7a)

In these hypermetric lines picturing Christ's death at the "hands" of His slayer (the Cross) variously as a sleep, a catharsis of exhaustion, a release, and a temporary rest, the poet uses the paradoxical *communicatio idiomatum*, wherein Divinity is mortalized: "carried away," "laid down," "watched," "set therein." Woolf comments on this device and its doctrinal and aesthetic significance:

> In the thirty lines of dramatic description of the Crucifixion . . . there are ten examples of the *communicatio idiomatum*, and each one stimulates a shock at the paradox. . . . The habit of variation in Anglo-Saxon poetic style and the richness of synonyms in Anglo-Saxon poetic diction assist the poet in each instance to use a fresh word or phrase to emphasize some attribute of God, His rule, majesty, omnipotence. . . . The theological point that the Christ who endured the Crucifixion is fully God and fully man is thus perfectly made. . . .[33]

The visionary Cross now briefly describes its own "death" and "burial" and subsequent invention (cf. *Elene*), decoration with gold and silver, and exaltation above all other "trees," even as Mary was honored by God above all women. From being the hardest of punishments, it has become the *vitae via* for all who fear it (ll. 70–94). In lines 95–121 it exhorts the Dreamer to reveal his vision to others, to make known that it is the true Cross on which Almighty God suffered for mankind's many sins and Adam's deeds of old. On it He tasted death, but arose and ascended to heaven, whence He will come again on Judgment Day to judge each according to his deeds on earth. He will ask then who has tasted death for Him, and only he who "bears the Cross in his breast" (has been penitent and made restitution?) will be saved.

In the poem's closing frame, ll. 122–56, the persona first presents the result of his vision: his own "conversion" to life through the Cross. What formerly was the *bana* 'slayer' of the Lord is now, ironically enough, the Dreamer's *mundbyrd* 'protector.' Like other Old English exiles (see chapter 12), the persona has few friends left alive and longs for the day when the Cross he saw here on earth will fetch him to partake of the heavenly banquet of joys, thus completing *his* transformation. The poem concludes on the triumphant notes of Christ's Harrowing of Hell and His Ascension.

Analysis of *The Dream of the Rood* reveals a richness and complexity in both content and style. Central is the fusion of God-Christ's divine and human attributes and the verbal identification of Cross, Christ, and Dreamer.[34] A small illustration of this density: in l. 14a, the Dreamer, as he watches the Cross, *[wæs] forwunded mid wommum* 'was badly wounded by sins'; in l. 62b, the Cross says, after the deposition, *eall ic wæs mid strælum forwundod* 'I was very badly wounded with darts (i.e., nails).' The identification of Cross and Dreamer, and by extension Christ's humanity, is achieved not only stylistically by the verbal and syntactic parallelism, but also figuratively through the implicit equation of the Dreamer's sins with the nails crucifying Christ (see the discussion of *Christ III* for explicit equation of mankind's sins and the Crucifixion). Further, the nails are called 'darts' or 'spears,' suggesting the heroic battle mode in a passage which utilizes intensively the Christian *communicatio idiomatum*. That *The Dream of the Rood* strikes us as finer than other Anglo-Saxon religious poems may owe something to its lyrical combination of narrative and drama, and, despite its penitential "program," to the absence of homiletic exhortation.[35]

In the later Middle Ages the Crucifixion was pictured predominantly in terms of Christ's human suffering and His divine triumph was reserved for the Harrowing of Hell motif, illustrated by the conclusion of *The Dream of the Rood*. In Old English poetry this motif finds independent expression in the Exeter's Book's *Descent into Hell*.[36] The *Descent* (called the *Harrowing of Hell* in some editions, though the poem does not cover the release of the patriarchs) is a 137-line piece of uncertain date. The motif of the Descent and Harrowing goes back to the apocryphal Gospel of Nicodemus, translated in the mid-eleventh century into Old English prose (see chapter 3); but surprisingly neither the Old English poem nor others in the corpus which use the motif, nor any prose works, seem to have known this Gospel.[37]

The poem begins narratively with the visit of the sorrowing Marys to Christ's tomb. The poet stresses their knowledge of His burial, their expectation of the permanence of His entombment. But, "quite another thing/these women knew when they turned back again" (ll. 15b–6b). Following a brief description of Christ's Resurrection (ll. 17–23a), the scene abruptly switches to John the Baptist in hell, laughingly telling its inhabitants about *his* expectation that on this day (Easter) his kinsman, "the victorious Son of God," will visit them (ll. 23b–32). Christ's conquest of hell is presented heroically, emphasizing the ease with which, without men or weapons, He was able to gain entry:

> Mankind's Lord moved swiftly on His way,
> heaven's Guardian would destroy hell's walls:
> the fiercest of all kings wished to crush
> and to plunder that city's power.
> To battle He brought no helmet-bearers,
> nor would He lead armed warriors
> to the fortress-gates; but its locks fell
> open, its bolts drew back. The King rode in.   (ll.   33–40)

The patriarchs and all other souls in hell throng to see Him. John perceives that He has indeed come and addresses Him in a long speech (ll. 59 ff.) which runs to the end of the poem.[38] In his speech John apostrophizes Gabriel, Mary, Jerusalem, and the River Jordan in a manner similar to the liturgically inspired lyrics of *Christ I*,[39] and concludes by imploring Christ to show "us" mercy and cast the water of baptism over

"all city-dwellers,
even as you and John in the Jordan
with baptism nobly inspired
all this world; thanks be to God forever." (ll. 134b–7)

The *Descent into Hell* combines narrative and lyric modes in celebrating this "leap's" importance for mankind's salvation, linking typologically the patriarchs and others in hell with all living men. From certain knowledge of death in the "expectation" of the Marys, the poem moves to the conquest of darkness by light in John's perception of Christ's victory at hell's gates (ll. 52–5a), to a universalized prayer for the beginning of life eternal for all mankind through baptism. Christ's heroic saving power is revealed not only in His action and John's apostrophe, but in the many variational changes rung on His nature: He is designated in John's final imploration (ll. 107 ff.) as "our Savior" (twice), "Lord Christ," "Creator of men," "Lord God of victory," "Ruler of nations," "powerful Lord," "best of (all) kings (twice,)" "God of hosts" (thrice), "joy of nobles," "beloved Prince." The final epithet, unique in the poem, is *Meotud* 'Measurer.' Though the poem abruptly shifts focus in its course, it is not without its own aesthetic power.[40]

The Harrowing of Hell motif receives fuller expression in the 729-line poem that concludes the Junius MS, *Christ and Satan*.[41] Part I, ll. 1–365, consists of a series of plaints by Satan after his unsuccessful revolt against God-Christ, plaints interspersed with homiletic exhortations to choose Christ and a radiant Heaven, the "green street" up to the angels, by eschewing sins. Part II, ll. 366–662, centers on the Harrowing, but also introduces accounts of the Resurrection, Ascension, and Last Judgment, with brief sermonizing after the first two. Part III, ll. 663–729, gives an abbreviated (there is a sizable gap in the MS) but dramatic version of Christ's Temptation in the Wilderness.[42] The different contents of these sections, the varying styles, and the unchronological placing of the Temptation have led some scholars to believe that separate poems have been here conjoined without much aesthetic sense; but others have argued for the thematic and structural unity of the whole. One sees the poem focusing on "the incommensurate might of God." Another sees the homiletic technique of exemplum-exhortation—in Part III exemplum alone—providing the structural principle for "the dual theme of the development and revelation of the character of Christ, and the implications of this revelation for man's moral life." Still another sees the central theme as an opposition between a "descending" Christ, whose *caritas* leads to exaltation, and a would-be "ascending" Satan, whose *cupiditas* leads to abasement.[43]

In Part I the poet establishes Christ's power by equating Him with God the Father in the process of Creation. Then Satan, a wretched figure taunted by his own followers, reveals his negative capability as he laments his folly in revolt and the torments of his fiery, windy, dragon-guarded abode. He sounds very much like an exiled thegn: "Here is no glory of blessed ones,/Wine-hall of the proud, nor joy of the world,/nor throng of angels. . . ." (ll. 92b–4a); "So must I, abased wretch, move more widely,/travel exile-paths deprived of glory,/parted from joys. . . ." (ll. 119–21a). Like mankind's sins, he cannot be hid, he laments—even in hell's wide hall with its mingled heat and cold.

Images of light and darkness play against each other throughout Part I, but are even more apparent in the Harrowing panel. There, Christ appears at hell's doors "in a fair light" and releases the prisoners. Eve must plead to be saved, and does so in a speech in which she accepts responsibility for eating the bright but deadly apple. Touchingly, she reaches her hand toward Christ, appealing to Him for Mary's sake: "Lo, you, Lord, were born from my daughter/on middle-earth as a help to man./Now it is clear you are God Himself,/eternal Author of all creation" (ll. 437–40). Christ quickly releases Eve and condemns Satan to chains and darkness. After the just proceed to Heaven, Christ speaks to His followers about the creation, man's disobedience, and His descent to earth and Crucifixion (ll. 469–511). The poet then tells of the Resurrection, Christ's forty days on earth, His Ascension, and the Last

Judgment, where the wicked are sent to hell's darkness and the saved rejoice in heaven's radiance.[44]

Christ's power to save mankind in Part II counterpoints Satan's powerlessness to exalt himself in Part I. But the full extent of Satan's abject misery is seen in Part III, where the poet briefly but magnificently takes us back to Christ's rejection of the tempter's offer to allow Him to rule this world and, uniquely, the *rodera rice* 'kingdom of heaven.' In response Christ says:

> "Depart, accursed, to the pit of torment:
> for you, proud Satan, punishment
> and not at all God's realm stands ready.
> I command you, by virtue of My might,
> that you bring no hope to those in hell,
> but you might tell them the greatest grief:
> that you met the Measurer of all things,
> mankind's King. Get you behind me!
> Know too, accursed, how wide and broad is
> hell's mournful hall: measure it by hand!
> Begin with the bottom, then go so
> you may feel its whole circumference:
> first measure from above to the abyss
> and how broad the black mist may be;
> then you will see more clearly that you strove
> with God, when you have measured by hand
> the height and depth of inmost hell,
> that grim grave-house. Go quickly to work,
> so that before two hours have flown by
> you will have measured your destined home."[45]   (ll. 693–709)

And Satan sinks into hell to commence his measuring, and "It seemed to him then that from there (the pit)/to the doors of hell were a hundred thousand/miles. . . ." With the curse of his own fiends on his head, "Lo, thus lie now in evil! Formerly you did not wish for good," the poem abruptly ends.

Christ and Satan is generally viewed as having been composed in the early ninth century.[46] In this chapter and the last, we have discussed Old English poems of the ninth and tenth centuries dealing with Christ and His saints as the heroes of narrative and lyric. We have observed the fusion or overlapping of secular heroic concepts and Christian tradition in a poetic style that fuses native Anglo-Saxon and Latin rhetorical techniques. Cynewulf figured prominently as the one Anglo-Saxon poet whose name we have in this connection, and though only four poems bear his runic signature, several others, as we have noted, have been viewed by stylistic critics as Cynewulfian in manner: *Dream of the Rood, Guthlac B,* and *Christ I. Christ and Satan* probably stands between the Cynewulfian and the earlier "Caedmonian" poems in the Junius MS. These poems, along with the later *Genesis B* and *Judith,* form a group which have Old Testament figures as their heroes and heroines. They are the subject of the next chapter.

NOTES

1. Cook 1909.

2. See Das 1942 and Schaar 1949.

3. See ASPR 3, pp. xxv–vi, though the editors are inconclusive, giving the three poems consecutive line numbers. See also Philip 1940.

4. Mildenberger 1948; Chase, C. 1974; Frese 1975. For summary remarks on the unity debate, see Calder 1981, pp. 42–4.

5. Ed. separately by Campbell, J. 1959, with translation. Burlin 1968 contains text and translation accompanying an extended commentary.

6. See Burgert 1921; and Burlin 1968, pp. 38–45; Rankin 1985.

7. Campbell, J. 1959 takes the former view; Anderson, E. 1983, pp. 50–4, the latter.

8. See Burlin 1968, pp. 56–9. This book offers a clear exposition of typological figuration and a running commentary on each of the lyrics.

9. Burlin 1968, p. 65.

10. See Lass 1966 and Cross 1964.

11. For textual criticism of this passage and others in Lyric II, see Pope 1981b.

12. See Burlin 1968, pp. 119–25; Foley 1975; Anderson, E. 1979.

13. Greenfield 1953. On thematic unity, see further Pàroli 1979; Anderson, E. 1983, pp. 50–64.

14. Ed. in ASPR 3; Cook 1909.

15. Clemoes 1971.

16. On the "gifts of men" theme in OE poetry, see Cross 1962; Anderson, E. 1983, pp. 28–44. On Cynewulf's extensive use of it in *Christ II* and the possible relation of the theme to the "unity" of the *Christ* poems, see Chase, C. 1974. For fuller discussion of this theme, see chapter 11. On "soul's need," see Rice 1977.

17. On heroic vocabulary in the poem, see Clemoes 1971, pp. 294–6;

Cherniss 1972, pp. 221–6 argues that the heroic connotations of that vocabulary are here minimal.

18. Calder 1981, p. 67. On backgrounds of the Descent-Ascent motif and its use in the poem, see Brown, G. 1974.

19. See Pope 1969, who clarifies the situation by analyzing the passage in terms of Bede's *Ascension Hymn*, which Cynewulf is utilizing here.

20. On rhetorical ornamentation in this passage, see Clemoes 1970, pp. 11–3.

21. See notes 16, 20.

22. On the "Harrowing" motif in the poem, see Campbell, J. 1982, pp. 145–7.

23. For interpretive problems with the runic signature, see Elliott 1953a; Page 1973, pp. 208–10; Frese 1975, pp. 327–34.

24. See Adams, R. 1974 on the centrality of the Ascension-Advent interaction. For detailed analysis of the poem, see Calder 1981, pp. 42–74; see also Letson 1980.

25. Anderson, E. 1983, p. 67.

26. Ed. in ASPR 3; Cook 1909.

27. See Hill, T. 1973; Kuznets/Green 1976; Chase, C. L. 1980. An extensive analysis of the poem is Caie 1976, pp. 160–4, 173–225; a brief appreciation of it is Shepherd 1966, pp. 19–22. For the alphabetic hymn, see Cook 1909, pp. 171 ff.

28. Ed. in ASPR 2; separately by Dickins/Ross 1954 and Swanton 1970.

29. For description and comment on the RC itself, see Swanton 1970, pp. 9–38. Both RC and BC inscriptions ed. in ASPR 6. For "reconstruction" and trans. of the RC inscription, see Howlett 1976a.

30. Braswell 1978.

31. On *Dream* and *Christ III*, see Payne, R. 1975 and Chase, C. L. 1980; on the paradox of Christ's Being, see Woolf 1958 and Swanton 1970, pp. 42–58. Fleming 1966 emphasizes the poem's eschatological and penitential elements; Burrow 1959, the persona's "progress" from sinner to saved; Leiter 1967, the interlocking transformations of Christ, Cross, and Dreamer. On Cross iconology, see Swanton (as above) and Schwab 1978. On liturgical influence, see Patch 1919 and Ó Carragáin 1982.

32. On *prosopopoeia* and the *Dream*, see Schlauch 1940.

33. Woolf 1958, pp. 151–2.

34. See n. 31; further, Hieatt 1971. For an interpretive analysis of the poem's syntax, see Pasternack 1984. For an appreciative commentary and sensitive poetic translation, see Gardner, H. 1970.

35. Gatch 1965 is undoubtedly right in seeing the Vercelli corpus, both homilies and poems, as a collection intended to inspire repentance; see further chapter 3.

36. Ed. in ASPR 3; Shippey 1976, with facing translation.

37. See Campbell, J. 1982 for an account of the motif and its various appearances in OE literature.

38. L. 135a, *Swylce git Johannis* 'even as you two, John (and Christ),' causes problems. Some critics emend the *git* or assume the speaker of ll. 59–137 is Adam. Others see ll. 134–7 as the persona's voice, speaking for all mankind (Conner 1980), or the combined universal voices of John, persona, and mankind (Trask 1971; Campbell, J. 1982, pp. 150–3). Kaske 1976 views *git* as comprising John and the baptismal water.

39. Conner 1980 attempts to link *Descent* directly to the Light and Baptismal services of Holy Saturday rites.

40. For literary analysis, see Shippey 1976, pp. 36–43.

41. Ed. in ASPR 1; separately by Clubb 1925; Finnegan 1977; (on microfiche in) Sleeth 1982.

42. No specific source has been identified—see Finnegan 1977, p. 37 for its "inspiration."

43. See respectively Huppé 1959, pp. 227–31; Finnegan 1977; Sleeth 1982.

44. See Campbell, J. 1982, pp. 153–8.

45. Hill, T. 1982 comments on wordplay here between Christ's appellation *Meotod* 'Measurer' and His command to Satan to *metan* 'measure' hell with his hands.

46. Sleeth 1982 places it as late as 850.

CHAPTER 9

Old Testament Narrative Poetry

Christ and Satan, recorded by three different scribes, occupies the second "book" of the Junius 11 MS; the two poems that constitute *Genesis,* as well as the *Exodus* and the *Daniel,* all in the hand of one scribe, make up the first. In addition to the poems, the MS contains forty-eight illustrations depicting scenes from *Genesis,* though they are not always faithful to the poetic text.[1] Scholars long felt that this manuscript contained poems written by the famed Caedmon himself, since Bede's account (*HE* 4:24) tells how, after miraculously receiving the gift of song, the humble cowherd composed pious verses:

> He sang first about the creation and about the origin of mankind, and all that story of Genesis . . .; in turn about the exodus of the Israelites from the land of the Egyptians and about the entrance into the promised land; and about many other stories of the Holy Scripture. . . .

But scholarship now recognizes different authors for the several poems, and firmly rejects attribution of any extant poems to Caedmon save for the *Hymn* (see chapter 10).

The first of the "Caedmonian" poems in the Junius MS runs to 2935 lines, divided by the scribe into forty-one fitts, but lines 235–

851 are in origin and style a separate poem on the Fall of Man. Lines 1–234 and 852–2935 are usually taken together as *The Earlier Genesis*, or *Genesis A*, and dated around 700; the inserted portion, fitted sequentially but awkwardly into the narrative, is known as *The Later Genesis*, or *Genesis B*, and dated mid-ninth century.[2] The former follows the biblical account of the First Book of Moses through 22:13—the sacrifice of Isaac—with expansions, omissions, and changes of various kinds, perhaps the most notable change being the addition of the apocryphal Fall of the Angels. There is evidently a lacuna in the manuscript after the creation of the sea on the third day (l. 168),[3] at which point the text jumps to the creation of Eve. More than half the extant lines are devoted to Abraham.

Earlier commentators viewed the nature, quality, and meaning of *Genesis A* reductively; they pointed to the Teutonizing of the biblical story, noting the "addition" of heroic formulas (cf. with "Saints' Lives," chapter 7). But since Huppé's seminal essay, many critics have found a figurative or allegorical signification, in the manner of Bede's *Commentary on Genesis*. Huppé proposes a unity for the narrative based upon man's need to praise God. He sees the poet developing

> those portions of the biblical story which trace figuratively the salvation and damnation of mankind, first symbolized in the actions of expelling Adam and Eve from Paradise. . . . It is on Abraham, as a figurative character, that the poet chiefly concentrates. . . . The sacrifice of Isaac represents the fulfillment of God's promise to Abraham of the birth of Christ and the Redemption of mankind.[4]

Huppé overstates the figurative case for details of the poem, however, as even those who accept his critical premise acknowledge.[5] For example, God does not, in *Genesis A*, promise Abraham "the birth of Christ and the Redemption of mankind"; rather, he promises him a son by Sarah, whom all men shall call "Isaac";

> By spirit's might I will give that man
> My divine grace, abundance of friends
> for his benefit; My blessing
> and special favor shall he receive,

My love and delight. From that leader
shall come a great people, brave princes,
who will be keepers of the kindgom,
worldly kings famous far and wide. (ll. 2330–7)

Though the grace bestowed is divine, the blessings are surely literal and secular (e.g., "*worldly* kings"), not figurative. Secular heroic values also seem built into the account of the battle between
the northern kings who fought and defeated the southern kings
of Sodom and Gomorrah, and into the description of Abraham's
ensuing rescue of his nephew Lot, taken captive in that conflict.
In the former battle scene, for example, the dewy-feathered raven
sings in expectation of carnage, and

There was hard fighting,
exchange of deadly spears, the din of war
and loud shouts of battle. From their sheaths
warriors drew with hands ring-adorned swords,
strong in their edges. (ll. 1989b–93a)

In Abraham's rescue operation, his warriors surprise the enemy
by attacking at night:

In the (enemy's) camp was noise
of shields and shafts, the death of shooters
and the shock of arrows; sharp spears bit
grievously beneath the men's garments,
and the enemies fell, foe after foe,
where laughing they had led away booty
as comrades in arms. . . .
Abraham gave
them war as tribute—not twisted gold—
for his brother's son: he struck and killed
the foe in the fighting. (ll. 2061b–72a)

Whether the most devout or the most learned Christian in any
Anglo-Saxon audience would have conceived Abraham here not
as a secular warrior but as "an ideal of Christian living" is doubtful.

Criticism of *Genesis A* has not only moved away from Huppé's
detailed figurative paraphrase, but it has also produced literal

interpretations. Boyd, for instance, sees the predominating themes of the poem as "wealth and *freondscipe*," and the narrative "a version of history on which the poet has superimposed a framework of moral values which is restricted to a purely secular concept of propriety and nobility"; Brockman believes the Cain and Abel episode had, for the poet's audience, a "more concretely secular, social meaning" than an exegetical one.[6] On a purely literal level, *Genesis A* contrasts those who obey and those who disobey God. The first fitt, ll. 1–81, is illustrative: it begins with the narrator's statement that it is right to praise and love God for His eternal power as King over the heavenly thrones (ll. 1–8a)[7]; it next describes the joy of the angels obedient to and loving their Lord (ll. 8b–21); then follows Lucifer's revolt *for oferhygde* 'for pride' and God's exiling the rebellious angels, depriving them of joys (ll. 22–77); and it concludes with peace and joy reestablished in heaven among the angelic *duguð* 'host, tried retainers' with their *drihten* 'Lord.' The poet clearly makes good use of his native stylistic medium, including "envelope" patterns, word collocations, and wordplay.[8] All the subsequent episodes and fitts employ similar stylistic patterns and themes—such as rewards for the faithful and exile for the disobedient. Abraham's willingness to sacrifice Isaac is literally consonant with Germanic notions of loyalty and obedience and provides a fitting conclusion. Nevertheless, patristic commentary does permeate the work in many ways.[9] Sixteen times the word *nergend* 'Savior' refers to God; and, at least for those familiar with exegesis, the biblical Genesis itself had accumulated typological meanings for its Old Testament figures and actions. Yet this poet, unlike the creator of *Exodus*, made no special effort to ensure that his audience would recognize such features. Even *nergend* seems to be a common (if anachronistic) choice of epithet for an Old English Christian writer.

Inserted in the midst of *Genesis A* is a poem on the temptation and fall of Adam and Eve, a poem that has often been compared with *Paradise Lost*. There has been some speculation that Milton may have known *Genesis B* through his acquaintance with Junius (see chapter 5, note 41), who had the manuscript in London. As early as 1875 Sievers advanced the hypothesis that this portion of *Genesis* was a translation of an Old Saxon (Low German) poem;

and his theory was triumphantly confirmed in 1894 with the discovery of an Old Saxon fragment in the Vatican Library corresponding to lines 790–816.[10] Since the Saxon poem clearly dates from the mid-ninth century, the Old English translation of it (probably made by a continental Saxon in England)[11] cannot be placed any earlier.

Genesis B opens in the middle of a speech by God to Adam and Eve, in which He is telling them to enjoy the fruits of Paradise, but not to taste those of the forbidden tree. A long flashback follows, recounting the Creation and Fall of the Angels. Satan here is similar to the proud and rebellious tyrant-hero of *Paradise Lost*, a conception of character that both the Old English poet and Milton may owe to the fifth-century *Poematum de Mosaicae Historiae Gestis Libri Quinque* of Avitus.[12] In raising his standard of defiance, Satan says,

> "I have great strength
> to establish a more stately throne,
> a higher in heaven. Why serve His will,
> yield Him homage? I can be God as well as He.
> Strong comrades, stout-hearted warriors, stand by me,
> loyal to me in battle. For their lord those brave men
> have chosen me; with such champions can one plan
> and bring it about. They are my bosom friends,
> true in their thoughts; in truth I can be their lord,
> rule in this realm. Thus it seems not right to me
> to grovel before God for any favors:
> no longer will I be His follower." (ll. 280b–91)

Even in defeat he is the undaunted Germanic warrior, not the lamenting exile of *Christ and Satan;*[13] bound in iron bands in hell as he is, he hurls words if not spears:

> "Alas! if I could use my hands
> and be without for only an hour,
> for a winter's hour, then I with this host—
> but iron bands bind me securely,
> chains ride hard upon me." (ll. 368b–70a)

Ironically, he urges the comitatus-thegn bond as reason for one of his fallen comrades (obviously unbound) to aid him by escaping

into the upper world; there he can seduce Adam and Eve into dis-
obeying God. Thus mankind will be prevented from gaining the
rebellious angels' now lost heritage, and Satan and his cohorts will
have their revenge on God.

With the acceptance of this task by an unnamed subordinate,
the Old Saxon poet moves from apocryphal story to biblical account; but there are several modifications, apart from the initial
substitution of the devil's disciple as tempter, that are unusual and
significant. For one thing, the tempter tries Adam first, telling him
that it is God's command that he eat of the fruit from the forbidden tree, here pictured as evil and ugly—a tree of death, not of
knowledge. Adam rejects the temptation, saying that he does not
understand the message, and that the messenger is unlike any
angel he has ever seen. Furthermore, Adam says, the messenger
bears no sign of God's favor, and God can command Adam directly from on high—He needs no ministering angel. Angered, the
devil turns to Eve (whom the Lord made, the poet tells us, with
a "weaker mind" [ll. 590b–1a]) with the story that Adam has for-
feited God's favor by rejecting His command to eat the fruit; that
Eve can regain His favor by playing the better part, eating and
persuading Adam to eat; and that he is indeed God's messenger.
He concludes, with some irony, "I am not like a devil." Eve suc-
cumbs, eats, and sees a vision of heaven, granted her by the devil,
which she takes for a token of the truth. With the devil's prompt-
ing, she thereupon urges Adam all the long day to that dark deed.
The deed done, the apple eaten, the devil gloats and returns to
hell. Adam and Eve recognize their error, repent, and pray for
punishment; there is no hint that they refuse to acknowledge their
guilt, as in biblical and Augustinian versions of the Fall, nor do
they seek to blame God.

Critics find an additional modification of the biblical story in the
poem: the appearance of the fiend as an angel of light in his deception of Adam and Eve.[14] Many details—the angelic disguise,
the poet's description of Eve, the "handwork of God," as both
deceived (ll. 626–30, 699–703, 821–3) and loyal (l. 708), and further Adam and Eve's insistence on a "sign" from God (ll. 540–1,
653, 713–4, 773b–4)—lead to the conclusion that the poet was not
stressing man's moral disobedience but the deception of inno-

cence by malevolence and fraud.[15] There are forces of destruction that lurk behind human choices and actions, however good their motivations. While the poet depicted Eve sympathetically—and in doing so contrasted Satan's fall through pride with Adam and Eve's fall through deception[16]—he did not portray her as innocent. In various ways, he alerted his audience to her moral guilt or culpable ignorance.[17] Whether we see Eve as wholly or partly guilty, we must recognize a subversion of hierarchical order, wherein reason yields, as it should not do, to sense. And there is probably a typological relationship between the two falls: the concepts of Promethean overreaching and subverted hierarchy work together in this poem, much as the triumph and passion of Christ and Cross do in *The Dream of the Rood*.[18] We cannot be certain, of course, that the original Saxon or English audience would have understood the poem in this way. But surely they were at least minimally aware of its fusion of Germanic poetic form, dramatic irony, and heroic concepts with the Christian idea that disloyalty to God entails the loss of Paradise and all that woe.

The literal-allegorical question posed by *Genesis* arises also over the interpretation of the following poem in the Junius MS, the 590-line *Exodus*.[19] This is in many ways the most difficult of the Caedmonian poems, and perhaps of all Old English poems. It adds a great deal to its main source, Exodus 12.29–30, 13.17–14.31. Its style is rather spasmodic; there are many unusual metaphors; lacunae exist in the manuscript; unrealistic details appear in the midst of realistically portrayed scenes; there is a digression on Noah and Abraham in the midst of the Red Sea crossing; and many individual words offer interpretative problems. Further, there is the overall "strategy" to consider: whether the poem "offers its message of human salvation largely in heroic terms, terms perhaps quite unfamiliar or uncongenial to Latin exegetes," or, whether the exodus itself "is being described in terms appropriate to the journey of all Christians through this life to the heavenly home."[20] In either case, *Exodus* is one of the most stirring and exciting of Old English poems.

It begins epically in a complex passage: *Hwæt, we feor and neah gefrigen habbað* 'Lo, we have heard far and near'; and it continues, with possible double reference, by praising Moses' laws (the Commandments/the Pentateuch), which offer the reward of heavenly life for the blessed after the "difficult journey" (of this life/of the Israelite exodus) and enduring counsel for those presently alive—"Let him hear who will!" (ll. 1–7). The poet then depicts Moses as a folk leader and battle champion, wise and dear to God; he gives a brief preview of Moses' victory over the Egyptians, "God's adversaries," and tells (unbiblically) how God had earlier revealed to Moses the story of Creation and His own name (ll. 8–29). Now the poem moves quickly to the tenth plague, the slaying of the Egyptians' firstborn sons, and the release of the Israelites. Moses leads his people forward under the protection of a pillar of cloud that shields them from the hot Ethiopian sun by day and a pillar of fire that staves off the terrors of the night. The Israelites encamp by the Red Sea on the fourth night and learn that the Egyptian host pursues them. At this point there is a gap in the manuscript (l. 141). With the resumption of the narrative, the Egyptians are approaching the encampment. In the following passage (ll. 154–204a), the poet shows considerable scenic skill in his use of the "cinematographic" technique of shifting point of view between the opposed forces as they converge.[21] First he shows the terrified Hebrews as they watch the approach of the "shining troop of horsemen," with the "beasts of battle" expecting carrion. Then he views the scene from the side of the advancing cavalry, with its king in bright armor. A brief parenthetical glance back at the entrapped Hebrews (ll. 178b–9), and then a long description of the number, organization, and determination of the Egyptians to gain vengeance on the slayers of their brothers (the firstborn). Again the "camera" swings back to the Israelites, as their fear rises to a crescendo in the sound of wailing; the enemy is resolute as the gap between the forces narrows, till suddenly God's angel intervenes, and scatters the foes in the night (ll. 204b–7).

At dawn Moses summons his people together, bids them organize their armies, and also to take heart and trust in the Lord. He describes the miracle he performed as he struck the waters of the Red Sea with his rod and the waves parted in ramparts on each side of the now revealed ancient sea bottom. Curiously, the poet does not give an account of the objective action itself. As the tribes cross, the poet comments that they all had "one father" (i.e., Abraham), a reference which leads to a brief account of Noah and the flood and to a longer one of Abraham and the sacrifice of Isaac. At the end of an account of God's covenant with Abraham, there is another large gap in the manuscript, and the narrative resumes with the already trapped Egyptians trying in vain to flee the closing walls of water. The drowning of the host is emphasized reiteratively and somewhat confusedly, reflecting, consciously or unconsciously, the Egyptians' panic. At the end of this passage (l. 515), the poet briefly touches on Moses' preaching to the Israelites on the seashore. Then he introduces a homiletic section contrasting transitory earthly joys and heaven's bliss, returns to Moses' address, and finally describes the Israelites despoiling the dead Egyptians of Joseph's wealth.

That the crossing of the Red Sea held allegorical meaning for biblical commentators is well known; we saw in chapter 3 that Ælfric, in the early tenth century, reproduced an exegetical treatment of it. The allegorical possibility for *Exodus* gives sense and depth to the apparently naive nautical imagery applied to the Israelites as they *march* toward the Promised Land and along the bottom of the Red Sea. While the metaphors may be part of the native Anglo-Saxon heroic apparatus with which the poem is liberally furnished, they can also point to the standard Christian interpretation of the sea voyage, a representation of man's journey as an exile to his spiritual home in heaven[22] (cf. Cynewulf's extended simile at the end of *Christ II* and interpretations of *The Seafarer*). Typological foreshadowing seems encouraged by the wording which describes Moses' binding of "God's adversaries" and his freeing of the Israelites in the early part of the poem: a foreshadowing of Christ's Harrowing of Hell. Lucas suggests something more about how the words work in unusual collocations to imply allegorical connections:

> In lines 88b–90a the 'sails' (a metaphor for the pillars of cloud and fire) are called *lyftwundor leoht* 'bright miracles of the air', a phrase more appropriate to the pillar in another metaphorical guise, as the Cross. . . . Thus the allegorical interpretation of the Israelites following the pillar as Christians . . . following the Cross is implied. This allegorical interpretation is specifically linked, as the mention of 'sails' has already

suggested, to nautical imagery. In lines 80b–87a the Israelites, elsewhere called "sea-men' . . ., are seen as on board a ship, with mast,
cross-bar and rigging, a clear allusion to the patristic commonplace
(though not from the exegesis of the exodus) of the Ship of the Church
together with the Mast of the Cross. The rigging of the ship merges
into a tent (85), an allusion to the Tabernacle of the Tent of the Presence of the Lord where God manifested his presence to the Israelites
(86–7a). Juxtaposition of these two concepts, 'Ship' and 'Tent', is possible because in allegorical exegesis both represented the Church, the
family of all Christians.[23]

For all such exegetical reading, Lucas does not see the poem as a
consistent allegory, but as a "chain of associated notions rather
than a fully developed structural element." The "allegorical di-
mension," as he calls it, has attracted many critics, who find the
poem revolves around the Sacrament of Baptism.[24] Others concentrate on the details of typological equations, such as the reference to the encampment at Etham as being "an allusion to the
gathering of the church from the gentiles."[25] The significance of
the "Patriarchal Digression" in the midst of the Red Sea crossing
has been much discussed, and its relevance for *Exodus* fairly well
established, whether literally in terms of covenants or typologically. It is skillfully introduced and poetically effective; the Noah
and Abraham episodes are thematically and imagistically consistent with the *Exodus* proper; and they share with the main story
Christological and sacramental typologies.[26]

Critics who are allegorically inclined often find an explicit call
for exegetical readings in the poet's comment that "if life's interpreter, the body's guardian bright in the breast, wishes to unlock
this ample good with the keys of the Spirit [i.e., the Holy Spirit],
the mystery will be made clear" (ll. 523 ff.). They take the *run*
'mystery' as a reference to the poet's own text, and find sanction
therein for such readings.[27] This may be so; but the poet seems
to be referring to spiritual interpretation of the Ten Commandments, to which he has just alluded in ll. 520–2: "Still men find
in the writings every law which God commanded them [the Isra-
elites] in true words on that journey."[28]

Allegorical or not, *Exodus* everywhere exhibits an epic tone and
grandeur in its account of the flight as a battle between armies.

For instance, when the tribe of Simeon enters the now exposed path at the bottom of the sea:

> Next the sons of Simeon went forth
> in powerful bands, troop after bold troop;
> a third mighty host, banners flying
> over dew-tipped spears, they pressed forward
> duly arrayed. Tumultuous day
> broke over waters, God's bright beacon
> sea-morning splendid. The host moved on.   (ll.   340–6)

Even the overwhelming of the Egyptians by the closing walls of water is viewed in martial terms:

> the watery slopes were spattered with blood,
> the sea spewed gore; an uproar split the waves,
> the water filled with weapons, poured forth death.
> The Egyptians turned back in their tracks,
> fled in fear perceiving their peril:
> they would seek their homes, sick of the battle,
> their boasting humbled. High-towering waves
> darkened over them. None of that army
> arrived home, for fate from behind
> engulfed them in waves. Where pathways once stood,
> the sea now raged.   (ll.   449–59a)[29]

The afflictors, God's adversaries, have become the afflicted; the treasurehoard (both the Israelites, metaphorically, and Joseph's treasure, literally) has been plundered.[30] Whether the poem's thematic unity lies in the ritual of baptism, or the help of God, the keeping of covenants, or salvation by faith and obedience, cannot be firmly established. Nevertheless, the poem's intensity and vigor have power to engage us.

Daniel, the last piece of Book I of Junius 11, does not present the same hermeneutic complexities as *Exodus*.[31] Although based upon the Vulgate Daniel 1–5, the 764-line Old English poem seems to concentrate on Nebuchadnezzar and on the three youths Hannaniah, Azariah, and Mishael and their miraculous salvation in the fiery furnace (ll. 1–485). Unlike his Vulgate counterpart, Daniel as seer and prophet is not even mentioned when the Babylonian king seeks out young scholars from among the now enslaved Jews for training as his counsellors. He appears only after the king's first dream, when the Chaldean wise men have failed to tell the monarch the disturbing dream he cannot recall (l. 149b). Moreover, this dream is not narrated in its literal details nor in Daniel's explanation, as it is in the Vulgate. It is quickly passed over, with a transition indicating the untouchability of Nebuchadnezzar's heart, to get to the building of the idol on the plain of Dura, the prelude to the furnace episode. Only after the king's temporary conversion to goodness as a result of the three-youths' miracle, and his backsliding into insolence, does Daniel play much of a role. The second dream, about the wondrous tree, *is* told in detail, as is the prophet's interpretation. Here the poem follows the Vulgate fairly closely, recounting the king's exile and return, Belshazzar's ultimate inheritance of the kingdom and its treasures, his feast, and the handwriting on the wall. The poem ends abruptly—or incompletely—in the midst of Daniel's denunciatory explication of the writing (see note 37).

Apart from the questionable ending, there are two related structural problems: (1) the salvation of the three youths is told twice; and (2) the "Song of Azarias," supplicating God for deliverance (ll. 279–332), comes *after* the first account of deliverance (ll. 271–8). Such anomalies suggest interpolation. Farrell, however, would absolve the Old English poet of structural blundering—and the poem of interpolation—by observing that on the first count there is a somewhat similar repetition in the Vulgate (3:19–24 and 3:47–51), and on the second that the Church Fathers, in their interpretation of Daniel, obviously felt that the biblical text itself indicates supplication after their deliverance.[32] However, the Vulgate says only, in Daniel 3:24, "And they walked in the midst of the flame, praising God and blessing the Lord"; not until *after* Azariah's prayer (3:49–50), does the angel actually descend into the furnace and drive the flames away. The structural problem posed by the "Song" in both the Vulgate and the Old English poem is obviated if one sees it, like the praise song of the three children after the (second) deliverance, as communal rather than personal, a prayer for the salvation of the Jews as a nation.[33]

The omissions and additions in the poem, and its shift of focus away from Daniel to Nebuchadnezzar, suggest that thematically *Daniel* is a warning against pride in times of prosperity.[34] The opening lines, referring interestingly enough to the exodus, describe the Jews' flourishing while they obeyed God's laws, sharing treasure and conquering other nations,

> until at feasting pride invaded them,
> and drunken thoughts led to devilish deeds. (ll. 17–8)

Their decimation, downfall, and captivity in Babylon follow their abandonment of the law and God. They set the stage for the "wolf-hearted" Nebuchadnezzar's pride, his refusal to acknowledge God despite the miracle he sees in the fiery furnace, and his seven-year exile with beasts. The climax of pride and insolence, feasting and drunkenness, divorce from God, comes with Belshazzar's defilement of the Jews' holy vessels; even Nebuchadnezzar, who had seized those treasures, was not that evil, Daniel explains. Belshazzar's punishment will thus be more severe—total destruction of his Chaldean nation. On a figurative level, we can see the opposition between the Augustinian "two cities," Jerusalem 'the high city' (l. 38) and the devilish Babylon, between the believing Hebrew youths and the heathen Chaldeans.[35] Though *Daniel* may display a "gracelessness" at times,[36] it nevertheless exhibits a balance between its beginning and end, a sense of climax, and a strong moral thematic development. It has taken a long time for it to achieve critical recognition as an effective Anglo-Saxon poem; but it is not unworthy to follow *Genesis* and *Exodus* in the Junius manuscript.[37]

The songs of Azariah and the three children exist in another version, in the Exeter Book, between *Guthlac B* and *The Phoenix*.[38] This 191-line poem consists mainly of Azariah's prayer (ll. 1–48), an account of the flame's dispersal (ll. 48–72), and the song of the three youths (ll. 73–179b); it concludes briefly with Nebuchadnezzar bidding the youths to come forth from the furnace, and with the poet's comment that their triumph over sin and fire was through their hearts' love and wisdoms' prudence. Beginning almost word for word like its counterpart in *Daniel*, *Azarias* develops the prayers at some length and with a number of differences.

This is particularly true of the praise song of the three youths, which is twice the length of the *Daniel* version. This song emphasizes the nature and function of the Lord's creatures who are called on to bless Him; the seas' and rivers' benefits to men and the habitation they provide for their amazing denizens; and the heavenly reward for those who are meritorious.[39] Additionally, the prayer of the three youths is more explicitly Christian. While the *Daniel* poet does have the three bless "the Lord of every nation, the Father Almighty,/the true Son of the Creator, Savior of souls/Helper of men, and you, Holy Spirit" (ll. 400–2; cf. *Az.* 155–7), the youths in *Azarias* invoke blessings on "Christ King" (l. 103) and ask mass priests to bless Him (l. 149); and the poet himself says "Christ shielded them" (l. 165). Further, unlike the trio in *Daniel* and the Vulgate, the youths in *Azarias* make their prayer personal, ending with praise for God's having sent His angel to protect them from fire and foes. Finally, it is a retainer of Nebuchadnezzar, a terrified *eorl*, rather than the king himself, who views the miracle in the furnace, and reports it to his lord in the hall.[40] This reworking of the Vulgate material thus has some interest in its own right.

The literal humbling of insolent and drunken pride, and the figurative defeat of the devil through faith, themes we saw in *Daniel*, are also present in the Old English *Judith*. This 349-line poem follows *Beowulf* in MS Cotton Vitellius A.xv, and is written in the same hand as that of the second scribe who copied the epic.[41] Earlier attributed to Caedmon by some scholars and to Cynewulf or a later ninth-century poet by others, and considered of Anglian provenience, it is now placed in the late tenth century and thought to be of West Saxon origin.[42] Based mainly on the apocryphal Old Testament Judith 12:10–15:1,[43] the Old English poem seems influenced by patristic tradition and by Latin and English saints' lives. Judith is a martial Christian saint, like Juliana and Elene before her; she even prays for guidance and aid to the Trinity (l. 86a). Her faith in God's grace is stressed throughout the poem; at the end the poet moralizes on her conquest over Holofernes and the earthly reward she receives from her nation—Holofernes' sword, helmet, armor, and treasures—treating this recompense as but a prelude to the greater reward she will receive in heaven.

The beginning of *Judith* is missing. When the narrative commences in the extant poem, at l. 7b, with the epic formula *Gefrægen ic* 'I have heard,' we are in the midst of Holofernes' feast on the "fourth day." Unlike the more decorous beer feasts of *Beowulf*, this is a riotous occasion:

> Care-less and proud, all his comrades in woe
> set to the feast, filled cup after cup with wine—
> bold armed warriors. There frequently deep bowls
> were borne along the benches, brimful pitchers
> and goblets to guests in the hall. Doomed they drank,
> famous shield-warriors, though the feared and mighty
> lord of men did not know that: Holofernes,
> gold-friend to men giving good cheer.
> He laughed and roared loudly, raged and ranted,
> till men far off could easily hear
> how that stern-hearted man stormed and yelled,
> proud in his cups encouraged all those
> jostling on benches to drink and enjoy.
> So all the day long the evil one
> poured the wine into his retinue:
> the fierce treasure-dispenser poured them so much
> that they lay in a swoon as if slain by death,
> drained of their senses. So their lord commanded
> those hall-guests be served, till the hastening night
> closed darkly upon them.   (ll.   15–34a)

After Judith is led to Holofernes' tent, where the lecher-tyrant lies in a swoon, she prays God for help. She draws Holofernes by the hair into a position suitable for her bloody vengeance, and with two strokes of his sword cuts through his neck. Judith and her servant return to Bethulia with Holofernes' head, and she announces her triumph to the Hebrews. My success augurs your victory, she says, and bids the army make haste to attack the now leaderless Assyrians. The ensuing battle is a vigorous epic expansion of the Vulgate, including the Germanic "beasts of battle" theme.[44] In fact, there is *no* such battle in the Vulgate, since there the Assyrians find Holofernes dead and flee before the Hebrews leave their city to pursue them; but in the Old English the discovery of the dead leader is made the climax of the military engagement that had begun at dawn and proceeded all morning long.

This narrative reorganization helps glorify the Jews who, victorious like those in *Exodus*, despoil the heathens of their armor and treasure. The Christian poet makes symbolic use of this treasure trove to extol the greater treasure of heaven.

The larger problems of interpreting *Judith* revolve around two not unrelated features: (1) the amount of material missing at the beginning, and (2) the poet's simplification of his Vulgate text in characterization and omission of proper names. As examples of the latter, Ozias, one of the two Bethulian rulers, who greets Judith on her return in the Vulgate, is not mentioned: there is only the splendid welcoming crowd. And the episode involving the renegade Achior, summoned by the biblical heroine, is altogether omitted by the Anglo-Saxon poet. On the score of the decapitated text: Is the poem basically complete as we have it, with but a few lines decollated, and thus a religious lay akin to the secular *Finnsburh Fragment* and *Maldon*? Or is it a fragment of a larger religious epic of some 1300 to 1400 lines, which included reworking of earlier sections of the Vulgate? On the second score: Do the poet's modifications and transformations of his Vulgate source argue for the poem's unity and coherence pretty much as it stands, or vice versa? And do they make a literal or an allegorical reading of the poem more probable?

The first question arises not only because there is more in the Book of Judith than the Old English poem preserves, but because fitt or section numbers in the MS margin begin with X, at l. 15, which seems to indicate a loss of almost nine fitts. But *Daniel* comprises only chapters 1–5 of the Vulgate text, we have seen, and *Exodus* concentrates on a single event and its consequences. As to the fitt numbering, Woolf contends that it is no indication of *authorial* numbering, since the Junius 11 poems *Genesis*, *Exodus*, and *Daniel*, though clearly by different poets, have seriatim fitt markings from I to LV.[45] Chamberlain, however, finds *Judith* quite different from the Junius poems, and argues that that MS is a special case of an editor's or lector's intentions. He suggests that it is "more reasonable to expect in *Judith* the separate numbering that appears in *Beowulf, Elene,* and *Christ and Satan*"—and so we more likely have only about a fourth of the poem.[46] In any case, considering the average length of the three complete fitts (107, 118, and

113 lines), about 100 lines, and not just "a few," are missing. Even though this last observation removes the unity which adherents of the short poem theory have seen established by verbal parallels at beginning and end of the extant text, Chamberlain concedes that "the *Judith* poet could certainly have added an excellent 100 lines that would not have jeopardized the present unity, but in fact, improved it."[47] He nevertheless not only argues for an original long poem on the basis of fitt numbers and the poet's modifications of the Vulgate text, but for a literal, nonexegetical reading of the poem as a religious and political exemplum of courage, faith, and nobility for a late tenth-century audience harassed by the growing incursions of the heathen Danes.

Chamberlain's literal interpretation is an argument against such allegorical readings of *Judith* as those by Huppé and Campbell, in which the poem is viewed as the Fathers interpreted the biblical heroine, typologically as *Ecclesia* or the Church in its victory over the devil, and tropologically as the monastic virtue of chastity.[48] Pringle advances the attractive reading that *Judith* embodies *both* the allegorical and the political, even as Ælfric in his homily on *Judith* made explicit the heroine's figurative meaning of chastity, and in his *Letter to Sigeweard* saw her as "an example to your own men that you should defend your country with weapons against an invading army."[49]

Whatever the original length of *Judith*, and however we interpret it, the poem is aesthetically forceful. In addition to aspects of style and technique already indicated, the poet uses the same or similar epithets for an ironic contrasting of Good and Evil; e.g., Judith has the greatest need for the grace *þæs hehstan Deman, þæt he hie wið þæs hehstan brogan/gefrioðde* 'of the highest Judge, that he should protect her against the greatest terror (i.e., Holofernes)', ll. 4–5a; and the poet calls God *þearlmod ðeoden gumena* 'mighty Prince of men' (l. 66a), while Judith, in her prayer to the Trinity, labels Holofernes by exactly the same term (l. 91a).[50] The poem also has a high proportion of end-rimes—higher than in any other Old English poem save for the *tour de force* of the *Riming Poem* (see chapter 12)—and many expanded or hypermetric lines.[51] Some examples may be seen in the passage translated above, where ll. 16–21 and 30–34 are hypermetric and l. 23b has rime in the Old

English *(hlynede ond dynede)*. The poet plays with sound patterns, as in ll. 15a, *Hie ða to ðam symle*, which begins the passage in normal verse and 22b, *on gytesalum*, where normal verse resumes after the first hypermetric section. There is the fine irony in ll. 29–32a, where Holofernes pours so much wine *into* his warriors that they are drained *out of* their senses, lying in a simulacrum of the death they will eventually achieve. And irony appears in such a detail as the poet's expansion on the Vulgate's *conopeum* 'bedcurtain' around the lecher's bed into a golden "fly-net" with a one-way transparency, whose connotations suggest Holofernes' ironic entrapment in the net of his own inner evil.[52]

Such poetic virtuosity indicates that Old English poetry, like its prose, was not decadent toward the end of the Anglo-Saxon period. As the late tenth-century *Maldon* reflects the earlier secular ethos in a brilliant use of the conventional poetic techniques, so the tenth-century *Judith*, with perhaps a greater experimentation in its verse, reflects the earlier glorification of religious heroism of both the Caedmonian and the Cynewulfian schools.

NOTES

1. For reproductions of the eleventh-century illustrations, see Kennedy, C. 1916 as well as the facsimile edition, Gollancz 1927. Five further drawings have been discovered by the use of ultraviolet light—see Ohlgren 1972a. For commentary on the illustrations and their relationship to the poem, see Ohlgren 1972b and 1975; Raw 1976. Kennedy, C. 1916 contains a prose translation of the whole Junius MS. On MS unity, and for bibliography, see n. 37 below.

2. Ed. in ASPR 1; *Genesis A* ed. separately by Doane 1978a; *Genesis B*, by Timmer 1954. On the question of "three poems or one?" and of dating, see Irving 1959.

3. All line numbers are those of ASPR 1.

4. Huppé 1959, pp. 131–216; quotation, pp. 206–7. Cf. Shepherd 1966 who, citing Bede's and Alcuin's similar use of Genesis, says, "Plainly this was considered the proper place to end. In Isaac is foreshadowed Christ, whose work should undo all that followed the revolt of Lucifer" (p. 30). Others comment on the syntactic and dictional ambiguity of l. 2887b, *Wudu bær sunu*— either 'the s[S]on carried the wood [Cross]' or 'the Cross bore the Son'—see Creed 1967a, p. 80.

5. Thus Doane 1978a, p. 43, who nevertheless sees the poet's modifications of his biblical source as primarily influenced by patristic commentary.

6. Boyd 1982, pp. 236–7; Brockman 1974.

7. Cf. *Caedmon's Hymn*, chapter 10. This opening probably reflects the Preface to the Canon of the Mass—see Michel 1947.

8. On rhetorical patterns and word collocations, see Hieatt 1980a; also Gardner, J. 1975, pp. 18–32. On wordplay, see Frank 1972, pp. 211–6. Lee, A. A. 1972, pp. 17–41 emphasizes the conceptual duality of a secular/heavenly *dryht* or *comitatus*.

9. For example, in the onomastic pun of the epithet "seed-bearing" for Seth, l. 1145a—see Robinson 1968, pp. 29–30.

10. Sievers 1875. For his later views on the structure of *Genesis*, see Sievers 1929; but see further Irving 1959.

11. See Timmer 1954 and Capek 1971.

12. There has been a question as to whether the sources of the OE poem's inspiration were literary, like Avitus' poem, or the theological tradition of the Jewish Apocrypha and Christian exegesis, like Gregory's *Moralia*—see Evans 1963 on the former, Woolf 1963 on the latter.

13. On the figure of Satan as a combination of Germanic and first-phase patristic accounts of the devil, see Woolf 1953. Cherniss 1972, pp. 151–70 stresses the secular heroic aspects of the poem.

14. The first edition of this *Critical History* suggested that the fiend remains a serpent throughout the temptation—l. 491a indicates he assumed a *wyrm's* shape in tempting Adam, and ll. 589–90a say that the *wyrmes geþeaht* the serpent's counsel' worked within Eve—giving added ironic thrust to Eve's failure to penetrate the deception. Critics have ignored this suggestion, dismissing l. 491a as a momentary "confusion" on the poet's part, and conveniently overlooking ll. 589–90a. But the only ground for the "angel-of-light" disguise *in the text* is Eve's statement *after* eating the fruit. Since her vision of heaven, which she describes to Adam in ll. 666b ff., is an illusion provided by the fiend, why should her description of the fiend in ll. 656b–7a as "this beautiful messenger, God's good angel" be any more "real"?

15. Cf. Evans 1963.

16. On verbal contrasts, repetitions, and irony, see Britton 1974. For a psychological analysis of Satan's self-deception, see Renoir 1967; on Eve's psychology, Klinck 1979.

17. See Woolf 1963 and Finnegan 1976. Vickrey 1969 suggests that the A-S audience would have recognized Eve's vision of God's throne in the south and east as ironically indicative of the Last Judgment: "the real point of the vision [is] that through disobedience is the way to Judgment" (p. 99).

18. Hill, T. 1975.

19. Ed in ASPR 1; separately by Irving 1953 (with textual corrections in 1972 and supplement to the Introduction in 1974) and Lucas 1977. The poem is of Anglian origin, probably Northumbrian; its date of composition, probably eighth century.

20. Respectively, Irving 1974, p. 220 and Lucas 1977, p. 46.

21. Cf. Renoir 1962, on *Judith*.

22. See Cross/Tucker 1960.

23. Lucas 1977, pp. 46–7.

24. See Green, B. 1981. Earl 1970 provides the fullest allegorical reading.

25. Helder 1975, p. 10.

26. Hauer 1981, pp. 89–90.

27. See Martin 1982.

28. Cf. Lucas 1977, notes to ll. 520–2, 523–6; also Shippey 1972, pp. 142–3. The latter finds *Exodus* and the other Junius MS poems "resistant to allegorical or figurative readings" (p. 153).

29. The poet is keenly attuned to the ironic interrelationship of sound and sense: in l. 458, for example, he plays *wæge* 'wave' against *wegas* 'ways'; ll. 455b–6a are synesthetic; and in l. 451b *wæl*—in the compound *wælmist* (trans. as "poured forth death" but literally 'slaughter-mist')—is probably meant to suggest its near homonym *wæl* 'a deep pool or gulf,' since it alliterates with *wæter* in the a-verse.

30. See Hill, T. 1980b and Vickrey 1972a and 1972b.

31. Ed. in ASPR 1; separately (with *Azarias*—see below) by Farrell 1974.

32. Farrell 1967. Solo 1973 would eliminate both problems by syntactic interpretation and seeing a shift in point of view.

33. Bjork 1980, pp. 223–6.

34. Caie 1978. The most notable addition is that of a *ræswa* 'counsellor,' who advises the king to release the three youths; it is he who recognizes the miracle as a demonstration of the true God's power.

35. See Solo 1973, pp. 358–64. Finnegan 1984 suggests that, for a time in the poem, Babylon is a type of the heavenly Jerusalem (p. 195), and that the poem demonstrates "man's curious incapacity to maintain faith with God" and God's repeated granting to man of opportunity for salvation (p. 211).

36. Shippey 1972, p. 147.

37. For suggestions about the "imaginative unity" of the entire MS, see Caie 1978 and Hall 1976. Caie 1979 provides a full bibliography on Junius 11 down through Lucas 1977. Lucas 1979 argues that some 48 lines are missing from *Daniel*.

38. The poem is known as *Azarias;* ed. in ASPR 3 and Farrell 1974. Farrell argues that it was intended as a conclusion to *Guthlac B*.

39. See Farrell 1974, p. 38 who observes that none of these emphases are in the Latin or in the OE *Daniel*.

40. For analysis of the art of *Azarias*, stressing the lord-retainer theme, see Kirkland/Modlin 1972.

41. Ed. in ASPR 4; separately by Timmer 1961.

42. But see Wenisch 1982, who resurrects the theory of Anglian provenience.

43. For the Vulgate text, see Timmer 1961, pp. 14–6.

44. On the cinematographic technique of this scene, see Renoir 1962.

45. Woolf 1955b.

46. Chamberlain 1975; p. 139. He observes that "the second scribe of the Nowell Codex shows that he is a faithful copyist . . . [and] might wish to leave an accurate impression about the poem's original length" (p. 141, n. 22). But the argument assumes the scribe was copying from an independent transcription of *Judith*, and not from an "anthology" like MS Junius 11. If the latter were the case, however, and especially if that "anthology" were already decapitated, the faithful scribe might well have copied extant fitt numbers.

47. Chamberlain 1975, p. 137. The possibility of so many missing lines should make critics chary of finding the precise kind of structural balance that Doubleday 1971 suggests.

48. Huppé 1970, 114–88; Campbell, J. 1971. See also Hermann 1976.

49. Pringle 1975, p. 87.

50. On diction and variation, see Brodeur 1968, pp. 105–9. Kaske 1982 calls attention to the heroic ideal of *sapientia et fortitudo* in the poet's presentation of Judith.

51. Cf. Hieatt 1980b.

52. Berkhout/Doubleday 1973.

CHAPTER 10

Miscellaneous Religious and Secular Poetry

In the present chapter we shall consider poems that do not properly fall into the generic categories of the final two chapters, "Lore and Wisdom" and "Elegiac Poetry." A number of short poems, as well as the longer *Phoenix*, will come under scrutiny, many of historical rather than intrinsic literary interest. But one of the shortest poems combines literary power and historical significance: it lies at the heart of the fusion between native Anglo-Saxon and Latin-Christian traditions in the Old English period. This poem is, of course, the nine-line *Hymn* of Caedmon—the only authentic extant work of the first English Christian poet.

Bede's account, in the *Historia Ecclesiastica (HE)*, of the miracle of poetic composition granted the unlettered cowherd should be quoted at length:

> In the monastery of this abbess [Hild] there was a certain brother specially distinguished by the divine grace, in that he used to compose songs suited to religion and piety. . . . By his songs the minds of many were often fired with contempt of the world and with desire for the heavenly life. . . . [H]e did not learn that art of singing from men, nor [was he] taught by man, but he received freely by divine aid the gift of singing. . . . [H]e had lived in the secular habit until he was well advanced in years, and had never learnt anything of versifying;

and for this reason sometimes at an entertainment, when it was resolved for the sake of merriment that all should sing in turn, if he saw
the harp approaching him, he would rise from the feast [the OE version adds "in shame"] and go out and return home.

   When he did this on one occasion, and having left the house where
the entertainment was, had gone to the stable of the cattle which had
been committed to his charge that night, and there at the proper time
had composed himself to rest, there appeared to him someone in his
sleep, and greeting him and calling him by his name, he said: "Caedmon, sing me something." But he replied: "I cannot sing; and for this
reason I left the entertainment and came away here, because I could
not sing." Then he who was speaking to him replied: "Nevertheless,
you must sing to me." "What," he said, "must I sing?" And the other
said: "Sing me of the beginning of creation." On receiving this answer,
he at once began to sing in praise of God the Creator, verses which he
had never heard, of which this is the sense: [Bede here gives a Latin
paraphrase of the poem and apologizes for the loss of beauty and grandeur in the paraphrase—see below for the OE and Latin.] Awakening
from his sleep, he remembered all that he had sung when sleeping,
and soon added more words in the same manner in song worthy of
God. [Having recounted his gift to the reeve this next morning, Caedmon was brought before Hild; and after proving his new-found powers
by turning a passage of Scripture or doctrine recited to him into poetry
overnight, he was joined to the brethren.] And remembering all that
he could learn by listening [from the scriptural stories read to him by
the brothers], and like, as it were, a clean animal chewing the cud, he
turned it into most harmonious song, and, sweetly singing it, he made
his teachers in their turn his hearers. [The OE version adds that his
teachers wrote down his songs.][1]

   In the Latin text, as the above translation indicates, Bede says
that he is giving only the *sensus* of Caedmon's Old English *Hymn*.
But the Old English poem itself must quickly have become popular in the religious houses, for versions of it are preserved in
twenty-one manuscripts: five in Caedmon's native Northumbrian
dialect, in manuscripts of the Latin text of the *HE*; eleven in the
West Saxon dialect in manuscripts of the Latin text; and five in
West Saxon in texts of the late ninth-century Old English translation of the *HE*. These manuscripts date from the early Moore
MS of 737 to the late fifteenth-century Paris MS.[2] To give some
notion of dialectial differences, we cite below both the Moore MS
version (Northumbrian) and the Tanner 10 MS (West Saxon), fol-

lowed by a literal translation; then, for comparison with Bede's paraphrase, the Latin *"sensus"* in the *HE:*

Nu scylun hergan   hefaenricaes uard
metudæs maecti   end his modgidanc
uerc uuldurfadur   sue he uundra gihuaes
eci dryctin   or astelidæ
he aerist scop   aelda barnū
heben til hrofe   haleg scepen.
tha middungeard   moncynnæs uard
eci dryctin   æfter tiadæ
firum fold^v frea allmectig.

Nu sculon herigean   heofonrices weard
meotodes meahte   7 his modgeþanc
weorc wuldorfæder   swa he wundra gehwæs
ece drihten   or onstealde.
he ærest sceop   eorðan bearnū^3
heofon to hrofe   halig scyppend.
þa middangeard   moncynnes weard
ece drihten   æfter teode
firum foldan   frea ælmihtig.

(Now let us praise the Keeper of the heavenly kingdom, the might of the Creator and His thought, the works of the glorious Father, how He of each of wonders, eternal Lord, established the beginning. He first created for the sons of men [Nthn.]/for the children of earth [WS] heaven as a roof, the holy Shaper; then middle-earth the Keeper of mankind, eternal Lord, afterwards made for men, [made] the earth, the Lord almighty.)

Nunc laudare debemus auctorem regni caelestis potentiam creatoris et consilium illius facta patris gloriae quomodo ille cum sit aeternus deus omnium miraculorum auctor extitit· qui primo filiis hominum caelum pro culmine tecti dehinc terram custos humani generis omnipotens creavit·^{4}

This seemingly simple poem in praise of God poses at least four interrelated problems, all of which impinge in one way or another upon larger interpretive matters. Since the *Hymn* is short, it may be instructive to go into some detail about these problems, as a case study of the difficulties involved in establishing definitive interpretations of Old English poems.

One problem concerns questions of syntax and meaning; in citing the Old English, we refer to the West Saxon forms: (1) is "the works of the glorious Father" part of the object of the verb *praise,* or is it the subject, in apposition with the missing but understood *we:* "Now ought we, the creatures of the Father of glory, to praise . . ."?[5] (2) does *teode,* l. 8, mean 'made' or 'adorned'?[6] (3) are *firum* and *foldan,* l. 9a, a syntactic unit meaning 'for the men of earth,' and thus a variation in the West Saxon version of l. 5b, 'for the children of earth' (though it would *not* have been such in Caedmon's original Northumbrian, 'the sons of men'); or is the literal translation given above the correct one?[7] A second problem is the nature of the miracle Bede saw in Caedmon's vision and performance: Was it the gift of traditional poetic language, "aristocratic" and heroic, to an illiterate for the expression of Christian ideas? Insight into Scripture, along with the gift of language? The gift of memory? The fact that God chose someone "unsullied by the trivial qualities of pre-Christian verse and a complete novice in composition" to herald "a clean break with the heathen past symbolized by all previous poetry"?[8]

A third problem concerns the nature of the poem's composition: did Caedmon, with his "gift," adapt oral formulas or formulaic systems he had heard in the "trivial" pagan songs to the expression of Christian thoughts, or did he only use the native alliterative meter and stylistic technique of variation as the vehicle for a vocabulary gleaned from "Genesis, Psalm 146, and the Nicene and Apostles' Creeds, which even an illiterate layman could have known orally"?[9] In connection with this problem, we should remember that Caedmon composed about the year 670, and his *Hymn*—apart possibly from some Charms, segments of *Widsith* and the like—is the earliest extant poem, secular or religious, that we possess. Further, it was composed less than one hundred years after Augustine's Christianizing mission landed in England and only about fifty years after the conversion of the Northumbrian King Edwin at York.

The fourth of the interrelated problems—and one not often discussed—is why Bede chose *not* to give Caedmon's Old English poem in the original, especially if he saw a miracle of language involved in its composition. As Orton notes, "the fact that [Bede] apologizes so profusely for his paraphrase as a poor substitute for the original indicates both his sense of its authenticity and also his intention not to record it." Since the paraphrase seems deliberately to circumvent—by omissions and by conceptual and syntactic changes—the poetic variations of the Old English poem, it is possible that, in order to stress the new order of Christian vernacular poetry Caedmon initiated, and its divorce from the pagan past, Bede chose not to cite the Old English poem to avoid calling attention to the *Hymn*'s roots in the secular tradition.[10]

The larger interpretive matters related in the hermeneutic circle[11] concern the poem's doctrine, structure, and stylistic movement. Most critics agree that the theology of the poem is Trinitarian, and that *heofonrices weard* in line 1 refers to the Father; but which of the three following terms, *if any*, refer to the Son and Holy Ghost has been variously argued or taken on faith.[12] That ll. 1–4 praise God's creation of the "ideas" of things in their eternal aspects and ll. 5–9 the creation of *this* world for men, and that the epithets *heofonrices weard* and *moncynnes weard* are thus appropriately placed in the poem's structure, seem clear enough. But is the chronological sequence in the second part tripartite—"first," "then," "afterwards"—to accord with the view of this part as creation of heaven, creation of earth, and adornment of earth, or is it bipartite, a simple creation of heaven and then earth (with *æfter* being just a variation of *þa*, and *no* adornment)? Caedmon uses nine epithets for God in nine lines, though not one in each line. But is there really the stylistic and structural balance in their arrangement and the numerological possibilities for interpretation that Schwab proclaims? Are there really close parallels to "praise" sections of *Beowulf*, as Bessinger suggests? However we read the *Hymn*—in its details, its doctrine, its subtleties of expression; in its relation to oral Germanic poetry and Christian parallels; in reference to Bede's statements about its creation and his Latin paraphrase—we can even today feel its affective power.

Since Caedmon's *Hymn* bears at least some resemblance to various of the psalms involving the praise of the Lord, it may be appropriate to consider next the Old English metrical translations of the psalms. A translation of all the canticles into Old English survives in the beautiful but mutilated mid-eleventh-century *Paris*

Psalter.[13] The Latin text is on the verso, the Anglo-Saxon on the recto, with the first fifty psalms written in West Saxon prose and often attributed to Alfred, while psalms 51–150 are written in verse.[14] The metrical translation was probably made in the tenth century as part of the Benedictine reform (see chapters 1 and 3). These verses are not very distinguished as poetry: meter and alliteration, however regular, are mechanical and uninspired, common adjectives and adverbs as well as unusual words are overworked as verse fillers, and the traditional poetic vocabulary finds little place therein.[15]

Fragments of the metrical psalter, undoubtedly transcribed from the original of the Paris MS, also appear in MS Junius 121, and a lengthy poetic paraphrase of Psalm 50 (Vulgate)—which appears as prose in the *Paris Psalter*—is found in MS Cotton Vespasian D.vi.[16] *Psalm 50*, a 157-line poem in a mixed West Saxon and Kentish dialect, probably also has a connection with the tenth-century monastic revival; but its translator was more of a poet than the Paris versifier. His poetic paraphrase, in about a six-to-one ratio of Old English to its Latin original, employs many of the conventional formulas and the technique of variation to good if not startling effect. After a thirty-line introduction, following the line of patristic exegesis of the psalm as David's repentance for his affair with Bathsheba, the poet expands upon each Latin verse, and concludes with a brief epilogue in which he prays that he and others, like David, may receive God's forgiveness. In the same manuscript is the 43-line *Kentish Hymn*, a conflation and paraphrase of the *Te Deum* and *Gloria*, presenting rather an exposition on the Trinity than a prayer for intercession and a confession of faith.[17]

There are also *Fragments of Psalms* which are part of the *Benedictine Office* compiled by Wulfstan (see chapter 3).[18] Further in the *Office* are the *Gloria I*, the *Lord's Prayer III*, and the *Creed*.[19] Like *Psalm 50*, the *Gloria I* quotes each phrase of its Latin text, here the *Gloria patri*, and then poetically expands upon its original; the opening extended paraphrase of the one word *Gloria* will illustrate:

Thy glory and praise be widely spread
among all nations, Thy grace and will,

Thy might and mercy and all heart's love,
peace for the righteous; and Thy judgment be
glorified in the world, as Thou canst rule
all earthly might and the heavenly,
wind and clouds. Thou rulest all rightly. (*Gloria I*, ll. 1–7)

The *Lord's Prayer III* follows the same pattern as the *Gloria I*, but is much less expansive in its versifying of the *Pater noster*; it provides a clear, straightforward paraphrase of the Latin liturgical text. The *Creed*, on the other hand, resembles the *Gloria I* in its lengthy paraphrase of the *Credo*. It is almost stanzaic in form: of the first five sections, four are of eight lines each; and the second section, which expatiates upon the only Son and gives prominence to the Annunication, is exactly twice as long. Like the other poems of the *Office*, the *Creed* seems already to have been in circulation when Wulfstan drew upon it for his compilation.[20]

Another text of the *Gloria I*, substantially the same, appears in MS CCCC 201; it is preceded there by another version of the Lord's Prayer, known as *Lord's Prayer II*.[21] The latter is similar to the former in technique, building up its expansion of the Latin text phrase by phrase, bearing touches of the liturgy and scriptural matter, owing little to earlier verse vocabulary but comfortable in its use of earlier metrical patterns. Both poems are almost surely by the same author, but the *Lord's Prayer II* differs sufficiently in style, length, and subject matter to warrant our considering it an independent poem from its namesake in the *Office*.[22]

The two poems preceding the *Lord's Prayer II* in the Corpus Christi College Cambridge MS are known as *An Exhortation to Christian Living* and *A Summons to Prayer*.[23] The former is an 82-line poem, homiletic in tone, urging the reader or listener to abstain from sin and to perform good deeds, especially almsgiving, so that his soul may be secured against the coming Judgment Day. It is not a very distinguished piece of poetry, being a loose collocation of urgings and using some of the conventional formulas rather mechanically. But it contains some concepts and verses with parallels in *The Seafarer* (see chapter 12) which may help throw some light on that elegy.[24] *A Summons to Prayer* is a 31-line macaronic poem, the first half-line of each full verse being in Old English, the second in Latin (cf. the ending of *Phoenix*).[25] It is a call to repentance through prayer to God the Creator, to His Son, to Mary (who receives the greatest attention), and finally to all the saints that they intercede for mercy for "thy soul" from the "great Judge." Whitbread, following Förster, suggests that *Exhortation* and *Summons* were added by the compiler of the Cambridge MS to *Judgment Day II* (*Be Domes Dæge*), so that the five poems, including the following *Lord's Prayer II* and *Gloria I*, would form a penitential sequence moving from contrition and confession to absolution and prayer.[26]

The almost stanzaic form of the Junius MS 121 *Creed* makes it resemble the *Seasons for Fasting*, a poetic calendar of sorts on the observance of fasts.[27] This poem was discovered in 1934 by Robin Flower in the sixteenth-century transcript of MS Cotton Otho B.xi made by Laurence Nowell. It consists of some 230 lines divided into stanzas of eight lines each, save for the fourth, which has six, the fifteenth, which has nine, and an incomplete last stanza. The first few stanzas deal with the Jews, their observance of Moses' Law and their fasts, after which the poet discusses the four Ember fasts, urging his audience to follow the custom established by Gregory rather than continental recommendations; that is, they should observe the Ember fasts in March in the first week of Lent, in June in the week after Pentecost Sunday, in September in the week before the equinox, and in the week before Christmas. The poet then devotes several stanzas to the forty-day Lenten fast. The age-old problem of sinful priests—we recall Bede's, *Guthlac A's* and Ælfric's wrestling with it—crops up in stanzas 25 ff. The last three stanzas present a vigorous portrait of the sinful priests who, instead of observing the fast, hurry after mass to the tapster and persuade him it is no sin to serve oysters and wine before noon, rationalizing as they sit and tipple that it is permissible to refresh oneself after mass. Although not remarkable as poetry, this probably late tenth-century piece is notable for its experimentation with the alliterative meter in stanzaic form; and it does reveal a logical and orderly structure, a knowledge of its subject, and an emotional sensitivity in its depiction of the sacerdotal sinners.

Seasons for Fasting only impinges upon the concept of the calendar. More clearly in that genre is the poetic *Menologium* which, like several Latin poetic martyrologies and the Old English prose *Menologium* which resembles it, gives a chronological account of the Christian year.[28] Simultaneously, it puts the liturgical facts into the perspective of the natural year.[29] The 231-line poem is preserved in MS Cotton Tiberius B.i, one of the manuscripts recording the Anglo-Saxon Chronicles; it seems to have been viewed by the scribe as a prologue to the Chronicles, though it was originally an independent piece. The poet's sources were the ecclesiastical calendars in missals and other liturgical books; the date is uncertain, probably late tenth-century.

Three minor religious pieces are *A Prayer, Thureth,* and *Aldhelm.*[30] The last is unique in its irregular macaronic composition and in its inclusion of Greek as well as Latin words; its seventeen lines praise the great Canterbury religious writer (see chapter 1), and are fittingly preserved in a manuscript of his prose *De Laude Virginitatis. Thureth,* extant in MS Cotton Claudius A.iii, is eleven lines long; it represents a *halgungboc* 'coronation liturgy' as interceding for Thureth (Thored), who commissioned its making. *A Prayer,* extant in MS Cotton Julius A.ii and in part in MS Lambeth Palace 427, is a 79-line poem in which the speaker rather tearfully and melodramatically beats his breast, acknowledging over and over his smallness as compared to the Lord's greatness and asking Him for grace for his soul.[31]

Man's soul comes off much better *poetically* in the longer *Soul and Body I* and *II,* preserved in the Vercelli and Exeter Books respectively.[32] The former is a more extended poem, 166 lines in length, though its ending is missing. It presents first the speech of a damned soul to its decaying body and a description of that body's disintegration that is unparalleled in English literature; then, at line 127, it turns to the speech of a saved soul to its former earthly habitation. The Exeter poem contains only the first address, in 121 lines; it is substantially the same as its Vercelli counterpart, but with numerous variants.

Orton, examining the two manuscript versions in detail, argues (1) that the Vercelli text section on the saved soul was a later addition to an original poem represented by the Exeter text and the first part of Vercelli, by an author who "drew directly on patterns of structure and expression in $V1/E$ for his own contribution"; and (2) that the two texts derive from an earlier written composition, with E being closer to the original than V.[33]

The soul and body *topos*[34] runs throughout medieval literature and has certain obvious affinities with the Doomsday theme (see chapter 3 and also below). It takes two forms: the address and the debate. In the former, the dead body lies, unanswering, as the soul castigates or (more rarely) blesses it for its deeds while living; in the latter, a dialogue ensues. Though the Old English poem is only a monologue, and thus technically an address, the silence of the body is not only necessitated by its awful condition, but thematically eloquent.[35] First the poet comments that a man had better ponder his soul's state before their separation by death; he then says that the soul must visit its body weekly for three hundred years, unless the world ends sooner. When the damned soul speaks, it reproaches the body for making it suffer in its earthly housing as well as now, and foretells their further punishment on Judgment Day. With some grim satisfaction it vilifies its former dwelling in anaphoric parallels:

> Now you are no more prized as companion
> by any man alive, by mother or father
> or any kinsman, than the dark raven
> since I journeyed out alone from you
> through His hand by whom I first was sent.
> Now red jewels cannot remove you hence,
> nor gold nor silver nor any of your goods;
> but here your bones, despoiled, must abide
> ripped from their sinews, and I your soul
> against my will must often seek you,
> with words revile you, as you wasted me.
> (ll. 49–59 of the Exeter text)

When the soul departs, the poet graphically describes the body, helpless to answer: with cloven head, disjointed hands, distended jaws, severed palate, sucked sinews, gnawed-through neck, and slit tongue. And he further shows the decomposing worms at work, with their leader Gifer,[36] who first descends into the grave:

> He slits the tongue and bores through the teeth
> and eats through the eyes up in the head
> and for other worms opens the way
> to an abundant feast. (ll. 114–7a)

The Exeter poem concludes with a brief exordium paralleling its opening one, but this time suggesting that the wise man should give serious thought to his *body's* fate.[37]

The damned soul's denunciation of its body makes living flesh creep. *Soul and Body I's* additional portrayal of the righteous soul's words of consolation to *its* decaying body while it awaits resurrection is pallid by comparison.[38] No specific source has been discovered for this tenth-century (?) poem, but there is probably some connection with the Book of Job and with Doomsday homiletic material; and one of the Vercelli homilies contains remarks on a similar theme (see chapter 3).

A less overtly didactic poem on the body's fate is *The Grave*, composed sometime in the century after the Norman Conquest and consequently not always accepted as part of the Old English poetic corpus.[39] Extant in the twelfth-century MS Bodley 343, it consists of 23 lines plus three additional ones in a later thirteenth-century hand. Unlike *Soul and Body*, this poem is not concerned with the Judgment Day, only with the body's earthly resting place, which it describes in a sustained metaphor as a house: "built before you were born," a low house *sans* door, in which "you will be long locked" (only "Death has the key"), an abode where "no friend will journey to see you" or ask you "how that house pleases you"—for, it concludes, "you are loathsome and unlovely to view." *The Grave* is not without poetic power, utilizing parallelism, antithesis, and other Latin tropes to good effect.[40]

The Domesday *topos* is evident, however, in the two poems called *Judgment Day I* and *II* which, like *Christ III* (see chapter 9), use it "as a vehicle to convey a moral truth: that the moment of apocalypse or 'revelation' and the judgment of man on each deed is ever-present, and that man's *dom* 'glory' is established by a lifetime of such favourable judgments."[41] *Judgment Day I* is an exhortative homiletic poem (late eighth- or early ninth-century?) of 119 lines preserved in the Exeter Book.[42] It depicts the end of the world and the suffering of the damned repetitively, as if to exemplify the poet's statement: "Therefore *ever* shall I teach the people that they glorify on high God's praise" (ll. 46–8a). Beginning with the simple announcement, *Þæt gelimpan sceal* 'that must befall,' the poet introduces the Apocalypse with an unbiblical flood that will submerge the world.[43] He then proceeds to the apocalyptic fire, which he merges with the fires of hell in which greedy, hard-hearted men shall burn. To avoid those fires, the individual must meditate upon his sins in this present life, the initial step in penance. Those who do so and free themselves from vice will live forever in the splendid mansion the Lord of victory will build. The poet employs images of journeying, transience, and "unaware" feasting, images more strikingly used in the elegies (see chapter 12), especially *The Seafarer*. He concludes by adjuring his audience to "repeat what this says: it will become clear that I cannot prevent that event under the heavens, but it must happen thus [*ac hit þus gelimpan sceal*] to everyone, a burning flame over all the bright homes. After that flame life will be permanent: he who thinks properly will possess wealth in glory."[44]

Judgment Day II (Be Domes Dæge) is much more esteemed by critics than its Exeter Book counterpart. It is preserved in the eleventh-century MS CCCC 201, an important manuscript record of minor poetical texts of the later Anglo-Saxon period, which also contains the OE *Apollonius of Tyre* and a nucleus of Wulfstan homilies (see chapter 3).[45] This poem is a close expanded translation, 306 compared with 157 lines originally, of the Latin hexametrical *De Die Judicii*, attributed by the rubrics to Bede, though felt by some scholars to be by Alcuin.[46] It is a late work, probably late tenth-century, which substitutes end rhyme for alliteration in a few lines and even combines the two poetic techniques several times; it also reveals the influence of the soul and body *topos* in its speaker's penitential exhortations to his flesh to forsake its earthly attachments:

> Why, flesh, do you lie in filth, filled with sins,
> weighed down by crimes? Why do you not cleanse
> your grievous sins with a gush of tears?
> Why not pray for poultice and plaster
> for yourself, life's physic from life's Lord? (ll. 77–81)

Or:

> Ah, flesh, what do you do? What feast on now?
> What can weeping help in that time's need?

Woe to you now who serves this world
and lives here happy in wantonness,
goading yourself with luxury's sharp spurs! (ll. 176–80)

The first of these passages contains two dominant images: those
of flowing water and of medical leechcraft. The former is enun-
ciated in the poem's opening lines, in a notable expansion on the
Latin source:

Latin:
While I sat sad and alone under the covering of a shady tree, among
the flowing grasses of the fertile earth, with the branches echoing on
every side from the wind's breath, I was suddenly disturbed by a bitter
lament. I sang these mournful songs because my mind was sad when
I remembered the sins I had committed.

JD II:
Lo! I sat alone within a grove
covered by the deep woods' canopy,
where water-streams melodiously ran
amid the meadow, all as I say.
There pleasant plants flourished and blossomed
luxuriantly on that peerless plain,
and the trees moved and made melody
through the wind's force, and the sky was churned
and my wretched spirit was all disturbed.
Then suddenly fearful and sad, I
poured forth in song these fearsome verses,
all as you declared,[47] recalled my sins. . . (ll. 1–12)

The garden image in these lines has been given various allegorical
interpretations: Huppé sees it as the Garden of Eden, with the Tree
being that of Knowledge and the speaker a figure of fallen Adam
hiding in its shade to escape God's wrath; Hoffman as "a kind of
earthly Paradise—in a good sense—with suggestion of the waters
of grace and the Tree of Life. . . . an allegorical representation of
the Church on earth"; Caie as the *hortus conclusus* of the Song of
Solomon, the Church in this world (the monastery in particular),
and anagogically as the pure, Christian soul—but at the same time
as an "amoral" place where man can make a hell for himself, if
he lives lustfully and leisurely, or a heaven, if he penitently re-

members this world's transience.[48] However we wish to understand its significance, the Old English poem's earthly garden, unlike Bede's, has an initial seductive security. It suggests the hiddenness of sins which must be *now* revealed to God through such an outpouring from the tear ducts[49] as the persona calls for in ll. 26 ff. The water streams, which the poet adds to his original, foreshadow the cleansing effect of these penitential tears that the poet evokes again and again.

In ll. 45 ff., the persona links penitential weeping to the revelation of sins' wounds to the "heavenly Leech, who alone can heal with virtue the errant spirit." He then uses the example of Dismas, the repentant thief on the cross, as a paradigm for sinners' salvation. Like the poet of *Christ III*, that of *Judgment Day II* emphasizes the need for inner probing of sin and for repentance *now*, since on Judgment Day *all* will be revealed. The terrors of the damned in hell are even more powerfully portrayed in this poem than in the former; and an interesting passage shows abstractions of vice, like those in the later morality plays, gliding away at the end of the world:

> Then drunkenness shall disappear, and feasting,
> and play and laughter depart together,
> and lust shall likewise pass from here,
> and stinginess steal far away,
> vice vanish, and each vanity then
> shall guilty glide into the dark,
> and wretched, enfeebled sloth shall flee,
> slinking backwards slack with slumber.   (ll.   234–41)[50]

The poem ends on the usual thematic note of eschatological poetry, with the bliss of the blessed in heaven, but it has the unusual feature, adapted from Bede's poem, of the Virgin Mary leading that white-clothed band "through the lovely bright kingdom/of the glorious Father" (ll. 296–7). This scene also suggests a garden image, a heavenly one to counterpoint the earthly one of the beginning, with "red heaps of roses" (martyrs?) and white virgins "hung with blossoms."

Comments on two other poems will complete our discussion of miscellaneous religious verse: *Physiologus* and *The Phoenix*. Unlike the poems discussed so far, they are explicitly allegorical. Both are extant in the Exeter Book. The former[51] deals with the broad themes of salvation and damnation. It describes the traits and actions of birds and animals—these do not necessarily bear any resemblance to natural history—and then didactically explicates their signification in terms of God, Christ, mankind, or the devil. The physiologus-bestiary genre has a long history, going back to Alexandria in pre-Christian times. Its great popularity in the Middle Ages is attested by the many European and non-European translations in which it is preserved.

The Old English poem consists of seventy-four lines on the Panther, eighty-nine on the Whale, and a fragmented sixteen on a bird whose identity has been questioned, but which is usually identified as the Partridge. The gap between the first line of the last section, which ends folio 97, and the remaining fifteen lines beginning folio 98, occasioned much controversy in the late nineteenth and early twentieth centuries. Was the poem a fragment of a large cycle (continental versions of the *Physiologus* can amount to fifty "stories"), with several leaves missing from the manuscript, or was it a short-cycle type, in which the Panther, Whale, and Partridge were often associated? Krapp and Dobbie remove all doubt that the Old English version is a short-cycle Physiologus, with only one leaf missing from the manuscript.[52] Apart from the evidence of the manuscript gatherings, the poem as it stands shows a structural unity: it begins with a generalization applicable to all beasts and birds, embracing earth, water, and air, before narrowing its focus to one representative of each category; it continues with the word "further" used as a transition between sections; and the word *Finit* at the end of "Partridge" explicitly calls attention to the completion of the poem.[53]

The "Panther" section characterizes that beast as one gentle and kind to all save the dragon, with a coat of many colors. After he has eaten his fill, he sleeps in a cave for three days, arising on the third with a wondrous-sounding roar and with such a fragrance emanating from his mouth that men and beasts all hasten to him. Then follows the *significatio:* the Panther is God-Christ, gentle to all but Satan; and his sleep and waking are His Death and Resurrection. Those who hurry to the fragrance are the righteous, performing good deeds for their salvation.

The "Whale" section depicts that beast (originally an asp-turtle) as he appears to mariners: like a rough rock or a mass of seaweed on dunes near the shore. Sea-weary sailors are deceived into believing him an island, and they moor on him and build a fire. When they feel most secure, "rejoicing in fair weather," the crafty whale suddenly plunges to the depths, drowning the sailors "in the halls of death." Significantly, this is the devil's deceptive way, luring men to pride and wicked deeds, then dragging them off to hell.[54] The Whale has another trick: when hungry, he opens wide his jaws, from which issues a sweet smell that attracts little fish to their doom. Here is a parallel to the fleshly joys whereby the devil entices men to hell. [55] The deliberate contrast in *Physiologus*, as in most bestiaries, between the sweet smell of Panther-Christ drawing men to good deeds and salvation and that of whale-devil luring men to fleshly lusts and damnation emphasizes the polarity of Good and Evil that is central to the poem.[56]

We cannot tell much about the poetic representation of "Partridge" because in its fragmentary condition we have only one line on the physical bird; in fact, our identification of the bird as a partridge stems from the similarity in its allegorical representation of the parental relationship between God and man to the corresponding explication in the ninth-century Bern *Physiologus*, in which there is also the larger parallel association of Panther, Whale, and Partridge. One critic has argued that its form is homiletic and that its three sections, respectively concerned with earth, hell, and heaven, are primarily typological, tropological, and anagogical in their allegorical significations.[57]

The allegorical nature of the Old English *Physiologus* is somewhat simple and its poetry, for the most part, mediocre. But Anglo-Saxon literature produced an outstanding poetic example of this genre in the radiantly complex *Phoenix*. This poem moves beyond the customary equation of story or fable with moral or spiritual truths: it achieves a symbolic density that only the best of its kind reveal.

The *Phoenix* is found on folios 55b–65b of the Exeter Book.[58] Once counted among Cynewulf's poems, it is no longer considered his, though it may contain some trace of the Cynewulfian style as well as that of the *Andreas* poet.[59] Its date of composition, like that of most Old English poems, is uncertain, perhaps the late ninth century. Of its 677 lines, the first 380 closely follow, though they expand upon, the fourth-century Latin poem *De Ave Phoenice*, attributed to Lactantius. The remaining lines, which furnish an explicit allegory, would seem to be the poet's own, though they obviously incorporate biblical material and probably exegetical writings on the Resurrection. For this fable about the mythical bird which renews its life through immolation lent itself readily to the Christian doctrine of resurrection through and after the flames of Judgment Day. The motif itself is of Oriental origin and, in its handling by Lactantius, connected with the worship of the sun.

In the opening section of the eight parts into which the manuscript divides the poem, we find a description of the Earthly Paradise presented in negatives and positives, with rhyme and near-rhyme; for instance:

> That is a fair plain, where green forests
> stretch their limbs. There neither rain nor snow
> nor frost's breath nor fire's blazing death
> nor hail's pounding fall nor hoarfrost's pall
> nor sun's quick heating nor cold congealing
> nor warm weather nor winter shower
> harms its plenty, but the plain remains
> ever flourishing: that finest land
> stands full-blown with blossoms. (ll. 13–21a)

The landscape is Lactantian, but with echoes of Genesis, Ezekiel, and Revelation. When the Phoenix is presented in the second section, it is associated with the sun: it bathes twelve times daily in the cold streams of Paradise before the sun rises, and then, rising swiftly into the air, offers its adoration in song and carol to God's bright token. This routine continues for 1000 years, when the bird, grown old, flies westward to a wood in Syria, attended for a while by a concourse of birds. But seeking seclusion, the Phoenix drives away its attendants and builds its nest atop a lofty tree named after itself. There, in Section 3, the bird's "solarium" is kindled by the sun; and nest, bird, and the sweet herbs the *anhaga* 'lone-dweller' has gathered are consumed together on the pyre. In the cooled ashes, however, an apple's likeness appears; from it emerges a wondrously fair worm, which grows into a fledgling Phoenix. The renewed bird eats nothing but honeydew till (Section 4) it seeks again the terrestrial Eden, once more attended by flocks of birds singing hosannahs. But again the birds must retire, this time when the Phoenix reaches the ideal land (Section 5); and the self-containment of the bird, and its lack of fear of death, are praised as the paraphrase of the Lactantian poem runs its course.

The Anglo-Saxon poet's interpretation of the fable commences in the middle of Section 5, mitigating the division between "cortex" and "nucleus" of his poem:

> The almighty Prince of men granted him [the Phoenix]
> that he should be just as beautiful
> again, as fine-feathered as he was
> before, though the fire had consumed him.
> So after misery each blessed man
> chooses his way through death's dark woe
> to eternal life, after earthly days
> enjoys God's gifts in joys continual;
> and endlessly in glory will he
> dwell as just reward for his past deeds.   (ll.   377–85)

Here is the central allegory, the parallel between the Phoenix's re-birth through fire and the resurrection of all good Christians. As part of this equation, the sweet herbs the old bird gathers become the good deeds men do on earth (ll. 465 ff.). But the allegory has other dimensions. The bird's departure from the Earthly Paradise is, early in the "interpretive" part, equated with the exile of Adam and Eve for eating the forbidden fruit (ll. 400–4). Towards the end, the poet compares the Phoenix with Christ—imagistically in ll. 591 ff. and explicitly in ll. 646b–9. In ll. 548b ff. he uses the figure of Job who, like the Phoenix, is certain in his faith, knowing he will rise again to enjoy happiness with the Lord (Job 29:18). The poem's texture is further enriched by the incorporation in the fable of an extended harvest-and-sowing image (ll. 243 ff.), which suggests that resurrection is a natural phenomenon, a familiar process of nature, as well as a mysterious and unique event like the renewal of the mythical Phoenix or a biblical asseveration like Job's. Moreover, the bird is anthropomorphized by terms from the heroic vocabulary, thus helping to identify its life with that of man, which it symbolizes in its life, death, and resurrection.

Although Cross reads the *Phoenix* as a four-level allegory, the text appears to resist such a reading.[60] The various strands seem, rather, more interlaced with a vision of heavenly beauty to produce a symbolic vision wherein "the world of grace . . . mirrors the art of God to man, so that man may be redeemed through the art of his own works and days, arriving, crowned at last, in the city of art, which is heaven itself."[61]

The *Phoenix* is a splendid piece of literature in its entirety, though often only the Lactantian fable receives attention. Of the remaining poems to be surveyed in this chapter, not so much can be said. As a bridge between the religious poems and the few secular poems, we have the philosophical-religious *Meters of Boethius* and a few metrical prefaces and epilogues. The *Meters* are preserved only in MS Cotton Otho A.vi, damaged in the Cottonian fire of 1731, and in a transcript made by Junius before the damage was incurred (MS Junius 12).[62] They are a poetic paraphrase of the earlier Old English prose translation, not of the Latin original; like that translation, they may on good grounds be attributed to King Alfred himself (see chapter 2).[63] As poetry they are not especially noteworthy, employing many fillers or tag verses; but comparisons with their prose originals, analyses of their formularity and originality, suggest that at times, at least, they tighten the conceptuality of the piece and reveal an "unexpectedly subtle use of connotations or play on sound patterns."[64] To give a small idea of the prose/poetic relationship, as well as that to Boethius' *Consolation*, we translate the first part of the Old English *Meter 4*, Boethius' prayer to the Creator (Bk. I, m. 5), along with the Anglo-Saxon prose version, and quote Green's translation[65] of the Latin original:

OE:
O You Creator of the bright stars,
of heaven and earth: on Your high throne You
reign eternally, and swiftly You turn
the whole heaven, and through Your holy might

You constrain the stars to obey You.
Likewise the sun dispels the shadows
of the dark nights through Your might.
With her pale light the moon tempers
the bright stars through the power of Your might,
at times also deprives the sun
of its bright light, when it comes about
that they get so near by necessity.

A-S Prose:
O You Creator of heaven and earth, You who rule on Your eternal seat,
You turn the heaven on its swift course, and You make the stars obedient to You, and You make the sun dispel the shadows of the dark
night with her bright light. Likewise does the moon with her pale light
that dims the bright stars in heaven, and sometimes deprives the sun
of its light when it comes between us and it.

Latin:
Creator of the star-filled universe, seated upon your eternal throne You
move the heavens in their swift orbits. You hold the stars in their assigned paths, so that sometimes the shining moon is full in the light of
her brother sun and hides the lesser stars; sometimes, nearer the sun
she wanes and loses her glory.

We note that both the Old English prose and verse change the
paling of the moon from its proximity to the sun to an eclipse;
that the Latin "star-filled universe" becomes "heaven and earth"
in the prose and that the *Meter* includes stars, heaven, and earth;
and that the several b-verses about "God's might" in the *Meter*
are obviously verse fillers. A greater transformation may be seen
by comparing ll. 1–8 of *Meter* 27 with a translation[66] of its Latin
equivalent, Book iv, m. 4:

OE:
Why must you ever with unrighteous hate
disturb your mind, even as the sea-flood's
waves agitate the ice-cold sea,
move before the wind? Why do you fault
your fate, which has no fatal power?
Why can you not abide for bitter death
which the Lord shaped for you by nature,
towards which He hastens you now each day?

Latin:
Why do you whip yourselves to frenzy, and ever seek your fate by self-destruction? If you look for death, she stands nearby of her own accord; she does not restrain her swift horses.

The sea image is Alfred's; and in his employment of the poetic vocabulary and formulas, as well as of the alliterative line, the king forged his *Meters* in the native poetic tradition, despite the intractability of much of the *Consolation's* subject matter.

The metrical prefaces and epilogues may be treated more briefly. There exist a verse Preface and a verse Epilogue to Alfred's translation of the *Pastoral Care* (see chapter 2), in the ninth-century MS Hatton 20, sent by Alfred's order to Wærferth, bishop of Worcester, as well as in two or three other manuscripts.[67] In the 16-line *Metrical Preface*, Gregory's work, personified, speaks briefly of its original composition in Rome, its transmission by Augustine to the English, and Alfred's translation and despatching of it to his bishops "because some of them, who least know Latin, needed it." This *Preface* has not received critical attention. The 30-line *Metrical Epilogue*, utilizing an extended but consistent water image to refer to the contents of the *Pastoral Care* as the living waters from which readers may drink if their containers are *fæst*, has been more fortunate.[68] There is also a 27-line verse Preface to Wærferth's translation of Gregory's *Dialogues* preserved in MS Cotton Otho C.i,[69] and a 10-line Epilogue to the Old English translation of Bede's *Historia Ecclesiastica* (the *Metrical Epilogue to MS 41, CCCC*).[70] Robinson has discussed this in its immediate manuscript context. He sees the scribe's prayer in this colophon—for his readers to "support with kindly power the scribe who wrote this book with his two hands so that he might complete yet many [more copies] with his hands according to his lord's desire"—as merging the scribe's voice with that of Bede, who had himself served as a scribe.[71]

Seven secular pieces remain to be mentioned. Five of them, found in four of the manuscripts of the Anglo-Saxon Chronicles, along with *Brunanburh* (see chapter 6), are therefore referred to as Chronicle poems.[72] They are, like that heroic poem celebrating Æthelstan's victory of 937, concerned with national history, but none of them compares with it in poetic quality. *The Capture of the Five Boroughs* commemorates King Edmund's victory over the Norsemen in 942, by which he liberated the boroughs from Viking rule. *The Coronation of Edgar* (973) describes the ceremony performed by Dunstan and Oswald at Bath when, fourteen years after his accession, King Edgar decided to be officially anointed. *The Death of Edgar*, rather than dealing with a single event, treats of five important happenings in the year 975.[73] One of these, the expulsion of Oslac, earl of Northumbria, illustrates the mechanical piling up of the older poetic formulas with little regard for specificity of meaning:

> And þa wearð eac adræfed   deormod hæleð,
> Oslac, of earde   ofer yða gewealc,
> ofer ganotes bæð,   gamolfeax hæleð,
> wis and wordsnotor,   ofer wætera geðring,
> ofer hwæles eðel,   hama bereafod. (ll. 24–8)

> (And there was also driven   the brave-hearted warrior,
> Oslac, from his dwelling,   over the rolling of waves,
> over the sea-mew's bath,   grey-haired warrior,
> wise and clever with words,   over the concourse of waters,
> over the whale's home,   deprived of [his] homes.)

Despite this overaccumulation of formulas, the last line is effective in its contrast of home with homelessness. *The Death of Alfred* (1036), only partially in verse, recounts the imprisonment and murder of Prince Alfred, Æthelred's son, at the hands of Earl Godwine; and *The Death of Edward* (1065) eulogizes Edward the Confessor for about thirty lines, ending with a brief mention of his alleged bequest of the crown to Harold. A sixth poem, also in the Chronicles (1087), is *William the Conqueror*.[74] This doggerel verse almost completely abandons Old English poetic techniques, using rhyme and greatly varying verse lengths in its description of William as a proud, greedy, mean man.

The seventh poem, and last, is chronologically the latest of all extant Anglo-Saxon poems. It is in the tradition of the *encomium urbis* or 'praise of the city,' a standard rhetorical exercise of the Middle Ages, an example being the Latin poem of Alcuin's on

York.[75] The 21-line Old English poem *De Situ Dunelmi*, or *Durham*, is in two parts: it begins with a description of the famous city, its stones, its fish-filled river, and its animal-filled forest; then it gives an account of the famous men whose relics rest therein: St. Cuthbert, Bede, Bishop Aidan, King Oswald, and others. The poem was composed between 1104–9, but is surprisingly regular in its use of the older vocabulary and meter.[76] Thus in *Durham*, a poem in praise of a city and of the saints who sleep there awaiting Doomsday, composed more than five centuries after the illustrious Caedmon had uttered his hymn in praise of the Creator, the Anglo-Saxon poetic tradition found its last exponent, before it became transformed in the freer Middle English alliterative poems like Layamon's *Brut* and in the later fourteenth-century poems of the Alliterative Revival.

NOTES

1. Quoted from Whitelock 1979, pp. 722–3.

2. Dobbie 1937 edits seventeen of the versions; Humphreys/Ross 1975 publishes four more. The *Hymn*, in one Northumbrian and one WS version, ed. also in ASPR 6; four Northumbrian versions ed. in Smith 1933.

3. On the variants *aelda barnu[m]/eorðan bearnu[m]*—which are *not* confined to the Northumbrian and WS versions respectively—see Schwab 1983, pp. 14–6.

4. Quoted from the Moore MS, with the original scribe's raised points.

5. Howlett 1974, p. 7. *Weorc* grammatically can be nom. or acc., sg. or pl.; the Latin *facta* can be nom. or acc. pl.

6. Huppé 1959, pp. 99–130, Bessinger 1974, and Howlett 1974 take it as the latter and build their critical interpretations in part upon this meaning; but there is no hard evidence to support it—see Schwab 1983, p. 17, n. 67.

7. Bede's paraphrase does not help answer the question, since Bede omits the phrase altogether; his *creavit* probably translates *scop*, and he omits *teode*. Such questions of syntax and meaning are complicated by the ambiguity as to the number of independent clauses in the poem.

8. See respectively Wrenn 1946; Huppé 1959, pp. 99–130; Fritz 1974; Orton 1983a, p. 165.

9. On the former, see Magoun 1955a and Fry 1974a; on the latter, Blake 1962 and Howlett 1974, p. 10.

10. Cf. Orton 1983a; quotation from pp. 168–9. For very different views, see Howlett 1974, p. 6 and Schwab 1983, pp. 12–4.

11. On circularity in interpreting textual and extra-textual data in the criticism of OE poems, see Greenfield 1972, chapter 1.

12. On this and the following points, see all items in previous notes.

13. Ed. Colgrave 1958.

14. On the prose psalms, see chapter 2; the metrical psalms ed. in ASPR 5.

15. Keefer 1979 shows that the poet often relied on OE interlinear glosses of the Latin Psalms. Diamond 1963 feels that the poet used the "fillers" artistically; he also argues that the diction is as formulaic as that of the older poetry.

16. Ed. in ASPR 6. A further fragment, in the *Eadwine Psalter*, which parallels the text of the *Paris Psalter* 90.16.1–95.2.1, is ed. by Baker 1984.

17. Ed. in ASPR 6. For discussion of sources, see Shepherd 1952.

18. Ed. in ASPR 6.

19. Ed. in ASPR 6. Texts and discussions also in Ure 1957. On *Gloria I,* see further Whitbread 1966b.

20. Cf. Bethurum 1957, p. 49 and Whitbread 1962.

21. Ed. in ASPR 6 and Ure 1957, Appendix A.

22. Whitebread 1962, n. 15. Ure 1957 argues for *LPr II* and *III* as variants of the same poem. There is a still briefer, workmanlike metrical translation, *LPr I,* in the Exeter Book, and a 3-line *Gloria II* preserved in MS Cotton Titus D.xxvii—ed. in ASPR 3 and 6 respectively.

23. Both ed. in ASPR 6.

24. Greenfield 1981. Whitbread 1951 feels there is little trace of the older poetic vocabulary in *Exhortation.* On textual problems, see Whitbread 1949. Two prose adaptations exist, one in Pseudo-Wulfstan Homily XXX (Napier's numbering), the other in Vercelli Homily XXI.

25. Ed. in ASPR 6. On the macaronic hymn tradition in medieval English literature, see Wehrle 1933, pp. 1–14.

26. Förster 1942; Whitbread 1957; Caie 1976, pp. 115–6; Frantzen 1983a, pp. 180–1.

27. Ed. in ASPR 6, separately by Grimaldi 1981, with Italian translation. For commentary, see Sisam, K. 1953, pp. 45–60. On technical calendrical matters, see Henel 1934.

28. Ed. in ASPR 6; see also Rositzke 1940, pp. 3–11. Malone 1969 provides a trans. On the prose *Menologium,* see Henel 1934.

29. Hennig 1952.

30. Ed. in ASPR 6.

31. For commentary on the poem *Aldhelm,* particularly on its use of Greek words, see Whitbread 1976, which also contains a translation. Raw 1978, pp. 123–6 provides a brief analysis of *A Prayer.*

32. Ed. in ASPR 2 and 3; also Willard 1935. Shippey 1976 edits the longer Vercelli text, with facing translation.

33. Orton 1979a, 1979b. Willard 1935 had seen *V* as the source for *E;*

and Gyger 1969 had suggested that differences between the two texts were the result of oral transmission.

34. Shippey 1976, pp. 29–36 provides a summary of the history of this *topos*.

35. Ferguson 1970.

36. See Kurtz 1929.

37. Ferguson 1970 and Orton 1979a call attention to the circular or symmetrical structure of *Soul and Body II*. Both find it poetically as well as doctrinally effective; but Bradley 1982, pp. 358–9 savagely denounces it on both scores.

38. Though Smetana 1967 claims it has "real poetic power," Orton 1979a, pp. 451–7 makes detailed argument to the contrary. On doctrinal problems in the poem, see Shippey 1976 and Frantzen 1982.

39. Not in ASPR. For text see Short 1976a; Anderson, G. 1966, p. 188–9 provides translation.

40. See Short 1976a; see also Dudley 1913 and Marino, C. 1981.

41. Caie 1976, p. 4; further on the Doomsday theme, see Whitbread 1967.

42. Ed. in ASPR 3; Shippey 1976, with facing translation.

43. A flood is not one of the Christian medieval signs of doom, though in Matthew 24:37–9 Christ *compares* Doomsday to Noah's flood. Perhaps the poet was influenced by Germanic apocalyptic tradition. Caie 1976, pp. 99–101, suggests the water is purgatorial, like that of baptism. On the signs of doom, see Caie's Appendix.

44. For analyses of *Judgement Day I*, see Caie 1976, pp. 95–114 and Shippey 1976, pp. 43–6.

45. On the "sequence" of penitential poems which begins with *Judgment Day II*, see n. 26, above.

46. OE and Latin texts ed. in Löhe 1907 (with German translation) and Lumby 1876 (with English translation); the OE text alone ed. in ASPR 6. For comparison of OE and Latin texts, and critical analyses, see Whitbread 1966a and Caie 1976, pp. 115–59; see also Hoffman 1968.

47. This verse, like l. 4b's "all as I say," are clearly not in the Latin. Despite some far-fetched conjectures about the referent of *you* in l. 12a, Whitbread 1966a, p. 648 is undoubtedly correct in seeing it reflecting the Latin epilogue's l. 158, where Bede addresses Bishop Acca: "I have composed these verses *just as you commanded*." The epilogue is otherwise omitted in the OE poem.

48. Huppé 1959, pp. 80–93; Hoffman 1968, p. 177; Caie 1976, pp. 120 ff. and 158–9.

49. Translators take the word *æddran*, l. 26a, as either "veins" or "fountains"; the Latin has "eyes." The OE word literally means "a channel for liquids," and a translation "tear ducts" makes more sense here.

50. The poet uses many rhetorical tropes; these and other aspects of

the poem's technique remain largely unexplored, despite the analyses cited above.

51. Ed. in ASPR 3; see also Cook 1919. For a verse translation, see Cook/Pitman 1921.

52. ASPR 3, pp. l–li.

53. See Cordasco 1949 and Letson 1979b.

54. The ME *Bestiary* contains a similar description of "Cethegrande." Milton draws on the same tradition for his simile comparing Satan to Leviathan in *Paradise Lost* I, ll. 200 ff.

55. The open jaws of hell are common in medieval pictorial representations—see the illuminations in the Junius MS facsimile, Gollancz 1927.

56. Cf. Campbell, T. 1978, who finds a relationship between the OE poem and Paul's Epistle to the Ephesians.

57. Letson 1979b.

58. Ed. in ASPR 3; see also Cook 1919. Separately by Blake 1964.

59. See chapter 7 and Hietsch 1955.

60. Cross 1967; argued against by Greenfield 1972, pp. 140–5 and Letson 1979b, pp. 17–8; Heffernan 1982 finds Marian symbolism in some of the imagery. For a typological reading, see Kantrowitz 1964.

61. Calder 1972c, p. 181. Stevick 1980 provides a reading in terms of mathematical proportions and number symbolism.

62. Ed. in ASPR 5.

63. See Sisam, K. 1953, pp. 293–7.

64. Monnin 1979, p. 360. See also Metcalf 1973 and Conlee 1970.

65. Green, R. 1962, pp. 14–5.

66. Ibid., p. 88.

67. Ed. in ASPR 6; texts and metrical translation in Hamer 1970.

68. See Cross 1969b, which contains a prose translation; also Isaacs 1968, pp 83–9.

69. Ed. in ASPR 6; separately by Yerkes 1980.

70. Ed. in ASPR 6.

71. Robinson 1980; translation quoted from pp. 19–20.

72. All ed. in ASPR 6.

73. Isaacs 1968, pp. 89–93 sees the poem as a "series of ways and images for expressing death."

74. Ed. in Fowler, R. 1966; not in ASPR. For comments, see Whiting 1949.

75. See Schlauch 1941. The OE poems ed. in ASPR 6.

76. Howlett 1976b finds the poem's structure conforming to the Golden Section.

CHAPTER 11

Lore and Wisdom

From poems celebrating God and His handiwork and man in his chronicle of years, we turn to verse more didactic in purpose, to verse emphasizing secular and Christian lore and wisdom. Such wisdom literature is "devoted . . . to rules for conduct or control of the environment or to information about nature and men" and intended to "suggest a scheme of life . . . to ensure its continuance, . . . to control life by some kind of order."[1] In a largely unlettered society like the Anglo-Saxon, such "rules" are apt to take a somewhat aphoristic form. Thus runes, charms, gnomes and proverbs, riddles, and some more pointedly homiletic Christian poems comprise the bulk of the poetry to be considered in this chapter.

Earlier we mentioned the use of runes in Germanic, and particularly in Old English, poetry (see chapter 5): the inscription on the Golden Horn of Gallehus, the runic signatures of Cynewulf, the inscription on the Ruthwell Cross containing verses found also in *The Dream of the Rood*. As these illustrations suggest, runes were employed to identify the maker (and sometimes the owner) of instruments of pleasure and warfare, to signify the poet who wished to have prayers said for his soul's salvation, or to inscribe a monument. They might also be used to convey a message of one sort or another, as in the *Riddles* and *The Husband's Message;* but they also had a magico-religious function. The word *rune* (OE *run*) means "mystery" or "secret"; and from the time of adoption of the *fuþark* (OE *fuþorc*), or runic alphabet, by Germanic tribes, possibly from North Italic models (c. 250–150 B.C.?), the formalized non-cursive script often served ritualistic purposes.[2]

The Germanic runic alphabet consisted of twenty-four letters, headed by those which give it its name: ᚠ (f) ᚢ (u) ᚦ (th) ᚨ (a) ᚱ (r) ᚲ (k). The Old English runic alphabet probably entered England in East Anglia with the Anglo-Saxon invaders, spread to the southwest and in the seventh century to the north, where it flourished.[3] The Anglo-Saxons modified the forms of the letters somewhat—for example, ᚦ became ᚦ , ᚨ became ᚪ , ᚲ became ᚻ —and they added nine more letters for a total representing thirty-three phonetic sounds. The runes had names, as their use in Cynewulf's signatures demonstrates. In large part these are taken from the Germanic world of gods and men, the world of natural powers, and treasured possessions. The first six Old English runes had the names *feoh* 'wealth,' *ur* 'aurochs, wild ox,' *þorn* 'thorn' (replacing Gmc. **þurisaz* 'giant'? or from **þuranaz* 'thorn'?), *os* 'mouth/god', *rad* 'riding,' and *cen* 'torch.'

The 94-line *Rune Poem,* preserved only in Hickes's *Thesaurus* transcript of 1705, since the manuscript perished in the Cottonian fire, furnishes us with a poeticized alphabet of twenty-nine characters.[4] The stanzas vary in length, but each describes what is named by the corresponding runic letter. We illustrate by translating the verses for the first six runes, and for the last:

> *Wealth* is welcome to those in this world;
> yet every man must spend it freely
> if he would gain glory from the Lord.
> *Aurochs* is awesome and over-horned,
> a fierce beast who fights with its horns,
> a known moor-treader; that's a mighty one.
> *Thorn* is a very sharp thing: to each thane
> who grasps it, pain, the greatest roughness
> to every man who lies among them.
> *Mouth* is the means by which all men speak,[5]
> the prop of wisdom welcome to the wise,

hope and happiness to every man.
Riding is no risk to the reveller
in the hall, but hard on him who sits
astride the stout steed mile after mile.
Torch is to the living told by its flame;
shining and bright it burns most often
inside where princes sit at ease

. . . .

Grave is gruesome to great and small
when flesh inexorably starts to fail,
the pale body cool, choose the cold earth
as its bedfellow: life's blossoms fade,
joys turn away, all covenants betray.   (ll.   1–18, 90–94)

The mnemonic, informative, and hortatory nature of the *Rune Poem* is evident in the translated stanzas. So, we hope, are some of the poetic qualities—such as the triple alliteration in the first line of each stanza, the humor in the "riding" stanza, and the parallelism and homoeoteleuton (similarity of inflectional ending: *fade, away, betray* reflect the OE *gedreosaþ, gewitaþ, geswicaþ*) in the last. The poem also employs a number of "heroic" formulas and kennings, such as *mære morstapa*, l. 6a (cf. *Beowulf* l. 203a, *mære mearcstapa*, of Grendel), and "gannet's bath" for the sea in l. 79a (cf. *Beowulf* 1861b). And though the Christian poet was restricted by the order imposed by the runic alphabet, he manages to come full circle, with the 4-line stanza 20 mediating both in length and ideationally between the first and the last:

Man in his mirth is dear to his kinsman;
yet each must someday betray the other,
since the Lord intends by His sentence
to give the wretched body back to earth.   (ll.   59–62).[6]

Akin to the runes in their magical properties are the charms. The oldest relics of Germanic literature, despite their Christianization in their Old English forms, the charms are openly rather than secretively magic. Their magic stems from three elements: a source in *cræft* 'cunning, knowledge' and *mægen* 'power,' an operational force that is nonphysical, and a ritual whose threefold purpose is to secure the power, transmit it to the desired site of operations, and utilize it effectively. "The rhetoric of charm," Northrop Frye observes, "is dissociative and incantatory: it sets up a pattern of sound so complex and repetitive that the ordinary processes of response are short-circuited. Refrain, rhyme, alliteration, assonance, pun, antithesis: every repetitive device known to rhetoric is called into play."[7]

Bald's *Leechbook* and *Lacnunga* (see chapter 4), together with three other volumes, contain the texts of the twelve extant Old English metrical charms: "For Unfruitful Land," the "Nine Herbs Charm," "Against a Dwarf," "For a Sudden Stitch," "For Loss or Theft of Cattle" (three charms), "For Delayed Birth," "For Water-Elf Disease," "For a Swarm of Bees," "A Journey Charm," and "Against a Wen."[8]

Something of the nature and character of the charms may be seen in one intended to keep bees from swarming (ASPR 6, no. 8; Storms, no. 1):

> [Against bees swarming, take earth, cast it with your right
> hand under your right foot and say:]
> I catch it under foot, I have found it.
> Lo, earth has power against all creatures,
> and against malice and against neglect,
> and against the mighty tongue of man [i.e., an evil spell].
> [Whereupon cast sand over them, when they swarm, and say:]
> Settle down, victory-women, sink to earth,
> never be wild and fly to the woods.
> Be as mindful of my welfare
> as is each man of eating and home.

Part one states the speaker's knowledge of the power residing in earth and of his control over the earth he throws under foot and thus "catches." The repetitive formula in the last two-and-a-half lines emphasizes the power in words themselves. In the second part, the speaker applies his power at the proper moment, when the bees start to swarm, casting sand which forms, as it were, a magic circle in the air, at the same time cajoling the bees with a "circle" of words. The image of the "victory-women" has sometimes been taken as a relic of the pagan Valkyries, but more likely it is a simple metaphor suggested by analogy of the bee's sting with the "sting" of a victorious sword.

In a longer and more complex charm, *Wið Færstice* "For a Sudden Stitch" or "Against Rheumatism" (ASPR 6, no. 4; Storms, no. 2), there is another reference to "mighty women"; but here it *is* to female spirits that were thought to cause the disease. Again, some have seen an allusion to Valkyries. The whole charm is against evil spirits, who have "shot spears" into the sick person; the conjurer will answer fire with fire. A prose statement to boil certain herbs in butter (into which, at the end of the charm, a knife will be plunged for applying the salve to the patient) precedes the charm. Then an introduction reminiscent of epic openings begins abruptly:[9]

> Loud they were, lo, loud, when they rode over the mound,
> fierce and resolute when they rode over the land.
> Shield yourself now to escape this evil:
> out, little spear, if you be in here.

Then comes the mention of the "mighty women," who plot how to use their *mægen* or supernatural strength, sending "screaming darts," which the speaker says he will requite in kind; and he repeats the "out, little spear, if you be in here" formula. A reference to a smith making a "little knife" follows, and again the incantatory refrain; then "six smiths made slaughterous spears,/out, spear, not in spear!" The referents and allusions in this first part have occasioned much debate, as has its structural relation to the "remedial" second part, at the end of which the speaker incants:

> If it were shot of Æsir, or shot of elves,
> or shot of witch, I will help you now.
> This your cure for shot of Æsir, this your cure for shot of elves,
> This your cure for shot of witch, I will help you.
> Fly there to the mountaintop [i.e., the "shot"]
> Be hale! May the Lord help you! [i.e., the patient]

That the "riders" who get their nefarious power from the burial mound, the mighty women, and the smiths of the first part are to be equated with the gods (Æsir), witches, and elves of the second makes an attractive reading that resolves many of the difficulties posed by this charm, both as magic and as poetry.[10]

Wið Færstice seems primarily pagan despite its Christian ending. Christianity in the charms may perhaps best be seen in the eleventh-century text of *Æcerbot* "For Unfruitful Land" or "Field Ceremonies" (ASPR 6, no. 1; Storms, no. 8). The first part (ll. 1–48) consists of ceremonies honoring the sun; yet for all its "rules" of turning to the east and bowing nine times, it includes saying a *Pater noster*, four masses, the names of the four Gospelers, a prayer to Mary, the litany, and a *Sanctus*. The second part (ll. 49–87) is a ceremony in honor of Mother Earth, with an apostrophe to a mysterious *Erce*, but with an immediate call upon the Christian God:

> Erce, Erce Erce, mother of earth,
> May the Almighty, eternal Lord, grant you
> fields sprouting with grain and fruitful,
> ever increasing and flourishing,
> tall shafts of corn and shimmering crops,
> and broad barley crops,
> and glistening white wheat crops,
> and all the crops of the earth.

The above is to be chanted as the seeds are placed on the body of the plough; further incantation is called for as one cuts the first furrow, and again when one places a baked loaf of many flours under it. The charm ends with a *Pater noster* said thrice. Niles suggests there is no need to substitute pagan elements for Christian ones to understand this charm: it is, rather, "an expression of the piety and anxiety of eleventh-century Christian Englishmen" who, having faced famine, invoke assistance from "the God of the Covenant, patron of agriculture, the One who . . . . 'has control over both times and seasons' (*Beowulf* 1610-11a)."[11]

Other Old English metrical charms have received interesting critical readings, such as "A Journey Charm," which has been seen as a supplication throughout life's "journey" for protection against earthly evils.[12] And the charms have received appreciative analysis for their various poetic techniques: their employment of formulas, variations, kennings, metrical patterns, and the like.[13]

The charms' practical value, their wisdom, was obviously very specialized, unlike that of the gnomes or maxims, which provided generalized reflections on the properties naturally inherent in creatures and objects, or offered up moral guides for large socio-religious areas of human endeavor. Like the charms, however, these sententious bits of wisdom have a long pedigree, and we may observe parallels in many different languages, from the Old Testament Book of Proverbs to the Greek Hesiod to the Old Icelandic *Hávamál*.[14] Strands of gnomic wisdom are found throughout Old English poetry encased in lyric or narrative form, in the elegies and in *Beowulf* in particular.[15] But there are two distinctive heterogeneous collections of apothegms, one in the Exeter Book, known as *Maxims I*, and a shorter one, *Maxims II*, in MS Cotton Tiberius B.i, following the *Menologium* (see chapter 10) and preceding one of the texts of the Anglo-Saxon Chronicles.[16] Attempts have been made to find pagan and Christian strata in these collections, but their ninth- or tenth-century authors were undoubtedly clerics who fused, however awkwardly, ancient and more contemporaneous aphoristic lore.

The Exeter Gnomes (*Maxims I*) come to 206 lines, divided into three sections; those may represent works of three different authors, or perhaps the divisions are merely scribal. *Maxims I A* begins as a riddling match or dialogue, the poet stressing that perceptive men should exchange their aphorisms: "Question me with wise words; do not let your understanding spirit be hidden." Then the poet proceeds to share *his* wisdom with us; ll. 18b–36 give some idea of his substance and technique:

> The wise man shall hold
> meeting with the wise. Their minds are alike:
> always they settle disputes, preach peace,
> which evil men earlier disturbed.
> Counsel goes with wisdom, justice with the wise,
> the good must be with good. Two are mates:
> woman and man shall bear in this world
> children through birth. A tree shall on earth
> lose its leaves, its branches mourn forlorn.
> The dying shall depart, the doomed die,
> struggling every day to his parting
> from the earth. Only the Ruler knows
> where the dead one arrives when he leaves this realm.[17]
> The new-born increase when death comes early:
> therefore there are so many men on earth;

mankind would spread measurelessly
if this world's Maker did not diminish them.
Foolish is he who knows not his Lord; death often comes unexpected.
Wise men care for their souls, keeping truth with justice.

Are these loosely collocated maxims, or is there some controlling structure? One critic finds the several members connected by association of ideas, through meaning and through sound.[18] The end of one gnome may suggest the next, or a central theme may run through a number of maxims, or both methods may be combined. In the above passage, we may see how the theme of the wise man runs through several verses and then leads, through the association of one good man with another, to the concept of a further grouping of two, wife and husband; and this in turn to their children, and to death. The tree gnome is perhaps a vivid image for parents mourning the death of children, a theme pursued in the following verses, with their Malthusian insight. At the end of the passage, there is a gnomic antithesis about folly and wisdom vis-à-vis salvation, a philosophical aphorism which also occurs in *The Seafarer*.

Maxims I A has other striking images. There are cliffs holding back storm-driven waves, both feeling the wind, seemingly associated with the strong mind necessary to "steer" one's life. This is followed by a simile: "as the sea is calm/when the wind does not stir it,/so peoples are peaceful when they have come to terms" (ll. 54–6). The whole poem reveals a sense of structure. After his introduction, the poet tells us first to praise God, because in the beginning He gave us life and transitory joys, which He will ask us to repay Him. At the end, after maxims about a king's sovereignty, warriors' duty, a woman's proper place at her own table, and fealty and the receiving of treasure, the poet says that we will have to repay the one [One] who gave us these favors. The poet thus creates a kind of envelope pattern.

Maxims I B and *C* have less force and unity. *B* begins with "natural" gnomes about frost freezing, fire burning wood, ice forming a bridge and locking up the earth's reproductive powers—a binding God alone loosens. It contains an oft-quoted passage on the joyous welcome the Frisian wife gives her sailor husband on his return, which leads into an admonition to women to remain faithful. *B* ends with a contrast between Woden, who made idols, and the true God, who made heaven. As part of the wisdom proffered in *C*, we find the philosophical-elegiac theme of man's solitariness in the world: how the exile must take wolves as companions, comrades who will tear him to pieces. Yet he who can sing and play the harp is less lonely than others, and it is better for a man to have a brother to help him in the hunt, in battle, and in pastime hours over the chessboard. *C* ends, after a section on murder and violence that started with Cain's killing Abel, on a heroic note,[19] telling how the shield must be at the ready, the spear-point on the shaft, courage in a brave man, but "ever for the faint-hearted shall be the least treasure." Shippey's summary comment on both *Maxims I* and *II* is apt, especially for the former:

> The central tenets . . . seem to be that misfortune is inevitable, but that wise men find ways of guarding against it, mitigating it, in the last resort accepting it. In this prudential process social controls are given high importance. For a modern reader the poems' charm often derives from their unfamiliar blend of the bold and the canny, the physical and the abstract, the banal and the suggestive.[20]

One problem in understanding the *Maxims* is determining the specific meanings of the reiterated *sceal* or *scyle*. In some cases the verb seems to have the force of moral obligation, fitness, or propriety; in others it merely suggests what is characteristic, customary, or inherent; in others it has a "sense of certainty which current dialectal varieties of the future (with *will*) bring out. . . ."[21] This problem is especially acute in the 66-line *Maxims II*; ll. 14–19a will illustrate:

> Good companions shall encourage
> the young prince in battle and in ring-giving.
> Courage shall be in a warrior. Sword shall see
> battle against helmet. The hawk, though wild,
> shall dwell on the glove. The wolf shall live
> in a grove, a wretched solitary.

All three possibilities of meaning for "shall" exist in these verses, but the parallelism and syntactic regularity which extends through

l. 54a "creates the expectation of a concomitant semantic consistency in the meaning of *sceal* in each of its occurrences."[22]

Beginning with a *sceal*-gnome, "A king shall rule a kingdom," the poem moves to a statement that "Cities, the skillful work of giants, . . . are visible from afar," and through a series of *bið* 'is' statements about the superlativeness of such phenomena as wind, thunder, fate, seasons, truth, treasure, and the wisdom of age and experience. After the long list of *sceal*-gnomes that begin at l. 14, the poem concludes with the statements that

> the future state is
> hidden and secret. The Lord alone,
> the saving Father, knows (it). None comes again
> hither under the roofs who can say here in truth
> to men what sort of thing is God's domain,
> the seats of the blessed, where He Himself dwells.

This final suggestion about the limitations of man's knowledge and wisdom gives *Maxims II* its special unity. In the beginning it was implied that men can see "from afar" the works of man, the *visibilia* of this world; the central part displays the specifics of man's experience and wisdom; the end states the impossibility of knowledge of the next world. Since the poem precedes a text of the Anglo-Saxon Chronicles in the Cotton MS, perhaps "the compiler saw a kind of propriety in prefacing an ambitious intellectual endeavor such as the *Chronicle[s]* with *Maxims II*, a poem on the limitations of knowledge."[23]

Similar to the gnomes and the proverbs in their exposition of wisdom through formulaic repetition are two more pointedly Christian poems of the Exeter Book, *The Gifts of Men* and *The Fortunes* (or *Fates*) *of Men*.[24] Both employ the anaphoric *sum* 'one'-pattern to display the various crafts and destinies that God in His wisdom distributes to men. Cynewulf used the "gifts" theme in *Christ II* (see chapter 8, n. 16). The ultimate Christian source is the parable of the talents in Matthew 25:14–30; perhaps the more immediate one was a key phrase in Gregory's *Homilia IX in Evangelia: Alius . . . tamen didicit artem qua pascitur*. In his *In Natale Unius Confessoris* Ælfric translated this as *Sum . . . leornode swa-þeah sumne cræft þe hine afet* 'One learned, however, a craft which fed him'—

the concept lending itself by easy extension to the various crafts that "feed" men.[25] But the theme as expressed in *Gifts* emphasizes aristocratic talents analogous to those found in Old Norse Eddic poetry, rather than practical or spiritual ones, and the poem undoubtedly represents a fusion of Christian and Germanic concepts.[26] The poet begins by stating that God gives some kind of natural endowment to every man lest he become depressed; nevertheless, He will grant no man too much lest he become arrogant (ll. 1–29). The body of the poem enumerates some forty secular and ecclesiastical talents (ll. 30–85; 86–97): among the former are such diverse occupations as gem-working, carpentry, minstrelsy, scholarship, and soldiering, and such natural aptitudes and capacities as beauty of form, swiftness of foot, agility in swimming, and wittiness at wine-taking; among the latter are the discernment to choose the grace of God above worldly treasures, fondness for fighting the devil, capability as a Church functionary, and skill in the arts of the scriptorium. The poem concludes (ll. 97–113) with reiteration of God's wisdom in not overendowing any one individual, and with a call to praise Him and His bounty.[27]

Although *The Fortunes of Men* has a structural outline similar to that of *Gifts*, it is a superior poem. Its enumeration of the evil fates and good fortunes which overtake and are allotted to men is more graphic and detailed. Further, its introduction seems more integral to the poem as a whole, setting forth succinctly the human ritual of begetting, birth, and rearing offspring, which leads to the challenging remark that "God alone knows what the years will bring to the growing boy." This observation in turn is developed in the central portion. First the poem vividly portrays the evil destinies of men: the wolf-devoured, the hunger-wasted, the storm-wrecked, the spear-slain, the sightless, the limb-injured. The poet describes at greater length one who falls from a high tree in the forest, sailing through the air like a bird, yet featherless, to lose his life at the roots;[28] one who swings on the gallows, where the raven plucks out his eyes and he is powerless to ward off the outrage; one who, becoming drunk, cannot hold his tongue and thereby loses his life. But another shall pass from adversity to prosperity; and here, around l. 64, the poet shifts gears. In de-

scribing the good fortunes God distributes to men, he picks up
the "gifts" theme. The theme receives quite different treatment in
Gifts and *Fortunes*, as the corresponding descriptions of the apti-
tude for harping reveal:

> One with his hands can play the harp,
> has skill to stir the gleewood deftly. (*Gifts*, ll. 49–50)

> One shall with his harp at his lord's
> feet sit, receiving gifts and treasure,
> and ever rapidly sweep the strings,
> let the leaping plectrum loudly sound,
> the nail make melody; he has great zeal. (*Fortunes*, ll. 80–4)

But though the poet of *Fortunes* has perhaps swerved from his
original intention of depicting the destinies of men, he draws both
the gifts and fates themes together in his conclusion (ll. 93–8):

> In this wondrous way the Lord of hosts
> shaped and bestowed the crafts of men
> throughout this world, and ruled the fortunes
> of each of mankind upon this earth.
> So now let each man say thanks to Him
> for all He in His mercy ordains for men.[29]

Gifts and *Fortunes* are concerned with the paths men follow in
this world. The famous short poem known as *Bede's Death Song*
deals directly with the preparation man makes for his eternal destiny:

> Before the fateful journey,[30] no one
> will be wiser than knowing the need
> to ponder before his departure
> what to his soul of good or evil
> after the death-day will be adjudged.

There is an enigmatic quality to this one-sentence poem, with its
compellingly balanced *before . . . before . . . after* sequence. It is
preserved in Northumbrian and West Saxon versions in some
thirty-three manuscripts of the *Epistola Cuthberti de Obitu Bedae*.[31]
The "death-day" seems to refer both to the individual's dying and

to the Day of Judgment. The acme of wisdom, the poem suggests, is the renunciation of all wisdom save that which conduces to good, since one will finally be judged as good or evil, and hence saved or damned, not by what one knows but by what one has done of good and evil in this world.[32] This "limitation of knowledge" may be compared with that in *Maxims II,* where good struggles with evil, the wise man considers the strife in this world, and the criminal hangs for his wicked deeds. Whether Bede was simply quoting a poem he knew (Caedmon's?), or whether he composed the *Death Song* as he lay dying, is not clear from Cuthbert's letter; but most scholars accept the attribution to Bede himself. There is, from the modern perspective at least, a certain irony in the thought that the eighth-century scholar *par excellence* should at the end have so depreciated his own worldly wisdom; but such depreciation was a *topos* in the Middle Ages.

Wisdom of a more didactic sort appears in several other minor poems, most of them recorded in the Exeter Book. One piece is a 94-line poem called variously *Precepts, A Father's Counsel,* or *A Father's Instructions to his Son.*[33] The poem follows the tradition of the "instruction genre" in its structure and in its use of imperatives (thirty-one in all), antithetically balancing in its sections—and at times its lines—good and bad behaviors, along with their corresponding rewards and consequences.[34] But it presents a rather uninspired series of admonitions. Ten times a father delivers himself of platitudes about not committing crimes, not associating with evil companions, guarding against the deadly sins, learning what is fitting to be learned, and other such common advice. The seventh section is more gnomic than perceptual, lacking an imperative; and the ninth, with only one injunction, bemoans the decline in observance of spiritual law.[35] Though a parallel with the Ten Commandments seems indicated in the poem, only the first injunction actually corresponds to any part of the Decalogue: honor thy father and mother.

The 84-line *Vainglory*[36] concentrates on the one admonitory theme of its modern title. It begins with an "autobiographical" introduction, stating that a poet long ago was instructed by a book-learned sage how to distinguish God's own son [Son?] from a sinful man. This opening leads to a picture of the babble in the wine-hall, where voice competes with voice "even as minds are unalike." The vainglorious person is then described: envious, boasting, deceiving, drinking, quarrelling. The devil's arrows pierce his defenses, and he in turn *hygegar leteð,/scurum sceoteþ* 'lets fly his mind-spear,/shoots with showers (of malicious barbs)' (ll. 34b–5a). Now, says the poet, you have been enabled to recognize such a one as a son of the devil "enclosed in flesh," whose soul "is destined for hell and worthless to God" (ll. 46b–50)—i.e., the antithesis of "God's own son[Son],/the welcome guest in the dwellings" (ll. 5b–6a; cf. ll. 80b–1a, where Christ is more surely the *immediate* referent). The source of man's presumption is then traced to the rebellious angels (ll. 57 ff); and the conclusion contrasts the humble with the proud and their respective eternal rewards. Like *Precepts*, this poem has its antithetical balance; but unlike that poem, it almost totally avoids admonition; it uses heroic formulas combined with Christian metaphors, is rich in compounds and *hapax legomena*, and poses more interpretive problems.[37] Shippey suggests that its aim is the same as that of *Precepts:* "to arouse a sense of danger, to make one aware of the mutual exclusiveness and intolerance of good and evil, so much so that one will approach cautiously any action or decision to be taken in life."[38]

The Order of the World, or *Wonders of Creation*, a poem of 102 lines, follows *Maxims I* in the Exeter Book.[39] In an "autobiographical" introduction similar to that of *Vainglory*, the poet asks his audience, a *fus hæle* 'man ready [to absorb knowledge?]', whether he is desirous of conversing with a much-travelled stranger, of asking him, a "wise seer/poet," to tell about the wonders of creation. The poet continues with a comment that it is through power of the word-hoard that men who have contemplated this "web of mysteries" pass on their knowledge. Yet one must learn, too, that God's power passeth man's understanding, and give thanks that the eternal King will grant us to ascend to heaven if we obey His commands (ll. 1–36). The body of the poem is a *herespel* 'eulogy' of God's creation and His ordering of the world so that all things keep their place, fulfilling His eternal commands. The daily course of the sun receives lengthy treatment as a symbol of this order. That part of its bright journey we observe would seem to be an image of the knowledge we *can* obtain. Yet, the poet cautions,

there lives no man so wise that can know
by his own power whence it comes,
how that gold-bright sun goes through the depth
into the dark under the waters' surge,
or what land-dweller can enjoy the light
after it departs over the sea (ll. 76–81)

—a limitation, again, on human knowledge. The poet returns to the stability of the elements under God's commands, "within the power of His bonds by which heaven and earth may be raised up." He ends the body of his poem with a glance at the eternal glory, feasting, and joy of the blessed, and concludes with a five-line coda, an exhortation to forsake vain desires, fleeting joys, and vices, and travel to the "better kingdom." There is a symmetry to *Order of the World* that consorts well with its subject; and if our interpretation is correct, the sun-symbol unifies the basic ideas: the glories of Creation, its order and stability, the "brightness" yet limitations of human knowledge, and the possibility through keeping God's commands of man's ascent into heaven.[40]

The 20-line *Homiletic Fragment II*[41] is seemingly addressed by way of consolation to one in distress. He receives the wisdom that, though the affairs of the world now seem uncertain and man betrays man, there is one faith, one living God, one baptism, one Father everlasting, one Lord of the people, Who created this earth, its blessings and joys. Contrasted with this present Sixth Age, with its possibility of redemption, is that of the tree-screened, darkness-covered world of unredeemed man before Christ's Advent (ll. 12–4). In the beginning the addressee is gnomically adjured to bind fast the thoughts of his heart, to guard his *hordlocan* 'treasure-chamber'; at the end the poet refers to the Nativity, to the dwelling of the Holy Spirit in the *hordfate* 'treasure chest' of the Virgin. Often considered fragmentary, the poem is complete, as this thematic and verbal linking suggests.[42]

The 47-line *Homiletic Fragment I*, extant in the Vercelli Book,[43] is also concerned about evil and this world's moral decline; but it focuses attention on calumniators in a "homily" which takes Psalm 28:3 for its text: "Draw me not away with the wicked, and with the workers of iniquity, which speak peace to their neighbors, but mischief is in their hearts." The psalm itself is paraphrased in ll.

9–15a. Isaacs demonstrates that the poem—at least the first thirty lines—is unified verbally around the metaphor of the bee, who has honey in its mouth but a poisonous sting in its tail (ll. 19b–23); so smooth-talking men promise truth with fair words, have in their promises *hunigsmæccas* 'tastes of honey,' but in their hearts a secret wound through the devil's craft (ll. 24–30).[44] The poem ends with the usual homiletic exhortation to consider how we may gain heaven's light and help for our souls to dwell with the angels when God destroys earthly life.

At the end of the late twelfth century MS l i. I.33, University Library, Cambridge, there is a collection of moral and religious metrical apothegms called by its first editor *Instructions for Christians*.[45] It consists of 264 lines in 41 verse paragraphs. Typical of its substance are ll. 4–9, which say that there are four things necessary to gain eternal life: man's labor, the monk's prayer, learning the Law, and fasting; there is also the typical vanity theme of ll. 36–8:

> It is vanity which you view here,
> and all you see here, it is like shadows;
> it will all depart like the dark shower.

The nine-line Exeter MS poem *Almsgiving*[46] is structured around Ecclesiasticus 3:33: "just as water extinguishes fire, so almsgiving extinguishes sin."[47] But it combines this with an opening paraphrase of Psalm 40's "Blessed is he who considers the poor," a conclusion further echoing the psalm's "Lord . . . heal my soul," and an organization based on the patristic tradition in which *considered* almsgiving, as contrasted with the habitual, is blessed both on earth and in heaven.[48] Such almsgiving will not only save one's own soul, the poem suggests, but is "(1) a means of releasing souls from purgatory, and (2) a quasi-sacramental analogue of baptism." It demonstrates in addition that the *reþehydig wer* 'man righteous of mind' of l. 2 continues "the redemptive work of the *reþust ealra cyninga*" 'the most righteous of all kings' (of the *Descent into Hell*).[49]

One final short religious "wisdom" piece to be mentioned here is the eight-line *Pharaoh*, which follows *Almsgiving* in the Exeter

MS.[50] It is a kind of riddle-dialogue in the genre of the prose *Solomon and Saturn* and *Adrian and Ritheus* (see chapter 3): the questioner asks how many warriors there were in Pharaoh's army when they pursued the Israelites. And the respondent replies, "I'm not sure, but there were 600 chariots when they were drowned." Perhaps the audience was supposed to know that each chariot contained three men, and that answer, as in the *Ioca Monachorum*, was 1800;[51] or perhaps the poet was being faintly ironic in asking about the number of men, pursuing, and answering with the number of chariots, drowning.

Our discussion of gnomic wisdom has led us down a path to homiletic verse of no great poetic distinction. But if we return to our starting point, we can take another direction and come thereby to the Old English *Riddles;* for the compressed observations of nature and characteristic behavior that constitute gnomic utterance are but a twist and turn of presentation from the riddle genre. There, too, we find representations of natural phenomena (storm, sun, fire, iceberg) and of the proprieties of civilized conduct. Some lines in the Exeter *Maxims* about the lord's lady's duty to tender the mead cup first to her husband have a counterpart in the "Horn" riddle's "Sometimes a ring-adorned maiden fills my bosom." But the riddles elaborate metaphorically upon their subjects with the deliberate ambiguities that are their generic essence. Riddles are psychologically close to the charms, yet in concept and method the obverse: whereas the charm takes us "into the mythological universe of traditional names and mysterious powers," the riddle "seems rather to take us into the actual world explored by sense experience, where the eye is overwhelmingly prominent, and the reason."[52]

Riddling is an ancient art, finding a place in many a narrative action. The incest riddle became something of a plot-motivating force in the Greek-Latin-Old English romance of *Apollonius of Tyre* (see chapter 3). Oedipus' solving of the riddle of the Sphinx ultimately led to that Greek hero's tragedy. Samson's riddle to the Philistines, "Out of the eater came forth meat, and out of the strong came forth sweetness" (Judges 14:12–4), played its role in the hostilities between Samson and his enemies. But the Old English riddles exist for sheer intellectual stimulation and titillation, even as they impart their wisdom—and in many cases are excellent poems. They are preserved in the Exeter Book in three groups: nos. 1–59; a second version of no. 30 and *Riddle 60* (the latter considered by some critics to be part of *The Husband's Message* [see chapter 12]); and nos. 61–95.[53] Many of the last group, occupying the latter part of the manuscript, unfortunately have been damaged by the action of some corrosive agent. Further, it is impossible to tell whether there were originally 100 riddles in imitation of the century of three-line hexameter *Ænigmata* of Symphosius (an unknown Latin author of c. fifth century), the 100 *Ænigmata* of the seventy-century Aldhelm (which range in length from four to eighty-three hexameter lines), and the combined 100 riddles of Tatwine (archbishop of Canterbury in 731) and Eusebius (Hwætberht, abbot of Wearmouth, 716–c.45, and friend of Bede?).[54] It is clear, however, that the Latin enigmas did exert some influence on the Old English vernacular collection, since *Riddles 47, 60, and 85* ("Bookworm/Moth," "Reed-pen," and "Fish and River") are indebted to Symphosius, and 35 and 40 ("Coat of Mail" and "Creation") are reworkings of the *lorica* and *creatura* enigmas of Aldhelm.[55] But sometimes that influence has been overstated.

The *Riddles* are a heterogeneous collection of verse on secular and Christian subjects, reflecting both oral or popular and literary or learned traditions. Although at one time the whole group was assigned to Cynewulf on the basis of a misreading of the elegiac *Wulf and Eadwacer* as "The First Riddle" (see chapter 12), the variety of technique, subject matter, and tone argues for multiplicity of authorship and a range in date of composition (eighth to tenth centuries?). The solutions to the riddles in many cases are questionable, since the Old English manuscript, unlike the Latin ones, does not identify the answers.[56] Among the subjects treated, in no discernible order, are domestic equipment like the loom and churn, agricultural implements like the rake and plow, various birds, animals, and natural phenomena, items of food and drink, artifacts connected with the pen, the sword, and priestly cloth, and even such an anomaly as a one-eyed seller of garlic. At one extreme in manner of presentation is the lyric, which by its obviousness places greater emphasis upon its thematic development than upon any residual ambiguity. Foremost in this category are the "Storm" *Riddles*, nos. 1 and 2–3—the last two are almost universally taken as one riddle, and a number of critics take all three as a unity, solving "Wind" or "the Power of Nature."[57] The first (or first part) depicts a storm on land; the seventy-two lines of no. 2–3 describe a series of storm or wind operations: (a) beneath the sea, (b) beneath the land (earthquake), (c) on the surface of the sea, and (d) on land. Segment (c) offers a striking picture of a shipwreck as the waves rise, fall, and smash upon the rocks:

> There the ship resounds
> with its sea-guests' cries; the steep stone cliffs
> calmly await the crash of waters,
> the thrashing waves, when the towering throng
> crowds up the slopes. There the ship must face
> a cruel battle if the sea bears it
> off in that fierce hour with its freight of souls,
> so that it will have lost control
> of its fate in that fighting, ride foaming
> on the backs of breakers.

The "Storm" or "Wind" *Riddles* are learned, fusing a knowledge of Graeco-Roman cosmology and medieval Christian science (Isidore of Seville, Bede).[58] At the other extreme of presentation we find several kinds of riddles whose kernels are more like kennings.[59] The aphoristic Christian "Chalice" (no. 48) is one kind:

> I heard a ring speak without tongue
> brightly on men's behalf, though it had
> neither a stout voice nor strong words.
> Silently that treasure spoke for men:
> "Save me, O Savior of souls."
> May men perceive the mystery,
> the red gold's incantation, wisely trust
> their souls to God, as the ring said.

The obscene *double entendre* of the "Ornamented Shirt" (no. 61) is quite a different type:[60]

> Often a lovely lady locked me
> in a chest: sometimes she took me out

with her hands and gave me to her lord,
her gracious master, as commanded.
Then he stuck his head into my center,
forced it upward where it was confined.
If he who received me had strength,
adorned as I was something rough was due
to fill me. Now guess what I mean.

A subtler, more metaphysical *double entendre* and punning have been
analyzed in the "Moth/Bookworm" *Riddle* (no. 47), a six-line riddle based on Symphosius' three-line *Tinea*, in which we are told
that the subject eats words but is none the wiser for swallowing
them: the poet's "puns make the poem self-referential in a complex and sophisticated way, forcing the words themselves to display the simultaneous reality and insubstantiality of language."[61]
In still a different vein is the paradoxical "Anchor" (no. 16):

Often I must fight with wave and wind,
strive against both when I seek the earth
shrouded by sea: that land is strange to me.
I am strong in strife if I stay at rest;
if I fail, they have more force than I,
and tearing me apart put me to flight:
they would plunder what I must defend.
I withstand them if my tail stands fast
and the stones can stoutly hold me
firm in place. Find out what I am called.

In form and formula the *Riddles* also vary considerably. Some
use runes rather straightforwardly to spell out their objects' names:
others use runes cryptographically.[62] Some use the opening formula "I saw . . ." and conclude with "Say how it is called"; others begin "I am . . ." and end with "Tell what my name is." One
of the finest, "Horn" (no. 14), employs an anaphoric *hwilum*
'sometimes'-series to characterize the wide-ranging uses of the instrument:[63]

I was a warrior's weapon; now a young
gallant covers me with gold and silver,
with filigree. Sometimes men kiss me;
sometimes my voice calls forth close friends

to battle; sometimes a horse bears me
across the land; . . . .

As a final illustration of the wisdom encapsulated in the *Riddles*,
of their humor, their seriousness, their Puckish quality, we cite
the following (no. 11):

My garment's gray, but bright ornaments,
red and gleaming, bedeck that robe.
I mislead the muddled and urge the foolish
to contrary ways; others I keep
from a useful course. I know not why,
made so foolish, their minds betrayed,
led astray in deed, they extol my
crooked ways to everyone. Woe to them
when they lead on high their dearest hopes,
their souls, if they have not ceased their folly.

The solution to this riddle would seem to be a cup or beaker of
wine—*in ænigmate veritas*.

Wisdom and truth of greater religio-philosophical depth are the
substance of the two poetical dialogues of *Solomon and Saturn*.[64]
These ninth- or tenth-century poems—presumably based on an
undetermined Latin source—survive in fragmentary form in two
manuscripts: CCCC 422 (MS A), which contains Poem I, a prose
dialogue, and Poem II; and CCCC 41 (MS B), which contains lines
1–93 of Poem I written in the margins of three pages of the Old
English translation of Bede's *Ecclesiastical History*. The dialogues offer
a strange combination of Oriental, Germanic, and Christian lore;
they employ runes, gnomes, and riddles, and have some properties of the charms. They thus make a suitable conclusion to this
chapter on lore and wisdom.

The *Solomon and Saturn* poems and the prose "continuation" of
Poem I in MS A should not be confused with the prose piece of
the same name (see chapter 3). All the English works, it is true,
have the unique Saturn (in the poems represented as a prince of
the Chaldeans) as Solomon's opponent in debate, whereas the later
Latin and continental vernacular versions have the name Marcolf.
The Old English prose is catechistic in nature and the poems, especially II, are more far-reaching in their substance and more

squarely in the dialogue genre. Saturn is the embodiment of pagan wisdom, while Solomon, as a type of Christ, represents Christian wisdom. Still, he preserves some of his Hebraic-Arabic character of magician and subduer of demons; as the latter, he further resembles Christ. Solomon's magical propensities are more pronounced in I. There the king expounds on the virtues of the *Pater noster:* he describes the manner in which each letter of the Lord's Prayer, personified as an angelic warrior, overcomes the devil. *P,* for example, has a long rod to scourge the devil (ll. 90–2a), and *T* stabs at the devil's tongue, twists his throat, and smashes in his cheeks (ll. 94–5).[65] This unique presentation of the *Pater noster* suggests the pagan-Christian exorcist rites of the charms; the magical association is reinforced on a more clearly pagan level by the manuscript use of the Germanic runic characters for each letter of the Lord's Prayer, and on a more Christian level by reference to the *Pater noster* as "palm-twigged," the palm being a traditional medieval symbol for victory over the devil.[66]

Poem II, probably the earlier of the two poems—and infinitely the superior—follows the separate and distinct, exaggerated and allegorized prose treatment of the contention between the devil and the hypostasized or personified *Pater noster* itself (rather than its letters). Its contestants are truly engaged in dialogue, and Saturn is not only the recipient of instruction but a propounder of difficult riddles in his own right, a worthy, if inferior, opponent to the great Solomon. Near the beginning, Solomon is the questioner, asking Saturn to tell him about "the land where no man can set foot"; the latter replies with what is known as the *Weallende Wulf* 'raging Wolf' passage, about a hero who killed twenty-five dragons there before he himself was killed. That land is now desolate, cannot be reached by water, air, or land, and is the source of all poisonous creatures. Yet, Saturn ends, Wolf's "brightly polished sword still shines, and over the graves its hilt gleams." This is followed by a riddle-like section on books, their power to impart wisdom to their user (Saturn says), salvation to those who love them (Solomon says). Then the king has a long passage satisfying Saturn's curiosity about the *Vasa Mortis* (literally, "receptacle[s] of death"), a demonic bird in the center of the Philistines' land, which Solomon had bound in chains to prevent its terror-

izing the Philistines. Another riddle-like question from Saturn about
"that wonder that travels throughout the world,/moves inexorably, beats at foundations,/raises tears of sorrow" (ll. 283–4a) and
Solomon discourses on the "answer," old age. Structurally, these
four sections may be considered Part I:[67] they seem to move from
heroic-mythic origins, to intellectual-spiritual wisdom, to shaman-
istic control of demonic terror, to the inevitability of worldly death.
The concluding lines about old age say "she overcomes the
wolf,/she outlasts the stones, she conquers steel,/she bites through
iron with rust, she will do likewise to us" (ll. 299b–301).

Part II contains a number of comments and gnomic wisdom that
suggest Maxims, Fortunes and other poems already considered. At
one point Saturn's gnomic speech (ll. 303 ff.) that "Night is the
darkest of weathers, need is the hardest of fates,/Sorrow is the
heaviest of burdens, sleep is most like death," provokes from Solomon the famous lines:

A little while the leaves are green;
then they fade and brown, fall to the earth
and perish, pass and turn into dust.
Thus then fall those who formerly long
committed crimes, remain in wickedness,
hoard rich treasure, ...[68]

The large issue of fate and man's destiny receive their due in this
part, culminating in Solomon's return to "myth" in an account of
Lucifer's revolt and fall, and a statement that every man has about
him a good and bad angel struggling for his soul (cf. Guthlac A,
chapter 7, n. 53).[69]

We quote in translation one further passage. Beginning with a
section suggestive of Fortunes 10–14, Solomon says that a mother
cannot control her son's destiny, but must weep therefore:

when he sets forth young,
he has wild hopes, a restless heart,
mind full of cares; frequently he errs,
wretched, joyless, bereft of honor.
Sometimes depressed he paces a hall,
lives far from his people; his only lord
often looks away from this luckless man. (ll. 378b–84)

The motif of the transitory nature of earthly splendor, so vividly depicted in the *lytle hwile leof beoð grene* passage (though the comparison is specifically with sinners who hoard treasure), and the formulaically expressed theme of exile in the mother-son lines, are but part of the rich pattern of wisdom and knowledge exhibited in the *contentio* of *Solomon and Saturn II*—a poem which, "by its human drama and combination of detail and mystery create(s) an impression of profundity beyond any of the other didactic poems."[70] But the motif and theme are centrally significant in Anglo-Saxon elegiac poetry the concern of our final chapter in this critical history.

NOTES

1. Bloomfield 1968, p. 17.
2. The origins of the Germanic runic alphabet are much debated. For general discussion, see Elliott 1959. For English runes in particular, see Page 1973. On English MS runes, the source of our runic-Roman equivalents and main evidence for A-S rune names, see Derolez 1954; see also Schneider, K. 1956.
3. Page 1973, p. 32.
4. Ed. in ASPR 6; Shippey 1976, with facing translation. Ed. separately by Halsall 1981, with Norwegian and Icelandic analogues; contains facing translations of all. Halsall dates and localizes the poem as tenth-century West Saxon.
5. Most scholars interpret "mouth" here, as a replacement of *os* (Gmc. **ansuz*) 'god' by the Latin homonym *os* 'mouth'; but the context supports also an allusion to Oðinn/Odin, the Germanic god of eloquence and wisdom. This possibility of wordplay also exists in the following stanza, since an OE homonym for *rad* 'riding' means 'modulation of tone,' (i.e. 'a boast'), a meaning also suitable to context: "*Rad* is easy for each of warriors in the hall." On such wordplay, see Hall 1977. On the poem's function of uniting and relating "homophonous variants of the [rune] names where they were perceived to exist," see Hamp 1976, p. 144.
6. The verb *(ge)swican* 'betray' occurs in this stanza and the last (see above); but Tir 'a guiding planet, star, or constellation, useful in navigation' (stanza 17; Halsall, p. 137) *næfre swiceþ* 'never fails.'
7. Frye 1976, p. 126; for comparison and contrast of charms and riddles in general (including OE), see pp. 123–47.
8. Ed. in ASPR 6; see also Storms 1948, with facing translations, and Grattan/Singer 1952.
9. This opening has been described as one which calls attention to the

charm as a "dramatic verbal performance in which the very act of saying creates its own magic"—Chickering 1971, p. 87.

10. See Hauer 1977. Chickering 1971 feels that claims of unity and equal literary power for the second part of the charm are "overingenious"—p. 104. See also Weston 1985.

11. Niles 1980a, p. 55.

12. Stuart 1981. For bibliography of the charms, see Lendinara 1978.

13. See Vaughan-Sterling 1983. Nelson, M. 1984b analyzes verbal-act fusion in the structures of "For a Swarm of Bees," "For Unfruitful Land," and "A Journey Charm."

14. Barley 1972 makes a distinction between *proverb* and *maxim:* the former is particular but metaphorical, the latter general but literal.

15. On OE poetry and wisdom literature, see Bloomfield 1968; Shippey 1972, pp. 67–8; Shippey 1976.

16. Ed. in ASPR 3 and 6 respectively; in Shippey 1976, with facing translations. Shippey's introduction covers OE gnomic poetry in general, as well as the *Maxims* poems; see also Williams, B. 1914. For bibliography, see Lendinara 1977.

17. This line is problematic: the translation "dead one" for OE *cwealm* 'death, pestilence' would be unique; but it seems to make more sense.

18. Dawson 1962. Nelson, M. 1984a finds *Maxims I* controlled by the idea of sharing knowledge.

19. See Taylor 1969 on "heroic ritual" in the *Maxims.*

20. Shippey 1976, p. 18.

21. Henry 1966, p. 103. For a finer discrimination in the range of meanings from "is typically" to "ought," see Nelson, M. 1984a.

22. Greenfield/Evert 1975; quotation, p. 345. The following analysis is based on this essay; for other analyses, see Lendinara 1971; Shippey 1976, pp. 13–5; Barley 1977.

23. Greenfield/Evert 1975, p. 354; cf. Bollard 1973. A smaller collection of popular wisdom, the *Durham Proverbs,* has been surveyed in chapter 3. Two brief Latin-English proverbs and the two-line *A Proverb from Winfrid's Time* are ed. in ASPR 6.

24. Ed. in ASPR 3; the latter also in Shippey 1976, with facing translation.

25. See Cross 1962.

26. On the Germanic paradigms, see Russom 1978b; on the fusion, Anderson, E. 1983, pp. 31–3.

27. On the possible influence of Gregory's pedagogic theory in his *Pastoral Care,* see Short 1976b.

28. Efforts to explain this image, along with that of tree climbing in *Christ II,* ll. 678b–9a, have not been successful: for summary, see Isaacs 1975.

29. On the poem's unity and artistry, see Shippey 1976, pp. 10–1 and Dammers 1976.

30. The "fateful journey" or "sudden danger" (the OE word is ambiguous) is, of course, "death."

31. The authorative discussions of the MSS of Cuthbert's letter on Bede's death are Dobbie 1937 and Humphreys/Ross 1975; the count of thirty-three is by Twomey 1983. The OE poem is ed. in ASPR 6 and Smith 1933.

32. Cf. Huppé 1959, pp. 78–9. On the ambiguous syntax of *godes ond yfles* (l. 4b) vis-à-vis "Symeon of Durham's" twelfth-century Latin translation of the *Death Song*, and for a "penitential" reading of the poem, see Twomey 1983. Chickering 1976 provides a reading against the *Epistola* from several perspectives: psychological, theological, and literary. Schwab 1972 gives a numerical/tectonic and symbolic analysis.

33. Ed. in ASPR 3; Shippey 1976, with facing translation.

34. See Hansen 1981.

35. Shippey 1976, p. 128 notes a strong monastic flavor and suggests the poet may have been a member of a later tenth-century Benedictine reformed house.

36. Ed. in ASPR 3; Huppé 1970; Shippey 1976—the latter two with facing translations.

37. On patristic psychology in the poem, see Regan 1970. Huppé 1970, pp. 8–26 suggests an influence of the psalms. The antithesis between God's son and the devil's also appears in Ælfric's homily on the Lord's Prayer—see chapter 3, n. 56.

38. Shippey 1976, p. 9.

39. Ed. in ASPR 3; Huppé 1970, with facing translation.

40. On sources, and for critical analyses, see Huppé 1970, pp. 34–61 and Cross 1972, pp. 75–82. Isaacs 1968, pp. 71–82 would see the poem as one about the creation of poetry.

41. Ed. in ASPR 3.

42. See Wittig 1969 on the poem's unity and influence upon it of the Epistle to the Ephesians.

43. Ed. in ASPR 2.

44. Isaacs 1968, pp. 99–106.

45. Rosier 1964a; ed. also by Grimaldi 1979, with Italian translation.

46. Ed. in ASPR 3.

47. This source was first observed by Whitbread 1945, who provides text, translation, notes, and commentary.

48. Trahern 1969.

49. Berkhout 1972.

50. Ed. in ASPR 3. See also Whitbread 1946, who provides text, translation, notes, and commentary.

51. See Trahern 1970.

52. Fry 1976, p. 141; see also Williamson 1982, pp. 25–41.

53. Ed. in ASPR 3, whose numbering we follow; separately by Williamson 1977. For translations of all the riddles, see Williamson 1982 and

Baum 1963; Crossley-Holland 1979 translates most of them. For bibliography, see Lendinara 1976 and Williamson 1977, pp. 467–82.

54. For Symphosius, see Ohl 1928; for Aldhelm, see Pitman 1925; for Tatwine-Eusebius, see De Marco 1968. On the Anglo-Latin *ænigmata*, see chapter 1.

55. Aldhelm's *Lorica* riddle was also translated into Northumbrian in the latter half of the eighth century—see the *Leiden Riddle*, ed. in ASPR 6 and Smith 1933. For textual readings and discussion, see Gerritsen 1969 and Parkes 1972. For critical comment, see Anderson, G. 1967.

56. The wide range of solutions to some riddles is astonishing; e.g. *Riddle 28* has been solved as Horn of Yew, Wine Cask, Tortoise-Lyre, Damascened Sword, John Barleycorrn; and *Riddle 39* as Speech, Dream, Death, Time, Moon, Cloud, Day. A convenient collation of solutions is Fry 1981.

57. Williamson 1977 and Campbell, J. 1975 respectively. See also Nelson, M. 1974, p. 433 on the unity of the three. Foley 1976b takes no. 1 by itself as "Apocalyptic Storm."

58. See Erhardt-Siebold 1949 and Williamson 1977, pp. 130–3.

59. On the relation between kennings and riddles, see Stewart 1979.

60. On *double entendre* in the riddles, see Stewart 1983 and Gleissner 1984, the latter especially on the obscene riddles.

61. Robinson 1975, p. 362. Russom 1977 analyzes the riddle as a statement about mortality; both he and Marino, M. 1978 make pleas for paying greater attention to the literary quality of individual riddles. See chapter 5 for an analysis of the "Swan"riddle.

62. See Eliason 1952.

63. See Nelson, M. 1974 on rhetorical devices in the *Riddles*.

64. Ed. in ASPR 6, with continuous numbering; so also in the separate edition of Menner 1941. Shippey 1976 edits Poem II with facing translation.

65. "The poet's text may be represented as follows: *Pater nos(ter), qui (es) (in) c(ae)l(is): (sancti)f(icetur) (no)m(en) (tuum). (A)d(veniat) (re)g(num) (tuum). (Fiat voluntas tua, sicut in caelo, et in terra.) (Panem nostrum) (quotidianum) (da) (no)b(is) h(odie).* The letters in parenthesis are those which have already occurred earlier in the prayer and are hence not repeated by the poet; after *hodie* only letters already used are found"—Menner 1941, pp. 36–7. Of the nineteen letters that should appear, only sixteen are found in the MS.

66. See further Kellermann/Haas 1982, pp. 387–93.

67. See Dane 1980 on the "controlled dialectic progression of argument"—p. 600. On possible sources of the *weallende wulf* and *vasa mortis* passages, see Menner 1941, pp. 59–62.

68. On this passage, see Hill, T. 1970.

69. See further Kellermann/Haas 1982, pp. 393–9.

70. Shippey 1976, p. 25.

CHAPTER 12

Elegiac Poetry

In the course of this history we have had occasion to notice the pervasiveness of the elegiac as well as the heroic in Old English poetry. Thus the epic *Beowulf* reveals in its larger patterning both moods; Andrew's disciples in *Andreas* mourn elegiacally when told they may be put ashore without their chieftain; so do Christ's followers on their leader's ascension in Cynewulf's poem; the devil in *Juliana* and Satan in *Christ and Satan* lament their states of exile; and poems of wisdom incorporate passages in the same spirit. We began our survey of the poetry with verse predominantly heroic in mood; we conclude with those poems, and some passages from *Beowulf*, which have been called *elegies*.[1]

The nine (ten?) poems to be considered are all extant in the Exeter Book: *The Ruin, The Wanderer, The Seafarer, Resignation (A and B?), The Riming Poem, Wulf and Eadwacer, The Wife's Lament, The Husband's Message,* and *Deor*—the titles, of course, are those of modern editors.[2] Though labelled *elegies*, they are neither in the classical mold of being composed in a specific meter nor in the post-Renaissance sense of being lamentations for the loss of specific persons or communites. Scholars have attempted to characterize and define this perceived Old English genre. One frequently quoted says that the poems "call attention in varying degrees to the transitory nature of the pleasures of this world" and are "relatively short reflective or dramatic poem[s] embodying a contrasting pattern of loss and consolation, ostensibly based upon a specific personal experience or observation and expressing an attitude towards that experience."[3] On the other hand, another suggests that they might better be thought of as "wisdom literature," being "planted without any mark of distinction" in "a very considerable block of admonitory, reflective verse . . . from which they differ only through their deliberate illusions of personality."[4] But the poems are really a heterogeneous lot, requiring some stretching to fit these Procrustean characterizations, and being distributed more widely in the Exeter Book than Shippey indicates. In fact different genres have been proposed for them singly or as parts of small groups. For example, *The Ruin* has been seen as an *encomium urbis*; *The Wanderer* as a *consolatio*, or together with *The Seafarer* as a *planctus*, or with the latter and *Resignation* as a penitential poem; *Wulf and Eadwacer* as a riddle.[5] If these lyrics indeed constitute a genre in Old English literature, they do so "by force of our present, rather than determinate historical, perspective; that is, by our 'feel' for them as a group possessing certain features in common."[6] Perhaps we should take the description of the Exeter Book in the list of Leofric's donations to Exeter Cathedral at its word: *.i. mycel englisc boc be gehwilcum þingum on leoð-wisan geworht* 'a large book about various subjects composed in verse,' and stop trying to impose our perspectives of generic commonality upon them.[7] But this does *not* mean that comparisons among them, or to other poems in the MS, or to other works in the Anglo-Saxon corpus, are frivolous or useless; or that Celtic, Norse, and Latin analogues and similarities in patristic commentary or Scripture should be ignored.[8]

We begin our survey with the 49-line *Ruin*, whose lines 12–8 and 42 ff. were damaged by the same destructive agent that obliterated so much of the *Riddles*.[9] *The Ruin* differs from the other "elegies" by having no first-person speaker. The poet instead speaks throughout. He begins with a panoramic view of the ruins of a nameless city, usually accepted as Bath, though the scene may be an imaginative amalgam of various locales:[10]

> Wondrous this wall-stone; wasted by fate,
> buildings crumbled; the work of giants decays.
> Roofs have collapsed, in ruin the towers,
> the high gate unbarred, hoar-frost on mortar,
> ramparts gaping: all rent, spent,
> undermined by age.   (ll.   1–6a)

The rulers and builders are similarly long since destroyed; but once, the poet continues, this was a fair city, filled with bathhouses and sounds of revelry. Then pestilence came, the people perished, tiles parted from the buildings' frames, until only

> ruins remained on the plain,
> fragments, where formerly many a man
> cheerful and sparkling in all his splendor,
> proud and wine-flushed flourished in armor;
> he gazed on treasure, silver, precious stones,
> on wealth, on land, on this wondrous jewel:
> the bright city of the broad kingdom.   (ll.   31b–7)

The end of the poem, or what can be deciphered of it, calls to the mind's eye the hot baths as they functioned in the city's prime.

The vanished splendor becomes, in the poet's treatment, a symbol of human impermanence. As such, it has obvious affinity with the ruined halls of Urien and Cynddylan lamented by the Old Welsh poets Llywarch Hen and Heledd, and with that in Venantius Fortunatus' sixth-century Latin poem *De Excidio Thoringae*.

The Ruin's specific quality, however, inheres in its use of alternation between the present devastation and past beauty, between the dead builders and rulers and the once-breathing and strutting warriors; and in its climax, which narrows in focus from the "broad kingdom" to the city's pride, its circular baths. As the two passages above suggest, compressed and separate images describe the decaying present, whereas a more sweeping syntactic movement conveys the reconstructed glories of the past.[11] The poet neither sentimentalizes nor moralizes: he presents his picture disinterestedly, though his poetic recreation of the prosperous city furnishes a kind of consolation for Fate's destructive embrace.[12]

The 115-line *Wanderer* is a much more complex poem.[13] It encompasses the exile theme, the ruin theme, and the *ubi sunt* motif[14] in a frame of Christian attitudes and values. The three *topoi* occupy successively the major segments of the poem's body, lines 8-110, which is the purported speech of a homeless exile or wanderer, a thegn who has lost his lord and kinsmen. The poet begins with a Christian commentary on the fate of and prospects for an exile:

Often the exile finds God's favor,
His mercy, though weary in mind and heart
on the ocean lanes he long had to
stir with his hands the ice-cold sea,
follow exile's path: Fate takes its course.

Lines 8 ff. launch into the *eardstapa*'s 'earth-stepper's' monologue:

"Often alone at dawn of day I
had to mourn my cares—no man now lives
to whom I dare make known my deepest
thoughts and feelings. I know for a fact
that nobility of soul demands
that a man bind fast his feelings,
guard well his thoughts, whatever he may think."

The gnomic mood of the last sentence continues as the speaker recounts his loss of lord and vain efforts to secure another. In a well-known passage he tells how an exile dreams of former days:

"When sorrow and sleep together
catch the care-worn exile in their toils,
in his mind he seems to clasp and kiss
his own dear lord, and on his knee lay
hand and head in fealty, as when
in by-gone days throne-gifts came his way." (ll. 39-44)

But even this consolation is but momentary, for

"straightway the friendless man awakes,
sees the dark waves dance before him,
sea-birds bathing, spreading their feathers,
frost and snow falling fast, mingled with hail." (ll. 45-8)

This self-centered tale of exile broadens in scope as the speaker places himself in the perspective of the evanescence of all worldly joys, recalling how suddenly warriors had "given up the hall" (i.e., died). Here he utilizes the ruin theme:

> "The wise man must see how awesome it will be
> when the wealth of all this world stands waste,
> as now in many areas of this earth
> walls stand swept by winds of place and time,
> bound with frost, the buildings deep in snow.
> The wine-halls crumble, rulers decay,
> deprived of joys, the proud host joins them
> beside the wall." (ll. 73–80a)

In the third part of his monologue, the sense of destruction leads the speaker to postulate a wise man who, understanding the re-morselessness of Fate, utters the *ubi sunt* lament and ends with an apocalyptic vision of the world become wasteland:[15]

> "Where the horse? where the hero? where he who lavished treasure?
> Where the seats of feasting? where the sound of hall-joys?
> Alas bright cup! Alas brave warrior!
> Alas prince's power! How time has passed,
> darkened into night, as it had never been!"

Leaving his *snottor on mode* 'wise in mind' speaker *sundor æt rune* 'apart in meditation' (l. 111), the poet himself then concludes with a gnomic-homiletic exhortation to find true security with the Father in heaven.[16]

The introductory and concluding frames echo each other in their references to God's mercy, His *ar* (ll. 1b, 114b). The former merely states that such mercy is often granted an exile, and leaves open the possibility of earthly amelioration of his lot; the latter expli-citly calls for seeking that mercy in heaven. In the former the ep-ithet for God is *Metud* 'Measurer,' in the latter *Fæder* 'Father.' Such parallelism and progression is matched in the body of the poem as the speaker moves from describing his personal difficulties, and attempts to find new accommodation in the world, to his recog-nition of earthly transience. (Unless one takes the last five lines as part of the *eardstapa*'s speech, the speaker does not achieve the

Christian understanding of salvation which the poem as a whole acknowledges.) Adjectives denoting an unhappy state of mind cluster in the early part, those denoting wisdom in the later. Various terms for "hall," the locus of warmth, friendship, the *comitatus*, reflect the exile's former hope of finding a new lord; the external forbidding "wall" symbolizes his more mature observations. Rhetorically, antithesis and correlatives predominate in the first section of the monologue, polysyndeton and anaphora in the second, and exclamations in the third. These stylistic strategies harmonize well with the respective emphases of the three parts: "the attempts to bind and hold fast to human ties and pleasures; the discovery by reflection of the negative and dissoluble nature of human life and its Ozymandian grandeur, and the somewhat apocalyptic final view that *onwendeð wyrda gesceaft weoruld under heofonum* 'Fate's decree changes the world beneath the heavens' (l. 107)."[17]

The idea that *The Wanderer* is a penitential poem[18] will not bear scrutiny; there is simply no mention of repentance anywhere in it. That it contains elements of the *planctus* or *consolatio* seems a more reasonable conjecture, though it is doubtful whether Boethius' *Consolation of Philosophy* was a specific influence upon it.[19] It is doubtful, too, that the exile *topos* of the first part is to be read as a Christian allegory of man's earthly existence as an exile from Eden, though the sea image may suggest the "*mare vitae*, a pervasive metaphor for the arbitrary turmoil of mortal life."[20] Sea-voyaging plays a more important role in *The Seafarer*, however, and critics have been more receptive to allegorical interpretations of *The Wanderer*'s "companion piece."

The Ruin, as we have observed, has no first-person speaker; and *The Wanderer*'s monologue is still tied to the poet's own voice at beginning and end. *The Seafarer* and the other elegies, however, are cut loose from the authorial voice, being spoken wholly by a fictitious "I," and for this reason, among others, have provoked even greater controversy about their speakers, actions, and meanings. The 124-line *Seafarer*,[21] with its syntactic and conceptual disjunctions, its "personal" and "homiletic" halves, and its interpretive cruxes, has been particularly a locus of critical disagreement.

Lines 1–64a ostensibly present the narrator's literal account of his past sufferings on the sea, which somehow *therefore (for þon)* prompt him to desire setting forth on another voyage.[22] The persona graphically describes his past experiences:

> I can sing a true song about myself,
> tell my travails, how in days of toil
> I often suffered distressful times,
> lodged bitter sorrows within my breast,
> navigated many halls of care,
> awful rolling waves, where anxiety
> often seized me at night-watch in ship's prow
> when tossing by the cliffs. With cold
> were my feet oppressed, by frost bound
> in cold fetters, where those cares sighed
> hot around my heart; hunger within tore
> the mind sea-weary.   (ll.   1–12a)

In contrast to the "wanderer," who twice invokes "one who knows," one who has experienced similar sorrow and loss (ll. 29b ff., 37b ff.), the "seafarer" thrice contrasts his lot with that of the prosperous man on land, one who does *not* know how the speaker had to dwell in exile or what he suffered there (ll. 12b ff., 29b ff., 55–7). He reinforces his sense of desolation and isolation by references to seabirds as his only companions and source of joy (ll. 19b–26). After the second allusion to the land-dweller who cannot believe what the speaker has endured, and a description of the earth bound by darkness, snow, frost, and hail (ll. 29–33a), he says *for þon* his spirit urges him to a sea-journey, "to seek far hence the home of foreigners/exiles" (ll. 33b–8).[23] Another *for þon* introduces an impersonal passage expressing every man's (and by implication the speaker's) trepidations about the outcome of a sea-journey (ll. 39–47). But the blossoming world and sad-voiced cuckoo (harbinger of summer) urge on the one who contemplates traveling far on the flood-waves (ll. 48–56a). *For þon* again introduces the "I":

> *For þon* now my heart and spirit, passing
> beyond my breast, bursts upon the sea,
> turns widely over the whale's terrain
> to its far corners, comes back to me

full of fierce longing: the lone-flier cries,
urges my heart upon the whale-path
to dare the sea, for dearer to me
are the Lord's joys than this earthly life,
dead and transient. (ll. 58–66a)[24]

Thus the "seafaring" portion of the poem passes over into the homiletic. What follows is essentially eschatological in nature. First, an acknowledgement of the inevitability of death; and *for þon*

for each man the praise of those
who live after is best memorial,
praise he can earn before he departs
by taking arms against enemies,
by noble deeds against the devil,
so that people afterwards will praise him,
and his fame will ever live on high
with angels, glory in life eternal,
bliss among the Hosts. (ll. 72–80a)

Then a comment on the decline of earthly splendor:

There are now no kings or emperors
or givers of gold as once there were
when they gave themselves to glory and
were monuments of magnificence.
All this host has perished, and their bliss;
the weaker live on and hold the world,
grind out small lives in grief. Glory fails,
the splendor of earth ages and fades,
as does every man on middle-earth. (ll. 82–90)[25]

Next a reminder that gold cannot help the sinful soul, that God's power is terrible and real, that death comes unexpected. Finally stress on the necessity to recognize and strive to reach our true home in heaven.

Like the speaker in *The Wanderer*, the persona of *The Seafarer* develops in his outlook as the poem progresses: from an attitutde of despair and suffering as he "relives" his former seafaring existence, he moves to a state in which he desires further travel, but of a different kind, to an unknown distant shore. Still, he has fears about such a journey, but when he thinks about the joys of God, all doubts and hesitations vanish; for in the mirror of eternity he recognizes the mutability of all earthly happiness and, unlike the "wanderer," in the sound of the sea he has heard the message of Christian salvation. The momentous "sea change" begs for some kind of resolution. We can take the proposed sea-journey literally, seeing in it an ascetic resolve to forsake the things of this world for a *peregrinatio pro amore Dei;*[26] or we can take it as an allegory of man's passage to the land from whence he was exiled in the Fall of Adam, the heavenly *patria,* and his early voyaging as an allegory for man's life on earth, as in the sea-voyage simile at the end of *Christ II* (see chapter 8). Or we can read it both ways.[27]

The poem bristles with many other interpretive cruxes, partially because of its deliberate ambiguity. But in that ambiguity lies much of its poetic fascination.[28] The same words in different contexts, for example, point up the contrast between the joys of comradeship in this world and in heaven (ll. 78–90), and between a man's earthly lord and the Lord (ll. 39–43). Or double meanings reside in the single use of a word or phrase, as possibly in the "home of foreigners/exiles," or as in the lovely

> Groves take blossoms, cities beautify,
> fields brighten, the fair world hastens on;
> all these admonish one ready in mind
> to depart. . . .   (ll.   48–51a)

Here the hastening of the world looks two ways: to the cyclical movement into springtime that is a call to travel, and to the degeneration of the world moving toward the millenium, an additional reason for the "seafarer's" embarkation on his literal-allegorical journey to the lasting security of heaven.[29]

The 118-line poem called *Resignation* in ASPR 3 has frequently been compared with *The Seafarer* and *The Wanderer,* since in its latter part it uses the exile theme in a fashion similar to theirs.[30] But Bliss and Frantzen have demonstrated that a leaf is missing from the Exeter Book after line 69, and that the two parts are so dissimilar in thought, syntax, and diction as to make it extremely unlikely they belong to the same poem; they therefore designate ll.

1–69 *Resignation A* and ll. 70–118 *Resignation B*.[31] The former is clearly a prayer, and might have been considered with the poem so called in chapter 10; but since *A* and *B* have subsequently received critical treatment as a scribal, if not authorial, elegiac unity,[32] we shall survey both poems here. (It is of course possible that the missing lines were still part of one and the same poem; stylistic and conceptual disjunctions, we have seen, are not uncommon in Old English poetry.)[33]

Resignation A is the first-person supplication of a self-accusing sinner, who asks God to have mercy on him, to save his soul from devils who would, if they could, lead it on a "hateful journey" to hell. The speaker does not seem to be at death's door, since he asks God to show him how to observe His will so that, though he has obeyed God more weakly than he should have, his soul may come to heaven (ll. 10–21). The poem uses many epithets for God— almost one every two lines—and is quite repetitive in diction and thought. It contains a number of conjunctive verses of no great distinction: l. 2b: *þu gesceope heofon ond eorþan* 'You created heaven and earth'; l. 5a: *micel ond manigfeald* 'great and manifold'; l. 7a: *ond min word ond min weorc* 'and my words and my deeds.'[34] Hardly an appealing poem, it nevertheless has some force as a versified prayer.

Resignation B is a narrative monologue in which the speaker tells about his punishment by God for his sins, some of which he cannot perceive. Wretched, friendless, and destitute, he is sad and sick at heart. He would take ship, but cannot afford to purchase a boat. "The forest may grow, await its destiny,/put forth twigs" (ll. 106–7a, Malmberg ed.), but the speaker cannot love anyone. His only hope for amelioration lies after this life in God; with stoic resignation he must meanwhile bear the fate he cannot change.

The poem resembles *The Seafarer* in several ways. First, the "I," even though still clearly in his native land, thinks of his punishments before men in this world as a kind of exile he can no longer endure (ll. 86b–98a).[35] Second, the "I" wishes, on account of his present sufferings, to take an exile journey, one which seems to be envisaged as both a literal *peregrinatio pro amore Dei* (ll. 99b–105) and a metaphoric one to the heavenly *patria* (ll. 73–7a, 11b–4). Third, the "forest-growing" passage is not unlike the springtime one in *The Seafarer*. But the speaker does not recognize the transience of this world, nor achieve the wisdom of either the "wanderer" or the "seafarer." He is frozen in the wretched here and now of his internal exile, however much he has prepared his spirit for the long journey "home" (ll. 71–7a).[36]

The speaker of *Resignation B* seems always to have suffered the slings and arrows of outrageous fortune, the "seafarer" always to have led a life of hardship. On the contrary, the "I" of the 87-line *Riming Poem* indicates that, like the "wanderer," he once prospered in the world.[37] Now, however, "what had been precious in the day flees in the night" (ll. 44b–5a). There are five main stages in the progress of the poem: (1) to l. 42, the former pleasures of rank and riches are detailed: feasts, horses, ships, company, music, and ultimately power as lord and protector, as distributor of treasure; (2) but the speaker's very largesse seems to have led to unspecified trouble, and in ll. 43–54 he indicates vexations of mind as he contemplates men's loss of courage, joys, and desires; (3) in ll. 55–69 he contemplates the slackness of the world in more general terms; (4) in ll. 70–9, returning to a first-person account, he recognizes the inevitability of the grave, the fate of his body; (5) in ll. 80–7 he stresses the good man's awareness of the path of righteousness, and exhorts his audience to hasten thereon to eternal bliss.[38]

The *Riming Poem* is a *tour de force* in which the first verse or half line not only alliterates with the second in the usual Old English metrical pattern, but rhymes with it. Further, pairs of lines frequently have the same rhyme scheme, and even four consecutive lines rhyme in two sections: ll. 13–6, 51–4. This metrical display is intensified by homoeoteleuton: thus the verses in ll. 29–37 all end with *-ade*. Because of the compression of thought enjoined by this scheme, the meaning of details is not always as clear, despite the clarity of the poem's thematic structure.[39] The sudden reversal of fortune after l. 42 is prepared for by ambiguous diction, in which "bad" senses of words seem to lie just beneath their "good" surface meanings in immediate context; even the beginning, "To me He loaned life, Who revealed this light," anticipates the end, where in heaven the saved "will see the true God, and ever rejoice in peace."[40] Such anticipations, the frequency of asyndetic para-

taxis, the use of *an* 'alone' as a verse unto itself in the climax of
the description of worms eating the dead body (l. 77, "until there
is just the bone, alone"), the parallelism of the microcosm of man
in his decline and the macrocosm of the world in its degeneracy,
the riddle-like quality of the opening and the homiletic nature of
the conclusion—all these help the poet achieve an esthetic density
and complexity commensurate with that of the verse form he attempted.[41]

The poems so far considered in this chapter treat of human misfortunes as concomitants of temporal existence. The next three deal
instead with patterns of concord and discord in the relations between men and women—at least insofar as the majority of critics
have read them. Two of these, if adjectival endings and context
are any guides, have first-person women speakers. They seem to
be impassioned laments about the *personas'* separations from their
beloveds, and might thus be generically classified along with similar medieval lyrics in other languages as *Frauenlieder*.[42] Both are
obscure, yet somehow haunting. The 19-line *Wulf and Eadwacer* was
early mis-taken as "The First Riddle" because of its enigmatic
quality and because it immediately precedes the first group of
Riddles.[43] It had best be presented in "a" complete translation:

> It's like a gift given my people;
> they'll take care of him if he comes to them.
>   It is differrent with us!
> Wulf's on an isle, I on another;
> 5 that island's secure, guarded by fens.
> Deadly-fierce men dwell in that isle;
> they'll take care of him if he comes to them.
>   It is different with us!
> For my Wulf's far-journeys I waited with hope:
> 10 when weather was rainy and I wept,
> when the battle-bold man embraced me,
> I took some pleasure, but it pained me too.
> Wulf, my Wulf, wanting you,
> your rare arrivals, have made me ill—
> 15 a sorrowing heart, not hunger for food.
>   Do you hear, Eadwacer? our poor whelp
>   Wulf bears to the woods,

It's easy to sever what never was seamed:
our song together.

The difficulties of interpretation are obvious. One commonly held reading is that Wulf, an outlaw, is the speaker's lover, and Eadwacer is her detested husband; the "whelp" is the latter's child, which Wulf is carrying away, thus destroying the mis-mated "love fruit." Some have taken Wulf to be the husband, outlawed, and Eadwacer her jailor, who has forced his intentions upon her; the "whelp" may be Wulf's. The situation seems so specific, despite its lack of clarity, that many critics attempted to base the poem on Germanic story, the Signy-Sigmund lay and the Wolfdietrich B saga being the leading candidates. But all such proposals fall short in some way of matching the details of the Old English poem. The situational difficulty is compounded, as all critics recognize, by dictional ambiguity;[44] and it is perhaps wiser to follow Renoir's "non-interpretational" lead, accepting the narrative obscurity and focusing instead, on the more obvious thematic patterns of union and separation, suffering and hostility.[45]

In any case, part of the poem's appeal lies in its obscurity. Some of it is in the thematic patterning, but much of it resides in the style: in the refrain; in the pathetic fallacy of rainy weather and weeping; in the shifts in syntax and line lengths; in its unmetrical and plaintive *Wulf min Wulf* (l.13).

The other poem with a female speaker is the 53-line *The Wife's Lament*.[46] As with *Wulf and Eadwacer*, the specificity of details has prompted suggestions of legendary plot sources, among them the Constance saga, the Crescentia tale, and the Old Irish *Liadain and Curithir*; but again none of them will quite do. Unlike *Wulf and Eadwacer*, this poem is not an apostrophe to the absent lover, though it shares many of that lyric's features. The wife, like the "seafarer," will tell a true tale about her sufferings, "never more than now." First, her husband-lord departed over the seas, and she suffered "dawn-care" as to where he might be. His departure was the result of his kinsmen's scheming to separate them. But he had ordered her to *folgað secan* 'take refuge-exile' in an oak grove, perhaps a heathen sanctuary, because she had few friends in his land.[47] She recalls here how well she and her husband were matched, the oaths they had sworn never to part;

> but that is now changed,
> utterly gone, as if our union
> had never been. I must far and near
> suffer from the feud of my beloved.   (ll.   23b–6)

In her oak grove she writhes with longing:

> Valleys are veiled in gloom, hills veer up,
> bitter asylum covered with briars,
> a land without joys; often my lord's
> leaving terrified me. Lovers on earth
> live happily at rest together,
> while I at dawn drag myself along
> under this oak tree throughout these caverns,
> where I must sit a summer-long day,
> where I can bemoan my miseries,
> my many cares, because I can never
> still the restlessness of my heart's grief,
> nor all the longings this life's decreed.   (ll.   30–41)

The last section, ll. 42–53, offers a knotty problem of interpretation. It is partly gnomic and partly a reflection on the concomitant fate of her husband: if outwardly fortunate, nevertheless bearing within a sorrowing spirit; if outwardly unfortunate, say in a desolate sea-surrounded hall, he will remember a happier dwelling, even as *she* does in her abode of sorrow.[48] The speaker concludes gnomically:

> Woe to that one
> who lives for the beloved in longing.

The emphasis in *The Wife's Lament* is upon the speaker's miserable state of mind, the contrast between happiness in love and the frustration of separation. The poem abounds in words for misery, sorrow, enduring, longing, trials, and tribulations. The location of the wife's abode in what seems to be a barrow or tumulus, the images of briars and water, add to the atmosphere of desolation and isolation. Parallels of phrasing further aid in the pathetic futility of mood: for instance, the wife says, l. 12b, that her lord's kinsmen secretly plotted *þæt hy todælden unc* 'that they would separate us' and later, in l. 22, that her husband and she had vowed *þæt unc ne gedælde nemne deað ana* 'that nothing save death would ever part us.'[49] Of all the Exeter Book "elegies," *The Wife's Lament* is most devoid of consolatory hope: there is no Christian God whose ultimate mercy can be relied on, nor any pleasure in the remembrance of things past. Only a stoic fortitude, frozen in time present,[50] can cope with the intense personal anguish.

The Husband's Message, on the contrary, is the least elegiac of the "elegies."[51] Yet it does have in common with most of the others the exile theme and a pattern of contrast between past and present; only in this case it is the present which is the better. It has often been paired with *The Wife's Lament,* as the other side of the coin, so to speak.[52] Here a messenger carrying a rune-incised piece of wood—or the personified *beam* itself—delivers a husband's call to his wife to join him over the sea. This prince or king had been driven into exile by a feud, but now has overcome his miseries; he can promise his wife that they will once more be able to distribute treasure from the high seat, for, says the messenger:

> now that man has
> conquered woes; he lacks nothing he wants,
> not horses or treasures or hall-joys,
> nor any of the world's noblest wealth,
> prince's daughter, save possessing you,
> as you two promised with pledge of old.
> I hear .S.R. together swearing
> with .EA.W. and M. by oath declaring
> that he will keep the faith and compact,
> and fully while he lives perform
> what you two often vowed in days of old. (ll. 44b–54)

We may mention a few of the difficulties that inhere in the text of this 54-line poem. In the first place, it follows a piece generally considered to be *Riddle 60* ("Reed-pen"); but some have preferred to view the riddle as a prologue to or part of *The Husband's Mes-*

sage, taking it as a piece of wood which speaks of its origins before it, itself, "delivers" the husband's summons.[53] The runes in the oath at the end of the poem—the .S.R.,.EA.W., and M. of the translation above—are not clear in themselves or in context.[54] And holes in the manuscript have effectively destroyed lines, words, and letters. However we wish to negotiate these problems, there seems to be a note of cautious optimism that runs through this dramatic lyric as the messenger tries to convince the lady—and evidently, for some unspecified reason, she needs convincing[55]—that her husband is indeed true and will honor the old vows they swore together as well as his new ones.[56]

It is with a return to the combination of heroic and elegiac that we bring this critical history to an end. The 42-line *Deor*, with its allusions to Germanic heroic story, is in some respects like *Widsith* (see chapter 6), even to having a fictitious scop as its *persona*.[57] Like *Wulf and Eadwacer*, it has a refrain: *þæs ofereode, þisses swa mæg* 'that passed away, [and] so will this.' The passing away of the specific misfortunes alluded to in the irregular-length stanzas may mean that improvement occurred and will occur, akin to the upturn of Fortune's wheel; or it may mean that the sorrows (and joys) of this world are transitory because they *are* of this world. In the latter case, the poem comes close in meaning to *The Wanderer* and *The Seafarer*.

Of the seven stanzas—some see only six, since there is no refrain after the "sixth"—the first five allude to specific characters and/or stories from the realm of Germanic legend: Weland's captivity by Nithhad; the captive smith's revenge upon the king's sons and daughter, Beadohild;[58] the love of Maethhild and Geat; Theodoric's exile; and Ermanaric's tyranny. The sixth is a gnomic reflection on the "gifts of men," on the wise Lord's granting of mercy to some and a portion of woes to others. The last stanza provides the fictious elegiac framework for the whole poem:

About myself I will say this much,
that once I was the Heodening's scop,
dear to my lord. Deor was my name.
For many years I was held with honor
in my master's heart, till Heorrenda,

that song-crafty man, usurped those rights
which the leader of men had given me.
    That passed away, and so will this." (ll. 35–42)

Like the other "elegies," *Deor* poses many individual cruxes as
well as problems of overall interpretation. Who *are* Maethhild and
Geat? Is Theodoric the Goth or the Frank? What are the structural
connections between the legendary stanzas? To what precisely do
the *that* and *this* of the refrain, especially in the last stanza, refer?
There is disagreement about even the emotional centers of the individual stanzas. An example of the last: the first stanza, about
Weland's suffering, has been seen by one critic as emphasizing
physical miseries, by another "the spiritual horror of the situation," and by a third the smith's "triumph over adversity through
his resolution of mind and skill in artifice."[59] In terms of its meaning as a whole and its generic associations, *Deor* has been taken
as a charm, a begging poem, and a wisdom poem suggesting "the
ability of the mind to control itself and resist its surroundings."[60]
It has also frequently been taken as an Anglo-Saxon *Consolation of
Philosophy*, even directly indebted to Alfred's Old English translation of Boethius.[61] If the Alfredian influence is true, we at least
have a terminus *a quo* for this elusive but affective poem.

The final pieces to be mentioned are two "set passages" in *Beowulf*. In "The Lament of the Last Survivor" in Part II of the epic,
the speaker contrasts his nation's former days of earthly wealth
and glory with the present: all are dead save him. He must now
bury in the earth the useless treasure that was once his people's
joy; it is the treasure the dragon will find, the source of Beowulf's
tragedy:

"Hold now, earth, what warriors cannot,
the wealth of heroes! Lo! it was yours
before good men obtained it from you.
Through war, dread and evil death has claimed
my people: each one has passed from life,
from joy in the hall. I have no one
to carry sword or clean the costly
plated cup: the company is gone.
The hard, gold-ornamented helmet
must lose its plates; the polishers sleep

whose task it was to shine the war-mask;
so too the war-coat, which once endured
the bite of swords over crashing shields,
decays with the man. Nor can ring-mail
travel far and wide with the war-lord,
by heroes' sides. No harp-joy sounds
from unplucked strings, no good hawk swings
through the hall, no swift horse stamps his feet
in the courtyard: baleful death has come
and swept far off many living men!" (ll. 2247–67)

The second passage also occurs in Part II, in the midst of the hero's account of Geatish history as he prepares to face the dragon (ll. 2435 ff.). Beowulf suggests King Hrethel's sorrow in his inability to take revenge upon his son Haethcyn for his accidental killing of his eldest brother. He does so by comparing the old king's plight to that of a father mourning his son who swings on the gallows, a fate which likewise cannot be avenged. Oddly for the context, he pictures the father viewing the desolate ruins of his son's erstwhile establishment, where

"Sorrowful, he sees in his son's dwelling
the empty wine-hall, waste and cheerless,
where winds only rest: riders, warriors,
sleep in their graves; no harp resounds,
no mirth fills the courts as formerly." (ll. 2455–9)

The ruin *topos* evidently had a metaphoric quality that made it applicable not only in poems like *The Ruin* and *The Wanderer*, but in elegiac verse in which it was literally uncalled for.[62]

The poems and passages discussed in this chapter have captured the attention and moved the hearts of generations of readers. They illustrate the *mana* residing in the conventional Old English formulas and themes. Adapted to different poetic situations, they could be made ever fresh by the tongues and pens of those to whom God, in his gifts to men, had granted the power of poetic song among the Anglo-Saxons.

This critical history has, we hope, presented convincing evidence for the stature of our earliest English literary heritage. In its special fusion of Christian and pagan materials and attitudes, in its aesthetic techniques so different from those of later ages, it reveals its particular nature as a body of literature. Though that nature is not ours, we can still understand and respond to it through the efforts of those historical, textual, and literary critics who have opened doors and windows for its illumination.

NOTES

1. On the elegiac mood in OE poetry, see Timmer 1942.

2. Ed. in ASPR 3; most also separately as a group in Kershaw 1922 and Sieper 1915, with English and German translations respectively. Other editions mentioned below; there are many translations. For study of the poems as a genre, see Greenfield 1966 and Green, M. 1983a.

3. Greenfield 1966, p. 143.

4. Shippey 1972, p. 67.

5. For a summary of the critical history of the "elegies," see Green, M. 1983a, pp. 11–28, which does not, however, consider *The Riming Poem*.

6. Greenfield 1972, p. 135. See Klinck 1984 on structural similarities in the OE genre.

7. The fact that the Exeter scribe, or his exemplar, began the compilation with the *Christ* poems, followed by *Guthlac*, may show some recognition of "appropriateness." On the other hand, the wide separation of the two explicit allegories, *Phoenix* and *Physiologus*, and the division of the riddles into several groups, do not give one confidence that MS placement is an infallible guide to generic similitude.

8. On Celtic links, see Pilch 1964 and Henry 1966. Harris 1983, comparing Old Norse and OE "elegies," claims a historical "Common Germanic heroic elegy" as the ancestor of both; he suggests a progression from specificity "toward generalization and finally allegory" in the OE group, with *Wulf and Eadwacer* being the earliest stage, *The Seafarer* the latest (p. 49).

9. Ed. Leslie 1961.

10. Other locations suggested are Chester and Hadrian's Wall. If Roman Bath was the inspirational site, as seems most likely, archaeological evidence indicates the early eighth century as time of composition: see Leslie 1961; Hotchner 1939; Wentersdorf 1977.

11. For elaboration on such contrasts, see Greenfield 1966, pp. 121–2; Calder 1971a; Renoir 1983. The poet is very conscious of sounds: e.g., ll. 4b and 5b in the OE are *hrim on lime* and *scorene gedrorene*.

12. Johnson 1980 argues that the detached perspective is consonant with reading the poem as a "body-city" riddle. Some have seen the poet's stance as Christian and adversative, taking the city to represent Babylon or the

City of Man—see respectively Keenan 1966 and Doubleday 1972b. Others have taken the poem as an *encomium urbis*, like *Durham* (see chapter 11)— see Lee, A.T. 1973 and Howlett 1976b.

13. Ed. separately by Leslie 1966 and Dunning/Bliss 1969; the former dates the poem eighth century, the latter tenth.

14. On the exile theme in OE poetry, see Greenfield 1955; on *ubi sunt*, see Cross 1956.

15. On the apocalyptic in the poem, see Green, M. 1975.

16. This outline of structure and movement is based on Greenfield 1951. Nineteenth-century criticism had disintegrated the poem (and its "companion piece" *The Seafarer*) into Christian and pagan strata; but since Lawrence 1902 most readers have found it unified and the product of the cloister—an exception is Hollowell 1983. Agreement on the number of "voices" and on speech boundaries has, however, been less than unanimous. For some of this controversy, see Huppé 1943; Lumiansky 1950; Pope 1965; Greenfield 1969—as well as other references throughout this commentary.

17. Greenfield 1966, p. 152; see pp. 147 ff. for stylistic analysis. Further on imagery, see Rosier 1964b and Clark S./Wasserman 1979.

18. Stanley 1955 and Henry 1966, pp. 161–75.

19. See Cross 1961b; Doubleday 1972a; Woolf 1975.

20. Osborn 1978b, p. 1. The allegorical reading is Smithers 1957; for strictures, see Calder 1971b.

21. Ed. separately by Gordon, I. L. 1960.

22. The connective *for þon*, which normally means "therefore" or "because," and which appears several times, has been variously construed as "truly," "indeed," and "yet." The suffering/desire paradox or disjunction led nineteenth-century critics to postulate a dialogue between an old and a young sailor. Pope 1965 finds two dramatic voices; Pope 1974 retracts this theory.

23. An important crux, *elþeodigra eard:* does it mean simply a literal journey to foreign shores, or is it a reference to heaven, the true home of fallen man as an exile in this world? Or does it mean both? Smithers 1957 first advanced the "heaven" reading. Vickrey 1982, pp. 72–4 suggests *eard* here can be the sea itself.

24. On the image of the mind as a lone-flier, see Clemoes 1969; also Salmon 1960 and Diekstra 1971. Some take the lone-flier to be a seabird or the cuckoo—so Gordon, I. L. 1960, pp. 41–2.

25. On the macrocosm-microcosm relation between the fading world and degenerating man, see Cross 1962. Horgan 1979 argues that the poem is based on Psalm 49 (48), and "is an indictment of the traditional values of Germanic civilization" (p. 49).

26. See Whitelock 1950.

27. Many allegorical readings have been made: see e.g., Anderson, O.

1937 and Smithers 1957. Leslie 1983 sees the earlier voyage as a voluntary exile for the soul's salvation, both "realistically" and metaphorically; Holton 1982 suggests that the sea of the first voyage is a metaphor for lack of grace, postlapsarian sin, chaos; cf. Vickrey 1982. On differences between the earlier and later voyages, see Osborn 1978b. Calder 1971b distinguishes between the allegorical mode of *The Seafarer* and the thematic one of *The Wanderer*.

28. See Greenfield 1954.

29. For the literal-metaphorical seasonal cycle in the poem, and a reading as psychological illumination and religious conversion, see Greenfield 1981.

30. See Stanley 1955 and Henry 1966.

31. Bliss/Frantzen 1976. Ed. separately as two poems by Malmberg 1979, but with continuous line numbering.

32. Nelson, M. 1983.

33. See discussion of *The Seafarer*; Pasternack 1984.

34. For other stylistic features, see Malmberg 1979, pp. 4–5.

35. Malmberg 1979 suggests it is "possible to regard the speaker as a kind of internal exile with no contact with those around him" (p. 7). Bliss/Frantzen 1976 deny the speaker is exiled; but the diction throughout this passage is rich in exile imagery. They further find *Resignation B* so different from *The Seafarer* as to preclude mutual illumination (p. 402).

36. Nelson, M. 1983, p. 144 sees his inability to "move" the result of the sin of fear.

37. Ed. separately by Macrae-Gibson 1983; see also Lehmann, R. 1970. Both contain translations. The former dates the poem as mid-tenth century.

38. Cf. Smithers 1957, part 2, pp. 8–9. Howlett 1978a finds a symmetry corresponding to the Golden Section.

39. Macrae-Gibson 1973 denies obscurity in the details; but the numerous extended notes here and in his 1983 edition would argue otherwise.

40. See Macrae-Gibson 1973 and 1983.

41. On microcosm-macrocosm, see Cross 1962; on the riddle quality, Lehmann, R. 1970.

42. See Malone 1962a. The two poems have much in common situationally and in mood; see further next note.

43. A riddle theory has been resurrected by Anderson, J. 1983, who would take the poem, along with the immediately preceding *Soul and Body II* and *Deor*, as a tripartite "first riddle." *The Wife's Lament*, it should be noted, immediately follows the first group of riddles.

44. Baker 1981 tries to disentangle unnecessary ambiguities created by loose readings from deliberately artful ones. A case in point of the latter may be *apecgan* 'take care of' in ll. 2 and 7: it can mean either "to feed" or "to kill."

45. Renoir 1965. A convenient review of interpretations may be found in Frese 1983, who suggests the speaker is a mother bewailing her son; see also Osborn 1983. If the poem's situation is a sexual one, perhaps Wulf, the "battle-bold man," and Eadwacer are one and the same person. The outlawed lover Wulf, *persona non grata* to the speaker's people and equally in danger from the fierce men on his island refuge (they would "take care of" him in one sense, she in another), has only rarely visited her. When he had, as in the scenario of ll. 9–11, the precariousness of the moment made it painful as well as pleasurable. Addressing Wulf as *Eadwacer* 'watchful of happiness,' she asks him *(in absentia)* to consider that he carries their easily destroyed happiness, represented in the metaphors of the whelp and the song, in his wanderings. Cf. Jensen 1979.

46. Ed. by Leslie 1961.

47. Wentersdorf 1981 aruges for this sequence of events.

48. These lines have also been taken as a curse on the husband or on a third party responsible for her position, or as a wish that her husband might experience the same kind of fate as she.

49. For the Germanic context of sorrowing women, see Renoir 1975, who also gives a brief summary of interpretations of the poem's speaker as "a dead woman, a live man, a sorceress-elect, a mistreated wife, a minor heathen deity, and an allegorical voice yearning for the union of Christ and the Church" (p. 236); see further Wentersdorf 1981, n. 1. On formal aspects, see Stevick 1960 and Greenfield 1966, pp. 165–9. Renoir 1977 analyzes the emotional impact of the poem.

50. Green, M. 1983b.

51. Ed. by Leslie 1961.

52. For efforts to link the poems via Germanic story, see Leslie 1961, pp. 10 and 20. Howlett 1978b sees them as a lyric diptych, one elegiac, the other consolatory.

53. On the problem of the speaker, see Orton 1981; though he separates *Riddle 60* from *The Husband's Message*, he argues that the messenger is the piece of wood. Leslie 1961, pp. 13–4 and Greenfield 1966, pp. 169–71 argue for a human messenger. Leslie 1968 makes the case for the riddle's integrity—see also Williamson 1977, pp. 315–8. Kaske 1967b takes the riddle as part of the lyric.

54. See Leslie 1961, pp. 15–8 and Elliott 1955. One common reading of them is "heaven (*Sigel-Rad* 'sun-path'), earth (*Eard-Wyn* 'earth-joy'), and man *(Monn)*."

55. Renoir 1981 feels there is not much likelihood of a happy answer (pp. 74–6).

56. Kaske 1967b reads the poem as a speech of the Cross; Greenfield 1972, pp. 145–53 argues against this reading. Goldsmith 1975 sees the poem spoken by a reed pen representing Holy Writ, calling the addressee to a Christian life.

57. Ed. separately by Malone 1966.

58. Of interest in connection with the Weland story is the scene carved on the left front panel of the whalebone casket of early Northumbrian provenience presented to the British Museum in 1867 by Sir Augustus W. Franks. This scene is reproduced as the frontispiece to this volume. The Franks Casket contains several other scenes and two sets of runic alliterative verse inscriptions—ed. in ASPR 6. See Elliott 1959 for interpretations and bibliography; further Becker 1972; Osborn 1974; Derolez 1981.

59. See respectively Mandel 1977, pp. 2–3; Tuggle 1977, p. 238; Boren 1975, p. 268. Despite such disagreement, these three essays among them provide a good assessment of the poet's art; see also Greenfield 1966, pp. 160–3 and Shippey 1972, pp. 75–8.

60. See respectively Bloomfield 1964; Eliason 1966 and 1969; Shippey 1972, p. 78. Condren 1981 would see the poem proclaiming art's power over adversity.

61. So Kiernan 1978. Markland 1968 first proposed this connection; see also Bolton 1971.

62. Cf. Stanley 1955.

Abbreviations

ABR	*American Benedictine Review*
ae	altenglisch—
ags	angelsächsisch—
AION	*Annali Istituto Universitario Orientale, Napoli*
AnM	*Annuale Mediaevale*
Archiv	*Archiv für das Studium der neueren Sprachen und Literaturen*
Arv	*Arv: Journal of Scandinavian Folklore*
A-S	Anglo-Saxon
ASE	*Anglo-Saxon England*
ASPR	The Anglo-Saxon Poetic Records, eds. G. P. Krapp and E. V. K. Dobbie
BaP	Bibliothek der ags Prosa
BGdSL	*Beiträge zur Geschichte der deutschen Sprache und Literatur*
CCCC	Corpus Christi College, Cambridge
CCSL	*Corpus Christianorum Series Latina*
ChR	*Chaucer Review*
CL	*Comparative Literature*
CM	*Communication Monographs*
CSEL	*Corpus Scriptorum Ecclesiasticorum Latinorum*
ed(s).	editor(s), edited, edition
EEMF	Early English Manuscripts in Facsimile
EETS	Early English Text Society
EETS,ss	Early English Text Society, Supplementary Series
EGS	*English and Germanic Studies*
EHR	*English Historical Review*
ELH	*ELH: Journal of English Literary History*
ELN	*English Language Notes*
ES	*English Studies*

E&S	Essays and Studies by Members of the English Association
JEGP	Journal of English and Germanic Philology
JAF	Journal of American Folklore
JEH	Journal of Ecclesiastical History
KHVL	Kungl. Humanistiska Vetenskapssamfundets i Lund
LeedsSE	Leeds Studies in English
MÆ	Medium Ævum
ME	Middle English
MGH	Monumenta Germaniae Historica
Migne	see PL
MLN	Modern Language Notes
MLQ	Modern Language Quarterly
MLR	Modern Language Review
MP	Modern Philology
MS(S)	M(m)anuscript(s)
MS	Mediaeval Studies
NDEJ	Notre Dame English Journal
Neophil	Neophilologus
NM	Neuphilologische Mitteilungen
N&Q	Notes and Queries
OE	Old English
OEN	Old English Newsletter
ON	Old Norse
PBA	Proceedings of the British Academy
PL	Patrologia Latina, ed. Migne
PLL	Papers on Language and Literature
PMLA	PMLA: Publications of the Modern Language Association of America
PQ	Philological Quarterly
QJS	Quarterly Journal of Speech
Rb	Revue bénédictine
RES	Review of English Studies
R(r)ev.	R(r)evised
Rpr.	Reprinted
SM	Studi Medievali
SN	Studia Neophilologica
SP	Studies in Philology
TPS	Transactions of the Philological Society
trans.	translator(s), translated
TRHS	Transactions of the Royal Historical Society
TSL	Tennessee Studies in Literature
TSLL	Texas Studies in Literature and Language
UTQ	University of Toronto Quarterly
W-S	West-Saxon
YES	Yearbook of English Studies
YSE	Yale Studies in English

Bibliography
of Works Cited

The following bibliography is in alphabetical order; it is not divided into subjects. For a list of items concerning any individual work or period, check the footnote references in the main text. In many cases, subtitles of books have been omitted.

Adams, E. 1917	Adams, Eleanor N. *OE Scholarship in England from 1566–1800*. YSE 55. New Haven 1917. Rpr. Hamden, Conn: Archon Books, 1970.
Adams, R. 1974	Adams, Richard W. "*Christ II:* Cynewulfian *Heilsgeschichte.*" ELN 12 (1974), 73–9.
Alford/Seniff 1984	Alford, John A. and Dennis P. Seniff. *Literature and Law in the Middle Ages*. New York and London: Garland, 1984.
Allott 1974	Allott, Stephen. *Alcuin of York*. York: William Sessions, 1974.
Amos 1980	Amos, Ashley C. *Linguistic Means of Determining the Dates of OE Literary Texts*. Cambridge, Mass.: The Medieval Academy of America, 1980.
Anderson, E. 1974	Anderson, Earl R. "Social Idealism in Ælfric's *Colloquy.*" ASE 3 (1974), 153–62.
Anderson, E. 1979	——. "The Speech Boundaries in Advent Lyric VII." *Neophil* 63 (1979), 611–8.
Anderson, E. 1983	——. *Cynewulf: Structure, Style and Theme in His Poetry*. Rutherford, N. J., London and Toronto: Fairleigh Dickinson University Press/Associated University Presses, 1983.

Anderson, G. 1966   Anderson, George K. *The Literature of the Anglo-Saxons.* Rev. ed. Princeton: Princeton University Press, 1966.

Anderson, G. 1967   ———. "Aldhelm and the *Leiden Riddle.*" In Creed 1967b, pp. 167–76.

Anderson, J. 1983   Anderson, James E. "*Deor, Wulf and Eadwacer, The Soul's Address:* How and Where the OE Exeter Book Riddles Begin." In Green, M. 1983a, pp. 204–30.

Anderson, L. 1903   Anderson, Lewis F. *The A-S Scop.* Toronto: Toronto University Library, the Librarian, 1903.

Anderson, O. 1937   Anderson (later Arngart), Olaf. "The Seafarer: An Interpretation." *KHVL Årsberättelse* 1. Lund: C. W. K. Gleerup, 1937–8.

Andersson 1976   Andersson, Theodore M. *Early Epic Scenery: Homer, Virgil, and the Medieval Legacy.* Ithaca and London: Cornell University Press, 1976.

Arngart 1942   Arngart, O., ed. *The Proverbs of Alfred.* 2 vols. Lund: C. W. K. Gleerup, 1942 and 1955.

Arngart 1951   ———. "The Distichs of Cato and the Proverbs of Alfred." *KHVL Årsberättelse* (1951–2), 95–118.

Arngart 1981   ———, ed. "The Durham Proverbs." *Speculum* 56 (1981), 288–300.

Arnold 1885   Arnold, Thomas, ed. *Symeonis Monachi Opera.* 2 vols. Rolls Series 75. London: Longman and Co., 1885.

ASPR 1   *The Junius Manuscript,* ed. G. P. Krapp. New York: Columbia University Press, 1931.

2   *The Vercelli Book,* ed. G. P. Krapp. New York: Columbia University Press, 1932.

3   *The Exeter Book,* ed. G. P. Krapp and E. V. K. Dobbie. New York: Columbia University Press, 1936.

4   *Beowulf and Judith,* ed. E.V.K. Dobbie. New York: Columbia University Press, 1953.

5   *The Paris Psalter and the Meters of Boethius,* ed. G. P. Krapp. New York: Columbia University Press, 1932.

6   *The A-S Minor Poems,* ed. E. V. K. Dobbie. New York: Columbia University Press, 1942.

Assmann 1889   Assmann, Bruno, ed. *Ags Homilien und Heiligenleben.* BaP 3. Kassel: G. H. Wigland, 1889. Rpr. with a supplementary intro. by Peter Clemoes. Darmstadt: Wissenschaftliche Buchgesellschaft, 1964.

Attenborough 1922   Attenborough, Frederick L., ed. *The Laws of the Earliest English Kings.* Cambridge: Cambridge University Press, 1922.

Atwood/Hill 1969   Atwood, E. Bagby and A. A. Hill. *Studies in Language, Literature, and Culture of the Middle Ages and Later.* Austin: University of Texas Press, 1969.

Ayres 1917   Ayres, Harry M. "The Tragedy of Hengest in *Beowulf.*" *JEGP* 16 (1917), 282–95.

Baker 1980   Baker, Peter S. "The OE Canon of Byrhtferth of Ramsey." *Speculum* 55 (1980), 22–37.

Baker 1981 ———. "The Ambiguity of *Wulf and Eadwacer.*" In Wittig 1981, pp. 39–51.

Baker 1982 ———. "Byrhtferth's *Enchiridion* and the Computus in Oxford, St John's College 17." *ASE* 10 (1982), 123–42.

Baker 1984 ———, ed. "A Little-Known Variant Text of the OE Metrical Psalms." *Speculum* 59 (1984), 263–81.

Barley 1972 Barley, N. F. "A Structural Approach to the Proverb and Maxim, with Special Reference to the A-S Corpus." *Proverbium* 20 (1972), 737–50.

Barley 1977 ———. "Structure in the Cotton Gnomes." *NM* 78 (1977), 244–9.

Barlow 1962 Barlow, Frank, ed. *Vita Ædwardi Regis.* London: Nelson and Sons, 1962.

Barlow 1979 ———. *The English Church 1000–1066.* 2nd ed. London: Longman Group, 1979.

Barraclough 1976 Barraclough, Geoffrey. *The Crucible of Europe: The Ninth and Tenth Centuries in European History.* Berkeley and Los Angeles: University of California Press, 1976.

Bartlett 1935 Bartlett, Adeline C. *The Larger Rhetorical Patterns in A-S Poetry.* New York: Columbia University Press, 1935. Rpr. AMS Press, 1966.

Bately 1978 Bately, Janet M. "The Compilation of *The A-S Chronicle,* 60 BC to AD 890: Vocabulary as Evidence." *PBA* 64 (1980 for 1978), 93–129.

Bately 1979 ———. "Bede and the A-S Chronicle." In King/Stevens 1979, vol. 1, pp. 233–54.

Bately 1980a ———. *The Literary Prose of King Alfred's Reign: Translation or Transformation?* London: King's College, University of London, 1980.

Bately 1980b ———, ed. *The OE Orosius.* EETS, ss 6. London 1980.

Bately 1982 ———. "Lexical Evidence for the Authorship of the Prose Psalms in the Paris Psalter." *ASE* 10 (1982), 69–95.

Baum 1963 Baum, Paull F., trans. *A-S Riddles of the Exeter Book.* Durham, NC: Duke University Press, 1963.

Bazire/Cross 1982 Bazire, Joyce and James E. Cross, eds. *Eleven OE Rogationtide Homilies.* Toronto, Buffalo, and London: University of Toronto Press, 1982.

Becker 1972 Becker, Alfred. *Franks Casket: Zu den Bildern und Inschriften des Runenkästchens von Auzon.* Regensburg: H. Carl, 1972.

Belfour 1909 Belfour, Algernon O., ed. *Twelfth-Century Homilies in MS Bodley 343. I. Text and Translation.* EETS 137. London 1909. Rpr. 1962.

Benson 1966 Benson, Larry D. "The Literary Character of A-S Formulaic Poetry." *PMLA* 81 (1966), 334–41.

Berger/Leicester 1974 Berger, Harry, Jr. and H. Marshall Leicester, Jr. "Social Structure as Doom: The Limits of Heroism in *Beowulf*." In Burlin/Irving 1974, pp. 37–79.

Berkhout 1972   Berkhout, Carl T. "Some Notes on the OE *Almsgiving*." *ELN* 10 (1972–3), 81–5.

Berkhout 1974   ———. "*Feld dennade*—Again." *ELN* 11 (1974), 161–2.

Berkhout/Doubleday 1973   —— and James F. Doubleday. "The Net in *Judith* 46b–54a." *NM* 74 (1973), 630–4.

Berkhout/Gatch 1982   —— and Milton McC. Gatch, eds. *A-S Scholarship: The First Three Centuries*. Boston: G. K. Hall, 1982.

Bessinger 1958   Bessinger, Jess B., Jr. "*Beowulf* and the Harp at Sutton Hoo." *UTQ* 27 (1958), 148–68.

Bessinger 1962   ———. "*Maldon* and the *Óláfsdrápa*: An Historical Caveat." *CL* 14 (1962), 23–35.

Bessinger 1967   ———. "The Sutton Hoo Harp-Replica and OE Musical Verse." In Creed 1967b, pp. 3–26.

Bessinger 1974   ———. "Homage to Caedmon and Others: A Beowulfian Praise Song." In Burlin/Irving 1974, pp. 91–106.

Bessinger/Creed 1965   —— and Robert P. Creed, eds. *Franciplegius: Medieval and Linguistic Studies in Honor of Francis Peabody Magoun, Jr.* New York: New York University Press, 1965.

Bessinger/Kahrl 1968   —— and Stanley J. Kahrl, eds. *Essential Articles for the Study of OE Poetry*. Hamden, Conn: Archon Books, 1968.

Bessinger/Smith 1969   —— and Philip H. Smith, Jr., eds. *A Concordance to Beowulf*. Ithaca: Cornell University Press, 1969.

Bessinger/Smith 1978   ———. *A Concordance to The A-S Poetic Records*. Ithaca and London: Cornell University Press, 1978.

Bessinger/Yeager 1984   —— and Robert F. Yeager, eds. *Approaches to Teaching Beowulf*. New York: Modern Language Association of America, 1984.

Bethurum 1932a   Bethurum, Dorothy. "The Form of Ælfric's *Lives of Saints*." *SP* 29 (1932), 515–33.

Bethurum 1932b   ———. "Stylistic Features of the OE Laws." *MLR* 27 (1932), 263–79.

Bethurum 1957   ———, ed. *The Homilies of Wulfstan*. Oxford: Clarendon Press, 1957.

Bethurum 1963   ———. "Episcopal Magnificence in the Eleventh Century." In Greenfield 1963b, pp. 162–70.

Bethurum 1966   ———. "Wulfstan." In Stanley 1966b, pp. 210–46.

Biddle 1975   Biddle, Martin. "*Felix Urbs Winthonia*: Winchester in the Age of Monastic Reform." In Parsons 1975, pp. 123–40.

Binns 1961   Binns, A. L. "Ohtheriana VI: Ohthere's Northern Voyage." *EGS* 7 (1961), 43–52.

Bischoff 1976   Bischoff, Bernhard. "Turning-Points in the History of Latin Exegesis in the Early Middle Ages." In *Biblical Studies: The Medieval Irish Contribution*, ed. Martin McNamara. Dublin: Dominican Publications, 1976, pp. 74–164.

Bjork 1980   Bjork, Robert E. "Oppressed Hebrews and the Song of Azarias in the OE *Daniel.*" *SP* 77 (1980), 213–26.

Bjork 1985   ———. *The OE Verse Saints' Lives: A Study in Direct Discourse and the Iconography of Style.* Toronto, Buffalo, and London: University of Toronto Press, 1985.

Blair   See Hunter Blair.

Blake 1962   Blake, N. F. "*Caedmon's Hymn.*" *N&Q* 207 [n.s. 9] (1962), 243–6.

Blake 1964   ———, ed. *The Phoenix.* Manchester: Manchester University Press, 1964.

Blake 1965   ———. "*The Battle of Maldon.*" *Neophil* 49 (1965), 332–45.

Blake 1978   ———. "The Genesis of *The Battle of Maldon.*" *ASE* 7 (1978), 119–29.

Bliss 1967   Bliss, Alan J. *The Metre of Beowulf.* Rev. ed. Oxford: Blackwell, 1967.

Bliss 1972   ———. "The Origin and Structure of the OE Hypermetric Line." *N&Q* 217 [n.s. 19] (1972), 242–8.

Bliss/Frantzen 1976   ——— and Allen J. Frantzen. "The Integrity of *Resignation.*" *RES* 27 (1976), 385–402.

Bloomfield 1964   Bloomfield, Morton. "The Form of *Deor.*" *PMLA* 79 (1964), 534–41.

Bloomfield 1968   ———. "Understanding OE Poetry." *AnM* 9 (1968), 5–25.

Boenig 1980   Boenig, Robert E. "*Andreas,* The Eucharist, and Vercelli." *JEGP* 79 (1980), 313–31.

Bollard 1973   Bollard, J. K. "The Cotton Maxims." *Neophil* 57 (1973), 179–87.

Bolton 1967   Bolton, Whitney F. *A History of Anglo-Latin Literature 597–1066: I. 597–740.* Princeton: Princeton University Press, 1967.

Bolton 1968   ———. " 'Variation' in *The Battle of Brunanburh.*" *RES* 19 (1968), 363–72.

Bolton 1971   ———. "Boethius, Alfred, and *Deor* Again." *MP* 69 (1971–2), 222–7.

Bolton 1985   ———. "How Boethian is Alfred's Boethius?" In Szarmach 1985, pp. 153–68.

Bonjour 1950   Bonjour, Adrien. *The Digressions in Beowulf.* Oxford: Blackwell, 1950.

Bonjour 1957   ———. "*Beowulf* and the Beasts of Battle." *PMLA* 72 (1957), 563–73. Rpr. with add. comment in Bonjour 1962.

Bonjour 1962   ———. *Twelve Beowulf Papers: 1940–1960, with Additional Comments.* Neuchâtel: Faculté des lettres, 1962.

Bonner 1973   Bonner, Gerald. "Bede and Medieval Civilization." *ASE* 2 (1973), 71–90.

Bonner 1976   ———, ed. *Famulus Christi.* London: S.P.C.K., 1976.

Bonser 1957   Bonser, Wilfrid. *An A-S and Celtic Bibliography (450–1087).* 2 vols. Oxford: Blackwell, 1957

Bonser 1963   ——. *The Medical Background of A-S England: A Study in History, Psychology, and Folklore.* London: The Wellcome Historical Medical Library, 1963.

Boren 1969   Boren, James L. "Form and Meaning in Cynewulf's *Fates of the Apostles.*" *PLL* 5 (1969), 115–22.

Boren 1975   ——. "The Design of the OE *Deor.*" In Nicholson/Frese 1975, pp. 264–76.

Bosworth 1859   Bosworth, Joseph, ed. *King Alfred's A-S Version of the Compendious History of the World by Orosius.* London: Longman, Brown, Green and Longmans, 1859.

Bosworth/Toller 1882   ——, ed. *An A-S Dictionary.* Oxford: Oxford University Press, 1882. With a *Supplement* by Toller. Oxford: Clarendon Press, 1921. *Enlarged Addenda and Corrigenda to the Supplement* by Alistair Campbell. Oxford: Clarendon Press, 1972.

Boyd 1982   Boyd, Nina. "Doctrine and Criticism: A Revaluation of *Genesis A.*" *NM* 83 (1982), 230–8.

Bradley 1982   Bradley, S. A. J., trans. *A-S Poetry.* London, Melbourne, and Toronto: J. M. Dent and Sons, 1982.

Brady 1943   Brady, Caroline. *The Legends of Ermanaric.* Berkeley and Los Angeles: University of California Press, 1943.

Braswell 1978   Braswell, Bruce K. "*The Dream of the Rood* and Aldhelm on Sacred Prosopopoeia." *MS* 40 (1978), 461–7.

Brearley/Goodfellow 1982   Brearley, D. and M. Goodfellow, trans. "Wulfstan's Life of St. Ethelwold: A Translation with Notes." *Revue de l'Université d'Ottawa* 52 (1985), 377–407.

Bridges 1979   Bridges, Margaret. "Exordial Tradition and Poetic Individuality in Five OE Hagiographical Poems." *ES* 60 (1979), 361–79.

Bridges 1984   ——. *Generic Contrast in OE Hagiographical Poetry.* Copenhagen: Rosenkilde and Bagger, 1984.

Bright/Ramsay 1907   Bright, James W. and Robert L. Ramsay, eds. *Liber Psalmorum: The W-S Psalms.* Boston and London: D. C. Heath and Co., 1907.

Britton 1974   Britton, G. C. "Repetition and Contrast in the OE *Later Genesis.*" *Neophil* 58 (1974), 66–73.

Brockman 1974   Brockman, Bennet A. " 'Heroic' and 'Christian' in *Genesis A:* The Evidence of the Cain and Abel Episode." *MLQ* 35 (1974), 115–28.

Brodeur 1959   Brodeur, Arthur G. *The Art of Beowulf.* Berkeley and Los Angeles: University of California Press, 1959.

Brodeur 1968   ——. "A Study of Diction and Style in Three A-S Narrative Poems." In *Nordica et Anglica: Studies in Honour of Stefán Einarsson,* ed. A. H. Orrick. The Hague and Paris: Mouton, 1968, pp. 98–114.

Brodeur 1970   ——. "*Beowulf:* One Poem or Three?" In *Medieval Lit-*

erature and Folklore Studies: Essays in Honour of Francis Lee Utley, eds. Jerome Mandel and Bruce A. Rosenberg. New Brunswick: Rutgers University Press, 1970, pp. 3–26.

Bromwich 1950   Bromwich, J. I'a. "Who was the Translator of the Prose Portion of the Paris Psalter?" In Fox/Dickins 1950, pp. 289–303.

Brooke 1970   Brooke, Christopher N. L. "Historical Writing in England between 850–1150." In *La Storiografia Altomedievale*, Settimane di studio del centro italiano di studi sull'alto medioevo 17 (1970), 223–47.

Brooks, K. 1961   Brooks, Kenneth R., ed. *Andreas and the Fates of the Apostles*. Oxford: Clarendon Press, 1961.

Brooks, N. 1984   Brooks, Nicholas. *The Early History of the Church of Canterbury*. Leicester: Leicester University Press, 1984.

Brown, A. 1980   Brown, Alan K. "The Firedrake in *Beowulf*." *Neophil* 64 (1980), 439–60.

Brown, G. 1974   Brown, George H. "The Descent-Ascent Motif in *Christ II* of Cynewulf." *JEGP* 73 (1974), 1–12.

Brown, P. 1969   Brown, Peter. *Augustine of Hippo: A Biography*. Berkeley and Los Angeles: University of California Press, 1969.

Brown, W. 1969   Brown, William H. "Method and Style in the OE *Pastoral Care*." *JEGP* 68 (1969), 666–84.

Brown/Foote 1963   Brown, Arthur and Peter Foote, eds. *Early English and Norse Studies*. London: Methuen and Co., 1963.

Bruce-Mitford 1975   Bruce-Mitford, Rupert L. S. *The Sutton-Hoo Ship Burial*. 3 vols. in 4. London: British Museum Publications, 1975–83.

Bruce-Mitford 1979   ——, et al. *The Sutton-Hoo Ship Burial: Reflections after Thirty Years*. York: William Session, 1979.

Bullough 1972   Bullough, D. A. "The Educational Tradition in England from Alfred to Ælfric: Teaching *Utriusque Linguae*." In *La Scuola nell'Occidente Latino dell'Alto Medioevo*, Settimane di studio del centro italiano di studi sull'alto medioevo 19 (1972), 453–94, 547–54.

Burchfield 1974   Burchfield, Robert W. "The Prosodic Terminology of A-S Scholars." In Burlin/Irving 1974, pp. 171–202.

Burgert 1921   Burgert, Edward. *The Dependence of Part I of Cynewulf's Christ upon the Antiphonary*. Washington, D.C.: Catholic University of America, 1921.

Burlin 1968   Burlin, Robert B. *The OE Advent: A Typological Commentary*. YSE 168. New Haven and London 1968.

Burlin/Irving 1974   —— and Edward B. Irving, Jr., eds. *OE Studies in Honour of John C. Pope*. Toronto and Buffalo: University of Toronto Press, 1974.

Burrow 1959   Burrow, John A. "An Approach to *The Dream of the Rood*." *Neophil* 43 (1959), 123–33.

Cable 1971   Cable, Thomas. "Constraints on Anacrusis in OE
                  Meter." *MP* 69 (1971–2), 97–104.
Cable 1984   ——. "OE Prosody." In Bessinger/Yeager 1984, pp.
                  173–8.
Caie 1976   Caie, Graham D. *The Judgment Day Theme in OE Po-
                  etry.* Copenhagen: Nova, 1976.
Caie 1978   ——. "The OE *Daniel:* A Warning Against Pride." *ES*
                  59 (1978), 1–9.
Caie 1979   ——. *Bibliography of Junius XI MS.* Copenhagen: De-
                  partment of English, University of Copenhagen,
                  1979.
Calder 1971a   Calder, Daniel G. "Perspective and Movement in *The
                  Ruin.*" *NM* 72 (1971), 442–5.
Calder 1971b   ——. "Setting and Mode in *The Seafarer* and *The Wan-
                  derer.*" *NM* 72 (1971), 264–75.
Calder 1972a   ——. "Setting and Ethos: The Pattern of Measure and
                  Limit in *Beowulf.*" *SP* 69 (1972), 21–37.
Calder 1972b   ——. "Theme and Strategy in *Guthlac B.*" *PLL* 8 (1972),
                  227–42.
Calder 1972c   ——. "The Vision of Paradise: A Symbolic Reading of
                  the OE *Phoenix.*" *ASE* 1 (1972), 167–81.
Calder 1975   ——. "*Guthlac A* and *Guthlac B:* Some Discrimina-
                  tions." In Nicholson/Frese 1975, pp. 65–80.
Calder 1979a   ——, ed. *OE Poetry: Essays on Style.* Berkeley and Los
                  Angeles: University of California Press, 1979.
Calder 1979b   ——. "The Study of Style in OE Poetry: A Historical
                  Introduction." In Calder 1979a, pp. 1–65.
Calder 1981   ——. *Cynewulf.* Boston: Twayne, 1981.
Calder 1982   ——. "Histories and Surveys of OE Literature: A
                  Chronological Review." *ASE* 10 (1982), 201–44.
Calder/Allen 1976 —— and M. J. B. Allen, trans. *Sources and Analogues
                  of OE Poetry: The Major Latin Sources in Translation.*
                  Cambridge and Totowa, NJ: D. S. Brewer/Rowman
                  and Littlefield, 1976.
Calder/et al. 1983 ——, R. E. Bjork, P. K. Ford, and D. F. Melia, trans.
                  *Sources and Analogues of OE Poetry II: The Major Ger-
                  manic and Celtic Texts in Translation.* Cambridge and
                  Totowa, NJ: D. S. Brewer/Barnes and Noble, 1983.
Camargo 1981   Camargo, Martin. "The Finn Episode and the Trag-
                  edy of Revenge in *Beowulf.*" In Wittig 1981, pp. 120–
                  34.
Cameron 1982   Cameron, M. L. "The Sources of Medical Knowledge
                  in A-S England." *ASE* 11 (1982), 135–55.
Cameron 1983   ——. "Bald's *Leechbook:* Its Sources and Their Use in
                  its Compilation." *ASE* 12 (1983), 153–82.
Campbell, A. 1938 Campbell, Alistair, ed. *The Battle of Brunanburh.* Lon-
                  don: W. Heinemann, 1938.
Campbell, A. 1949 ——, ed. *Encomium Emmae Reginae.* Camden 3rd ser.
                  London: Royal Historical Society, 1949.

Campbell, A. 1950 ——, ed. *Frithegodi Monachi Breviloquium Vitae Beati Wilfredi et Wulfstani Cantoris Narratio Metrica de Sancto Swithuno*. Zurich: Thesauri Mundi, 1950.

Campbell, A. 1953 ——, ed. *The Tollemache Orosius*. EEMF 3. Copenhagen: Rosenkilde and Bagger, 1953.

Campbell, A. 1962a —— ed. *The Chronicle of Æthelweard*. London: Nelson and Co., 1962.

Campbell, A. 1962b ——. "The Old English Epic Style." In *English and Medieval Studies: Presented to J. R. R. Tolkien on the Occasion of his 70th Birthday*, eds. N. Davis and C. L. Wrenn. London: George Allen and Unwin, 1962, pp. 13–26.

Campbell, A. 1967 ——, ed. *Æthelwulf De Abbatibus*. Oxford: Clarendon Press, 1967.

Campbell, J. 1951 Campbell, Jackson J. "The Dialect Vocabulary of the OE Bede." *JEGP* 50 (1951), 349–72.

Campbell, J. 1959 ——, ed. *The Advent Lyrics of the Exeter Book*. Princeton: Princeton University Press, 1959.

Campbell, J. 1965 ——. "Learned Rhetoric in OE Poetry." *MP* 63 (1965–6), 189–201.

Campbell, J. 1971 ——. "Schematic Technique in *Judith*." *ELH* 38 (1971), 155–72.

Campbell, J. 1972 ——. "Cynewulf's Multiple Revelations." *Medievalia et Humanistica* 3 (1972), 257–77.

Campbell, J. 1975 ——. "A Certain Power." *Neophil* 59 (1975), 128–38.

Campbell, J. 1978 ——. "Adaptations of Classical Rhetoric in OE Literature." In *Medieval Eloquence: Studies in the Theory and Practice of Medieval Rhetoric*, ed. J. J. Murphy. Berkeley and Los Angeles: University of California Press, 1978, pp. 173–97.

Campbell, J. 1982 ——. "To Hell and Back: Latin Tradition and Literary Use of the 'Descensus ad Inferos' in OE." *Viator* 13 (1982), 107–58.

Campbell, Jas. 1982 Campbell, James, ed. *The Anglo-Saxons*. Ithaca: Cornell University Press, 1982.

Campbell, T. 1978 Campbell, Thomas P. "Thematic Unity in the OE *Physiologus*." *Archiv* 215 (1978), 73–9.

Capek 1971 Capek, Michael J. "The Nationality of a Translator: Some Notes on the Syntax of *Genesis B*." *Neophil* 55 (1971), 89–96.

Carlson 1975 Carlson, Ingvar, ed. *The Pastoral Care Edited from British Museum MS Cotton Otho B. ii*, Part I. Stockholm Studies in English 34 (1975).

Carlson 1978 ——, ed. *The Pastoral Care Edited from British Library MS Cotton Otho B. ii*, Part II, completed by Lars-G. Hallander, with Mattias Lofvenberg and Alarik Rynell. Stockholm Studies in English 48 (1978).

Carlton 1970 Carlton, Charles. *Descriptive Syntax of the OE Charters*. The Hague: Mouton, 1970.

Carnicelli 1969 — Carnicelli, Thomas A., ed. *King Alfred's Version of St. Augustine's Soliloquies*. Cambridge, Mass: Harvard University Press, 1969.

Carroll 1952 — Carroll, Benjamin H. "An Essay on the Walther Legend." *Florida State Univ. Studies* 5 (1952), 123–79.

Cassidy 1965 — Cassidy, Frederic G. "How Free was the A-S Scop?" In Bessinger/Creed 1965, pp. 75–85.

Cassidy/Ringler 1971 — —— and Richard N. Ringler, eds. *Bright's OE Grammar and Reader*. 3rd ed. New York: Holt, Rinehart and Winston, 1971.

CCSL

De Marco 1968 — De Marco, Maria, ed. *Ars Tatvini*. Vol. 133. Turnhout: Typographi Brepols, 1968.

Fraipont 1955 — Fraipont, J., ed. *Bedae Venerabilis Opera:* Pars IV. *Opera Rhythmica*. Vol. 122. Turnhout: Typographi Brepols, 1955.

Gebauer/Löfstedt 1980 — Gebauer, G. J. and Bengt Löfstedt, eds. *Bonifati (Vnfreth) Ars Grammatica*. Vol. 133B. Tourhout: Typographi Brepols, 1980.

Glorie 1968 — Glorie, F., ed. *Collectiones Aenigmatum Merovingicae Aetatis*. Vol. 133. Turnhout: Typographi Brepols, 1968.

Jones, C./et al. 1955 — Jones, C. W., et al. eds. *Bedae opera*. Vols. 118–23 (eventually comprising 10 vols.). Turnhout: Typographi Brepols, 1955–.

Chadwick, H. 1981 — Chadwick, Henry. *Boethius: The Consolations of Music, Logic, Theology and Philosophy*. Oxford: Clarendon Press, 1981.

Chadwick, H. M. 1912 — Chadwick, Hector M. *The Heroic Age*. Cambridge: Cambridge University Press, 1912.

Chamberlain 1975 — Chamberlain, David. "*Judith*: A Fragmentary and Political Poem." In Nicholson/Frese 1975, pp. 135–59.

Chambers 1912 — Chambers, Raymond W., ed. *Widsith: A Study in OE Heroic Legend*. Cambridge: Cambridge University Press, 1912.

Chambers 1932 — ——. *On the Continuity of English Prose from Alfred to More and His School*. EETS 191A. London 1932.

Chambers 1959 — ——. *Beowulf. An Introduction to the Study of the Poem*. 3rd ed. With supplement by C. L. Wrenn. Cambridge: Cambridge University Press, 1959.

Chambers/et al. 1933 — ——, Max Förster, and Robin Flower, eds. *The Exeter Book of OE Poetry*. Bradford: P. Lund, Humphries and Co., 1933.

Chaplais 1973 — Chaplais, P. "Who Introduced Charters into England? The Case for Augustine." In *Prisca Munimenta*, ed. F. Ranger. London: University of London Press, 1973, pp. 88–107.

Chase, C. 1974 — Chase, Colin. "God's Presence Through Grace as the

Theme of Cynewulf's *Christ II* and the Relationship of this Theme to *Christ I* and *Christ III.*" *ASE* 3 (1974), 87–101.

Chase, C. 1981 ——, ed. *The Dating of Beowulf.* Toronto, Buffalo, and London: University of Toronto Press, 1981.

Chase, C. L. 1980 Chase, Christopher L. "*Christ III, The Dream of the Rood,* and Early Christian Passion Piety." *Viator* 11 (1980), 11–33.

Chase, W. 1922 Chase, Wayland J., ed. and trans. *The Distichs of Cato.* Madison: University of Wisconsin Press, 1922.

Cherniss 1972 Cherniss, Michael D. *Ingeld and Christ.* The Hague: Mouton, 1972.

Chickering 1971 Chickering, Howell D. "The Literary Magic of 'Wið Færstice'." *Viator* 2 (1971), 83–104.

Chickering 1976 ——. "Some Contexts for Bede's *Death-Song.*" *PMLA* 91 (1976), 91–100.

Chickering 1977 ——, ed. and trans. *Beowulf: A Dual-Language Edition.* Garden City, NY: Anchor Press/Doubleday, 1977.

Cilluffo 1980 Cilluffo, Gilda. "Il dialogo in prosa *Salomone e Saturno* del MS CCCC 422." *AION,* Filologia germanica 23 (1980), 121–46.

Cilluffo 1981 ——, ed. and trans., *Il Salomone e Saturno in prosa del MS CCCC 422,* with appendix by Patrizia Lendinara. Quaderni di filologia germanica 2. Palermo 1981.

Clark, C. 1968 Clark, Cecily. "Ælfric and Abbo." *ES* 49 (1968), 30–6.

Clark, C. 1971 ——. "The Narrative Mode of *The A-S Chronicle* before the Conquest." In Clemoes/Hughes 1971, pp. 215–35.

Clark, G. 1965 Clark, George. "The Traveller Recognizes his Goal: A Theme in A-S Poetry." *JEGP* 64 (1965), 645–59.

Clark, G. 1968 ——. "*The Battle of Maldon:* A Heroic Poem." *Speculum* 43 (1968), 52–71.

Clark, G. 1979 ——. "The Hero of *Maldon:* Vir Pius et Strenuus." *Speculum* 54 (1979), 257–82.

Clark Hall/Meritt 1960 Clark Hall, J. R., ed. *A Concise A-S Dictionary.* 4th ed. with supplement by H. D. Meritt. Cambridge: Cambridge University Press, 1960.

Clark, S./Wasserman 1979 Clark, Sue L. and Julian N. Wasserman. "The Imagery of *The Wanderer.*" *Neophil* 63 (1979), 291–6.

Clement 1985 Clement, Richard W. "The Production of the *Pastoral Care:* King Alfred and His Helpers." In Szarmach 1985, pp. 129–52.

Clemoes 1959a Clemoes, P. A. M., ed. *The Anglo-Saxons: Studies in Some Aspects of Their History and Culture Presented to Bruce Dickins.* London: Bowes and Bowes, 1959.

Clemoes 1959b ——. "The Chronology of Ælfric's Work." In Clemoes 1959a, pp. 212–47.

Clemoes 1960 ——. "The OE Benedictine Office, CCCC MS 190, and the Relations between Ælfric and Wulfstan: a Reconsideration." *Anglia* 78 (1960), 265–83.

Clemoes 1966 ——. "Ælfric." In Stanley 1966b, pp. 176–209.

Clemoes 1969 ——. "*Mens absentia cogitans* in *The Seafarer* and *The Wanderer*." In Pearsall/Waldron 1969, pp. 62–77.

Clemoes 1970 ——. *Rhythm and Cosmic Order in OE Christian Literature: An Inaugural Lecture*. Cambridge: Cambridge University Press, 1970.

Clemoes 1971 ——. "Cynewulf's Image of the Ascension." In Clemoes/Hughes 1971, pp. 293–304.

Clemoes 1974 ——. "The Composition of the OE Text." In *The OE Illustrated Hexateuch*, eds. C. R. Dodwell and Peter Clemoes. EEMF 18. Copenhagen: Rosenkilde and Bagger, 1974, pp. 42–53.

Clemoes 1979 ——. "Action in *Beowulf* and Our Perception of It." In Calder 1979a, pp. 147–68.

Clemoes/Hughes 1971 —— and Kathleen Hughes, eds. *England before the Conquest: Studies in Primary Sources Presented to Dorothy Whitelock*. Cambridge: Cambridge University Press, 1971.

Clover 1980 Clover, Carol J. "The Germanic Context of the Unferþ Episode." *Speculum* 55 (1980), 444–68.

Clubb 1925 Clubb, Merrel D., ed. *Christ and Satan: An OE Poem*. YSE 70. New Haven 1925. Rpr. Hamden, Conn: Archon Books, 1972.

Cockayne 1864 Cockayne, Thomas O., ed. *Leechdoms, Wortcunning, and Starcraft of Early England*. 3 vols. London: Her Majesty's Stationary Office, 1864–6. Rpr. Kraus Reprint, 1965.

Colgrave 1927 Colgrave, Bertram, ed. *The Life of Bishop Wilfrid by Eddius Stephanus*. Cambridge: Cambridge University Press, 1927.

Colgrave 1940 ——, ed. *Two Lives of Saint Cuthbert*. Cambridge: Cambridge University Press, 1940.

Colgrave 1956 ——, ed. *Felix's Life of Saint Guthlac*. Cambridge: Cambridge University Press, 1956.

Colgrave 1958 ——, ed. *The Paris Psalter*. EEMF 8. Copenhagen: Rosenkilde and Bagger, 1958.

Colgrave 1959 ——. "The Earliest Saints' Lives Written in England." *PBA* 44 (1959), 35–60.

Colgrave 1968 ——, ed. *The Earliest Life of Gregory the Great*. Lawrence, Kansas: University of Kansas Press, 1968.

Colgrave/Mynors 1969 —— and R. A. B. Mynors, eds. and trans. *Bede's Ecclesiastical History of the English People*. Oxford: Clarendon Press, 1969.

Condren 1981 Condren, Edward I. "Deor's Artistic Triumph." In Wittig 1981, pp. 62–76.

Conlee 1970 Conlee, John W. "A Note on Verse Composition in the *Meters of Boethius*." *NM* 71 (1970), 576–85.

Conner 1980   Conner, Patrick W. "The Liturgy and the OE 'De-
                   scent into Hell'." *JEGP* 79 (1980), 179–91.
Cook 1909   Cook, Albert S., ed. *The Christ of Cynewulf.* 2nd ed.
                   Boston: Ginn and Co., 1909. Rpr. with Preface
                   by J. C. Pope. Hamden, Conn: Archon Books,
                   1964.
Cook 1919   ——, ed. *The OE Elene, Phoenix, and Physiologus.* New
                   Haven: Yale University Press, 1919.
Cook/Pitman 1921   ——, ed. *The OE Physiologus. Text and Prose Transla-
                   tion. Verse Translation by James Hall Pitman.* New
                   Haven: Yale University Press, 1921.
Cordasco 1949   Cordasco, Francesco. "The OE *Physiologus:* Its Prob-
                   lems." *MLQ* 10 (1949), 351–5.
Courcelle 1967   Courcelle, Pierre P. *La Consolation de philosophie dans
                   la tradition littéraire.* Paris: Études augustinennes,
                   1967.
Cox 1972   Cox, Robert S., ed. "The OE Dicts of Cato." *Anglia* 90
                   (1972), 1–42.
Crawford 1921   Crawford, Samuel J., ed. *Exameron Anglice, or the OE
                   Hexameron.* BaP 10. Hamburg: Henri Grand, 1921.
Crawford 1922   ——. *The OE Version of the Heptateuch, Ælfric's Treatise
                   on the Old and New Testament and his Preface to Gen-
                   esis.* EETS 160. London 1922.
Crawford 1927   ——, ed. *The Gospel of Nicodemus.* Edinburgh: I. B.
                   Hutchen, 1927.
Crawford 1929   ——, ed. *Byrhtferth's Manual (A. D. 1011).* EETS 177.
                   London 1929.
Creed 1959   Creed, Robert P. "The Making of an A-S Poem." *ELH*
                   26 (1959), 445–54. Rpr. in Bessinger/Kahrl 1968, pp.
                   363–73.
Creed 1967a   ——. "The Art of the Singer: Three OE Tellings of the
                   Offering of Isaac." In Creed 1967b, pp. 69–92.
Creed 1967b   ——, ed. *OE Poetry: Fifteen Essays.* Providence: Brown
                   University Press, 1967.
Creed 1975   ——. "Widsith's Journey Through Germanic Tradi-
                   tion." In Nicholson/Frese 1975, pp. 376–87.
Cross 1956   Cross, James E. " 'Ubi Sunt' Passages in Old En-
                   glish—Sources and Relationships." *Vetenskaps-So-
                   cietetens i Lund, Årsbok* (1956), pp. 25–44.
Cross 1957   ——. "The Dry Bones Speak— A Theme in Some OE
                   Homilies." *JEGP* 56 (1957), 434–9.
Cross 1961a   ——. "Ælfric and the Medieval Homiliary—Objection
                   and Contribution." *Scripta Minora Regiae Societatis
                   Humaniorum Litterarum Lundensis* 1961–2, no. 4.
Cross 1961b   ——. "On the Genre of *The Wanderer.*" *Neophil* 45
                   (1961), 63–75. Rpr. in Bessinger/Kahrl 1968, pp. 515–
                   32.
Cross 1962   ——. "The OE Poetic Theme of 'The Gifts of Men'."
                   Neophil 46 (1962), 66–70.

Cross 1963   ——. "Aspects of Microcosm and Macrocosm in OE Literature." In Greenfield 1963b, pp. 1–22.

Cross 1964   ——. "The 'Coeternal Beam' in the OE Advent Poem (*Christ I*) ll. 104–129." *Neophil* 47 (1964), 72–81.

Cross 1965   ——. "Oswald and Byrhtnoth: A Christian Saint and a Hero who is Christian." *ES* 46 (1965), 93–109.

Cross 1967   ——. "The Conception of the OE *Phoenix*." In Creed 1967b, pp. 129–52.

Cross 1969a   ——. "Ælfric—Mainly on Memory and Creative Method in Two *Catholic Homilies*." *SN* 41 (1969), 135–55.

Cross 1969b   ——. "The Metrical Epilogue to the OE Version of Gregory's *Cura Pastoralis*." *NM* 70 (1969), 381–6.

Cross 1972   ——. "The Literate A-S—On Sources and Disseminations." *PBA* 58 (1972), 67–100.

Cross 1974   ——. "Mainly on Philology and the Interpretative Criticism of *Maldon*." In Burlin/Irving 1974, pp. 235–53.

Cross 1977   ——. "Two Saints in the OE *Martyrology*." *NM* 78 (1977), 101–7.

Cross 1981   ——. "The Influence of Irish Texts and Traditions on the OE *Martyrology*." *Proceedings of the Royal Irish Acad.* 81C (1981), 173–92.

Cross 1982   ——. "Saints' Lives in OE: Latin Manuscripts and Vernacular Accounts: the OE *Martyrology*." *Peritia* 1 (1982), 38–62.

Cross 1985a   ——. "The Latinity of the Ninth-Century OE Martyrologist." In Szarmach 1985, pp. 275–99.

Cross 1985b   ——. "On the Library of the OE Martyrologist." In Lapidge/Gneuss 1985, pp. 227–49.

Cross/Hill 1982   —— and Thomas D. Hill, eds. *The Prose Solomon and Saturn and Adrian and Ritheus*. Toronto, Buffalo and London: University of Toronto Press, 1982.

Cross/Tucker 1960   —— and Susie I. Tucker. "Allegorical Tradition and the OE *Exodus*." *Neophil* 44 (1960), 122–7.

Crossley-Holland 1979   Crossley-Holland, Kevin, trans. *The Exeter Book Riddles*. Harmondsworth: Penguin Books, 1979.

Crowne 1960   Crowne, David K. "The Hero on the Beach: An Example of Composition by Theme in A-S Poetry." *NM* 61 (1960), 362–72.

CSEL
  Huemer 1885   Huemer, Johann, ed. *Sedulii Opera Omnia*. Vol. 10. Vienna: C. Gerold and Son, 1885.

  Huemer 1981   ——, ed. *Gai Vetti Aquilini Iuvenci: Evangeliorum Liber Quattuor*. Vol. 24. Vienna: F. Tempsky, 1891.

  McKinlay 1951   McKinlay, Arthur P., ed. *Aratoris Subdiaconi De Actibus Apostolorum*. Vol. 72. Vienna: Hoelder-Pichler-Tempsky, 1951.

Cummings 1980   Cummings, Michael. "Paired Opposites in Wulfstan's *Sermo Lupi ad Anglos.*" *Revue de l'Université d'Ottawa* 50 (1980), 233–43.

Curtius 1953 — Curtius, Ernst R. *European Literature and the Latin Middle Ages.* Trans. Willard R. Trask. New York: Pantheon Books, 1953. Rpr. Princeton: Princeton University Press, 1973.

Dalbey 1969 — Dalbey, Marcia A. "Hortatory Tone in the Blickling Homilies: Two Adaptations of Caesarius." *NM*, 70 (1969), 641–58.

Dalbey 1973 — ——. "Patterns of Preaching in the Blickling Easter Homily." *ABR* 24 (1973), 478–92.

Dalbey 1978 — ——. "Themes and Techniques in the Blickling Lenten Homilies." In Szarmach/Huppé 1978, pp. 221–39.

Dalbey 1980 — ——. " 'Soul's Medicine': Religious Psychology in the Blickling Rogation Homilies." *Neophil* 64 (1980), 470–7.

Damico 1984 — Damico, Helen. *Beowulf's Wealhtheow and the Valkyrie Tradition.* Madison: University of Wisconsin Press, 1984.

Dammers 1976 — Dammers, Richard H. "Unity and Artistry in *The Fortunes of Men.*" *ABR* 27 (1976), 461–9.

Dane 1980 — Dane, Joseph A. "The Structure of the OE *Solomon and Saturn II.*" *Neophil* 64 (1980), 592–603.

Das 1942 — Das, S. K. *Cynewulf and the Cynewulf Canon.* Calcutta: University of Calcutta, 1942.

Davis 1971 — Davis, R. H. C. "Alfred the Great: Propaganda and Truth." *History* 56 (1971), 169–82.

Dawson 1962 — Dawson, R. MacGregor. "The Structure of the OE Gnomic Poems." *JEGP* 61 (1962), 14–22.

Day 1974 — Day, Virginia. "The Influence of the Catechetical *Narratio* on OE and Some Other Medieval Literature." *ASE* 3 (1974), 51–61.

Deanesly 1961 — Deanesly, Margaret. *The Pre-Conquest Church in England.* London and New York: A. and C. Black, 1961.

De Marco 1968 — See *CCSL.*

Derolez 1954 — Derolez, René. *Runica Manuscripta: The English Tradition.* Brugge: De Tempel, 1954.

Derolez 1971 — ——. "The Orientation System in the OE Orosius." In Clemoes/Hughes 1971, pp. 253–68.

Derolez 1981 — ——. "A Key to the Auzon Casket." *ES* 62 (1981), 94–5.

Deug-Su 1983 — Deug-Su, I. *L'opera agiografica di Alcuino.* Spoleto: Centro italiano di studi sull' alto medioevo, 1983.

De Vriend 1984 — De Vriend, Hubert J., ed. *The OE Herbarium and Medicina De Quadrupedibus.* EETS 286. London 1984.

Diamond 1963 — Diamond, Robert E. *The Diction of the A-S Metrical Psalms.* The Hague: Mouton, 1963.

Dickins/Ross 1954 — Dickins, Bruce and A. S. C. Ross, eds. *The Dream of the Rood.* 4th ed. London: Methuen, 1954.

Diekstra 1971 — Diekstra, F. N. M. "*The Seafarer* 58–66a: The Flight of the Exiled Soul to Its Fatherland." *Neophil* 55 (1971), 433–46.

Dien 1975 Dien (later Hollis), Stephanie. *"Sermo Lupi ad Anglos: The Order and Date of the Three Versions." NM* 76 (1975), 561–70.

Dieterich 1983 Dieterich, Lana S. "Syntactic Analysis of Beowulf's Fight with Grendel." *Comitatus* 14 (1983), 5–17.

Dionisotti 1982 Dionisotti, A. C. "On Bede, Grammars, and Greek." *Rb* 92 (1982), 111–41.

Doane 1978a Doane, A. N., ed. *Genesis A: A New Edition*. Madison: University of Wisconsin Press, 1978.

Doane 1978b ——. "Legend, History and Artifice in *The Battle of Maldon*." *Viator* 9 (1978), 39–66.

Dobbie 1937 Dobbie, E. V. K., ed. *The MSS of Caedmon's Hymn and Bede's Death Song*. New York: Columbia University Press, 1937.

Donaghey 1964 Donaghey, Brian S. "The Sources of King Alfred's Translation of Boethius's *De Consolatione Philosophiae*." *Anglia* 82 (1964), 23–37.

Donner 1972 Donner, Morton. "Prudery in OE Fiction." *Comitatus* 3 (1972), 91–6.

Doubleday 1971 Doubleday, James F. "The Principle of Contrast in *Judith*." *NM* 72 (1971), 436–41.

Doubleday 1972a ——. "The Limits of Philosophy: A Reading of *The Wanderer*." *NDEJ* 7 (1972), 14–22.

Doubleday 1972b ——. "*The Ruin*: Structure and Theme." *JEGP* 71 (1972), 369–81.

Dubois 1943 Dubois, Marguerite-Marie. *Ælfric, sermonnaire, docteur et grammairien*. Paris: Libraire E. Droz, 1943.

Duckett 1951 Duckett, Eleanor S. *Alcuin, Friend of Charlemagne*. New York: Macmillan, 1951.

Duckett 1955 ——. *Saint Dunstan of Canterbury*. New York: Norton, 1955.

Duckett 1956 ——. *Alfred the Great: The King and His England*. Chicago: University of Chicago Press, 1956; London: Collins, 1957.

Dudley 1913 Dudley, Louise. " 'The Grave'." *MP* 11 (1913–4), 429–42.

Duff 1934 Duff, John W. and Arnold M., eds. *Minor Latin Poets*. London and Cambridge, Mass: W. Heinemann/Harvard University Press, 1934.

Dümmler 1881 See *MGH*.
Dümmler 1895 See *MGH*.
Dumville/Lapidge 1985 Dumville, David and Michael Lapidge, eds. *The Annals of St. Neots with the Vita Prima Sancti Neoti*. Woodbridge: Boydell and Brewer, 1985.

Dunning/Bliss 1969 Dunning, Thomas P. and Alan J. Bliss, eds. *The Wanderer*. London and New York: Methuen/Appleton-Century-Crofts, 1969.

Earl 1970   Earl, James W. "Christian Traditions in the OE *Exodus*." *NM* 71 (1970), 541–70.

Earl 1975   ——. "Typology and Iconographic Style in Early Medieval Hagiography." *Studies in the Literary Imagination* 8 (1975), 15–46.

Earl 1980   ——. "The Typological Structure of *Andreas*." In Niles 1980b, pp. 66–89, 167–70.

Ehwald 1919   See *MGH*.

Eis 1960   Eis, Gerhard. "Waltharius-Probleme: Bemerkungen zu dem lateinischen *Waltharius*, dem ags *Waldere* und dem voralthochdeutschen *Walthari*." In *Britannica. Festschrift für Hermann M. Flasdieck*, eds. Wolfgang Iser and H. Schabram. Heidelberg: Carl Winter, 1960, pp. 96–112.

Ekblom 1960   Ekblom, Richard. "King Alfred, Ohthere and Wulfstan: Reply to a Critique." *SN* 32 (1960), 3–13.

Eliason 1952   Eliason, Norman E. "Four OE Cryptographic Riddles." *SP* 49 (1952), 553–65.

Eliason 1966   ——. "Two OE Scop Poems." *PMLA* 81 (1966), 185–92.

Eliason 1969   ——. "*Deor*—A Begging Poem?" In Pearsall/Waldron 1969, pp. 55–61.

Eliason/Clemoes 1966   ——and Peter Clemoes, eds. *Ælfric's First Series of Catholic Homilies*. EEMF 13. Copenhagen: Rosenkilde and Bagger, 1966.

Elliott 1953a   Elliott, R. W. V. "Cynewulf's Runes in *Christ II* and *Elene*." *ES* 34 (1953), 49–57.

Elliott 1953b   ——. "Cynewulf's Runes in *Juliana* and *Fates of the Apostles*." *ES* 34 (1953), 193–204.

Elliott 1955   ——. "The Runes in *The Husband's Message*." *JEGP* 54 (1955), 1–8.

Elliott 1959   ——. *Runes: An Introduction*. Manchester: Manchester University Press, 1959.

Elliott 1962   ——. "Byrhtnoth and Hildebrand: A Study in Heroic Technique." *CL* 14 (1962), 53–70.

Emerton 1940   Emerton, E., trans. *The Letters of Saint Boniface*. New York: Columbia University Press, 1940.

Endter 1922   Endter, Wilhelm, ed. *König Alfreds des Grossen Bearbeitung der Soliloquien des Augustinus*. BaP 11. Hamburg: Henri Grand, 1922.

Erhardt-Siebold 1949   Erhardt-Siebold, Erika von. "The Storm Riddles." *PMLA* 64 (1949), 884–8.

Esposito 1913   Esposito, M. "La vie de sainte Vulfhilde par Goscelin de Cantorbéry." *Analecta Bollandiana* 32 (1913), 10–26.

Evans 1963   Evans, John. "*Genesis B* and Its Background." *RES* 14 (1963), 1–16, 113–23.

Evans/Serjeantson 1933   Evans, Joan and Mary S. Serjeantson, eds. *English Mediaeval Lapidaries*. EETS 190. Oxford 1933.

Fadda 1977   Fadda, Anna M. Luiselli, ed. *Nuove Omelie anglosassoni della rinascenza benedettina*. Filologia germanica, Testi e studi 1. Florence: F. Le Monnier, 1977.

Farrell 1967   Farrell, R. T. "The Unity of OE *Daniel*." *RES* 18 (1967), 117–35.

Farrell 1974   ——, ed. *Daniel and Azarias*. London: Methuen and Co., 1974.

Fehr 1914   Fehr, Bernhard, ed. *Die Hirtenbriefe Ælfrics*. BaP 9. Hamburg: Henri Grand, 1914. Rpr. with a supplementary intro. by Peter Clemoes. Darmstadt: Wissenschaftliche Buchgesellschaft, 1966.

Fell 1984   Fell, Christine. *Women in A-S England*. Bloomington: Indiana University Press, 1984.

Ferguson 1970   Ferguson, Mary H. "The Structure of the *Soul's Address to the Body* in OE." *JEGP* 69 (1970), 72–80.

Finnegan 1976   Finnegan, Robert E. "Eve and 'Vincible Ignorance' in *Genesis B*." *TSLL* 18 (1976), 329–39.

Finnegan 1977   ——, ed. *Christ and Satan: A Critical Edition*. Waterloo, Ont: Wilfrid Laurier University Press, 1977.

Finnegan 1984   ——. "The OE *Daniel*: The King and His City." *NM* 85 (1984), 194–211.

Fischer 1979   Fischer, Olga. "A Comparative Study of Philosophical Terms in the Alfredian and Chaucerian *Boethius*." *Neophil* 63 (1979), 622–39.

Fish 1975   Fish, Varda. "Theme and Pattern in Cynewulf's *Elene*." *NM* 76 (1975), 1–25.

Fisher 1952   Fisher, D. J. V. "The Church in England between the Death of Bede and the Danish Invasions." *TRHS*, 5th Ser. 2 (1952), 1–19.

Fleming 1966   Fleming, John V. " 'The Dream of the Rood' and A-S Monasticism." *Traditio* 22 (1966), 43–72.

Förster 1913   Foerster, Massimiliano [Max Förster], ed. *Il Codice Vercellese con Omelie e Poesie in Lingua Anglosassone*. Rome: Danesi, 1913.

Förster 1932   ——, ed. *Die Vercelli-Homilien*, I: *I.–VIII. Homilie*. BaP 12. Hamburg: Henri Grand, 1932.

Förster 1942   ——. "Zur Liturgik der ags Kirche." *Anglia* 66 (1942), 1–52.

Förster 1955   ——. "A New Version of the Apocalypse of Thomas in OE." *Anglia* 73 (1955), 6–36.

Foley 1975   Foley, John M. "*Christ* 164–213: A Structural Approach to the Speech Boundaries in 'Advent Lyric VII'." *Neophil* 59 (1975), 114–8.

Foley 1976a   ——. "Formula and Theme in OE Poetry." In *Oral Literature and the Formula*, eds. Benjamin A. Stolz and Richard S. Shannon III. Ann Arbor: Center for the Coordination of Ancient and Modern Studies, University of Michigan, 1976, pp. 207–32.

Foley 1976b   ——. " 'Riddle I' of the *Exeter Book:* The Apocalyptic Storm." *NM* 77 (1976), 347–57.

Foley 1983a   ——. "Literary Art and the Oral Tradition in OE and Serbian Poetry." *ASE* 12 (1983), 183–214.

Foley 1983b   ——. *The Oral-Formulaic Theory: An Annotated Bibliography.* New York: Garland, 1983.

Forsey 1928   Forsey, G. F. "Byrhtferth's Preface." *Speculum* 3 (1928), 505–22.

Fowler, D. 1976   Fowler, David. *The Bible in Early English Literature.* Seattle: University of Washington Press, 1976.

Fowler, R. 1965   Fowler, Roger, ed. "A Late OE Handbook for the Use of a Confessor." *Anglia* 83 (1965), 1–34.

Fowler, R. 1966   ——, ed. *OE Prose and Verse.* London: Routledge and Kegan Paul, 1966.

Fowler, R. 1972   ——, ed. *Wulfstan's Canons of Edgar.* EETS 266. London 1972.

Fox/Dickins 1950   Fox, C. and B. Dickins, eds. *The Early Cultures of North-West Europe: H. M. Chadwick Memorial Studies.* Cambridge: Cambridge University Press, 1950.

Fox/Pálsson 1974   Fox, Denton and Hermann Pálsson, trans. *Grettir's Saga.* Toronto: University of Toronto Press, 1974.

Fraipont 1955   See *CCSL.*

Frank 1972   Frank, Roberta. "Some Uses of Paronomasia in OE Scriptural Verse." *Speculum* 47 (1972), 207–26.

Franklin/Meyvaert 1982   Franklin, C. Vircillo and Paul Meyvaert. "Has Bede's Version of the *Passio S. Anastasii* Come Down to Us in BHL 408?" *Analecta Bollandiana* 100 (1982), 373–400.

Frantzen 1982   Frantzen, Allen J. "The Body in *Soul and Body I.*" *ChR* 17 (1982), 76–88.

Frantzen 1983a   ——. *The Literature of Penance in A-S England.* New Brunswick, NJ: Rutgers University Press, 1983.

Frantzen 1983b   ——. "The Tradition of Penitentials in A-S England." *ASE* 11 (1983), 23–56.

French 1945   French, Walter H. "*Widsith* and the Scop." *PMLA* 60 (1945), 623–30.

Frese 1975   Frese, Dolores W. "The Art of Cynewulf's Runic Signatures." In Nicholson/Frese 1975, pp. 312–34.

Frese 1983   ——. "*Wulf and Eadwacer:* The Adulterous Woman Reconsidered." *NDEJ* 15 (1983), 1–22.

Fritz 1974   Fritz, Donald W. "Caedmon: A Monastic Exegete." *ABR* 25 (1974), 351–63.

Fry 1967   Fry, Donald K. "OE Formulas and Systems." *ES* 48 (1967), 193–204.

Fry 1968a   ——. "OE Formulaic Themes and Type-Scenes." *Neophil* 52 (1968), 48–54.

Fry 1968b   ——. "Some Aesthetic Implications of a New Definition of the Formula." *NM* 69 (1968), 516–22.

Fry 1969 ———. *Beowulf and The Fight at Finnsburh: A Bibliography*. Charlottesville: University Press of Virginia, 1969.

Fry 1974a ———. "Caedmon as a Formulaic Poet." *Forum for Modern Language Studies* 10 (1974), 227–47.

Fry 1974b ———, ed. *Finnsburh: Fragment and Episode*. London: Methuen, 1974.

Fry 1980a ———. *Norse Sagas Translated into English: A Bibliography*. New York: AMS Press, 1980.

Fry 1980b ———. "Two Voices in *Widsith*." *Mediaevalia* 6 (1982 for 1980), 37–56.

Fry 1981 ———. "Exeter Book Riddle Solutions." *OEN* 15, no. 1 (Fall 1981), 22–33.

Fry 1985 ———. "Bede Fortunate in His Translator: The Barking Nuns." In Szarmach 1985, pp. 345–62.

Frye 1976 Frye, Northrop. "Charms and Riddles." In his *Spiritus Mundi: Essays on Literature, Myth, and Society*. Bloomington and London 1976: Indiana University Press, pp. 123–47.

Funke 1962a Funke, Otto. "Some Remarks on Wulfstan's Prose Rhythms." *ES* 43 (1962), 311–8.

Funke 1962b ———. "Studien zur Alliterierenden und Rhythmisierenden Prosa in der älteren ae Homiletik." *Anglia* 80 (1962), 9–36.

Gaites 1982 Gaites, Judith. "Ælfric's Longer *Life of St Martin* and its Latin Sources: A Study in Narrative Technique." *LeedsSE* 13 (1982), 23–41.

Gardner, H. 1970 Gardner, Helen. "*The Dream of the Rood*." In *Essays and Poems Presented to Lord David Cecil*. London: Constable, 1970, pp. 18–36.

Gardner, J. 1975 Gardner, John. *The Construction of Christian Poetry in OE*. Carbondale and Edwardsville, Ill: Southern Illinois University Press, 1975.

Gardner, T. 1969 Gardner, Thomas. "The OE Kenning: A Characteristic Feature of Germanic Poetical Diction?" *MP* 67 (1969–70), 109–17.

Gardner, T. 1972 ———. "The Application of the Term 'Kenning'." *Neophil* 56 (1972), 464–8.

Garmonsway 1953 Garmonsway, G. N., trans. *The A-S Chronicle*. London: J. M. Dent and Sons, 1953.

Garmonsway 1959 ———. "The Development of the Colloquy." In Clemoes 1959a, pp. 248–61.

Garmonsway 1978 ———, ed. *Ælfric's Colloquy*. Corrected ed. Exeter: University of Exeter, 1978.

Garmonsway/Simpson 1968 ———. and Jacqueline Simpson, trans. *Beowulf and its Analogues*. London: J. M. Dent and Sons, 1968.

Gaskoin 1904 Gaskoin, C. J. B. *Alcuin: His Life and his Work*. London: C. J. Clay and Sons, 1904.

Gatch 1964   Gatch, Milton McC. "Two Uses of Apocrypha in OE
               Homilies." *Church History* 33 (1964), 379–91.

Gatch 1965   ——. "Eschatology in the Anonymous OE Homilies."
               Traditio 21 (1965), 117–65.

Gatch 1976   ——. "Beginnings Continued: A Decade of Studies of
               OE Prose." *ASE* 5 (1976), 225–43.

Gatch 1977   ——. *Preaching and Theology in A-S England: Ælfric and
               Wulfstan*. Toronto: University of Toronto Press,
               1977.

Gatch 1978   ——. "The Achievement of Ælfric and His Col-
               leagues in European Perspective." In Szar-
               mach/Huppé 1978, pp. 43–73.

Gatch 1985   ——. "King Alfred's Version of Augustine's *Sololi-
               quia*: Some Suggestions on its Rationale and Unity."
               In Szarmach 1985, pp. 17–45.

Gebauer/Löfstedt 1980   See *CCSL*.

Gem 1912   Gem, Samuel H. *An A-S Abbot: Ælfric of Eynsham, A
               Study*. Edinburgh: T and T. Clark, 1912.

Gerould 1924   Gerould, Gordon H. "Abbott Ælfric's Rhythmic
               Prose." *MP* 22 (1924–5), 353–66.

Gerritsen 1969 Gerritsen, Johan, "The Text of the *Leiden Riddle*." *ES*
               50 (1969), 529–44.

Gibson 1981   Gibson, Margaret, ed. *Boethius: His Life, Thought and
               Influence*. Oxford: Blackwell, 1981.

Giles 1854   Giles, J. A., ed. *Vita Quorundum Anglo-Saxonum*. Lon-
               don: Caxton Society, 1854.

Glauche 1970   Glauche, G. *Schullektüre im Mittelalter: Entstehung und
               Wandlungen des Lektürekanons bis 1200*. Munich: Ar-
               beo-Gesellschaft, 1970.

Gleissner 1984 Gleissner, Reinhard. *Die 'zweideutigen' ae Rätsel des
               Exeter Book in ihrem zeitgenössischen Kontext*. Frank-
               furt am Main and New York: Peter Lang, 1984.

Glorie 1968   See *CCSL*.

Gneuss 1968   Gneuss, Helmut. *Hymnar und Hymnen im englischen
               Mittelalter*. Tübingen: M. Niemeyer, 1968.

Gneuss 1972   ——. "The Origin of Standard OE and Æthelwold's
               School at Winchester." *ASE* 1 (1972), 63–83.

Gneuss 1976a   ——. *Die Battle of Maldon als historisches und literar-
               isches Zeugnis*. Bayerische Akademie der Wissen-
               schaften, Philos.-hist. Klasse, Sitzungsberichte 1976,
               no. 5. Munich 1976.

Gneuss 1976b   ——. "*The Battle of Maldon* 89: Byrhtnoð's *ofermod* Once
               Again." *SP* 73 (1976), 117–37.

Gneuss 1981   ——. "A Preliminary List of MSS Written or Owned
               in England up to 1100." *ASE* 9 (1981), 1–60.

Gneuss 1986   ——. "King Alfred and the History of A-S Libraries."
               Forthcoming.

Godden 1973   Godden, Malcolm. "The Development of Ælfric's

Second Series of *Catholic Homilies*." *ES* 54 (1973), 209–16.

Godden 1978 — — . "Ælfric and the Vernacular Prose Tradition." In Szarmach/Huppé 1978, pp. 99–117.

Godden 1979 — — , ed. *Ælfric's Catholic Homilies: The Second Series, Text.* EETS, ss 5. London 1979.

Godden 1980 — — . "Ælfric's Changing Vocabulary." *ES* 61 (1980), 206–23.

Godden 1981 — — . "King Alfred's Boethius." In Gibson 1981, pp. 419–24.

Godfrey 1962 — Godfrey, John. *The Church in A-S England.* Cambridge: Cambridge University Press, 1962.

Godman 1981 — Godman, Peter. "The Anglo-Latin *opus geminatum*: from Aldhelm to Alcuin." *MÆ* 50 (1981), 215–29.

Godman 1982 — — , ed. and trans. *Alcuin: The Bishops, Kings, and Saints of York.* Oxford: Clarendon Press, 1982.

Goldsmith 1970 — Goldsmith, Margaret E. *The Mode and Meaning of Beowulf.* London: Athlone Press, 1970.

Goldsmith 1975 — — . "The Enigma of *The Husband's Message*." In Nicholson/Frese 1975, pp. 242–63.

Gollancz 1927 — Gollancz, Israel, ed. *The Caedmon MS of A-S Biblical Poetry.* Oxford: Oxford University Press, 1927.

Gollancz/Mackie 1895 — — , ed. *The Exeter Book. Part I. Poems I—VIII.* EETS 104. London 1895. Mackie, W. S., ed. *The Exeter Book. Part II. Poems IX–XXXII.* EETS 194. London 1934.

Gonser 1909 — Gonser, Paul, ed. *Das ags Prosa-leben des hl. Guthlac.* Anglistische Forschungen 27. Heidelberg: Carl Winter, 1909.

Goolden 1958 — Goolden, Peter, ed. *The OE Apollonius of Tyre.* London: Oxford University Press, 1958.

Gordon, E. 1937 — Gordon, E. V., ed. *The Battle of Maldon.* London: Methuen, 1937. Rpr. with supplement by D. G. Scragg 1976.

Gordon, I. A. 1966 — Gordon, Ian A. *The Movement of English Prose.* Bloomington and London: Longmans, 1966.

Gordon, I. L. 1960 — Gordon, Ida L., ed. *The Seafarer.* London: Methuen, 1960.

Gordon, R. 1954 — Gordon, Robert K., trans. *A-S Poetry.* Rev. ed. London: J. M. Dent and Sons, 1954.

Gottschaller 1973 — Gottschaller, E. *Hugeburc von Heidenheim.* Munich: Arbeo-Gesellschaft, 1973.

Gradon 1958 — Gradon, Pamela O. E., ed. *Cynewulf's Elene.* London: Methuen, 1958. Rpr. 1966.

Gransden 1974 — Gransden, Antonia. *Historical Writing in England c. 550 to c. 1307.* London: and Boston: Routledge and Kegan Paul, 1974.

Grattan/Singer 1952 — Grattan, J. H. G and Charles Singer. *A-S Magic and*

Medicine: Illustrated Specially from the Semi-Pagan Text Lacnunga. London: Oxford University Press, 1952.

Green, B. 1981 Green, Brian. "The Mode and Meaning of the OE *Exodus.*" *English Studies in Africa* 24 (1981), 73–82.

Green, M. 1975 Green, Martin. "Man, Time, and Apocalypse in *The Wanderer, The Seafarer,* and *Beowulf.*" *JEGP* 74 (1975), 502–18.

Green, M. 1983a ——, ed. *The OE Elegies: New Essays in Criticism and Research.* Rutherford, NJ. and London: Fairleigh Dickinson University Press/Associated University Presses, 1983.

Green, M. 1983b ——. "Time, Memory, and Elegy in *The Wife's Lament.*" In Green, M. 1983a, pp. 123–32.

Green, R. 1962 Green, Richard H., trans. *Boethius: The Consolation of Philosophy.* New York: Bobbs-Merrill, 1962.

Greenfield 1951 Greenfield, Stanley B. "*The Wanderer:* A Reconsideration of Theme and Structure." *JEGP* 50 (1951), 451–65.

Greenfield 1953 ——. "The Theme of Spiritual Exile in *Christ I.*" *PQ* 32 (1953), 321–8.

Greenfield 1954 ——. "Attitudes and Values in *The Seafarer.*" *SP* 51 (1954), 15–20.

Greenfield 1955 ——. "The Formulaic Expression of the Theme of 'Exile' in A-S Poetry." *Speculum* 30 (1955), 200–6. Rpr. in Bessinger/Kahrl 1968, pp. 352–62.

Greenfield 1962 ——. "*Beowulf* and Epic Tragedy." *CL* 14 (1962), 91–105.

Greenfield 1963a ——. "Geatish History: Poetic Art and Epic Quality in *Beowulf.*" *Neophil* 47 (1963), 211–7.

Greenfield 1963b ——, ed. *Studies in OE Literature in Honor of Arthur G. Brodeur.* Eugene, OR: University of Oregon Books 1963. Rpr. New York: Russell and Russell, 1973.

Greenfield 1966 ——. "The OE Elegies." In Stanley 1966b, pp. 142–75.

Greenfield 1967 ——. "Grendel's Approach to Heorot: Syntax and Poetry." In Creed 1967b, pp. 275–84.

Greenfield 1969 ——. "*Min, Sylf,* and 'Dramatic Voices' in *The Wanderer* and *The Seafarer.*" *JEGP* 68 (1969), 212–20.

Greenfield 1972 ——. *The Interpretation of OE Poems.* London and Boston: Routledge and Kegan Paul, 1972.

Greenfield 1976 ——. "The Authenticating Voice in *Beowulf.*" *ASE* 5 (1976), 51–62.

Greenfield 1979 ——. "Esthetics and Meaning and the Translation of OE Poetry." In Calder 1979a, pp. 91–110.

Greenfield 1981 ——. "*Sylf,* Seasons, Structure and Genre in *The Seafarer.*" *ASE* 9 (1981), 199–211.

Greenfield 1982a ——, trans. *A Readable Beowulf.* Carbondale and Edwardsville, Ill: Southern Illinois University Press, 1982.

Greenfield 1982b ——. "A Touch of the Monstrous in the Hero, or Beowulf Re-Marvellized." *ES* 63 (1982), 294–300.

Greenfield 1985 ——. "Beowulf and the Judgment of the Righteous." In Lapidge/Gneuss 1985, pp. 393–407.

Greenfield/Evert 1975 ——and Richard Evert. "*Maxims II:* Gnome and Poem." In Nicholson/Frese 1975, pp. 337–54.

Greenfield/Robinson 1980 ——and Fred C. Robinson. *A Bibliography of Publications on OE Literature to the End of 1972.* Toronto, Buffalo, and London: University of Toronto Press, 1980.

Grendon 1909 Grendon, Felix, ed. "The A-S Charms." *JAF* 22 (1909), 105–237.

Gretsch 1973 Gretsch, Mechthild. *Die Regula Sancti Benedicti in England.* Munich: Fink, 1973.

Gretsch 1974 ——. "Æthelwold's Translation of the *Regula Sancti Benedicti* and its Latin Exemplar." *ASE* 3 (1974), 125–51.

Grierson 1941 Grierson, P. "Relations between England and Flanders before the Norman Conquest." *TRHS* 4th ser. 32 (1941), 71–112.

Grimaldi 1979 Grimaldi, Maria, ed. "Precetti per i Cristiani." *AION,* filologia germanica 22 (1979), 59–78.

Grimaldi 1981 ——, ed. and trans. "*The Seasons for Fasting.*" *AION,* filologia germanica 24 (1981), 71–92.

Grünberg 1967 Grünberg, Madeleine, ed. *The W-S Gospels: A Study of the Gospel of St. Matthew with Text of the Four Gospels.* Amsterdam: Scheltema and Holkema, 1967.

Guerreau-Jalabert 1982 Guerreau-Jalabert, A. ed. *Abbo Floriacensis: Quaestiones Grammaticales.* Paris: "Belles lettres," 1982.

Gyger 1969 Gyger, Alison. "The OE *Soul and Body* as an Example of Oral Transmission." *MÆ* 38 (1969), 239–44.

Haarder 1975 Haarder, Andreas. *Beowulf: The Appeal of a Poem.* Copenhagen: Akademisk Forlag, 1975.

Haber 1931 Haber, Tom Burns. *A Comparative Study of the Beowulf and the Aeneid.* Princeton: Princeton University Press, 1931.

Hadden/Stubbs 1869 Hadden, A. W. and W. Stubbs, eds. *Councils and Ecclesiastical Documents relating to Great Britain and Ireland.* 3 vols. Oxford: Clarendon Press, 1869.

Hall 1976 Hall, J. R. "The OE Epic of Redemption: The Theological Unity of MS Junius 11." *Traditio* 32 (1976), 185–208.

Hall 1977 ——. "Perspective and Wordplay in the OE *Rune Poem.*" *Neophil* 61 (1977), 453–60.

Halsall 1981 Halsall, Maureen, ed. *The OE Rune Poem: A Critical Edition.* Toronto, Buffalo, and London: University of Toronto Press, 1981.

Hamer 1970   Hamer, Richard, ed. and trans. *A Choice of A-S Verse.* London: Faber, 1970.

Hamilton 1972   Hamilton, David. "The Diet and Digestion of Allegory in *Andreas.*" *ASE* 1 (1972), 147–58.

Hamilton 1975   ——. "*Andreas* and *Beowulf:* Placing the Hero." In Nicholson/Frese 1975, pp. 81–98.

Hamp 1976   Hamp, Eric P. "On the Importance of OS in the Structure of the Runic Poem." *Studia Germanica Gandensia* 17 (1976), 143–51.

Hanning 1966   Hanning, Robert W. *The Vision of History in Early Britain: from Gildas to Geoffrey of Monmouth.* New York and London: Columbia University Press, 1966.

Hanning 1974   ——. "*Beowulf* as Heroic History." *Medievalia et Humanistica* 5 (1974), 77–102.

Hansen 1976   Hansen, Elaine Tuttle. "Women in OE Poetry Reconsidered." *Michigan Academician* 9 (1976), 109–17.

Hansen 1981   ——. "*Precepts:* An OE Instruction." *Speculum* 56 (1981), 1–16.

Hargrove 1902   Hargrove, Henry L., ed. *King Alfred's OE Version of St. Augustine's Soliloquies.* YSE 13. New York 1902.

Hargrove 1904   ——, trans. *King Alfred's OE Version of St. Augustine's Soliloquies.* YSE 22. New York 1904.

Harmer 1914   Harmer, Florence E., ed. *Select English Historical Documents of the Ninth and Tenth Centuries.* Cambridge: Cambridge University Press, 1914.

Harmer 1952   ——, ed. and trans. *A-S Writs.* Manchester: Manchester University Press, 1952.

Harris 1983   Harris, Joseph. "Elegy in OE and ON: A Problem in Literary History." In Green, M. 1983a, pp. 46–56.

Hart 1972.   Hart, Cyril. "Byrhtferth and his *Manual.*" *MÆ* 41 (1972), 95–109.

Hart 1982   ——. "Byrhtferth's Northumbrian Chronicle." *EHR* 97 (1982), 558–82.

Hauer 1977   Hauer, Stanley R. "Structure and Unity in the OE Charm *Wið Færstice.*" *ELN* 51 (1977–8), 250–7.

Hauer 1981   ——. "The Patriarchal Digression in the OE *Exodus,* Lines 362–446." In Wittig 1981, pp. 77–90.

Healey 1978   Healey, Antonette di Paolo, ed. *The OE Vision of St. Paul.* Speculum Anniversary Monographs 2. Cambridge, Mass: The Medieval Academy of America, 1978.

Healey/Venezky 1980   ——and Richard L. Venezky, comps. *A Microfiche Concordance to OE.* Toronto: Center for Medieval Studies, University of Toronto, 1980.

Hecht 1900   Hecht, Hans, ed. *Bischof Waerferths von Worcester Übersetzung der Dialoge Gregors des Grossen.* 2 vols. BaP 5. Leipzig: Georg H. Wigland, 1900–7.

Heffernan 1982   Heffernan, Carol F. "The OE 'Phoenix': A Reconsideration." *NM* 83 (1982), 239–54.

Helder 1975 Helder, Willem. "Etham and the Ethiopians in the OE *Exodus.*" *AnM* 16 (1975), 5–23.

Helm 1963 Helm, P. J. *Alfred the Great.* London: Robert Hale, 1963.

Henel 1934 Henel, Heinrich. *Studien zum ae Computus.* Beiträge zur englischen Philologie 26. Leipzig: B. Tauchnitz, 1934.

Henel 1942 ——, ed. *Ælfric's De Temporibus Anni.* EETS 213. London 1942.

Henel 1943 ——. "Byrhtferth's *Preface:* The Epilogue of His *Manual?*" *Speculum* 18 (1943), 288–302.

Hennig 1952 Hennig, John. "The Irish Counterparts of the A-S *Menologium.*" *MS* 14 (1952), 98–106.

Henry 1966 Henry, P. L. *The Early English and Celtic Lyric.* London: Allen and Unwin, 1966.

Hermann 1976 Hermann, John P. "The Theme of Spiritual Warfare in the OE *Judith.*" *PQ* 55 (1976), 1–9.

Herren 1981 Herren, M. W., ed. *Insular Latin Studies.* Toronto: Pontifical Institute of Medieval Studies, 1981.

Heyne/von Schaubert 1958 Heyne, Moritz, ed. *Beowulf.* 17th ed. Rev. by Else von Schaubert. Paderborn: F. Schöningh, 1958–9.

Hickes 1703 Hickes, George. *Linguarum veterum Septentrionalium Thesaurus Grammatico-criticus et Archaeologicus.* 2 vols. Oxford: Sheldonian Theatre, 1703–5.

Hieatt 1971 Hieatt, Constance B. "Dream Frame and Verbal Echo in the *Dream of the Rood.*" *NM* 72 (1971), 251–63.

Hieatt 1974 ——. "*The Fates of the Apostles:* Imagery, Structure, and Meaning." *PLL* 10 (1974), 115–25.

Hieatt 1976 ——. "The Harrowing of Mermedonia: Typological Patterns in the OE *Andreas.*" *NM* 77 (1976), 49–62.

Hieatt 1980a ——. "Divisions: Theme and Structure of *Genesis A: NM* 81 (1980), 243–51.

Hieatt 1980b ——. "*Judith* and the Literary Function of OE Hypermetric Lines." *SN* 52 (1980), 251–7.

Hietsch 1955 Hietsch, Otto. "On the Authorship of the OE *Phoenix.*" In *Anglo-Americana,* ed. Karl Brunner. Vienna: W. Braumüller, 1955, pp. 72–9.

Hill, J. 1981 Hill, Joyce. "The Soldier of Christ in OE Prose and Poetry." *LeedsSE* 12 (1981), 57–80.

Hill, J. 1983 ——, ed. *OE Minor Heroic Poems.* Durham: Durham and St. Andrews Medieval Texts, 1983.

Hill, T. 1969 Hill, Thomas D. "Figural Narrative in *Andreas:* The Conversion of the Mermedonians." *NM* 70 (1969), 261–73.

Hill, T. 1970 ——. "The Falling Leaf and Buried Treasure: Two Notes on the Imagery of 'Solomon and Saturn'." *NM* 71 (1970), 571–6.

Hill, T. 1971 ——. "Sapiential Structure and Figural Narrative in the OE *Elene.*" *Traditio* 27 (1971), 159–77.

Hill, T. 1973 ——. "Vision and Judgement in the OE *Christ III.*" *SP* 70 (1973), 233–42.

Hill, T. 1975   ——. "The Fall of Angels and Man in the OE *Genesis B.*" In Nicholson/Frese 1975, pp. 279–90.

Hill, T. 1979   ——. "The Middle Way: *idel-wuldor* and *egesa* in the OE *Guthlac A.*" *RES* 30 (1979), 182–7.

Hill, T. 1980a   ——. "Bread and Stone, Again: *Elene* 611–18." *NM* 81 (1980), 252–7.

Hill, T. 1980b   ——. "The *Virga* of Moses and the OE *Exodus.*" In Niles 1980b, pp. 57–65, 165–7.

Hill, T. 1981   ——. "The Age of Man and the World in the OE *Guthlac A.*" *JEGP* 80 (1981), 13–21.

Hill, T. 1982   ——. "The Measure of Hell: *Christ and Satan* 695–722." *PQ* 60 (1982 for 1981), 409–14.

Hoffman 1968   Hoffman, Richard L. "Structure and Symbolism in the *Judgment Day II.*" *Neophil* 52 (1968), 170–8.

Holder-Egger 1887   See *MGH.*

Hollis 1977   Hollis, Stephanie. "The Thematic Structure of the *Sermo Lupi.*" *ASE* 6 (1977), 175–95.

Hollowell 1977   Hollowell, Ida M. "Linguistic Factors Underlying Style Levels in Four Homilies of Wulfstan." *Neophil* 61 (1977), 287–96.

Hollowell 1978   ——. "*Scop* and *Woðbora* in OE Poetry." *JEGP* 77 (1979 for 1978), 317–29.

Hollowell 1980   ——. "Was Widsið a *scop?*" *Neophil* 64 (1980), 583–91.

Hollowell 1982   ——. "On the Two-Stress Theory of Wulfstan's Rhythm." *PQ* 61 (1982), 1–11.

Hollowell 1983   ——. "On the Identity of the Wanderer." In Green, M. 1983a, pp. 82–95.

Holton 1982   Holton, Frederick S. "OE Sea Imagery and the Interpretation of *The Seafarer.*" *YES* 12 (1983), 208–17.

Horgan 1979   Horgan, A. D. "The Structure of *The Seafarer.*" *RES* 30 (1979), 41–9.

Hotchner 1939   Hotchner, Cecilia A. *Wessex and OE Poetry, with Special Consideration of the Ruin.* New York: New York University Press, 1939.

Howlett 1974   Howlett, D. R. "The Theology of Caedmon's Hymn." *LeedsSE* 7 (1974), 1–12.

Howlett 1975   ——. "*Se Giddes Begang* of *The Fates of the Apostles.*" *ES* 56 (1975), 385–9.

Howlett 1976a   ——. "A Reconstruction of the Ruthwell Crucifixion Poem." *SN* 48 (1976), 54–8.

Howlett 1976b   ——. "Two OE Encomia." *ES* 57 (1976), 289–93.

Howlett 1978a   ——. "The Structure of The Rhyming Poem." *NM* 79 (1978), 330–2.

Howlett 1978b   ——. "*The Wife's Lament* and *The Husband's Message.*" *NM* 79 (1978), 7–10.

Huemer 1885   See *CSEL.*

Huemer 1891   See *CSEL.*

Humphreys/Ross 1975   Humphreys, K. W. and A. S. C. Ross. "Further MSS of Bede's *Historia Ecclesiastica,* of the *Epistola Cuth-*

berti de Obitu Bedae, and Further A-S Texts of *Caedmon's Hymn* and *Bede's Death Song.*" *N&Q* 220 [n.s. 22] (1975), 50–5.

Hunt 1961 — Hunt, Richard W., ed. *St. Dunstan's Classbook from Glastonbury: Cod. Bibl. Bodl. Oxon. Auct. F. 4. 32.* Umbrae Codicum Occidentalium, IV. Amsterdam: North Holland Publishing Co., 1961.

Hunter Blair 1956 — Hunter Blair, Peter. *An Introduction to A-S England.* Cambridge: Cambridge University Press, 1956.

Hunter Blair 1970 — ———. *The World of Bede.* London: Secker and Warburg, 1970.

Hunter Blair 1985 — ———. "Whitby as a Centre of Learning in the Seventh Century." In Lapidge/Gneuss 1985, pp. 3–32.

Huppé 1943 — Huppé, Bernard F. "*The Wanderer:* Theme and Structure." *JEGP* 42 (1943), 516–38.

Huppé 1959 — ———. *Doctrine and Poetry: Augustine's Influence on OE Poetry.* Albany: SUNY Press, 1959.

Huppé 1970 — ———. *The Web of Words.* Albany: SUNY Press, 1970.

Huppé 1975 — ———. "The Concept of the Hero in the Early Middle Ages." In *Concepts of the Hero in the Middle Ages and the Renaissance,* eds. Norman T. Burns and C. J. Reagan. Albany: SUNY Press, 1975, pp. 1–26.

Huppé 1978 — ———. "Alfred and Ælfric: A Study of Two Prefaces." In Szarmarch/Huppé 1978, pp. 119–37.

Hurt 1972 — Hurt, James. *Ælfric.* New York: Twayne, 1972.

Ineichen-Eder 1981 — Ineichen-Eder, C. E. "The Authenticity of the *Dicta Candidi, Dicta Albini* and Some Related Texts." In Herren 1981, pp. 179–93.

Irving 1953 — Irving, Edward B., Jr., ed. *The OE Exodus.* New Haven: Yale University Press, 1953. Rpr. with "Errata" and "Supplement to the Bibliography." Hamden, Conn: Archon Books, 1970. Revisions and additional notes and commentary in *Anglia* 90 (1972), 289–324; see also Irving 1974.

Irving 1959 — ———. "On the Dating of the OE Poems *Genesis* and *Exodus.*" *Anglia* 77 (1959), 1–11.

Irving 1961 — ———. "The Heroic Style in *The Battle of Maldon.*" *SP* 58 (1961), 457–67.

Irving 1968 — ———. *A Reading of Beowulf.* New Haven: Yale University Press, 1968.

Irving 1974 — ———. "*Exodus* Retraced." In Burlin/Irving 1974, pp. 203–23.

Irving 1983 — ———. "A Reading of *Andreas:* the Poem as Poem." *ASE* 12 (1983), 215–37.

Isaacs 1968 — Isaacs, Neil D. *Structural Principles in OE Poetry.* Knoxville: University of Tennessee Press, 1968.

Isaacs 1975 — ———. "Up a Tree: To See *The Fates of Men.*" In Nicholson/Frese 1975, pp. 363–75.

Jaager 1935   Jaager, Werner, ed. *Bedas metrische Vita sancti Cuthberti*. Leipzig: Mayer and Müller, 1935.

James 1929   James, Montague R., ed. *Marvels of the East*. Oxford: Oxford University Press, 1929.

Jenkins 1935   Jenkins, C. "Bede as Exegete and Theologian." In Thompson 1935, pp. 152–200.

Jensen 1979   Jensen, Emily. "Narrative Voice in the OE *Wulf*." *ChR* 13 (1979), 373–83.

Johnson 1980   Johnson, William C., Jr. "*The Ruin* as a Body-City Riddle." *PQ* 59 (1980), 397–411.

Jones, C. 1943   Jones, Charles W., ed. *Bedae Opera de Temporibus*. Cambridge, Mass: The Medieval Academy of America, 1943.

Jones, C. 1947   ——. *Saints' Lives and Chronicles in Early England*. Ithaca: Cornell University Press, 1947.

Jones, C./*et al.* 1955   See *CCSL*.

Jones, G. 1961   Jones, Gwyn, trans. *Eirik the Red and Other Icelandic Sagas*. London and New York: Oxford University Press, 1961. Rpr. 1975.

Jones, G. 1972   ——. *Kings, Beasts and Heroes*. London: Oxford University Press, 1972.

Jones, P. 1928   Jones, P. F. "The Gregorian Mission and English Education." *Speculum* 3 (1928), 335–48.

Jost 1950   Jost, Karl H. *Wulfstanstudien*. Swiss Studies in English 23. Bern 1950.

Jost 1959   ——, ed. *Die Institutes of Polity, Civil and Ecclesiastical*. Swiss Studies in English 47. Bern 1959.

Jurovics 1978   Jurovics, Raachel. "*Sermo Lupi* and the Moral Purpose of Rhetoric." In Szarmach/Huppé 1978, pp. 203–20.

Kantrowitz 1964   Kantrowitz, Joanne Spencer. "The A-S *Phoenix* and Tradition." *PQ* 43 (1964), 1–13.

Kaske 1958   Kaske, Robert E. "*Sapientia et Fortitudo* as the Controlling Theme of *Beowulf*." *SP* 55 (1958), 423–56.

Kaske 1967a   ——. "The *Eotenas* in *Beowulf*." In Creed 1967b, pp. 285–310.

Kaske 1967b   ——. "A Poem of the Cross in the Exeter Book: *Riddle 60* and *The Husband's Message*." *Traditio* 23 (1967), 41–71.

Kaske 1976   ——. "The Conclusion of the OE *Descent into Hell*." In *Parádosis: Studies in Memory of Edwin A. Quain*. New York: Fordham University Press, 1976, pp. 47–59.

Kaske 1982   ——. "*Sapientia et fortitudo* in the OE *Judith*." In *The Wisdom of Poetry*, eds. Larry D. Benson and Siegfried Wenzel. Kalamazoo: Medieval Institute Publications, Western Michigan University, 1982, pp. 13–29, 264–8.

Keefer 1979   Keefer, Sarah Larratt. *The OE Metrical Psalter: An An-
                         notated Set of Collation Lists with the Psalter Glosses.*
                         New York and London: Garland, 1979.
Keenan 1966   Keenan, Hugh T. "*The Ruin* as Babylon." *TSL* 11
                         (1966), 109–17.
Kellermann/Haas 1982   Kellermann, Günter and Renate Haas. "Magie und
                         Mythos als Argumentationsmittel in den ae Dial-
                         oggedichten *Salmon und Saturn.*" In *Festschrift für Karl
                         Schneider,* eds. Ernst Dick and Kurt Jankowsky.
                         Amsterdam and Philadelphia: Benjamins, 1982, pp.
                         387–403.
Kelly 1971   Kelly, Henry Ansgar. "The Metamorphoses of the
                         Eden Serpent during the Middle Ages and Renais-
                         sance." *Viator* 2 (1971), 301–27.
Kennedy, A. 1983   Kennedy, A. G. "Cnut's Law Code of 1018." *ASE* 11
                         (1983), 57–81.
Kennedy, C. 1916   Kennedy, Charles W., trans. *The Caedmon Poems.*
                         London and New York: George Routledge and Sons,
                         1916. Rpr. Gloucester, Mass: Peter Smith, 1965.
Kennedy, C. 1943   ——. *The Earliest English Poetry.* London: Oxford Uni-
                         versity Press, 1943. Rpr. London and Totowa, NJ:
                         Methuen/Rowman and Littlefield, 1971.
Ker 1956   Ker, Neil R., ed. *The Pastoral Care; King Alfred's Trans-
                         lation of St. Gregory's Regula Pastoralis.* EEMF 6. Co-
                         penhagen: Rosenkilde and Bagger, 1956.
Ker 1957   ——. *Catalogue of MSS Containing A-S.* Oxford: Clar-
                         endon Press, 1957.
Kershaw 1922   Kershaw, Nora, ed. *A-S and Norse Poems.* Cambridge:
                         Cambridge University Press, 1922.
Keynes 1980   Keynes, Simon. *The Diplomas of King Æthelred The Un-
                         ready: 978–1016.* Cambridge: Cambridge University
                         Press, 1980.
Keynes/Lapidge 1983   ——and Michael Lapidge, trans. *Alfred the Great.*
                         Harmondsworth: Penguin Books, 1983.
Kiernan 1978   Kiernan, Kevin S. "*Deor:* the Consolations of an A-S
                         Boethius." *NM* 79 (1978), 333–40.
Kiernan 1981   ——. *Beowulf and the Beowulf MS.* New Brunswick, NJ:
                         Rutgers University Press, 1981.
Kiernan 1983   ——. "Thorkelin's Trip to Great Britain and Ireland,
                         1786–1791." *The Library* 5 (1983), 1–21.
King/Stevens 1979   King, Margot H. and Wesley M. Stevens, eds. *Saints,
                         Scholars, and Heroes: Studies in Medieval Culture in
                         Honor of Charles W. Jones.* 2 vols. Collegeville, Minn:
                         Hill Monastic MS Library, St. John's Abbey and
                         University, 1979.
Kirby 1983   Kirby, D. P. "Bede, Eddius Stephanus and the *Life of
                         Wilfrid.*" *EHR* 98 (1983), 101–14.
Kirby/Woolf 1949   Kirby, Thomas A. and Henry B. Woolf, eds. *Philolo-*

gica: The Malone Anniversary Studies. Baltimore: Johns Hopkins Press, 1949.

Kirkland/Modlin 1972   Kirkland, James W. and Charles E. Modlin. "The Art of *Azarias".* MÆ 41 (1972), 9–15.

Kitson 1978   Kitson, Peter. "Lapidary Traditions in A-S England: Part I, the Background; the OE Lapidary." *ASE* 7 (1978), 9–60.

Klaeber 1923   Klaeber, Fr. "Zu König Ælfreds Vorrede zu seiner Übersetzung der Cura Pastoralis." *Anglia* 47 (1923), 53–65.

Klaeber 1950   ——, ed. *Beowulf and The Fight at Finnsburg.* 3rd ed. Boston: D.C. Heath and Co., 1950.

Klinck 1979   Klinck, Anne L. "Female Characterisation in OE Poetry and the Growth of Psychological Realism in *Genesis B* and *Christ I."* *Neophil* 63 (1979), 597–610.

Klinck 1984   ——. "The OE Elegy as a genre." *English Studies in Canada* 10 (1984), 129–40.

Knappe 1906   Knappe, Fritz. *Das ags Prosastück Die Wunder des Osten.* Berlin: G. Bernstein, 1906.

Knowles 1963   Knowles, Dom David. *The Monastic Order in England.* 2nd ed. Cambridge: Cambridge University Press, 1963.

Kobayashi 1979   Kobayashi, Eichi. "On the 'Lost' Portions in the OE *Apollonius of Tyre."* In *Explorations in Linguistics: Papers in Honor of Kazuko Inoue,* eds. George Bedell, Eichi Kobayashi, and Masatake Muraki. Tokyo: Kenkyusha, 1979, pp. 244–50.

Korhammer 1985   Korhammer, M. "The Orientation System in the OE Orosius: Shifted or Not?" In Lapidge/Gneuss 1985, pp. 251–69.

Kotzor 1981   Kotzor, Günter, ed. *Das ae Martyrologium.* Bayerische Akademie der Wissenschaften, Philos.-hist. Klasse, Neue Forschung 88.1–2. Munich:Bayerischen Akademie der Wissenschaften, 1981.

Kotzor 1985   ——. "The Latin Tradition of Martyrologies and the OE *Martyrology."* In Szarmach 1985, pp. 301–33.

Kuhn 1947   Kuhn, Sherman M. "Synonyms in the OE Bede." *JEGP* 46 (1947), 168–76.

Kuhn 1972a   ——. "The Authorship of the OE Bede Revisited." *NM* 73 (1972), 172–80.

Kuhn 1972b   ——. "Cursus in OE: Rhetorical Ornament or Linguistic Phenomenon?" *Speculum* 47 (1972), 188–206.

Kuhn 1973   ——. "Was Ælfric a Poet?" *PQ* 52 (1973), 643–62.

Kurtz 1926   Kurtz, Benjamin P. *From St. Anthony to St. Guthlac.* University of California Publications in Modern Philology 12. Berkeley 1926.

Kurtz 1929   ——. "Gifer the Worm: An Essay Toward the History of an Idea." *University of California Publications in English* 2, no. 2 (1929), 235–61.

Kuznets/Green 1976 — Kuznets, Lois R. and Martin Green. "Voice and Vision in the OE *Christ III*." *PLL* 12 (1976), 227–45.

Kylie 1911 — Kylie, Edward J, trans. *The English Correspondence of St Boniface.* London: Chatto and Windus, 1911.

Ladner 1967 — Ladner, Gerhart B. "*Homo Viator:* Medieval Ideas on Alienation and Order." *Speculum* 42 (1967), 233–59.

Laistner 1935 — Laistner, M. L. W. "The Library of the Venerable Bede." In Thompson 1935, pp. 237–66.

Langenfelt 1959 — Langenfelt, Gösta. "Studies on *Widsith.*" *Namn och Bygd* 47 (1959), 70–111.

Lapidge 1972 — Lapidge, Michael. "Three Latin Poems from Æthelwold's School at Winchester." *ASE* 1 (1972), 85–137.

Lapidge 1975a — ——. "The Hermeneutic Style in Tenth-Century Anglo-Latin Literature." *ASE* 4 (1975), 67–111.

Lapidge 1975b — ——. "Some Remnants of Bede's Lost *Liber Epigrammatum.*" *EHR* 90 (1975), 798–820.

Lapidge 1979a — ——. "Aldhelm's Latin Poetry and OE Verse." *CL* 31 (1979), 209–31.

Lapidge 1979b — ——. "Byrhtferth and the *Vita S. Ecgwini.*" *MS* 41 (1979), 331–53.

Lapidge 1980 — ——. "St. Dunstan's Latin Poetry." *Anglia* 98 (1980), 101–6.

Lapidge 1981a — ——. "The Present State of Anglo-Latin Studies." In Herren 1981, pp. 45–82.

Lapidge 1981b — ——. "Some Latin Poems as Evidence for the Reign of Athelstan." *ASE* 9 (1981), 61–98.

Lapidge 1982a — ——. "*Beowulf,* Aldhelm, and the *Liber Monstrorum* and Wessex." *SM* 23 (1982), 151–92.

Lapidge 1982b — ——. "Byrhtferth of Ramsey and the Early Sections of the *Historia Regum* Attributed to Symeon of Durham." *ASE* 10 (1982), 97–122.

Lapidge 1982c — ——. "The Cult of St. Indract at Glastonbury." In *Ireland in Early Medieval Europe,* eds. D. Whitelock, R. McKitterick and D. Dumville. Cambridge: Cambridge University Press, 1982, pp. 179–212.

Lapidge 1982d — ——. "The Sudy of Latin Texts in Late A-S England: 1. The Evidence of Latin Glosses." In *Latin and the Vernacular Languages in Early Medieval Britain,* ed. Nicholas Brooks. Leicester: Leicester University Press, 1982, pp. 99–140.

Lapidge 1985 — ——. "Surviving Booklists from A-S England." In Lapidge/Gneuss 1985, pp. 33–89.

Lapidge/Gneuss 1985 — ——and Helmut Gneuss, eds. *Learning and Literature in A-S England.* Cambridge: Cambridge University Press, 1985.

Lapidge/Herren 1979 — ——and Michael Herren, trans. *Aldhelm: The Prose*

Lapidge/Hunter Blair 1984

Lapidge/Rosier 1985

Lass 1966

Law 1982

Law 1983

Lawler 1973

Lawrence 1902

Lee, A. A. 1972

Lee, A. T. 1973

Lehmann, R. 1970

Lehmann, W. 1956

Leinbaugh 1982

Leiter 1967

Lendinara 1971

Lendinara 1976

Lendinara 1977

Lendinara 1978

Works. Woodbridge and Totowa, N.J.: D. S. Brewer/Rowman and Littlefield, 1979.

——and P. Hunter Blair, eds. *A-S Northumbria.* London: Variorum Reprints, 1984.

——and James L. Rosier, trans. *Aldhelm: The Poetic Works.* Woodbridge: Boydell and Brewer, 1985.

Lass, Roger. "Poem as Sacrament: Transcendence of Time in the *Advent Sequence* from the Exeter Book." *AnM* 7 (1966), 3–15.

Law, Vivien. *The Insular Latin Grammarians.* Woodbridge: Boydell and Brewer, 1982.

——. "The Study of Latin Grammar in Eighth-Century Southumbria." *ASE* 12 (1983), 43–71.

Lawler, Traugott. "*Brunanburh:* Craft and Art." In *Literary Studies: Essays in Memory of Francis A. Drumm,* ed. John H. Dorenkamp. Wetteren, Belgium: Cultura Press, 1973, pp. 52–67.

Lawrence W. W. "*The Wanderer* and *The Seafarer.*" *JEGP* 4 (1902), 460–80.

Lee, Alvin A. *The Guest-Hall of Eden.* New Haven: Yale University Press, 1972.

Lee, Anne Thompson. "*The Ruin:* Bath or Babylon? A Non-Archaeological Investigation." *NM* 74 (1973), 443–55.

Lehmann, Ruth P. M. "The OE *Riming Poem:* Interpretation, Text, and Translation." *JEGP* 69 (1970), 437–49.

Lehmann, Winfred P. *The Development of Germanic Verse Form.* Austin: University of Texas Press, 1956.

Leinbaugh, Theodore H. "Ælfric's *Sermo e Sacrificio in Die Pascae:* Anglican Polemic in the Sixteenth and Seventeenth Centuries." In Berkhout/Gatch 1982, pp. 51–68.

Leiter, Louis H. "*The Dream of the Rood:* Patterns of Transformation." In Creed 1967b, pp. 93–127.

Lendinara, Patrizia. "I *Versi Gnomici* anglosassoni." *AION,* filologia germanica 14 (1971), 117–38 [summary, p. 611].

——. "Gli enigmi del Codice Exoniense: una ricerca bibliografica." *AION,* filologia germanica 19 (1976), 231–329.

——. "I cosidetti 'Versi Gnomici' del Codice Exoniense e del MS Cotton Tiberius B i: una ricerca bibliografica." *AION,* filologia geramanica 20 (1977), 281–314.

——. "Gli incantesimi del periodo anglosassone: una ricera bibliografica." *AION,* filologia germanica 21 (1978), 299–362.

Leslie 1959   Leslie, Roy F. "Analysis of Stylistic Devices and Effects in A-S Literature." In Paul Böckmann, ed. *Stil-und Form-probleme in der Literatur*. Heidelberg: Carl Winter, 1959, pp. 129–36. Rpr. in Bessinger/Kahrl 1968, pp. 255–63.

Leslie 1961   ——, ed. *Three OE Elegies*. Manchester: Manchester University Press, 1961.

Leslie 1966   ——, ed. *The Wanderer*. Manchester: Manchester University Press, 1966.

Leslie 1968   ——. "The Integrity of Riddle 60." *JEGP* 67 (1968), 451–7.

Leslie 1979   ——. "The Editing of OE Poetic Texts: Questions of Style." In Calder 1979a, pp. 111–25.

Leslie 1983   ——. "The Meaning and Structure of *The Seafarer*." In Green, M. 1983a, pp. 96–122.

Letson 1978   Letson, D. R. "The Poetic Content of the Revival Homily." In Szarmach/Huppé 1978, pp. 139–56.

Letson 1979a   ——. "The Form of the OE Homily." *ABR* 30 (1979), 399–431.

Letson 1979b   ——. "The OE *Physiologus* and the Homiletic Tradition." *Florilegium* 1 (1979), 15–41.

Letson 1980   ——. "The Homiletic Nature of Cynewulf's Ascension Poem." *Florilegium* 2 (1980), 192–216.

Levison 1905   See *MGH*.

Levison 1935   Levison, Wilhelm. "Bede as Historian." In Thompson 1935, pp. 111–51.

Levison 1946   ——. *England and the Continent in the Eighth Century*. Oxford: Clarendon Press, 1946.

Leyerle 1965   Leyerle, John. "Beowulf the Hero and the King." *MÆ* 34 (1965), 89–102.

Leyerle 1967   ——. "The Interlace Structure of *Beowulf*." *UTQ* 37 (1967), 1–17.

Liebermann 1903   Liebermann, Felix, ed. *Die Gesetze der Angelsachsen*. 3 vols. Halle: M. Niemeyer, 1903–16.

Liggins 1970   Liggins, Elizabeth M. "The Authorship of the OE *Orosius*." *Anglia* 88 (1970), 289–322.

Liggins 1985   ——. "Syntax and Style in the OE *Orosius*." In Szarmach 1985, pp. 245–73.

Linderski 1964   Linderski, Jerzy. "Alfred the Great and the Tradition of Ancient Geography." *Speculum* 39 (1964), 434–9.

Lipp 1969   Lipp, Frances R. "Ælfric's OE Prose Style." *SP* 66 (1969), 689–718.

Loewe 1969   Loewe, R. "The Medieval History of the Latin Vulgate." In *The Cambridge History of the Bible*. 2. *The West from the Fathers to the Reformation*. Cambridge: Cambridge University Press, 1969, pp. 102–54, esp. 133–40.

Löhe 1907   Löhe, Hans, ed. *Be Domes Dæge*. Bonn: P. Hanstein, 1907.

Lord 1960   Lord, Albert B. *The Singer of Tales.* Cambridge, Mass: Harvard University Press, 1960. Rpr. New York: Atheneum, 1978.

Lucas 1977   Lucas, Peter, ed. *Exodus.* London: Methuen, 1977.

Lucas 1979   ——. "The Incomplete Ending of *Daniel.*" *Anglia* 97 (1979), 46–59.

Lumby 1876   Lumby, Joseph Rawson, ed. *Be Domes Dæge. De Die Judicii, An OE Version of the Latin Poem Ascribed to Bede.* EETS 65. London 1876.

Lumiansky 1950   Lumiansky, Robert M. "The Dramatic Structure of the OE *Wanderer.*" *Neophil* 34 (1950), 104–12.

Lutz 1977   Lutz, C. E. *Schoolmasters of the Tenth Century.* Hamden, Conn: Archon Books, 1977.

Machielsen 1961   Machielsen, L. "Fragments patristiques non-identifiés du ms. Vat. Pa. 577." *Sacris Erudiri* 12 (1961), 488–539.

McIntosh 1950   McIntosh, Angus. "Wulfstan's Prose." *PBA* 35 (1950), 109–42.

Mackay 1976   Mackay, T. W. "Bede's Hagiographical Method: His Knowledge and Use of Paulinus of Nola." In Bonner 1976, pp. 77–92.

McKinlay 1951   See *CSEL.*

McKinnell 1975   McKinnell, John. "On the Date of *The Battle of Maldon.*" *MÆ* 44 (1975), 121–36.

McNeill/Gamer 1938   McNeill, John T. and Helena M. Gamer, trans. "Penitentials of the A-S Church." In their *Medieval Handbooks of Penance.* New York: Columbia University Press, 1938, pp. 179–248.

MacQueen 1961   MacQueen, W. W., trans. "*Miracula S. Nyniae.*" In *Dumfriesshire and Galloway Natural History and Antiquarian Society Transactions,* 3rd ser. 37 (1961), 21–57.

Macrae-Gibson 1973   Macrae-Gibson, O. D. "The Literary Structure of *The Riming Poem.*" *NM* 74 (1973), 62–84.

Macrae-Gibson 1983   ——, ed. *The OE Riming Poem.* Cambridge: D. S. Brewer, 1983.

McTurk 1981   McTurk, R. W. " 'Cynewulf and Cyneheard' and the Icelandic Sages." *LeedsSE* (1981), 81–127.

Magoun 1953   Magoun, Francis P., Jr. "Oral-Formulaic Character of A-S Narrative Poetry." *Speculum* 28 (1953), 446–67. Rpr. in Bessinger/Kahrl 1968, pp. 319–51.

Magoun 1955a   ——. "Bede's Story of Caedman: The Case History of an A-S Oral Singer." *Speculum* 30 (1955), 49–63.

Magoun 1955b   ——. "The Theme of the Beasts of Battle in A-S Poetry." *NM* 56 (1955), 81–90.

Magoun 1958   ——. "*Beowulf A*': A Folk-Variant." *Arv* 14 (1958), 95–101.

Magoun 1963   ——. "*Beowulf B*: A Folk-Poem on Beowulf's Death." In Brown/Foote 1963, pp. 127–40.

Magoun/Smyser 1950   ——and H. M. Smyser, eds. and trans. *Walter of Aquitaine: Materials for the Study of His Legend.* Connecticut College Monograph 4. New London, Conn: Connecticut College, 1950.

Malmberg 1979   Malmberg, Lars, ed. *Resignation.* Durham and Fife: Durham and St. Andrews Medieval Texts, 1979.

Malone 1951   Malone, Kemp, ed. *The Thorkelin Transcripts of Beowulf.* EEMF 1. Copenhagen: Rosenkilde and Bagger, 1951.

Malone 1959   ——. "The Tale of Ingeld." In *Studies in Heroic Legend and Current Speech,* eds. Stefán Einarsson and N. E. Eliason. Copenhagen: Rosenkilde and Bagger, 1959, pp. 1–62.

Malone 1962a   ——. "Two English *Frauenlieder.*" *CL* 14 (1962), 106–17.

Malone 1962b   ——, ed. *Widsith.* 2nd ed. Copenhagen: Rosenkilde and Bagger, 1962.

Malone 1963   ——, ed. *The Nowell Codex.* EEMF 12. Copenhagen: Rosenkilde and Bagger, 1963.

Malone 1966   ——, ed. *Deor.* 4th ed. London: Methuen, 1966.

Malone 1967   ——. "The Middle Ages: the OE Period (to 1100)." In *A Literary History of England,* Vol. 1, ed. Albert C. Baugh. 2nd ed. New York: Appleton–Century–Crofts, 1967, pp. 3–105. Also printed separately.

Malone 1969   ——. "The OE Calendar Poem." In Atwood/Hill 1969, pp. 193–9.

Mandel 1977   Mandel, Jerome. "Exemplum and Refrain: The Meaning of *Deor.*" *YES* 7 (1977), 1–9.

Marenbon 1981   Marenbon, John. *From the Circle of Alcuin to the School of Auxerre.* Cambridge: Cambridge University Press, 1981.

Marino, C. 1981   Marino, Cinzia. "Il poeme anglosassone 'The Grave'." *AION,* filologia germanica 24 (1981), 201–10.

Marino, M. 1978   Marino, Matthew. "The Literariness of the *Exeter Book* Riddles." *NM* 79 (1978), 258–65.

Markland 1968   Markland, Murray F. "Boethius, Alfred, and *Deor.*" *MP* 66 (1968–9), 1–4.

Marquardt 1938   Marquardt, Hertha. *Die ae Kenningar.* Halle: M. Niemeyer, 1938.

Martin 1982   Martin, Ellen E. "Allegory and the African Woman in the OE *Exodus.*" *JEGP* 81 (1982), 1–15.

Mayr-Harting 1972   Mayr-Harting, Henry. *The Coming of Christianity to A-S England.* London: B. T. Batsford, 1972.

Meaney 1984   Meaney, Audrey L. "Variant Versions of OE Medical Remedies and the Compilation of Bald's *Leechbook.*" *ASE* 13 (1984), 235–68.

Meindl 1964   Meindl, Robert J. "The Artistic Unity of *Widsith.*" *Xavier University Studies* 3 (1964), 19–28.

Mellinkoff 1979   Mellinkoff, Ruth. "Cain's Monstrous Progeny in *Beowulf.*" *ASE* 8 (1979), 143–62; *ASE* 9 (1981), 183–97.

Menner 1941   Menner, Robert J., ed. *The Poetical Dialogues of Solomon and Saturn.* New York: The Modern Language Association of America, 1941.

Menner 1949   ——. "The Anglian Vocabulary of the *Blickling Homilies.*" In Kirby/Woolf 1949, pp. 56–64.

Metcalf 1973   Metcalf, Allan A. *Poetic Diction in the OE Meters of Boethius.* The Hague and Paris: Mouton, 1973.

Meyvaert 1976   Meyvaert, Paul. "Bede the Scholar." In Bonner 1976, pp. 40–69.

MGH
Auctores antiquissimi:
    Ehwald 1919   Ehwald, R. ed. *Aldhelmi Opera.* Vol. 15. Berlin: Weidmann, 1919

    Mommsen 1898   Mommsen, Theodor, ed. *Chronica Maiora.* Vol. 13. Berlin: Weidmann, 1898, pp. 247–327.

    Peiper 1883   Peiper, Rudolf, ed. *Alcimi Ecdicii Aviti.* Vol. 6.2. Berlin: Weidmann, 1883.

Epistolae:
    Dümmler 1895   Dümmler, Ernst, ed. *Epistolae Karolini Aevi.* Vol. 4. Berlin: Weidmann, 1895.

    Tangl 1916   Tangl, Michel, ed. *S. Bonifatii et Lulli Epistolae, Epistolae Selectae,* Vol. 1. Berlin: Weidmann, 1916.

Poeti Latini Aevi Carolini:
    Dümmler 1881   Dümmler, Ernst, ed. *Poetae Latini Aevi Carolini.* Vol. 1. Berlin: Weidmann, 1881.

    Strecker 1923   Strecker, Karl ed. *Poetae Latini Aevi Carolini.* Vol. 4.3. Berlin: Weidmann, 1923.

Scriptores in Folio:
    Holder-Egger 1887   Holder-Egger, O., ed. *Vita SS. Willibaldi et Wynnebaldi.* Vol. 15.1. Hanover: Hannsche Buchhandlung, 1887.

Scriptores rerum Germanicarum in usum scholarum separatim editi:
    Levison 1905   Levison, Wilhelm, ed. *Vitae Sancti Bonifatii Archiepiscopi Moguntini.* Vol. 57. Hanover and Leipzig: Hannsche Buchhandlung, 1905.

Michel 1947   Michel, Laurence. "*Genesis A* and the *Praefatio.*" *MLN* 62 (1947), 545–50.

Middleton 1973   Middleton, Anne. "Ælfric's Answerable Style: The Rhetoric of the Alliterative Prose." *Studies in Medieval Culture* 4 (1973), 83–91.

Mildenberger 1948   Mildenberger, Kenneth. "Unity of Cynewulf's *Christ* in the Light of Iconography." *Speculum* 23 (1948), 426–32.

Miller 1890   Miller, Thomas, ed. and trans. *The OE Version of Bede's Ecclesiastical History of the English People.* EETS 95, 96, 110, 111. London 1890–8.

Minkoff 1976   Minkoff, Harvey. "Some Stylistic Consequences of Ælfric's Theory of Translation." *SP* 73 (1976), 29–41.

Mitchell 1975   Mitchell, Bruce. "Linguistic Facts and the Interpretation of OE Poetry." *ASE* 4 (1975), 11–28.

Mitchell 1985   ——. *OE Syntax.* 2 vols. Oxford: Clarendon Press, 1985.

Mitchell/Robinson 1982   ——and Fred C. Robinson, eds. *A Guide to OE, Revised with Texts and Glossary.* Toronto and Buffalo: University of Toronto Press, 1982.

Moloney 1982   Moloney, Bernadette. "Another Look at Ælfric's Use of Discourse in Some Saints' Lives." *ES* 63 (1982), 13–9.

Mommsen 1898   See *MGH.*

Monnin 1979   Monnin, Pierre-Eric. "Poetic Improvements in the OE *Meters of Boethius.*" *ES* 60 (1979), 346–60.

Moore 1976   Moore, Bruce. "The Relevance of the Finnsburh Episode." *JEGP* 75 (1976), 317–29.

Moore/Knott 1955   Moore, Samuel and Thomas Knott. *The Elements of OE.* 10th ed. Ann Arbor: George Wahr, 1955.

Morrell 1965   Morrell, Minnie Cate. *A Manual of OE Biblical Materials.* Knoxville: University of Tennessee Press, 1965.

Morris 1874   Morris, Richard, ed. *The Blickling Homilies of the Tenth Century.* EETS 58, 63, 73. London, 1874–80.

Morrish 1985   Morrish, Jennifer. "King Alfred's Letter as a Source on Learning in England." In Szarmach 1985, pp. 87–107.

Murphy 1970   Murphy, James J. "The Rhetorical Lore of the *Boceras* in Byrhtferth's *Manual.*" In Rosier 1970b, pp. 111–24.

Napier 1883   Napier, Arthur S., ed. *Wulfstan: Sammlung der ihm zugeschriebenen Homilien nebst Untersuchungen über ihre Echtheit.* Berlin: Weidmann, 1883. Rpr. with a bibliographical supplement by Klaus Ostheeren. Berlin, Dublin, Zurich: Weidmann, 1966.

Napier 1916   ——, ed. *The OE Version of the Enlarged Rule of Chrodegang; An OE Version of the Capitula of Theodulf; An Interlinear OE Rendering of the Epitome of Benedict of Aniane.* EETS 150. London 1916.

Nelson, J. 1967   Nelson, Janet L. "The Problem of King Alfred's Royal Anointing." *JEH* 18 (1967), 145–63.

Nelson, M. 1974   Nelson, Marie. "The Rhetoric of the Exeter Book Riddles." *Speculum* 49 (1974), 421–40.

Nelson, M. 1983   ——. "On *Resignation.*" In Green, M. 1983a, pp. 133–47.

Nelson, M. 1984a   ——. " 'Is' and 'Ought' in the Exeter Maxims." *Southern Folklore Quarterly* 45 (1984 for 1981), 109–21.

Nelson, M. 1984b   ——. " 'Wordsige and Worcsige': Speech Acts in Three OE Charms." *Language and Style* 17 (1984), 57–66.

Nichols 1968   Nichols, Ann E. "Ælfric's Prefaces: Rhetoric and Genre." *ES* 49 (1968), 215–23.

Nichols 1971 ———. "Ælfric and the Brief Style." *JEGP* 70 (1971), 1–12.

Nicholson 1980 Nicholson, Lewis E. "The Art of Interlace in *Beowulf.*" *SN* 52 (1980), 237–49.

Nicholson/Frese 1975 ——and D. W. Frese, eds. *A-S Poetry: Essays in Appreciation for John C. McGalliard.* Notre Dame: University of Notre Dame Press, 1975.

Niles 1980a Niles, John D. "The *Æcerbot* Ritual in Context." In Niles 1980b, pp. 44–56.

Niles 1980b ———, ed. *OE Literature in Context.* Cambridge and Totowa, NJ: D. S. Brewer/Rowman and Littlefield, 1980.

Niles 1983 ———. *Beowulf: The Poem and its Tradition.* Cambridge, Mass. and London: Harvard University Press, 1983.

Nitzsche 1981 Nitzsche, Jane C. "The A-S Woman as Hero: The Chaste Queen and the Masculine Woman Saint." *Allegorica* 5 (1981 for 1980), 139–48.

Norman 1949 Norman, Frederick, ed. *Waldere.* 2nd ed. London: Methuen, 1949.

Ó Carragáin 1982 Ó Carragáin, Eamonn. "Crucifixion as Annunciation: The Relation of 'The Dream of the Rood' to the Liturgy Reconsidered." *ES* 63 (1982), 487–505.

Oetgen 1975 Oetgen, Jerome. "The OE *Rule* of St. Benedict." *ABR* 26 (1975), 38–53.

Ohl 1928 Ohl, Raymond T., ed. and trans. *The Enigmas of Symphosius.* Philadelphia: University of Pennsylvania, 1928.

Ohlgren 1972a Ohlgren, Thomas H. "Five New Drawings in the MS *Junius 11:* Their Iconography and Thematic Significance." *Speculum* 47 (1972), 227–33.

Ohlgren 1972b ———. "The Illustrations of the Caedmonian *Genesis:* Literary Criticism through Art." *Medievalia et Humanistica* 3 (1972), 199–212.

Ohlgren 1975 ———. "Some New Light on the OE *Cædemonian Genesis.*" *Studies in Iconography* 1 (1975), 38–73.

Olsen 1981 Olsen, Alexandra H. *Guthlac of Croyland: A Study of Heroic Hagiography.* Washington: University Press of America, 1981.

O'Neill 1981 O'Neill, Patrick P. "The OE Introductions to the Prose Psalms of the Paris Psalter: Sources, Structure, and Composition." In Wittig 1981, pp. 20–38.

Opland 1980 Opland, Jeff. *A-S Oral Poetry.* New Haven and London: Yale University Press, 1980.

Orton 1979a Orton, P. R. "Disunity in the Vercelli Book *Soul and Body.*" *Neophil* 63 (1979), 450–60.

Orton 1979b ———. "The OE 'Soul and Body': A Further Examination." *MÆ* 48 (1979), 173–97.

Orton 1981 ———. "The Speaker in *The Husband's Message.*" *LeedsSE* 12 (1981), 43–56.

Orton 1983a   ——. "Caedmon and Christian Poetry." *NM* 84 (1983), 163–70.

Orton 1983b   ——. "King Alfred's Prose *Preface* to the OE *Pastoral Care*, ll. 30–41." *Peritia* 2 (1983), 140–8.

Osborn 1974   Osborn, Marijane. "The Picture-Poem on the Front of the Franks Casket." *NM* 75 (1974), 50–65.

Osborn 1978a   ——. "The Great Feud: Scriptural History and Strife in *Beowulf*." *PMLA* 93 (1978), 973–81.

Osborn 1978b   ——. "Venturing upon Deep Waters in *The Seafarer*." *NM* 79 (1978), 1–6.

Osborn 1983   ——. "The Text and Context of *Wulf and Eadwacer*." In Green, M. 1983a, pp. 174–89.

Otten 1964   Otten, Kurt. *König Alfreds Boethius*. Tübingen: M. Niemeyer, 1964.

Paetzel 1913   Paetzel, Walther. *Die Variationen in der altgermanischen Alliterationspoesie*. Berlin: Mayer and Müller, 1913.

Page 1973   Page, R. I. *An Introduction to English Runes*. London: Methuen, 1973.

Page 1982   ——. "A Tale of Two Cities." *Peritia* 1 (1982), 335–51.

Palmer 1959   Palmer, R. B. "Bede as Textbook Writer: A Study of his *De Arte Metrica*." *Speculum* 34 (1959), 573–84.

Panzer 1910   Panzer, Friedrich. *Studien zur germanischen Sagengeschichte. I. Beowulf*. Munich: C. H. Beck, 1910.

Parkes 1972   Parkes, M. B. "The MS of the *Leiden Riddle*." *ASE* 1 (1972), 207–17.

Pàroli 1979   Pàroli, Teresa. "Il *Christo I* anglosassone: tematica e struttura." *AION*, studi nederlandesi, studi nordici 22 (1979), 209–34.

Parsons 1975   Parsons, David, ed. *Tenth-Century Studies: Essays in Commemoration of the Millennium of the Council of Winchester and Regularis Concordia*. London and Chichester: Phillimore and Co., 1975.

Pasternack 1984   Pasternack, Carol Braun. "Stylistic Disjunction in *The Dream of the Rood*." *ASE* 13 (1984), 167–86.

Patch 1919   Patch, Howard R. "Liturgical Influence in *The Dream of the Rood*." *PMLA* 34 (1919), 233–57.

Patch 1935   ——. *The Tradition of Boethius*. New York: Oxford University Press, 1935.

Payne, F. 1968   Payne, F. Anne. *King Alfred and Boethius: An Analysis of the OE Version of the Consolation of Philosophy*. Madison: University of Wisconsin Press, 1968.

Payne, R. 1975   Payne, Richard C. "Convention and Originality in the Vision Framework of *The Dream of the Rood*." *MP* 73 (1975–6), 329–41.

Pearsall 1977   Pearsall, Derek. *OE and ME Poetry*. London and Boston: Routledge and Kegan Paul, 1977.

Pearsall/Waldron 1969   ——and Ronald A. Waldron, eds. *Medieval Literature and Civilization: Studies in Memory of G. N. Garmonsway*. London: Athlone Press, 1969.

Peiper 1883   See *MGH.*

Philip 1940   Philip, Br. Augustine. "The Exeter Scribe and the Unity of the *Crist.*" *PMLA* 55 (1940), 903–9.

Phillpotts 1929   Phillpotts, Bertha S. "*The Battle of Maldon:* Some Danish Affinities." *MLR* 24 (1929), 172–90.

Pilch 1964   Pilch, Herbert. "The Elegiac Genre in OE and Early Welsh Poetry." *Zeitschrift für Celtische Philologie* 29 (1964), 209–24.

Pitman 1925   Pitman, James H., ed. and trans. *The Riddles of Aldhelm.* New Haven: Yale University Press, 1925. Rpr. Hamden, Conn: Archon Books, 1970.

Planchart 1977   Planchart, A. E. *The Repertory of Tropes at Winchester.* 2 vols. Princeton: Princeton University Press, 1977.

Plummer 1892   Plummer, Charles, ed. *Two of the Saxon Chronicles Parallel,* with supplementary extracts from the others. A revised text . . . on the basis of an edition by John Earle, M. A. 2 vols. Oxford: Clarendon Press, 1892–9.

Plummer 1896   ——, ed. *Venerabilis Baedae Opera Historica.* 2 vols. Oxford: Clarendon Press, 1896.

Pope 1965   Pope, John C. "Dramatic Voices in *The Wanderer* and *The Seafarer.*" In Bessinger/Creed 1965, pp. 164–93. Rpr. in Bessinger/Kahrl 1968, pp. 533–70.

Pope 1966   ——. *The Rhythm of Beowulf.* Rev. ed. New Haven and London: Yale University Press, 1966.

Pope 1967   ——, ed. *Homilies of Ælfric: A Supplementary Collection.* EETS. 259, 260. London 1967–8.

Pope 1969   ——. "The Lacuna in the Text of Cynewulf's *Ascension* (*Christ II,* 556b). In Atwood/Hill 1969, pp. 210–9.

Pope 1974   ——. "Second Thoughts on the Interpretation of *The Seafarer.*" *ASE* 3 (1974), 75–86.

Pope 1981a   ——, ed. *Seven OE Poems.* 2nd ed. New York and London: W. W. Norton, 1981.

Pope 1981b   ——. "The Text of a Damaged Passage in the Exeter Book: *Advent* (*Christ I*) 18–32." *ASE* 9 (1981), 137–56.

Porsia 1976   Porsia, Franco, ed. *Liber Monstrorum.* Bari: Dedalo, 1976.

Potter 1939   Potter, Simeon. "The OE *Orosius.*" *TPS* (1939), 44–53.

Potter 1947   ——. "The OE *Pastoral Care.*" *TPS* (1947), 114–25.

Potter 1949   ——. "King Alfred's Last Preface." In Kirby/Woolf 1949, pp. 25–30.

Potter 1953   ——. "Commentary on King Alfred's *Orosius.*" *Anglia* 71 (1953), 385–437.

Pringle 1975   Pringle, Ian. "*Judith:* The Homily and the Poem." *Traditio* 31 (1975), 83–97.

Proppe 1973   Proppe, Katherine. "King Alfred's *Consolation of Philosophy.*" *NM* 74 (1973), 635–48.

Puhvel 1979   Puhvel, Martin. *Beowulf and the Celtic Tradition*. Wa-
                     terloo, Ont: Wilfrid Laurier University Press, 1979.
Quentin 1908   Quentin, H. *Les martyrologes historiques du moyen âge*.
                     Paris: J. Gabalda, 1908.
Quirk 1963   Quirk, Randolph. "Poetic Language and OE Metre."
                     In Brown/Foote 1963, pp. 150–71.
Quirk/Wrenn 1958   Quirk, Randolph and C. L. Wrenn. *An OE Grammar*.
                     2nd ed. London and New York: Methuen/Henry
                     Holt and Co., 1958.
Raine 1879   Raine, James, ed. *The Historians of the Church of York
                     and its Archbishops I*. Rolls Series 71. London: Long-
                     man and Co., 1879.
Raith 1933   Raith, Josef, ed. *Die ae Version des Haltigar'schen Buss-
                     buches (sog. Poenitential Pseudo-Ecgberti)*. BaP 13.
                     Hamburg: Henri Grand, 1933. Rpr. with a new in-
                     troduction. Darmstadt: Wissenschaftliche Buchge-
                     sellschaft, 1964.
Raith 1956   ——, ed. *Die alt- und mittelenglischen Apollonius-
                     Bruchstücke*. Munich: Max Hueber, 1956.
Rankin 1985   Rankin, Susan. "The Liturgical Background of the OE
                     Advent Lyrics: A Reappraisal." In Lapidge/Gneuss
                     1985, pp. 317–40.
Raw 1976   Raw, Barbara. "The Probable Derivation of Most of
                     the Illustrations in Junius 11 from an Illustrated OS
                     Genesis." *ASE* 5 (1976), 133–48.
Raw 1978   ——. *The Art and Background of OE Poetry*. London:
                     Edward Arnold, 1978.
Ray 1976   Ray, R. D. "Bede, the Exegete, as Historian." In Bon-
                     ner 1976, pp. 125–40.
Regan 1970   Regan, Catherine A. "Patristic Psychology in the OE
                     Vainglory." *Traditio* 76 (1970), 324–35.
Reichardt 1974   Reichardt, Paul F. "*Guthlac A* and the Landscape of
                     Spiritual Perfection." *Neophil* 58 (1974), 331–8.
Reinsma 1977   Reinsma, Luke M. "Rhetoric in England: The Age of
                     Ælfric, 970–1020." *CM* 44 (1977), 390–403.
Renoir 1962   Renoir, Alain. "*Judith* and the Limits of Poetry." *ES*
                     43 (1962), 145–55.
Renior 1965   ——. "*Wulf and Eadwacer*: A Noninterpretation." In
                     Bessinger/Creed 1965, pp. 147–63.
Renoir 1967   ——. "The Self-Deception of Temptation: Boethian
                     Psychology in *Genesis B*." In Creed 1967b, pp. 47–
                     67.
Renoir 1975   ——. "A Reading Context for *The Wife's Lament*." In
                     Nicholson/Frese 1975, pp. 224–41.
Renoir 1977   ——. "A Reading of *The Wife's Lament*." *ES* 58 (1977),
                     4–19.
Renoir 1978a   ——. "*Beowulf*: A Contextual Introduction." In *Heroic
                     Epic and Saga*, ed. F. J. Oinas. Bloomington and
                     London: Indiana University Press, 1978, pp. 99–119.

Renoir 1978b —. "The Ugly and the Unfaithful: *Beowulf* through the Translator's Eye." *Allegorica* 3 (1978), 161–71.

Renoir 1981 —. "The Least Elegiac of the Elegies: A Contextual Glance at *The Husband's Message*." *SN* 53 (1981), 69–76.

Renoir 1983 —. "The OE *Ruin*: Contrastive Structure and Affective Impact." In Green, M. 1983a, pp. 148–73.

Renoir/Hernández 1982 —and Ann Hernández, eds. *Approaches to Beowulfian Scansion*. OE Colloquium Series No. 1. Berkeley: Department of English, University of California, Berkeley, 1982.

Reuter 1980 Reuter, T., ed. *The Greatest Englishman*. Exeter: Paternoster Press, 1980.

Reynolds 1953 Reynolds, Robert L. "Le poème a-s *Widsith*: réalité et fiction." *Le Moyen Âge* 59 (1953), 299–324.

Rice 1977 Rice, Robert C. "The Penitential Motif in Cynewulf's *Fates of the Apostles* and in His Epilogues." *ASE* 6 (1977), 105–19.

Richards 1985 Richards, Mary. "The Manuscript Contexts of the OE Laws: Tradition and Innovation." In Szarmach 1985, pp. 171–92.

Roberts 1971 Roberts, Jane. "A Metrical Examination of the Poems *Guthlac A* and *Guthlac B*." *Proceedings of the Royal Irish Academy* 71C (1971), 91–137.

Roberts 1979 —, ed. *The Guthlac Poems of the Exeter Book*. Oxford: Clarendon Press, 1979.

Roberts 1985 —. "The OE Prose Translation of Felix's *Vita sancti Guthlaci*." In Szarmach 1985, pp. 363–79.

Robertson, A. 1925 Robertson, Agnes J., ed. *The Laws of the Kings of England from Edmund to Henry I*. Cambridge: Cambridge University Press, 1925.

Robertson, A. 1939 —, ed. *A-S Charters*. Cambridge: Cambridge University Press, 1939.

Robertson, D. 1951 Robertson, D. W. "The Doctrine of Charity in Medieval Literary Gardens: A Topical Approach through Symbolism and Allegory." *Speculum* 26 (1951), 24–49.

Robinson 1968 Robinson, Fred. C. "Some Uses of Name-meanings in OE Poetry." *NM* 69 (1968), 161–71.

Robinson 1970 —. "Lexicography and Literary Criticism: A Caveat." In Rosier 1970b, pp. 99–110.

Robinson 1975 —. "Artful Ambiguities in the OE 'Book-Moth' Riddle." In Nicholson/Frese 1975, pp. 355–62.

Robinson 1976 —. "Some Aspects of the *Maldon* Poet's Artistry." *JEGP* 75 (1976), 25–40.

Robinson 1979a —. "God, Death, and Loyalty in *The Battle of Maldon*." In *J. R. R. Tolkien, Scholar and Storyteller*, eds. M. Salu and R. T. Farrell. Ithaca and London: Cornell University Press, 1979, pp. 76–98.

Robinson 1979b ———. "Two Aspects of Variation in OE Poetry." In Calder 1979a, pp. 127–45.

Robinson 1980 ———. "OE Literature in Its Most Immediate Context." In Niles 1980b, pp. 11–29, 157–61.

Robinson 1984 ———. "History, Religion, Culture." In Bessinger/Yeager 1984, pp. 107–22.

Robinson 1985 ———. Beowulf and the Appositive Style. Knoxville: University of Tennessee Press, 1985.

Rogers 1971 Rogers, H. L. "Rhymes in the Epilogue to Elene: A Reconsideration." LeedsSE 5 (1971), 47–52.

Rogers 1985 ———. "The Battle of Maldon: David Casley's Transcript." N&Q 230 [n.s. 32] (1985), 161–9.

Rollason 1982 Rollason, D. W. The Mildrith Legend: A Study in Early Medieval Hagiography in England. Leicester: Leicester University Press, 1982.

Rollman 1982 Rollman, David A. "Widsith as an A-S Defense of Poetry." Neophil 66 (1982), 431–9.

Roper 1962 Roper, Alan H. "Boethius and the Three Fates of Beowulf." PQ 41 (1962), 386–400.

Rosier 1962 Rosier, James L., ed. The Vitellius Psalter. Ithaca: Cornell University Press, 1962.

Rosier 1964a ———, ed. " 'Instructions for Christians': A Poem in OE." Anglia 82 (1964), 4–22; 84 (1966), 74.

Rosier 1964b ———. "The Literal-Figurative Identity of The Wanderer." PMLA 79 (1964), 366–9.

Rosier 1970a ———. "Death and Transfiguration: Guthlac B." In Rosier 1970b, pp. 82–92.

Rosier 1970b ———, ed. Philological Essays: Studies in Old and Middle English Language and Literature in Honour of Herbert Dean Meritt. The Hague and Paris: Mouton, 1970.

Rositzke 1940 Rositzke, Harry A., ed. The C-Text of the OE Chronicles. Beiträge zur englischen Philologie 30. Bochum: Heinrich Pöppinghaus, 1940.

Russom 1977 Russom, Geoffrey R. "Exeter Riddle 47: A Moth Laid Waste to Fame." PQ 56 (1977), 129–36.

Russom 1978a ———. "Artful Avoidance of the Useful Phrase in Beowulf, The Battle of Maldon, and Fates of the Apostles." SP 75 (1978), 371–90.

Russom 1978b ———. "A Germanic Concept of Nobility in The Gifts of Men and Beowulf." Speculum 53 (1978), 1–15.

Rypins 1924 Rypins, Stanley, ed. Three OE Prose Texts in MS Cotton Vitellius A xv. EETS 161. London 1924 (for 1921).

Salmon 1960 Salmon, Vivian. "The Wanderer and The Seafarer, and the OE Conception of the Soul." MLR 55 (1960), 1–10.

Sauvage 1885 Sauvage, E. P., ed. "Translatio et Miracula S. Swithuni." Analecta Bollandiana 4 (1885), 367–410.

Sawyer 1957 Sawyer, Peter, ed. Textus Roffensis. EEMF 7, Pt. 1;

EEMF 11, Pt. 2. Copenhagen: Rosenkilde and Bagger, 1957 and 1962.

Schaar 1949   Schaar, Claes. *Critical Studies in the Cynewulf Group.* Lund: C. W. K. Gleerup, 1949. Rpr. New York: Haskell, 1967.

Schaar 1956   ———. "On a New Theory of OE Poetic Diction." *Neophil* 40 (1956), 301–5.

Schelp 1960   Schelp, H. "Die Deutungstradition in Ælfrics Homilae Catholicae." *Archiv* 196 (1960), 273–95.

Schepss 1895   Schepss, G. "Zu König Alfreds Boethius." *Archiv* 94 (1895), 149–60.

Schieffer 1972   Schieffer, Theodor. *Winfrid-Bonifatius und die christliche Grundlegung Europas.* Rev. ed. Darmstadt: Wissenschaftliche Buchgesellschaft, 1972.

Schipper 1899   Schipper, Jakob M., ed. *König Alfreds Übersetzung von Bedas Kirchengeschichte.* BaP 4. Leipzig: G. H. Wiegand, 1899.

Schlauch 1931   Schlauch, Margaret. "*Widsith, Vithförull,* and Some Other Analogues." *PMLA* 46 (1931), 969–87.

Schlauch 1940   ———. "The *Dream of the Rood* as Prosopopoeia." In *Essays and Studies in Honor of Carleton Brown.* New York: New York University Press, 1940, pp. 23–34. Rpr. in Bessinger/Kahrl 1968, pp. 428–41.

Schlauch 1941   ———. "An OE *Encomium Urbis.*" *JEGP* 40 (1941), 14–28.

Schmidt 1934   Schmidt, Karl H. *König Alfreds Boethius-Bearbeitung.* Göttingen: Universität Göttingen, 1934.

Schneider, C. 1978   Schneider, Claude. "Cynewulf's Devaluation of Heroic Tradition in *Juliana.*" *ASE* 7 (1978), 107–18.

Schneider, K. 1956   Schneider, Karl. *Die germanischen Runennamen.* Meisenheim am Glam: A. Hain, 1956.

Schroeder 1974   Schroeder, Peter R. "Stylistic Analogies Between OE Art and Poetry." *Viator* 5 (1974), 185–97.

Schröer 1885   Schröer, Arnold, ed. *Die ags Prosabearbeitungen der Benediktinerregel.* BaP 2. Kassel: G. H. Wiegand, 1885–8. 2nd ed. Rpr. with an appendix by H. Gneuss. Darmstadt: Wissenschaftliche Buchgesellschaft, 1964.

Schütt 1957   Schütt, Marie. "The Literary Form of Asser's *Vita Alfredi.*" *EHR* 72 (1957), 209–20.

Schwab 1967   Schwab, Ute, ed. *Waldere. Testo e commento.* Messina: Libreria peloritana, 1967.

Schwab 1972   ———. "Ær-æfter: Das *Memento Mori* Bedas als Christliche Kontrafaktur. Eine philologische Interpretation." In *Studi di Letteratura Religiosa Tedesca in memoria di Sergio Lupi,* ed. Claudio Magris. Florence: L. S. Olschki, 1972, pp. 5–134.

Schwab 1978   ———. "Das Traumgesicht von Kreuzesbaum: ein ikonologischer Interpretationsansatz zu dem ags

Dream of the Rood." In *Philologische Studien: Gedenkschrift für Richard Kienast*, eds. U. Schwab and E. Stutz. Heidelberg: Carl Winter, 1978, pp. 131–92.

Schwab 1979 ——. "Nochmals zum ags *Waldere* neben dem *Waltharius*." BGdSL 101 (1979), 229–51, 347–68.

Schwab 1983 ——. "The Miracles of Caedmon." *ES* 64 (1983), 1–17.

Scragg 1973 Scragg, D. G. "The Compilation of the Vercelli Book." *ASE* 2 (1973), 189–207.

Scragg 1979 ——. "The Corpus of Vernacular Homilies and Prose Saints' Lives before Ælfric." *ASE*, 8 (1979), 223–77.

Scragg 1981 ——, ed. *The Battle of Maldon*. Manchester: Manchester University Press, 1981.

Sedgefield 1899 Sedgefield, Walter J., ed. *King Alfred's OE Version of Boethius De Consolatione Philosophiae*. Oxford: Clarendon Press, 1899; trans. 1900. Rpr. Darmstadt: Wissenschaftliche Buchgesellschaft, 1968.

Sheerin 1978 Sheerin, D. J. "The Dedication of the Old Minster, Winchester, in 980." *Rb* 88 (1978), 261–73.

Shepherd 1952 Shepherd, Geoffrey. "The Sources of the OE *Kentish Hymn*." *MLN* 67 (1952), 395–7.

Shepherd 1966 ——. "Scriptural Poetry." In Stanley 1966b, pp. 1–36.

Sherley-Price 1955 Sherley-Price, L. *Bede: A History of the English Church and People*. Harmondsworth: Penguin Books, 1955. Rpr. and rev. 1965.

Shippey 1972 Shippey, T. A. *OE Verse*. London: Hutchinson and Co., 1972.

Shippey 1976 ——, ed. *Poems of Wisdom and Learning in OE*. Cambridge and Totowa, NJ: D. S. Brewer/Rowman and Littlefield, 1976.

Shippey 1978 ——. *Beowulf*. London: Edward Arnold, 1978.

Shippey 1979 ——. "Wealth and Wisdom in King Alfred's *Preface* to the OE *Pastoral Care*." *EHR* 94 (1979), 346–55.

Shook 1960 Shook, Laurence K. "The Burial Mound in *Guthlac A*." *MP* 58 (1960–1), 1–10.

Shook 1961 ——. "The Prologue of the OE *Guthlac A*." *MS* 23 (1961), 294–304.

Short 1976a Short, Douglas. D "Aesthetics and Unpleasantness: Classical Rhetoric in the Medieval English Lyric *The Grave*." *SN* 48 (1976), 291–9.

Short 1976b ——. "The OE *Gifts of Men* and the Pedagogic Theory of the *Pastoral Care*." *ES* 57 (1976), 497–501.

Short 1980a ——. "*Beowulf* and Modern Critical Tradition." In *A Fair Day in the Affections: Literary Essays in Honor of Robert B. White, Jr.*, eds. J. D. Durant and M. T. Hester. Raleigh, NC: Winston Press, 1980, pp. 1–23.

Short 1980b — ———. *Beowulf Scholarship: An Annotated Bibliography.* New York and London: Garland, 1980.

Short 1984 — ———. "Translations of *Beowulf.*" In Bessinger/Yeager 1984, pp. 7–14.

Sieper 1915 — Sieper, Ernst, ed. *Die ae Elegie.* Strassburg: K. J. Trübner, 1915.

Sievers 1875 — Sievers, Eduard, ed. *Der Heliand und die ags Genesis.* Halle: M. Niemeyer, 1875.

Sievers 1893 — ———. *Altgermanische Metrik.* Halle: M. Niemeyer, 1893. Partially trans. in Bessinger/Kahrl 1968, pp. 267–88.

Sievers 1929 — ———. "Caedmon und *Genesis.*" In *Britannica. Max Förster zum 60. Geburtstage.* Leipzig: B. Tauchnitz, 1929, pp. 57–84.

Sigerson 1922 — Sigerson, George, trans. *The Easter Song of Sedulius.* Dublin: The Talbot Press, 1922.

Sisam, C. 1953 — Sisam, Celia. "An Early Fragment of the *OE Martyrology.*" *RES* 4 (1953), 209–20.

Sisam, C. 1955 — ———. Review of Vleeskruyer 1953. *RES* 6 (1955), 302–3.

Sisam, C. 1976 — ———, ed. *The Vercelli Book.* EEMF 19. Copenhagen: Rosenkilde and Bagger, 1976.

Sisam, K. 1932 — Sisam, Kenneth. "Cynewulf and His Poetry." *PBA* 18 (1932), 1–28. Rpr. in Sisam, K. 1953, pp. 1–28.

Sisam, K. 1953 — Sisam, Kenneth. *Studies in the History of OE Literature.* Oxford: Clarendon Press. 1953.

Sisam, K. 1965 — ———. *The Structure of Beowulf.* Oxford: Clarendon Press, 1965.

Sisam, C./K. 1958 — Sisam, Celia and Kenneth Sisam. "V. The Psalm Texts." In Colgrave 1958, pp. 15–7.

Skeat 1881 — Skeat, Walter W., ed. *Ælfric's Lives of Saints.* EETS 76, 82, 94, 114. London 1881–1900.

Sleeth 1982 — Sleeth, Charles R. *Studies in Christ and Satan.* Toronto, Buffalo, and London: University of Toronto Press, 1982.

Smalley 1983 — Smalley, Beryl. *The Study of the Bible in the Middle Ages.* 3rd rev. ed. Oxford: Blackwell, 1983.

Smetana 1959 — Smetana, C. J. "Ælfric and the Early Medieval Homiliary." *Traditio* 15 (1959), 163–204.

Smetana 1961 — ———. "Ælfric and the Homiliary of Haymo of Halberstadt." *Traditio* 17 (1961), 457–69.

Smetana 1967 — ———. "Second Thoughts on *Soul and Body I.*" *MS* 29 (1967), 193–205.

Smith 1933 — Smith, A. H., ed. *Three Northumbrian Poems.* London: Methuen, 1933.

Smithers 1957 — Smithers, G. V. "The Meaning of *The Seafarer* and *The Wanderer.*" *MÆ* 26 (1957), 137–53; 28 (1959), 1–22, 99–104.

Solo 1973 — Solo, Harry Jay. "The Twice-Told Tale: A Reconsideration of the Syntax and Style of the OE *Daniel*, 245–429." *PLL* 9 (1973), 347–64.

Spindler 1934 — Spindler, Robert, ed. *Das ae Bussbuch (sog. Confessionale Pseudo-Ecberti)*. Leipzig: B. Tauchnitz, 1934.

Stafford 1978 — Stafford, P. A. "Church and Society in the Age of Ælfric." In Szarmach/Huppé 1978, pp. 11–42.

Stanley 1955 — Stanley, E. G. "OE Poetic Diction and the Interpretation of *The Wanderer*, *The Seafarer*, and *The Penitent's Prayer*." *Anglia* 73 (1955), 413–66. Rpr. in Bessinger/Kahrl 1968, pp. 458–514.

Stanley 1966a — ———. "*Beowulf*." In Stanley 1966b, pp. 104–41.

Stanley 1966b — ———, ed. *Continuations and Beginnings: Studies in OE Literature*. London: Thomas Nelson and Sons, 1966.

Stanley 1971 — ———. "Studies in the Prosaic Vocabulary of OE Verse." *NM* 72 (1971), 385–418.

Stanley 1974 — ———. "Some Observations on the A3 Lines in *Beowulf*." In Burlin/Irving 1974, pp. 139–64.

Stanley 1975 — ———. *The Search for Anglo-Saxon Paganism*. Cambridge and Totowa, NJ: D. S. Brewer/Rowman and Littlefield, 1975. Rpr. of articles from *N&Q* 1964–5.

Stanley 1979 — ———. "Two OE Poetic Phrases Insufficiently Understood for Literary Criticism: Ðing Gehegan and Seonoð Gehegan." In Calder 1979a, pp. 67–90.

Stenton 1925 — Stenton, F. M. "The South-Western Element in the OE Chronicle." In *Essays in Medieval History presented to Thomas Frederick Tout*, eds. A. G. Little and F. M. Powicke. Manchester: n.p., 1925, pp. 15–24. Rpr. in *Preparatory to A-S England*, ed. Doris Mary Stenton. Oxford: Clarendon Press, 1970, pp. 106–15.

Stenton 1955. — ———. *The Latin Charters of the A-S Period*. Oxford: Clarendon Press, 1955.

Stenton 1971 — ———. *A-S England*. 3rd ed. Oxford: Clarendon Press, 1971.

Stepsis/Rand 1969 — Stepsis, Robert and Richard Rand. "Contrast and Conversion in Cynewulf's *Elene*." *NM* 70 (1969), 273–82.

Stevenson 1904 — Stevenson W. H., ed. *Asser's Life of King Alfred*. Oxford: Clarendon Press, 1904. New Impression with an article on "Recent Work on Asser's Life of Alfred" by Dorothy Whitelock. Oxford: Clarendon Press, 1959.

Stevenson 1929 — ———, ed. *Early Scholastic Colloquies*. Oxford: Clarendon Press, 1929.

Stevick 1960 — Stevick, Robert D. "Formal Aspects of *The Wife's Lament*." *JEGP* 59 (1960), 21–5.

Stevick 1980 — ———. "Mathematical Properties and Symbolism in *The Phoenix*." *Viator* 11 (1980), 95–121.

Stewart 1979 — Stewart, Ann Harleman. "Kenning and Riddle in OE." *PLL* 15 (1979), 115–36.

Stewart 1983 ——. "Double Entendre in the OE Riddle." *Lore and Language* 3, no. 8 (1983), 39–52.

Storms 1948 Storms, Godfrid. *A-S Magic*. The Hague: Martinus Nijhoff, 1948.

Storms 1956 ——. "The Weakening of OE Unstressed *i* to *e* and the Date of Cynewulf." *ES* 37 (1956), 104–10.

Strecker 1923 See *MGH*.

Strunk 1904 Strunk, William, ed. *Juliana*. Boston: D.C. Heath and Co., 1904.

Stuart 1981 Stuart, Heather. " 'Ic me on þisse gyrde beluce': The Structure and Meaning of the OE *Journey Charm*." *MÆ* 50 (1981), 259–73.

Stuart 1982 ——. "The Meaning of *Maldon*." *Neophil* 66 (1982), 126–39.

Stubbs 1874 Stubbs, W., ed. *Memorials of St. Dunstan*. Rolls Series 63. London: Longman and Co., 1874, pp. 3–52.

Swanton 1968 Swanton, Michael J. "*The Battle of Maldon*: A Literary Caveat." *JEGP* 67 (1968), 441–50.

Swanton 1970 ——, ed. *The Dream of the Rood*. Manchester: Manchester University Press, 1970.

Swanton 1977 ——. "Heroes, Heroism and Heroic Literature." *E&S* 30 (1977), 1–21.

Sweet 1871 Sweet, Henry, ed. *King Alfred's W-S Version of Gregory's Pastoral Care*. EETS 45 and 50. London 1871–2.

Sweet 1883 ——, ed. *King Alfred's Orosius*. Pt. I: *OE Text and Latin Original*. EETS 79. London 1883.

Symons 1953 Symons, Thomas, ed. and trans. *Regularis Concordia*. New York and London: T. Nelson and Sons, 1953.

Symons 1975 ——. "*Regularis Concordia*: History and Derivation." In Parsons 1975, pp. 37–59.

Szarmach 1978 Szarmach, Paul E. "The Vercelli Homilies: Style and Structure." In Szarmach/Huppé 1978, pp. 241–67.

Szarmach 1980 ——. "The Meaning of Alfred's *Preface* to the *Pastoral Care*." *Mediaevalia* 6 (1982 for 1980), 57–86.

Szarmach 1981a ——. "Another OE Translation of Gregory the Great's *Dialogues?*" *ES* 62 (1981), 97–109.

Szarmach 1981b ——, ed. *Vercelli Homilies IX—XXIII*. Toronto, Buffalo, and London: University of Toronto Press, 1981.

Szarmach 1985 ——, ed. *Studies in Earlier OE Prose*. Albany: SUNY Press 1985.

Szarmach/Huppé 1978 —— and Bernard F. Huppé, eds. *The OE Homily and Its Backgrounds*. Albany: SUNY Press, 1978.

Talbot 1954 Talbot, C. H. *The A-S Missionaries in Germany*. London and New York: Sheed and Ward, 1954.

Talbot 1955 ——. "The *Liber Confortatorius* of Goscelin of Saint-Bertin." *Studia Anselmiana* 37 (1955), 1–117.

Talbot 1959 ——. "The Life of St. Wulsin of Sherborne by Goscelin." *Rb* 69 (1959), 68–85.

Talbot 1967 ———. *Medicine in Medieval England.* London: Old-bourne Book Co., 1967.

Tandy 1978 Tandy, Keith A. "Verbal Aspect as a Narrative Structure in Ælfric's *Lives of Saints.*" In Szarmach/Huppé 1978, pp. 181–202.

Tanenhaus 1962 Tanenhaus, G. H. "Bede's *De Schematibus et Tropis*— A Translation." *QJS* 48 (1962), 237–53.

Tangl 1916 See *MGH*.

Taylor 1969 Taylor, Paul B. "Heroic Ritual in the OE Maxims." *NM* 70 (1969), 387–407.

Thompson 1935 Thompson, Alexander H., ed. *Bede, his Life, Times and Writings.* Oxford: Clarendon Press, 1935.

Thomson 1949 Thomson, H. J., ed. *Prudentius.* 2 vols. London and Cambridge, Mass: W. Heinemann/Harvard University Press, 1949.

Thorpe 1840 Thorpe, Benjamin, ed. *Ancient Laws and Institutes of England.* 2 vols. London: Eyre and Spottiswoode, 1840.

Thorpe 1844 ———, ed. *The Homilies of the A-S Church. The First Part, Containing the Sermones Catholici, or Homilies of Ælfric.* 2 vols. London: Ælfric Society, 1844–6.

Thorpe 1861 ———, ed. and trans. *The A-S Chronicle.* 2 vols. London: Longman, Green, Longman, and Roberts, 1861.

Thorpe 1873 ———, ed. and trans. *Alfred's A-S Version of Orosius.* Appended to (Georg) Reinhold Pauli, *The Life of Alfred the Great* (trans. from the German). London: G. Bell and Sons, 1873.

Timmer 1942 Timmer, Benno J. "The Elegiac Mood in OE Poetry." *ES* 24 (1942), 33–44.

Timmer 1954 ———, ed. *The Later Genesis.* Rev. ed. Oxford: Scrivner Press, 1954.

Timmer 1961 ———, ed. *Judith.* 2nd ed. London: Methuen 1961. Rpr. 1966.

Tolkien 1936 Tolkien, J. R. R. "*Beowulf:* The Monsters and the Critics." *PBA* 22 (1936), 245–95.

Tolkien 1953 ———. "The Homecoming of Beorhtnoth Beorhthelm's Son." *E&S* 6 (1953), 1–18.

Tolkien/Bliss 1982 ———. *Finn and Hengest: The Fragment and the Episode,* ed. A. J. Bliss. London and Boston: George Allen and Unwin, 1982.

Towers 1963 Towers, Tom H. "The Thematic Unity in the Story of Cynewulf and Cyneheard." *JEGP* 62 (1963), 310–6.

Trahern 1969 Trahern, Joseph B., Jr. "The OE *Almsgiving.*" *N&Q* 214 [n.s. 16] (1969), 46–7.

Trahern 1970 ———. "The *Ioca Monachorum* and the OE *Pharaoh.*" *ELN* 7 (1970–1), 165–8.

Trahern 1976 ———. "Caesarius of Arles and OE Literature." *ASE* 5 (1976), 105–19.

Trask 1971 — Trask, Richard M. "*The Descent into Hell* of the Exeter Book." *NM* 72 (1971), 419–35.

Tristram 1970 — Tristram, Hildegard L. C., ed. *Vier ae Predigten aus der heterodoxen Tradition.* Freiburg: Albert-Ludwigs Universität, 1970.

Tuggle 1977 — Tuggle, Thomas T. "The Structure of *Deor.*" *SP* 74 (1977), 229–42.

Turville-Petre 1974 — Turville-Petre, Joan. "The Narrative Style in OE." In *Iceland and the Medieval World: Studies in Honour of Ian Maxwell,* eds. G. Turville-Petre and J. S. Martin. Melbourne: n.p., 1974, pp. 116–25.

Twomey 1983 — Twomey, Michael W. "On Reading *Bede's Death Song.*" *NM* 84 (1983), 171–81.

Ure 1957 — Ure, James M., ed. *The Benedictine Office: An OE Text.* Edinburgh: Edinburgh University Press, 1957.

van de Vyver 1935 — van de Vyver, A. "Les œuvres inédites d'Abbon de Fleury." *Rb* 47 (1935), 123–69.

van Dratt 1916 — van Draat, P. Fijn. "The Authorship of the OE Bede: A Study of Rhythm." *Anglia* 39 (1916), 319–46.

Vaughan-Sterling 1983 — Vaughan-Sterling, Judith A. "The A-S *Metrical Charms*: Poetry as Ritual." *JEGP* 82 (1983), 186–200.

Vickrey 1969 — Vickrey, John F. "The Vision of Eve in *Genesis B.*" *Speculum* 44 (1969), 86–102.

Vickrey 1972a — ———. "*Exodus* and the Battle in the Sea." *Traditio* 28 (1972), 119–40.

Vickrey 1972b — ———. "*Exodus* and the Treasure of Pharaoh." *ASE* 1 (1972), 159–65.

Vickrey 1977 — ———. "The Narrative Structure of Hengest's Revenge in *Beowulf.*" *ASE* 6 (1977), 91–103.

Vickrey 1982 — ———. "Some Hypotheses Concerning *The Seafarer,* Lines 1–47." *Archiv* 219 (1982), 57–77.

Vleeskruyer 1953 — Vleesskruyer, R., ed. *The Life of St. Chad.* Amsterdam: North Holland, 1953.

Voigts 1979 — Voigts, Linda E. "A-S Plant Remedies and the Anglo-Saxons." *Isis* 70 (1979), 250–68.

von Antropoff 1965 — von Antropoff, R. *Die Entwicklung der Kenelm-Legende.* Bonn: Universität Bonn, 1965.

Wallace-Hadrill 1971a — Wallace-Hadrill, J. M. "A Background to St. Boniface's Mission." In Clemoes/Hughes 1971, pp. 35–48.

Wallace-Hadrill 1971b — ———. *Early Germanic Kingship in England and on the Continent.* Oxford: Clarendon Press, 1971.

Walsh 1977 — Walsh, Marie M. "The Baptismal Flood in the OE 'Andreas': Liturgical and Typological Depths." *Traditio* 33 (1977) 137–58.

Walsh 1981 — ———. "St. Andrew in A-S England: the Evolution of an Apocryphal Hero." *AnM* 20 (1981), 97–122.

Wanley 1705 — Wanley, Humphrey. *Librorum Veterum Septentrional-*

ium, qui in Angliae Bibliothecis extant . . . Catalogus Historico-Criticus. Vol. II of Hickes 1703. Oxford: Sheldonian Theatre, 1705.

Waterhouse 1969 Waterhouse, Ruth. "The Theme and Structure of 755 A-S *Chronicle.*" *NM* 70 (1969), 630–40.

Waterhouse 1976 ———."Ælfric's Use of Discourse in Some Saints' Lives." *ASE* 5 (1976), 83–103.

Waterhouse 1978 ———. "Affective Language, Especially Alliterating Qualifiers, in Ælfric's Life of St Alban." *ASE* 7 (1978), 131–48.

Waterhouse 1980 ———. "Stylistic Features as a Factor in Detecting Change of Source in the Ninth-Century *A-S Chronicle.*" *Parergon* 27 (1980), 3–8.

Waterhouse 1982 ———. "Structuring in Ælfric's Lives of Saints XII and XIII." *Parergon* 32 (1982), 3–12.

Waterhouse 1985 ———. "Tone in Alfred's Version of Augustine's *Soliloquies.*" In Szarmach 1985, pp. 47–85.

Watts 1969 Watts, Ann Chalmers. *The Lyre and the Harp: A Comparative Reconsideration of Oral Tradition in Homer and OE Epic Poetry.* New Haven: Yale University Press, 1969.

Webb/Farmer 1983 Webb, J. F. and D. H. Farmer, eds. *The Age of Bede.* Harmondsworth: Penguin Books, 1983.

Wehrle 1933 Wehrle, W. O. *The Macaronic Hymn Tradition in Medieval English Literature.* Washington, D.C.: The Catholic University of America, 1933.

Wenisch 1982 Wenisch, Franz. "*Judith*—eine westsächsische Dichtung?" *Anglia* 100 (1982), 273–300.

Wentersdorf 1977 Wentersdorf, Karl P. "Observations on *The Ruin.*" *MÆ* 46 (1977), 171–80.

Wentersdorf 1978 ———. "*Guthlac A:* The Battle for the *beorg.*" *Neophil* 62 (1978), 135–42.

Wentersdorf 1981 ———. "The Situation of the Narrator in the OE *Wife's Lament.*" *Speculum* 56 (1981), 492–516.

Westom 1985 Weston, L. M. C. "The Language of Magic in Two OE Charms." *NM* 86 (1985), 176–86.

Whallon 1969 Whallon, William. *Formula, Character, and Context: Studies in Homeric, OE, and Old Testament Poetry.* Cambridge, Mass: Harvard University Press, 1969.

Whatley 1975 Whatley, E. Gordon. "Bread and Stone: Cynewulf's *Elene* 611–618." *NM* 76 (1975), 550–60.

Whatley 1981 ———. "The Figure of Constantine the Great in Cynewulf's 'Elene'." *Traditio* 37 (1981), 161–202.

Whitbread 1944 Whitbread, Leslie. "A Study of Bede's *Versus de Die Iudicii.*" *PQ* 23 (1944), 193–221.

Whitbread 1945 ———. "The OE Poem 'Alms-Giving'." *N&Q* 189 (1945), 2–4.

Whitbread 1946 ———. "The OE Poem 'Pharaoh'." *N&Q* 190 (1946), 52–4.

Whitbread 1949 ———. "The OE *Exhortation to Christian Living:* Some Textual Problems." *MLR* 44 (1949), 178–83.

Whitbread 1951 ———. "Notes on the OE *Exhortation to Christian Living.*" *SN* 23 (1951), 96–102.

Whitbread 1957 ———. "Notes on Two Minor OE Poems." *SN* 29 (1957), 123–9.

Whitbread 1962 ———. "The OE Poems of the *Benedictine Office* and Some Related Questions." *Anglia* 80 (1962), 37–49.

Whitbread 1966a ———. "The OE Poem *Judgment Day II* and its Latin Source." *PQ* 45 (1966), 635–56.

Whitbread 1966b ———. "Notes on Two Minor OE Poems." *ELN* 4 (1966–7), 241–3.

Whitbread 1967 ———. "The Doomsday Theme in OE Poetry." *BGdSL* (Halle) 89 (1967), 452–81.

Whitbread 1970 ———. "The Pattern of Misfortune in *Deor* and other OE Poems." *Neophil* 54 (1970), 167–83.

Whitbread 1976 ———. "The OE Poem *Aldhelm.*" *ES* 57 (1976), 193–7.

White 1898 White, Caroline L. *Ælfric: A New Study of His Life and Writings.* New York: Lamson, Wolff and Co., 1898. Rpr. with a supplementary bibliography by M. Godden. Hamden, Conn: Archon Books, 1974.

Whitelock 1930 Whitelock, Dorothy, ed. *A-S Wills.* Cambridge: Cambridge University Press, 1930.

Whitelock 1942 ———. "Archbishop Wulfstan, Homilist and Statesman." *TRHS,* 4th ser. 24 (1942), 25–45.

Whitelock 1950 ———. "The Interpretation of *The Seafarer.*" In Fox/Dickins 1950, pp. 259–72. Rpr. in Bessinger/Kahrl 1968, pp. 442–57.

Whitelock 1951 ———. *The Audience of Beowulf.* Oxford: Clarendon Press, 1951.

Whitelock 1961 ———, with David C. Douglas and Susie I. Tucker, trans. *The A-S Chronicle: A Revised Translation.* London: Eyre and Spottiswoode, 1961; New Brunswick, NJ: Rutgers University Press, 1962.

Whitelock 1962 ———. "The OE Bede." *PBA* 48 (1962), 57–90.

Whitelock 1963 ———, ed. *Sermo Lupi ad Anglos.* 3rd ed. London: Methuen, 1963.

Whitelock 1966 ———. "The Prose of Alfred's Reign." In Stanley 1966b, pp. 67–103.

Whitelock 1968a ———. *The Genuine Asser.* Reading: University of Reading, 1968.

Whitelock 1968b ———, ed. and trans. *The Will of Æthelgifu.* Oxford: Oxford University Press, 1968.

Whitelock 1970 ———. "The Authorship of the Account of King Edgar's Establishment of Monasteries." In Rosier 1970b, pp. 125–36.

Whitelock 1978 ———. "The Importance of the Battle of Edington A. D. 878." *Report for 1975, 1976 and 1977 of the Society*

of the Friends of the Priory Church of Edington, Wilt-
shire. 1978, pp. 6–15.

Whitelock 1979 ——, ed. English Historical Documents c. 500–1042. 2nd
ed. London and New York: Eyre Methuen/Oxford
University Press, 1979.

Whiting 1949 Whiting, Bartlett J. "The Rime of King William." In
Kirby/Woolf 1949, pp. 89–96.

Wieland 1983 Wieland, G. R., ed. The Latin Glosses on Arator and
Prudentius in Cambridge University Library MS Gg. 5.
35. Toronto: Pontifical Institute of Mediaeval Studies, 1983.

Willard 1935 Willard, Rudolph, ed. "The Address of the Soul to the
Body." PMLA 50 (1935), 957–83.

Willard 1960 ——, ed. The Blickling Homilies. EEMF 10. Copenhagen: Rosenkilde and Bagger, 1960.

Williams, B. 1914 Williams, Blanche Colton. Gnomic Poetry in A-S. New
York: Columbia University Press, 1914.

Williams, E. 1958 Williams, Edna Rees. "Ælfric's Grammatical Terminology." PMLA 73 (1958), 453–62.

Williamson 1977 Williamson, Craig, ed. The OE Riddles of the Exeter Book.
Chapel Hill: University of North Carolina Press,
1977.

Williamson 1982 ——, trans. A Feast of Creatures: A-S Riddle-Songs.
Philadelphia: University of Pennsylvania Press, 1982.

Wilmart 1934 Wilmart, A. "Eve et Goscelin." Rb 46 (1934), 414–38;
50 (1938), 42–83.

Wilmart 1938 ——. "La légende de sainte Edith en prose et vers par
le moine Goscelin." Analecta Bollandiana 56 (1938),
5–101, 265–307.

Wilson 1952 Wilson, Richard M. The Lost Literature of Medieval England. London: Methuen, 1952.

Wilson 1959 ——. "On the Continuity of English Prose." In Mé-
langes de Linguistique et de Philologie: Fernand Mossé
in Memoriam. Paris: Didier, 1959, pp. 486–94.

Winterbottom 1967 Winterbottom, Michael. "The Style of Æthelweard."
MÆ 36 (1967), 109–18.

Winterbottom 1972 ——, ed. Three Lives of English Saints. Toronto: Pontifical Institute of Mediaeval Studies, 1972.

Winterbottom 1977 ——. "Aldhelm's Prose Style and its Origins." ASE 6
(1977), 39–76.

Wittig 1969 Wittig, Joseph S. "Homiletic Fragment II and The Epistle to the Ephesians." Traditio 25 (1969), 358–63.

Wittig 1975 ——. "Figural Narrative in Cynewulf's Juliana." ASE
4 (1975), 37–55.

Wittig 1981 ——, ed. Eight A-S Studies. SP 78, no. 5 (1981).

Wittig 1983 ——. "King Alfred's Boethius and its Latin Sources: a
Reconsideration." ASE 11 (1983), 157–98.

Woolf 1953 Woolf, Rosemary. "The Devil in OE Poetry." RES 4

(1953), 1–12. Rpr. in Bessinger/Kahrl 1968, pp. 164–79.

Woolf 1955a ——, ed. *Juliana*. London: Methuen, 1955.

Woolf 1955b ——. "The Lost Opening to the *Judith*." *MLR* 50 (1955), 168–72.

Woolf 1958 ——. "Doctrinal Influences on *The Dream of the Rood*." *MÆ* 27 (1958), 137–53.

Woolf 1963 ——. "The Fall of Man in *Genesis B* and the *Mystère d'Adam*."In Greenfield 1963b, pp. 187–99.

Woolf 1966 ——. "Saints' Lives." In Stanley 1966b, pp. 37–66.

Woolf 1975 ——. "*The Wanderer, The Seafarer*, and the Genre of the *Planctus*." In Nicholson/Frese 1975, pp. 192–207.

Woolf 1976 ——. "The Ideal of Men Dying with Their Lord in *Germania* and in *The Battle of Maldon*." *ASE* 5 (1976), 63–81.

Wormald, F. 1948 Wormald, Francis. *The Miniatures in the Gospels of St. Augustine*. Cambridge: Cambridge University Press, 1948.

Wormald, F. 1959 ——. *The Benedictional of St. Ethelwold*. London: Faber and Faber, 1959.

Wormald, P. 1978 Wormald, Patrick. "Æthelred the Lawmaker." In *Ethelred the Unready: Papers from the Millenary Conference*, ed. David Hill. Oxford: British Archaeological Reports, 1978, pp. 47–80.

Wrenn 1933 Wrenn, Charles L. "Standard OE." *TPS* (1933), 65–88.

Wrenn 1940 ——. "A Saga of the Anglo-Saxons." *History* 25 (1940–1), 208–15.

Wrenn 1946 ——. "The Poetry of Caedmon." *PBA* 32 (1946), 277–95. Rpr. in Bessinger/Kahrl 1968, pp. 407–27.

Wrenn 1958 ——. "On the Continuity of English Poetry." *Anglia* 76 (1958), 41–59.

Wrenn 1962 ——. "Two A-S Harps." *CL* 14 (1962), 118–28.

Wrenn 1967 ——. *A Study of OE Literature*. London: Harrap, 1967; New York: W. W. Norton, 1968.

Wrenn/Bolton 1973 ——, ed. *Beowulf with the Finnesburg Fragment*. 3rd ed., rev. by Whitney F. Bolton. New York: St. Martin's Press, 1973.

Wright, C. 1939 Wright, Cyril E. *The Cultivation of Saga in A-S England*. Edinburgh: Oliver and Boyd, 1939.

Wright, C. 1955 ——, ed. *Bald's Leechbook*. EEMF 5. Copenhagen: Rosenkilde and Bagger, 1955.

Wright, H. 1957 Wright, Herbert G. "Good and Evil; Light and Darkness; Joy and Sorrow in *Beowulf*." *RES* 8 (1957), 1–11.

Wright, R. 1982 Wright, Roger. *Late Latin and Early Romance in Spain and Carolingian France*. Liverpool: Cairns, 1982.

Wyatt/Chambers 1920 Wyatt, Alfred J., ed. *Beowulf with the Finnsburg Frag-*

ment. Rev. by R. W. Chambers. 2nd ed. Cambridge: Cambridge University Press, 1920.

Yerkes 1979   Yerkes, David. *The Two Versions of Wærferth's Translation of Gregory's Dialogues: An OE Thesaurus.* Toronto, Buffalo, and London: University of Toronto Press, 1979.

Yerkes 1980   ——, ed. "The Full Text of the Metrical Preface to Wærferth's Translation of Gregory." *Speculum* 55 (1980), 505–13.

Yerkes 1982   ——. *Syntax and Style in OE: A Comparison of the Two Versions of Wærferth's Translation of Gregory's Dialogues.* Binghamton, NY: Center for Medieval and Early Renaissance Studies, 1982.

Yerkes 1984   ——, ed. *The OE Life of Machutus.* Toronto, Buffalo, and London: University of Toronto Press, 1984.

Yerkes 1985   ——. "The Translation of Gregory's *Dialogues* and its Revision: Textual History, Provenance, Authorship." In Szarmach 1985, pp. 335–43.

Zettersten 1979   Zettersten, Arne, ed. *Waldere.* Manchester and New York: Manchester University Press/Barnes and Noble, 1979.

Zupitza 1880   Zupitza, Julius, ed. *Ælfric's Grammar und Glossar.* Berlin: Weidmann, 1880. Rpr. with a preface by H. Gneuss. Berlin: Weidmann, 1966.

Zupitza 1959   ——. *Beowulf: Autotypes of the Unique Cotton MS Vitellius A. xv.* 2nd ed. with introductory note by Norman Davis. EETS 245. London 1959.

Index

THIS INDEX is designed to cover fully Anglo-Latin and Old English authors and works mentioned in the text and footnotes. In other respects, it is highly selective; it contains no references to modern scholars mentioned either in text or footnotes. It does not cover the Bibliography.

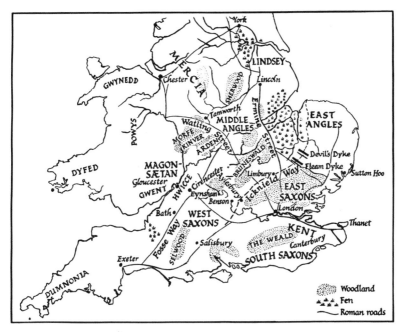

The early kingdoms of the southern English

England in the tenth century